Good Judgment in
Foreign Policy

Good Judgment in Foreign Policy

Theory and Application

Edited by Stanley A. Renshon
and Deborah Welch Larson

ROWMAN & LITTLEFIELD PUBLISHERS, INC.
Lanham • Boulder • New York • Oxford

ROWMAN & LITTLEFIELD PUBLISHERS, INC.

Published in the United States of America
by Rowman & Littlefield Publishers, Inc.
An Imprint of the Rowman & Littlefield Publishing Group
4720 Boston Way, Lanham, Maryland 20706
www.rowmanlittlefield.com

12 Hid's Copse Road, Cumnor Hill, Oxford OX2 9JJ, England

The tables in chapter 3, "Appraising Good Judgment Before It Matters," are used by
permission of The Pew Research Center for the People and the Press.

Portions of chapter 7, "Culture and Emotion as Obstacles to Good Judgment," were
previously published as "Remember the Falklands? Missed lessons of a misunderstood war,"
in *International Journal*, vol 52, no. 3 (Summer 1997), pp. 483–507. Reprinted by permission.

An earlier version of chapter 10, "Analysis and Judgment in Policymaking," was published
in *Education in a Research University*, ed. K. Arrow et al. (Stanford, Calif.: Stanford University
Press, 1996).

British Library Cataloguing in Publication Information Available

Library of Congress Cataloging-in-Publication Data

Good judgment in foreign policy : theory and application / [edited by],
Stanley A. Renshon and Deborah Welch Larson.
    p.   cm.
    Includes bibliographical references and index.
    ISBN 0-7425-1006-9 (cloth : alk. paper)—ISBN 0-7425-1007-7 (pbk. :
alk. paper)
    1. International relations—Decision making. 2. International
relations—Psychological aspects. 3. Judgment. I. Renshon, Stanley
Allen. II. Larson, Deborah Welch, 1951–
JZ1253 .G66 2002
327.1'01—dc21   2002004176

Printed in the United States of America

∞ ™ The paper used in this publication meets the minimum requirements of American
National Standard for Information Sciences—Permanence of Paper for Printed Library
Materials, ANSI/NISO Z39.48–1992.

Contents

Preface

Nowhere is the judgment of leaders more important than in the making of foreign policy decisions. Good judgments can avoid wars or win them. Alternatively, poor judgments can start wars or lose them. Judgment is the arena in which a leader's psychology and experience intersect with political realities to produce the consequences that can make or break a leader—or a country.

Yet, the importance of making good judgments is not confined to the great issues of war and peace. It is also to be found in the many decisions, large and often small, whose consequences may appear or echo long after a leader has left office or moved on to other concerns.

Surprisingly, in view of its importance, good political and policy judgment is more discussed than examined. Most are familiar with Richard Neustadt's classic formulation that a president must preserve his reputation for skill and willingness to use power domestically and internationally. Neustadt says he does so by successful bargaining, but to what end? His theory has led scholars to focus on instrumentalities instead of purpose. Whether the president has chosen wisely is an issue that is often overlooked. In hindsight, for example, many scholars would say that General George Marshall or President Dwight D. Eisenhower showed good judgment in their foreign policy thinking. However, they would be hard-pressed to explain why. Alternatively, Lyndon Johnson's foreign policy judgments in Vietnam or Bill Clinton's in Bosnia would not receive high marks, but for reasons that remain latent and unarticulated.

Contemporary political history is full of disastrous decisions and avoidable miscalculations. Why? What makes otherwise smart leaders blunder, at huge costs to themselves and those they lead? To date, we have clues—misperception, inadequate appraisal of alternatives, and so on. However, we have no overall framework for analysis that asks a most central question: Why do some leaders, and not others, make use of the benchmarks for high-quality decisions that have been established?

It seems clear that good procedures do not automatically result in either good or successful policy judgments. Why? Clearly judgment is related to the process by which one arrives at it, but it would seem inadequate to say that good process is the same as good judgment. How, then, are they related, and what can a focus on either separately tell us about how they operate together?

The purpose of this book is to provide a framework for the analysis of such questions. As well, we want to begin to fill the substantive vacuum left by an overreliance on "cost-benefit" analysis and a focus on routinized procedures at the expense of dynamic analysis. The focus of the book therefore is not primarily about "decision making" but rather questions about the quality of thought, analysis, and reflection that informs, or misinforms, judgments.

This is a book framed by many more questions than authoritative answers. Indeed, it is important to make clear that the purpose of this book is to help *develop* theory, not to provide conclusions. Toward that end we have drawn together a carefully selected and, we think, distinguished group of contributors from both the academic and real world of making foreign policy judgments. A number of contributors span both worlds.

The framework of the analyses presented herein is interdisciplinary. Our contributors are trained in psychology, political science, and policy analysis. Most represent several disciplinary perspectives.

In keeping with the attempt to develop useful theory, we make use of theoretical analyses but also detailed case studies from which useful inferences might be drawn. Also, in keeping with our purpose and casting a wide net, we examine good judgment through the lenses of different levels of analysis. We examine the issues surrounding good judgment from the individual, small-group, and institutional levels of analysis, often with attention to how these issues play out as one moves from one level to other.

The book's title is *Good Judgment in Foreign Policy*. However, most of analyses focus on American famed case studies and draw on those who have spent considerable professional time studying or serving in the American foreign policy apparatus. The focus is not inadvertent.

We considered structuring the book more specifically using a comparative framework with authors from different cultures, and chapters focused on those cultures. We decided against such a course and why we did so deserves brief comment. As noted, this book is an attempt to try to *build* a theory of good judgment, not test one we already have. Given this fact, it seemed prudent to first develop a framework and fill in the substantive theoretical underpinnings of a theory of good judgment in one culture, before rushing off to apply what didn't yet exist, elsewhere.

Wouldn't a focus on good judgment among Indian or Russian leaders increase the universe of understandings from which we hope to develop a theory. Possibly, yes, but at a steep price. That price is the assumption that culture, history, and political organization play no role in the development of good judgment within a particular country. Just stating the point in that way underscores what a poor basis on which to proceed that assumption would be. We thought it prudent to begin to build a framework within which to develop a theory in one domain and then apply it outward to see what, if any, modifications are necessary. Starting with the United States is the equivalent of holding culture, history, and political organization and practice somewhat constant, so that we can have a purer look at the phenomenon that interests us: good judgment.

That said, it is true of course that there is a built-in comparative element to all the chapters. How? Simply because all of the case studies and theoretical chapters deal with the United States and some other country. We are not arguing that this is the same as an explicitly comparative basis for the book, but a comparative focus is inherent in the nature of the undertaking.

Finally, we have begun the process of reaching out more specifically to comparative case studies that make use of non–United States actors in chapter 7 by Welch on the war between the United Kingdom and Argentina over the Falkland Islands. His chapter represents a useful first step in the direction of political and cultural comparisons because it focuses on a Latin American country and culture and a Western political culture. It is valuable as well because the United States was involved in the events leading up to the war as mediator.

THE BOOK'S FRAMEWORK

The book and its subject matter is divided into five parts: Part I: "The Nature of Good Judgment," Part II: "The Dynamics of Good Judgment: Appraisals and Images," Part III: "Judgments and Misjudgments in Foreign Policy Decisions," Part IV: "Improving the Quality of Judgment in Foreign Policy Decision Making," and Part V: "Reflections on Good Judgment in a Dangerous World."

The first section contains chapters dealing with the nature of good judgment—what is it, who has it, and how do they get it. The second part addresses issues of the ingredients and dynamics of good judgment. Part III contains historical case studies that clarify the nature of good and poor judgment. The fourth section examines the methods by which good judgments in foreign policy analysis might be augmented or improved. In the fifth and final section, Renshon examines George W. Bush's foreign policy judgment before and after September 11 and Larson examines politics, uncertainty, and values in relation to good judgment. Brief descriptions of the individual chapters can be found on pages 18–19.

ACKNOWLEDGMENTS

Every book is composite effort, and this one is no exception. Both editors have been very fortunate in having as an intellectual mentor Alexander L. George. His work on the psychology of decision making served as both a model and an inspiration to us both. He is truly the father of this collaboration.

We have also been very fortunate in having the opportunity to work with a thoughtful and responsive group of contributors. We have learned a lot from them in the process, and we are hopeful and confident you will share our appreciation of their work.

Jennifer Knerr of Rowman & Littlefield saw merit in our ideas. Her enthusiasm for this effort is sincerely appreciated.

Stanley Renshon would like to acknowledge, with love and appreciation, his family: his wife, Judith, and their children, David and Jonathan. They truly represent the best and the most fulfilling judgment he ever made. For expert research assistance and perceptive comments on judgment, Deborah Welch Larson is grateful to Jennifer Kibbe and Alexei Shevchenko.

We hope you are as stimulated by the questions posed herein as we are hopeful that you will find our attempts to frame answers to them informative and useful.

Part I

THE NATURE OF
GOOD JUDGMENT

· 1 ·

Good Judgment in Foreign Policy

Social Psychological Perspectives

Deborah Welch Larson

$\mathcal{W}$hat is good judgment in foreign policy? Can the necessary skills or competences be taught? Or is good judgment innate? Is good judgment an elusive
talent, like that of a first-class novelist? A master politician like Franklin Delano
Roosevelt may be inimitable. Nevertheless, we can try to identify characteristics of good judgment in foreign policy to see whether it is possible to improve
the quality of decisions. This essay will offer only preliminary answers to these
questions, which are treated in greater depth in the volume. I shall outline
some aspects of good political judgment and illustrate them with examples
from American foreign policy.

EFFORTS TO IMPROVE THE QUALITY OF
FOREIGN POLICY DECISION MAKING

Since the cold war, we have learned that good judgment does not depend on
having smart advice, a coherent, well-run bureaucratic organization, or even
rationality. In the 1950s and 1960s, academics tried to improve the quality of
foreign policy decisions by applying tools of economics and rational choice
theory such as systems analysis to strategic issues facing the U.S. government.
By the mid-1960s, however, the U.S. involvement in Vietnam caused many
policy-oriented academics to wonder what had gone wrong. The May group
of scholars at Harvard, named after Ernest R. May, tried to find an answer in
the ability of bureaucracies to deflect decisions away from the national interest
toward more parochial concerns such as maximizing their autonomy and budget share.

Academics made several proposals in the 1970s for restructuring the president's advisory system to improve the quality of advice and information reach-

3

ing the president.[1] What finally emerged from all the studies was the conclusion that no one organizational structure is best—it all depends on the cognitive style and informational needs of the individual president.[2]

Distinguished scholars Alexander George, Richard Neustadt, and Ernest May have given guidance to policymakers to enable them to avoid making major mistakes and to improve the overall quality of foreign policy decisions. Their suggestions, for the most part, concern ways to make more effective use of available information and sharpen the analysis that frames decisions. In *Presidential Decisionmaking*, George draws on a large body of research in social psychology, organization theory, and sociology as well as historical examples to develop prescriptions for avoiding biases and errors in the use of information about foreign policy issues. George cautions decision makers to avoid making particular types of cognitive errors such as being unwilling to accept information that contradicts their beliefs or imputing too much coherence to the adversary's behavior. He identifies several decision aids that policymakers may use to deal with uncertainty, such as the use of a "satisficing" decision rule, incrementalism, consensus politics, and ideological beliefs and other general principles. These cognitive shortcuts are not necessarily harmful to the quality of decision. The principal danger, George writes, is that the decision maker will resort to one of these cognitive aids prematurely or rely too heavily on it, closing himself off to in-depth information and analysis from his advisers and his organizational system. On some issues, the president might want to encourage "multiple advocacy," a structured debate among his advisers of alternative policy options.[3]

Although George does not address questions of political feasibility or the substance of good political judgment, he does outline the key issues for future research. He argues that a decision maker should try to harmonize the search for quality decisions with the need to attain adequate political support and the constraints on time and other analytical resources. An effective decision maker will find a balance between concern for the political acceptability of a policy and its contribution to the national interest. He or she should also avoid putting too many analytical and political resources into one area, while neglecting other issues.[4]

Neustadt and May propose various analytical tools or "minimethods" to improve the quality of analysis that goes into making decisions.[5] They suggest that policymakers use history more effectively, that they avoid inappropriate analogies and put foreign policy problems in historical context. To reduce the risk that following the "lessons of history" will blind governmental decision makers to important aspects of the current political situation, Neustadt and May suggest drawing up a checklist of similarities and differences between the historical parallel and the problem facing policymakers. Before moving directly to "what do we do," policymakers should try to distinguish what is known from what is merely presumed or unclear. What policymakers think they should do may reflect assumptions that are questionable or untrue. Above all, foreign policy officials should consider that they might well be wrong and try to identify in advance what events would undermine their presumptions.

Neustadt and May also provide a few tools for evaluating the political feasibility of policy options. Policymakers should think of "time as a stream"— that is, consider current issues as the outcome of a historical series of events, to predict what the future may hold and how it can be altered.[6] Placing issues on a historical time line provides clues about what is possible based on what worked or failed in the past. In selecting events for this chronology, staff members should be attuned to points where politics affected the outcome. Political leaders are by necessity concerned with accountability and reelection. A narrative history of the issue may also help policymakers empathize with the perspective and concerns of the other state's leadership by identifying the events that may have shaped their outlook.

Neustadt and May's minimethods are designed to help policymakers ask questions that bring out considerations that bear on the political feasibility of a goal or option. Better use of history would contribute to improving political judgment by encouraging political leaders to be more realistic about what they can achieve and therefore more prudent. Adopting a historical perspective is not enough to ensure good judgment, though, because it does not deal with problems of uncertainty and political trade-offs. While Neustadt and May recommend that policymakers challenge their own presumptions, the exercise of judgment entails going *beyond* the information available. Under conditions of acute uncertainty and pressure to make a decision, a president does not need to hear what he *doesn't* know. A historical analogy may help the president understand the essence of an unfamiliar situation, even if a checklist of similarities and dissimilarities would suggest that the two cases are more different than alike. Political acceptability is not the only desideratum of good foreign policy judgment. Exercising wise judgment may require going against what the public and advisers currently want or prefer.

WHAT IT MEANS TO EXERCISE
GOOD POLITICAL JUDGMENT

The prescriptions of George, Neustadt, and May aim to improve the analytical quality and accuracy of staff work and advice. Even the most competent policy analysis, however, is only an aid to, not a substitute for, the judgment of the decision maker.[7] As the former director of Strategic Studies for RAND, and later secretary of defense, James Schlesinger writes, "[A]nalysis is not a scientific procedure for reaching decisions which avoid intuitive elements, but rather a mechanism for sharpening the intuitions of the decision-maker." Consequently, while "poor or haphazard analysis may contribute to poor decisions . . . good analysis by itself cannot insure correct decisions."[8]

The president must take into consideration a wider range of values than can be addressed in a policy memoranda. He cannot simply calculate what the national interest requires without also weighing political feasibility and conflicts among objectives. He must make decisions on ultimate values, where many lives may be at stake.

Moreover, foreign policy decisions are often made under extreme uncertainty, where how the adversary will react cannot be predicted. As an illustration of the need for judgment, Herbert Simon gives the example of a commander deciding whether to order an infantry attack. The outcome of the attack will depend on objective factors such as the disposition of the enemy's forces, the terrain, his troops' morale, the accuracy and strength of artillery support, and other factors that cannot be known with any certainty in advance and are therefore a matter of the commander's judgment.[9] A political leader may be just as capable as an expert at predicting how an adversary will respond to conciliatory gestures, how he will react to coercive moves, or the degree of public support a policy will enjoy at home.[10] Indeed, a politician may be more capable of predicting the responses of his counterpart than experts who have more substantive knowledge: because of their shared role and situation, political leaders can better understand the domestic constraints under which the other is operating.[11]

Good political judgment entails integrating and balancing competing values and considerations to come up with a practical course of action. Philosopher Isaiah Berlin describes political judgment as "a capacity for integrating a vast amalgam of constantly changing, multicoloured, evanescent, perpetually overlapping data." By integration, Berlin means "to see the data . . . as elements in a single pattern, with their implications, to see them as symptoms of past and future possibilities, to see them pragmatically, that is, in terms of what you or others can or will do to them, and what they can or will do to others or to you."[12]

General George C. Marshall displayed the capacity to weigh a wide range of relevant factors and their interrelationship, as it would affect the outcome of different actions. Secretary of State Dean Acheson recalled many long conversations where Marshall explained the decision to invade Nazi-occupied Europe from England across the Channel rather than going up through the Balkans, as Winston Churchill preferred. "What impressed me was the wide scope of the factors he had weighed. They went beyond the purely military considerations and the usual political ones." Marshall had thought of the amount of shipping involved in shifting the Allied army from England to another location eastward, of the political implications of delaying the final move against Japan, which would lead to a million additional casualties. He considered President Roosevelt's deteriorating health and the 1946 congressional election:

> All elements of the problem were held, as it were, in solution in his mind until it was ready to precipitate a decision. This is the essence and the method—or rather the art—of judgment in its highest form. Not merely military judgment, but judgment in great affairs of state, which requires both mastery of precise information and apprehension of imponderables.[13]

Related to this ability to entertain many considerations simultaneously is the capacity to navigate through a complicated set of arguments to arrive at a net assessment. Director of the State Department Policy Planning Staff Robert Bowie recalled President Dwight Eisenhower's effectiveness in National Security Council (NSC) meetings:

> Often the discussion would be marked by impressive analysis by various individuals, who, as intellectuals, struck you as sometimes more articulate than he. But at the end, I felt that he frequently came out with a common sense appraisal . . . which was wiser than the input which he'd received from the separate advisers. Somehow, almost in an intuitive way, in a way which quite clearly wasn't a one, two, three, lawyer's type of analysis, he nevertheless came out with a net judgment which often struck me as wiser or more sensible than the specific positions taken by any one individual.[14]

Good judgment is not necessarily associated with academic knowledge or theoretical expertise. A president can make judgments on environmental policy, fiscal issues, diplomatic treaties, and strategic policy without being an expert in those areas.[15] As the chapters show, Ronald Reagan and Harry S. Truman were not experts in foreign policy, yet they often made good, commonsense judgments. Good judgment resides in the experience and intuition of the decision maker. Howard Gardner's theory of multiple intelligences holds that individuals may have competences and capabilities that are not captured by standard intelligence tests.[16] Good political judgment entails having practical intelligence.

Exercising good political judgment does require some understanding of politics. Former Secretary of State James Baker argues that "theoretical knowledge is not an absolute necessity for success as Secretary of State, because at its core, the Secretary of State's job is political, just on an international stage." Baker recalls that he always considered at least three political dimensions to any proposal: "Will we be able to build a domestic consensus in support of it? What kind of political reaction will it create in the capitals of our adversaries and allies? And, finally, how will it change the nature of our political relations internationally?"[17]

JUDGMENT TASKS

What are the various factors that a political decision maker should entertain in arriving at good judgments? One way to develop knowledge about a seemingly insoluble problem is to divide it up into smaller, more manageable components. Sir Geoffrey Vickers distinguishes between value, reality, and instrumental judgments. Reality and value judgments are interdependent, "for facts are relevant only in relation to some judgment of value and judgments of value are operative only in relation to some configuration of fact." Instrumental judgment "produces apt solutions to the problems set by such surveys of 'reality.'"[18]

George proposes seven types of judgments that policymakers may have to make in a given situation. The president may have to exercise judgment on any of the following questions.

Trade-offs among Time, Acceptability, and Quality

Leaders must decide how much time and political capital to allocate to reaching a high-quality decision. There may be conflicts between the *quality* of a foreign policy decision, the *time and resources* spent in formulating a solution, and its political *acceptability*.[19] The president must try to strike a balance between competing considerations, trading off what seems to be ideal according to one criterion to meet the other two constraints. Individuals with different personalities and cognitive styles may deal with the trade-offs in distinctive ways. In theory, spending more time should improve the quality of a decision. If a president makes a decision too hastily, he may err due to insufficient information or an incomplete analysis of the costs and risks. This was Truman's problem. Truman was insecure about his ability to step into Roosevelt's place. He also believed that the president's job was to make decisions. "I am here to make decisions," Truman told British Foreign Secretary Anthony Eden, "and whether they prove right or wrong I am going to take them." Sometimes, particularly in his first months in office, Truman approved policies without reading them over carefully and was later surprised and horrified at what he had done. Henry Wallace comments that "it is more and more evident that the President arrives at decisions on the spur of the moment on the basis of partial evidence. He does *so* like to agree with whomever is with him at the moment."[20]

Truman's decision style seemingly violates the tenets of normative theory, which holds that a decision maker should consider a reasonable number of options and choose the one that is likely to have the best outcome, discounted for its probability. In the political world, though, there are financial, political, and opportunity costs to gathering additional information and allocating analytical resources. Many decision papers come over the president's desk daily. Sometimes he can put them off for a while until the situation clarifies itself or he can gain additional analyses from staff members; often he cannot. David Gergen, a former adviser to Presidents Nixon, Reagan, and Clinton, writes, "[O]ne thing that he cannot do is dither."[21]

Increased effort does not necessarily yield better decisions. Overwork and fatigue, for example, can cause policymakers to make mistakes and misjudgments. President Lyndon B. Johnson tried to deal with Vietnam as he had coped with crises in the past: by working longer hours than anyone else and mastering all the details. Johnson in turn praised Defense Secretary Robert McNamara for being "the first one at work and the last one to leave. He is there every morning at 7:00 A.M. including Saturday. The only difference is that on Saturday he wears a sportcoat." Secretary of State Dean Rusk took off only twelve days in eight years.[22] After being elected and well into the first part of his presidency, Bill Clinton, in a state of euphoria, tried to get by with as little as four hours' sleep. He appeared puffy-eyed, distracted, impatient, and unable to carry on a serious conversation with his advisers. A Cabinet officer told journalist Elizabeth Drew, "He said to me he's dog tired, that he's sixteen months tired." Clinton's mishandling of several political issues in his early presidency, such as his trying to integrate gays openly into the military, may have stemmed from simple fatigue. His communications director George Stephanopoulos recalls, "A lot of the mistakes we made in the first weeks were because we were so tired."[23]

If the president spends *too* much time, he may appear indecisive, inefficient, or overwhelmed. President Jimmy Carter also tried to cope with his declining political popularity by working longer and longer hours, exercising leadership by example instead of exhortation. He aged visibly in his first year of office. The public came to believe that Carter had to work harder because he was overwhelmed by his responsibilities, as conveyed by a *New Republic* article titled "Can Carter Cope?"[24] Clinton was criticized for having endless White House talkfests. In April 1993, he engaged in lengthy discussions with his principal foreign policy advisers on what the United States could do to end the violence in Bosnia. The policy debates seemed to go nowhere. "It wasn't policymaking. It was group therapy—an existential debate over what is the role of America, etc.," a high-level official recalled. Emotionally upset over televised images of atrocities, Clinton made strong statements indicating that he planned to take strong action, including the use of U.S. military forces. When he did nothing because of allied opposition and concerns over the domestic public reaction, Clinton looked weak and ineffectual.[25]

More often than they would admit, policymakers do not analyze a problem extensively but instead use their "gut instincts." Psychologists distinguish between analytic and intuitive modes of thought. Intuition refers to "a cognitive process that somehow produces an answer, solution, or idea without the use of a conscious, logically defensible, step-by-step process."[26] Intuitive decision making is rapid, automatic, and outside conscious awareness. Analytic decision making is slow, deliberate, under conscious control.[27]

Intuition may guide a decision maker to the correct decision without need for deliberation or calculation.[28] Intuition is not mystical; it is the distillation of experience. As a result of dealing with different types of situations over time, experienced managers have accumulated much "tacit knowledge" about what to do that they cannot articulate.[29] As indicated in chapters 5 and 6, Truman and Reagan were both intuitive decision makers. Truman customarily made decisions rapidly, without much if any deliberation or calculation. Lou Cannon, a journalist who covered Reagan throughout his political career, observed that "he understood all manner of things that suggested powers of analysis without possessing any visible analytical ability."[30]

Intuition can be a useful tool to decide what *not* to do as well as what to do. Vague feelings of uneasiness or apprehension may indicate that a leader has overlooked risks or moral considerations and that he or she should reconsider the selected policy.[31] Sometimes, presidents would have been better advised to heed their instincts. Before he approved the fateful U-2 flight over the Soviet Union, Eisenhower worried that if one of these planes were shot down when he was apparently discussing peace, it would destroy his greatest asset in dealing with foreign leaders—his reputation for honesty.[32] Nevertheless, Eisenhower went against his instincts and approved the U-2 flight, which was shot down and led to the collapse not only of the Paris summit but also U.S.-Soviet cooperation. In his conversations with Senate Majority Leader Richard Russell and others in 1964, before he made the fateful escalation decisions, President Johnson agonized over whether to send ground troops to Vietnam. To National Security Adviser McGeorge Bundy, Johnson lamented, "I don't think it's worth fighting for and I don't think that we can get out. It's just the biggest damned mess that I ever saw." He continued, "What the hell is Vietnam worth to me? What is Laos worth to me? What is it worth to the country?"[33] He worried that the American people would not support a limited war of attrition. "If you make a commitment to jump off a building and you find out how high it is, you may want to withdraw that commitment," he said.[34] Again, Johnson did not follow through on his perceptive insight.

Political leaders must consider whether a given policy will have adequate political support both within the executive branch and among the general public. Even the best policy will not enhance decision makers' political goals if it is politically infeasible. On the other hand, giving too much attention to a policy's political popularity may sacrifice quality considerations. For example, Johnson always thought in terms of the political feasibility of policies rather than being guided primarily by their substantive merits. Johnson mastered the art of committing a bill to memory, so that if you gave him a sentence from it, he could paraphrase the whole page and everything after it. But once the bill had passed, he wouldn't remember the contents or even the name of the report even if was only a week later.[35] Like many legislators, Johnson conceived of policies in terms of getting bills passed instead of carrying them out.[36] Columnist James Reston criticized Johnson for citing public opinion polls as proof of the effectiveness of his Vietnam policy. "Popular support and sound policy are obviously not the same thing," Reston wrote in November 1965. "Nothing was more popular or more disastrous than the isolationist policy of the United States before the two World Wars."[37] Johnson obtained public support for the early phases of the war in Vietnam by not being honest about the scope of the U.S. commitment—he mortgaged his political future to get the Great Society legislation through Congress.[38]

Not all officials, however, regard domestic politics as a legitimate influence on foreign policy. At the opposite extreme, President Carter believed that "politics" was immoral. Carter separated politics from government; politics was a necessary evil, a means to gain entrée to the sphere of government. Once he was elected, Carter believed that he should use his own judgment about what was best for the country, without being affected by political considerations. Vice President Walter Mondale's chief of staff recalled that when they had meetings and someone would make a political argument, Carter would say, "I don't want to hear any political arguments. I just want the arguments on substance. I will make the political decisions." In practice, however, Carter often made decisions such as the cancellation of the B-1 bomber, completely oblivious to political considerations. Mondale later commented that "Carter's got the coldest political nose of any politician I ever met."[39] Carter followed a rational, apolitical, "technocratic" approach to decision making; his inability to achieve important goals highlights how political judgment differs from rational choice.

A president may tinker with a policy so that it achieves adequate support within and outside the executive branch, at the cost of its effectiveness, reflecting the trade-off between quality and acceptability. Johnson committed U.S.

troops in Vietnam gradually, with little explanation, to mislead Congress and the American people about the extent of the planned U.S. commitment. He feared that mobilization of the nation for war would arouse a divisive debate in Congress that would jeopardize passage of his massive domestic legislative program, the Great Society. In 1965, Johnson committed U.S. ground troops to preserving a noncommunist Vietnam without asking for legislative authority from Congress, requesting supplemental appropriations to pay for the war, or calling up the reserves.[40] It has been argued that the incremental U.S. escalation also gave the North Vietnamese time to react to each move and undermined its psychological impact.

Faced with the decision whether to renew or increase funding for Johnson's Antiballistic Missile (ABM) system called Sentinel, President Richard Nixon decided to approve a defensive system that would protect missile sites instead of cities, ostensibly to avoid threatening the other side's deterrent capability. The components of LBJ's Sentinel system, however, were not suited for hard-target defense. Nixon adopted the goal of defending missiles to accommodate city residents who objected to having missile interceptors stationed nearby, arms control advocates who opposed any departure from mutual assured destruction, and student protesters who were less likely to picket missile sites in North Dakota. Although the ABM system made little sense from the standpoint of strategic doctrine or technological efficacy, it was admirably political.[41]

Similarly, President Clinton was criticized for putting politics ahead of strategy when he explicitly ruled out the use of ground troops in Kosovo in a public statement on March 24, 1999. He did so because he would otherwise not have been able to maintain the support of U.S. allies and domestic public opinion for the NATO intervention in Yugoslavia. But by removing ground troops as an option, Clinton may have contributed to Yugoslav President Slobodan Milosevic's determination to hold out in the face of bombing. Certainly, knowing that he faced no imminent danger of land conflict provided Milosevic with additional time to accelerate the effort to drive ethnic Albanians out of Kosovo.[42]

Good political judgment entails balancing the need for public support with achieving foreign policy objectives. President Truman is renowned for making important and difficult decisions—the Truman Doctrine, the Marshall Plan, the Berlin airlift, NATO, the Korean War. What would have happened if Truman had decided that proposing a large-scale foreign aid program for Western Europe would hurt his chances for reelection in 1948? Truman put aside his personal and political interests in choosing what he perceived was best for the United States. At the same time, though, Truman tried to maintain bipartisan support for his foreign policy by consulting with Republicans, inviting them to represent the United States at important international conferences, and by being willing to share the credit for major foreign policy initiatives such as NATO or the Marshall Plan. Truman was more concerned to see that his foreign policy retained adequate support than to take personal credit. In a stroke of genius, he persuaded Marshall to become secretary of state. Marshall commanded great respect in Congress for his self-command and personal integrity; he seemed to rise above parties and politics. Truman insisted that the Marshall Plan for aid to Europe not be named the "Truman Plan" because "anything that is sent up to the Senate and House with my name on it will quiver a couple of times and die."[43] In what was to become a famous memorandum that set down the strategy for Truman's 1948 presidential campaign, political advisers Clark Clifford and Jim Rowe urged that Truman assume personal credit for such popular aspects of his foreign policy, rather than allowing Marshall to be the spokesman. Although he was far behind in the polls, Truman declined to take this advice.[44]

Leaders must calculate not only *what* level of domestic political support is adequate but also *whose* consent is essential. In general, presidents are more concerned about obtaining support from Congress than from public opinion. For example, during the 1960 presidential campaign, John F. Kennedy argued in favor of foreign aid although the majority of the American public opposed it because he wanted to reassure elites about his fitness to be president.[45]

The difficulty of obtaining adequate public support varies greatly. When a foreign policy enjoys legitimacy at home, the president need not spend a great deal of time and energy justifying individual actions he wants to take because he can present them as steps toward achieving long-range foreign policy objectives, for which he has already gained understanding and support. He can also survive occasional policy defeats or missteps. Policy legitimacy is like money in the bank; it provides credit that allows the president a margin of error and enough flexibility to maintain a consistent policy. As an academic, Henry Kissinger wrote that "the acid test of a policy is its ability to obtain domestic support. This has two aspects: the problem of legitimizing a policy within the government apparatus . . . and that of harmonizing it with the national experience." Unfortunately, that was the very test that his détente policy did not pass.[46]

Setting an Agenda

Presidents should consider how a decision might affect their overall political standing and agenda, domestic as well as foreign. Foreign policy issues are embedded in a political context. A decision on one issue may jeopardize the president's ability to gain his wishes on another important question. Presidents have a limited amount of political capital to spend, and using too much of it to obtain congressional support for one policy may jeopardize their ability to obtain other objectives. Some of his advisers believed that Carter should have postponed seeking congressional ratification of the Panama Canal treaty until after he had reached an agreement with the Soviet Union on SALT II (the Strategic Arms Limitation Treaty).[47]

Similarly, Clinton should not have taken on the controversial issue of integrating gays into the military as the first act of his term. Determined military opposition forced Clinton to accept a compromise that pleased no one. He looked weak and vacillating, unable to stand up to pressure from gay rights groups or to talk back to the Joint Chiefs of Staff. Clinton's approval rating went down twenty points in two weeks, and the damage was enduring.[48] As Richard Neustadt points out, a president's ability to govern depends on part on his professional reputation among Washingtonians.[49]

Leaders should consider how to schedule major policy decisions so as to maximize political support. There are risks with trying to overload the political agenda. People cannot comprehend too many issues simultaneously. Carter tried to achieve too many worthwhile objectives at once, regardless of their priority or conflicts with each other. A week after he took office, Carter wrote in his diary that "everybody has warned me not to take on too many projects so early in the administration, but it's almost impossible for me to delay something that I see needs to be done." Zbigniew Brzezinski, his national security adviser, developed a forty-three-page document outlining the administration's policy priorities, including achieving a settlement to the Cyprus issue in 1978, ratifying a new SALT treaty by the end of 1978, moving South Africa toward democracy, achieving a more equitable relationship between industrial and developing states, and making human rights a priority. Career diplomats in the State Department were shocked by the lengthy list.[50]

President Reagan's advisers were determined to learn from Carter's mistakes. They believed that Carter had tried to do too much and as a result accomplished too little. Reagan and his advisers decided to concentrate on economic issues shortly after Reagan was elected president. Reagan even postponed for three weeks the State Department's release of a "white paper" documenting communist countries' shipment of weapons to the guerrillas in El Salvador. That the media then covered El Salvador and the increase of U.S. assistance and advisers confirmed the Reagan team's belief that foreign policy issues should not be allowed to take over the national agenda until the economic program had been passed. Secretary of State Al Haig was asked to restrict his television appearances for a while.[51]

Formulation of Goals

Presidents must decide *what* values to pursue and at what level of costs and risks. Now that the cold war is over, it is unclear what goals the United States should pursue with what degree of effort, such as extending democracy, promoting U.S. exports, defending human rights, or pursuing humanitarian goals such as alleviating poverty or limiting environmental pollution.[52]

Policymakers may have to decide what level of cost and risk to accept in pursuit of their goals. Political leaders may seek to avoid excessive risks not by avoiding action entirely, but by carefully monitoring and controlling the level of risk so as to adjust their policy accordingly. Clinton intervened to protect Kosovo, but he did so by using air power to reduce the number of U.S. casualties. Particularly for military intervention, leaders should also engage in some form of cost-benefit analysis, deciding in advance when the costs outweigh potential benefits. In hindsight, Johnson should have set an upper threshold for U.S. troop involvement and casualties beyond which saving Vietnam was not worth the cost. In a memorandum to the president, McGeorge Bundy asked, "What is the upper limit of our liability?"[53] It was a question that Johnson did not answer until it was too late and the United States had committed over half a million troops.

Time Perspective

Presidents may have to decide whether to strive for short-term payoffs or goals that will take much longer to be achieved. By the nature of their role, political advisers to the president focus on the most recent opinion poll or the next election. The president, however, has to keep in mind potential foreign policy problems that may erupt into crises during his term for which he will be held accountable. When considering his historical legacy, the president may often want to achieve something positive, such as an arms control agreement or other major treaty. As Jentleson and Bennett discuss, the State Department Policy Planning Staff can assist the president in this endeavor by gathering information on and analyzing emerging problems that are not currently on the agenda.

President Eisenhower always considered the long-term ramifications of specific policies for the health of the U.S. economy. Continued high levels of defense spending, he feared, would require controls on the economy and restrictions on civil liberties, ultimately leading America to become a garrison state. In 1955, Eisenhower commented privately that we had to address the problem in terms of not six months but forty years. The Soviets would always attempt to keep America off balance, he said. Anyone who ever read Lenin knew that the communist objective was to make the United States spend itself into bankruptcy. The United States had to hold the line until the Soviets educated their own people. By doing so, they would sow the seeds of destruction of communist power. Despite the hysteria over the Soviets' orbiting of *Sputnik,* Eisenhower refused to increase defense spending because he argued that the United States had to maintain sufficient resources for confrontation with the Soviets over the long haul.[54]

Maximize or Satisfice

In pursuing his goals, a president needs to decide whether to aim for the maximum or a satisfactory outcome. Both Reagan and Bush pursued maximal agreements with the Soviet Union and drove hard bargains with Soviet General Secretary Mikhail Gorbachev. In his first term, Reagan could have gotten an agreement limiting medium-range missiles in Europe, but he wanted to eliminate them entirely, the "zero option." The Bush administration's strategy was to redirect Western policy from recognizing existing facts to a more ambitious vision of an independent, free Eastern Europe.[55] Reagan and Bush could successfully pursue a maximizing strategy because Gorbachev was a receptive interlocutor. Carter, on the other hand, provoked Soviet outrage and set back the SALT II negotiations by a few years when he proposed "deep cuts" in strategic arsenals in March 1977, rather than settling for the totals that had been agreed on by Leonid Brezhnev and Gerald Ford at Vladivostok.[56] Carter had unrealistic expectations and fundamentally misperceived the domestic political constraints operating on Brezhnev.

Value Trade-offs

Policymakers may have to deal with value complexity, the presence of multiple competing values embedded in a situation. Some of the values involved in a decision may conflict with each other—for example, promoting human rights in China versus improving access for U.S. companies to the Chinese market. For Clinton to uphold the human rights of Albanians in Kosovo against persecution and deportations by the Yugoslavian regime contradicted the norms of sovereignty and nonintervention in country's internal affairs.

Presidents may resolve, accept, or avoid difficult conflicts between values.[57] The president may be able to resolve the conflict by crafting a policy that satisfies some of the competing considerations to some extent. President Truman's decision to send supplies to Berlin by air during the 1948 blockade preserved U.S. credibility with the Germans while avoiding war with the

Soviet Union. Alternatively, the president may be able to take other actions either now or later to compensate for neglecting a value.

If he cannot avoid sacrificing some value, the president may have to set priorities, according one value precedence over another. According to normative theory, people should be willing trade a high value on one attribute for a low on another, for example, choosing a car that meets high safety standards but is less fuel-efficient. Although he had criticized the 1989–93 Bush administration for "coddling dictators" in China, Clinton subsequently believed that it was more important in the long run to keep China engaged in the world economy, open to the liberalizing influence of trade and the Internet, than to insist on human rights for dissidents.[58]

Making value trade-offs is stressful, and often people try to avoid them. Experimental subjects faced with conflicting values are more likely to select alternatives that meet a minimal threshold on all important attributes.[59] In a survey, business executives stated that they would be unwilling to give up any of their authority, even in return for a salary increase.[60] Often leaders are unwilling to admit even privately that trade-offs must be made. In such cases, presidents may use psychological methods of coping with painful decisions, such as downgrading the importance of the value not chosen or denying that any sacrifice has been made.[61] When faced with the morally and politically difficult decision to drop the bomb on Japan, President Truman was unwilling to admit to himself that Japanese women and children would also be killed. After he approved the final list of possible targets for the A-bomb, in which Nagasaki and Kokura were substituted for the national treasures of Kyoto, Truman wrote in his diary, "I have told Sec. of War . . . Stimson to use it so that military objectives and soldiers and sailors are the target and not women and children."[62] Yet, Truman knew the power of the bomb, and hitting a city could not help but kill women and children.

President Reagan was characteristically unwilling to make trade-offs. He believed that he could have a balanced budget, tax cuts, increased defense spending, and no cuts in entitlement programs like Social Security. Reagan used supply side economics to justify his predilections, which were to improve U.S. defenses while lowering the tax burden on the American people. According to supply side economics, a tax cut would yield increased business investment, which would eventually augment tax revenues. When the deficit ballooned, Reagan saw the opportunity to use the deficit to force Congress to make cuts in domestic programs. Besides, he thought, given enough time, supply side economics might work. Reagan tried to defer making the difficult choices as long as possible.[63] Political considerations reinforce the innate psychological tendency to deny the need to sacrifice important values; a choice might harm some domestic constituency.[64]

Timing of Action

The president must decide whether a decision is needed immediately or can be postponed. The situation itself may impose deadlines for decision—an upcoming summit meeting, a scheduled speech, a coup in another state. But even external pressures are susceptible to differing interpretations, affording the opportunity for judgment. This raises the question of how leaders decide that an emerging problem is important enough to warrant action. How did President Bush know that it was an opportune moment to work for German unification? The president may believe that he must take advantage of the favorable political climate for action even though he does not have all the necessary facts or a well-defined strategy to begin with to achieve an important goal.

Just as important as knowing when to act is knowing when to wait—for the situation to clarify itself, for the emergence of different alternatives, for a chance to probe the other side's intentions. Presidents have blundered when they believed, falsely, that they had no choice but to make an immediate decision.

PLAN OF THE VOLUME

The essays that follow consider good judgment from a variety of perspectives. Renshon uses character psychology to derive insights into the nature of good judgment—the quality of analysis, reflection, and insight that informs consequential decisions. Analyzing judgment from the "inside out," he suggests that good judgment depends on having a strong personal and political identity, self-esteem, and empathy. He proposes that some of the traits that contribute to good judgment may be exhibited by the candidates during the presidential campaign. Wayne argues that demonization of "enemy" impairs the quality of foreign policy judgments by creating perceptual blinders and domestic political constraints.

Several case studies investigate these preliminary ideas about what it means to exercise good political judgment in foreign policy. Larson analyzes why Truman ignored the recommendation of his expert advisers in approving an airlift of supplies to the West Berlin population during the 1948 Soviet blockade of West Berlin, a decision that ultimately proved to be more realistic and effective than courses of action advocated by those more knowledgeable about military and diplomatic matters. Farnham discusses how and why Reagan, often criticized as being intellectually incurious and dogmatic, could exercise good judgment in his dealings with Soviet leader Mikhail Gorbachev. Welch, on the other hand, shows how emotion and cultural biases can lead to misjudgment, particularly by political novices.

Jentleson and Bennett maintain that policy planning can improve foreign policy judgments by putting "hot" issues into a longer-term, more analytical perspective. They support the idea of using policy planners as independent source of advice, one that is less biased by parochial organizational concerns. From his experience in government and as a foreign policy analyst, Haass identifies some of the difficult conceptual issues involved in evaluating foreign policy judgment. He argues for a more careful consideration of the situation as it appeared to policymakers at the time and the role that implementation and fortune might have played in contributing to the outcome. We don't always know good foreign policy judgment when we see it. He offers some suggestions for improving foreign policy judgment by applying general knowledge to the problem and enhancing competition between alternative sources of analysis and advice. George provides a framework for analyzing good judgment and describes the various trade-offs that political decision makers may have to address. To carry out these judgmental tasks effectively requires what George calls "political rationality." Renshon identifies the character traits that enabled George W. Bush, a neophyte in foreign policy who was widely ridiculed during the presidential campaign for his lack of basic knowledge, to effectively handle the war in Afghanistan and national security issues arising from the 9/11 attacks. Ending the book, Larson draws on the case studies and more theoretical chapters for insights about what good foreign policy judgment is and how to improve its exercise by future foreign policymakers.

NOTES

1. Irving M. Destler, *Presidents, Bureaucrats, and Foreign Policy* (Princeton, N.J.: Princeton University Press, 1972); Graham Allison and Peter Szanton, *Remaking Foreign Policy: The Organizational Connection* (New York: Basic Books, 1976); Stephen Hess, *Organizing the Presidency* (Washington, D.C.: Brookings Institution, 1976).

2. Alexander L. George, *Presidential Decisionmaking in Foreign Policy: The Effective Use of Information and Advice* (Boulder, Colo.: Westview, 1980).

3. George, *Presidential Decisionmaking*, 39–47, 191–208.

4. George, *Presidential Decisionmaking*, 2–3.

5. Richard E. Neustadt and Ernest R. May, *Thinking in Time: The Uses of History for Decision-Makers* (New York: Free Press, 1986).

6. Neustadt and May, *Thinking in Time*, 248–56.

7. Alexander L. George, *Bridging the Gap: Theory and Practice in Foreign Policy* (Washington, D.C.: U.S. Institute of Peace, 1993), 21.

8. James R. Schlesinger, "Uses and Abuses of Analysis," *Survival* 10 (October 1968): 35.

9. Herbert A. Simon, *Administrative Behavior: A Study of Decision-Making Processes in Administrative Organizations*, 4th ed. (New York: Free Press, 1997), 60.

10. Robert Jervis, "Intelligence and Foreign Policy: A Review Essay," *International Security* 11 (1986/87): 151–52.

11. Ernest R. May, *Strange Victory: Hitler's Conquest of France* (New York: Hill & Wang, 2000), 460–61.

12. Isaiah Berlin, "Political Judgment," in Isaiah Berlin, *The Sense of Reality: Studies in Ideas and Their History*, ed. Henry Hardy (New York: Farrar, Straus & Giroux, 1996), 46.

13. Dean Acheson, *Present at the Creation: My Years in the State Department* (New York: Norton, 1969), 141.

14. Columbia Oral History interview, August 10, 1987, quoted in John P. Burke and Fred I. Greenstein, *How Presidents Test Reality: Decisions on Vietnam, 1954 and 1965* (New York: Russell Sage Foundation, 1989), 63. I am indebted to Fred Greenstein for bringing this quote to my attention.

15. Benjamin Barber, *The Conquest of Politics: Liberal Philosophy in Democratic Times* (Princeton, N.J.: Princeton University Press, 1988), xii.

16. Howard Gardner, *Frames of Mind: The Theory of Multiple Intelligences* (New York: Basic Books, 1993).

17. James A. Baker, *Politics and Diplomacy* (New York: Putnam's, 1995), 38–39.

18. Sir Geoffrey Vickers, *The Art of Judgment: A Study of Policy Making* (London: Chapman & Hall, 1965), 40, 73–74.

19. See also George, *Presidential Decisionmaking in Foreign Policy;* George, *Bridging the Gap;* George, "Analysis and Judgment in Policymaking," in *Education in a Research University*, ed. K. J. Arrow, B. C. Eaves, and O. Ingram (Stanford, Calif.: Stanford University Press, 1996).

20. Anthony Eden, *The Reckoning* (Boston: Houghton Mifflin, 1973), 621; Wallace diary, December 11, 1945, *The Price of Vision: The Diary of Henry A. Wallace, 1942–1946*, ed. John M. Blum (Boston: Houghton Mifflin, 1973), 528.

21. David Gergen, *Eyewitness to Power: The Essence of Leadership, Nixon to Clinton* (New York: Simon & Schuster, 2000), 293.

22. George C. Herring, *LBJ and Vietnam: A Different Kind of War* (Austin: University of Texas Press, 1994), 7.

23. Gergen, *Eyewitness to Power,* 261–62; Elizabeth Drew, *On the Edge: The Clinton Presidency* (New York: Simon & Schuster, 1994), 37.

24. Peter G. Bourne, *Jimmy Carter: A Comprehensive Biography from Plains to Postpresidency* (New York: Simon & Schuster, 1997), 423.

25. Drew, *On the Edge,* 146–60, quotation on 150.

26. Kenneth R. Hammond, *Human Judgment and Social Policy: Irreducible Uncertainty, Inevitable Error, Unavoidable Injustice* (New York: Oxford University Press, 1996), 60. See also Jerome Bruner, *The Process of Education* (Cambridge, Mass.: Harvard University Press, 1960), 13.

27. Daniel Kahneman and Amos Tversky, "On the Study of Statistical Intuitions," in

Judgment under Uncertainty: Heuristics and Biases, ed. Daniel Kahneman, Paul Slovic, and Amos Tversky (Cambridge: Cambridge University Press, 1982), 494; Kenneth S. Bowers, "Intuition and Discovery," in *Theories of the Unconscious and Theories of the Self*, ed. Raphael Stern (Hillsdale, N.J. Analytic Press, 1987), 78–79; Robyn M. Dawes, *Rational Choice in an Uncertain World* (New York: Harcourt, Brace, 1988), 5; K. R. Hammond, "Intuitive and Analytical Cognition: Information Models," in *Concise Encyclopedia of Information Processing in Systems and Organizations*, ed. Andrew P. Sage (Oxford: Pergamon, 1990), 309–10; Ray W. Cooksey, *Judgment Analysis: Theory, Methods, and Applications* (New York: Academic Press, 1996), 14.

28. K. R. Hammond, R. M. Hamm, J. Grassia, and T. Pearson, "Direct Comparison of the Efficacy of Intuitive and Analytical Cognition in Expert Judgment," *IEEE Transactions on Systems, Man, and Cybernetics SMC-17* (1987): 753–70.

29. Michael Polanyi, *Personal Knowledge: Towards a Post-critical Philosophy* (Chicago: University of Chicago Press, 1958); Herbert L. Dreyfus and Stuart E. Dreyfus with Tom Athansiou, *Mind over Machine: The Power of Human Intuition and Expertise in the Era of the Computer* (New York: Blackwell, 1986), 29.

30. Lou Cannon, *The President: The Role of a Lifetime* (New York: Simon & Schuster, 1991), 138.

31. Irving L. Janis, *Crucial Decisions: Leadership in Policymaking and Crisis Management* (New York: Free Press, 1989), 72.

32. Stephen A. Ambrose, *Eisenhower*, vol. 2: *The President* (New York: Simon & Schuster, 1984), 528.

33. Michael R. Beschloss, ed., *Taking Charge: The Johnson White House Tapes, 1943–1949* (New York: Simon & Schuster, 1997), 370.

34. Larry Berman, *Planning a Tragedy: The Americanization of the Vietnam War* (New York: Norton, 1982), 119.

35. Alfred Steinberg, *Sam Johnson's Boy: A Close-up of the President from Texas* (New York: Macmillan, 1968), 500, cited in John P. Burke and Fred I. Greenstein, *How Presidents Test Reality: Decisions on Vietnam, 1954 and 1965* (New York: Russell Sage Foundation, 1989), 12.

36. Burke and Greenstein, *How Presidents Test Reality*, 189; Herring, *LBJ and Vietnam*, 185.

37. *New York Times*, November 21, 1965, quoted in Walter LaFeber, "Johnson, Vietnam, and Tocqueville," in *Lyndon Johnson Confronts the World: American Foreign Policy, 1963–1968*, ed. Warren I. Cohen and Nancy Bernkopf Tucker (Cambridge: Cambridge University Press, 1994), 48.

38. Brian VanDeMark, *Into the Quagmire: Lyndon Johnson and the Escalation of the Vietnam War* (New York: Oxford University Press, 1991); Herring, *LBJ and Vietnam*, 125–30.

39. Bourne, *Jimmy Carter*, 420–21.

40. Burke and Greenstein, *How Presidents Test Reality*, 214, 247; Herring, *LBJ and Vietnam*, 127.

41. James Reston, "Washington: President Nixon's Priorities," *New York Times*, March 16, 1969.

42. R. W. Apple Jr., "A Domestic Sort with Global Worries," *New York Times*, August 25, 1999, 1.

43. David McCullough, *Truman* (New York: Simon & Schuster, 1992), 564.

44. "Memorandum for the President," November 19, 1947, Clark Clifford Papers, Political File, "Clifford-Rowe Memorandum of November 19, 1947, [1 of 2.], HSTL, Independence, Mo. Although Rowe wrote the memorandum, which Clifford revised, Clifford signed it, because Truman did not like Rowe and would not have read it otherwise. See Clark Clifford with Richard Holbrooke, *Counsel to the President: A Memoir* (New York: Random House, 1991), 190–91.

45. Lawrence R. Jacobs and Robert Y. Shapiro, "Issues, Candidate Image and Priming: The Use of Private Polls in Kennedy's 1960 Presidential Campaign," *American Political Science Review* 88 (September 1994): 534.

46. Cited in Gordon Craig and Alexander L. George, *Force and Statecraft,* 3d ed. (New York: Oxford University Press, 1995), 123. On legitimation, see B. Thomas Trout, "Rhetoric Revisited: Political Legitimation and the Cold War," *International Studies Quarterly* 19 (1975): 251–84; and Alexander L. George, "Domestic Constraints on Regime change in U.S. Foreign Policy: The Need for Policy Legitimacy," in *Change in the International System,* ed. Ole R. Holsti, Randy M. Siverson, and Alexander L. George (Boulder, Colo.: Westview, 1980).

47. Erwin C. Hargrove, *Jimmy Carter as President: Leadership and the Politics of the Public Good* (Baton Rouge: Louisiana State University Press, 1988), 123.

48. Drew, *On the Edge,* 42–48.

49. Richard E. Neustadt, *Presidential Power and the Modern Presidents: the Politics of Leadership from Roosevelt to Reagan* (New York: Free Press, 1990).

50. Bourne, *Jimmy Carter,* 373, 383.

51. Lou Cannon, *President Reagan: The Role of a Lifetime,* 111, 196–97.

52. Richard N. Haass, "Paradigm Lost," *Foreign Affairs* 74 (January/February 1995): 43–58.

53. Neustadt and May, *Thinking in Time,* 80–81.

54. Ambrose, *Eisenhower,* 520.

55. Robert L. Hutchings, *American Diplomacy and the End of the Cold War: An Insider's Account of U.S. Policy in Europe, 1989–1992* (Baltimore: Johns Hopkins University Press, 1997), 46; Michael R. Beschloss and Strobe Talbott, *At the Highest Levels: The Inside Story of the Cold War* (Boston: Little, Brown, 1993), chap. 4; Philip Zelikow and Condoleezza Rice, *Germany Unified and Europe Transformed* (Cambridge, Mass.: Harvard University Press, 1997), 24–32.

56. Strobe Talbott, *Endgame: The Inside Story of SALT II* (New York: Harper & Row, 1979). See also Neustadt and May, *Thinking in Time,* 111–33.

57. George, *Presidential Decisionmaking,* 28–36.

58. Steven Erlanger and David E. Sanger, "On Global Stage, Clinton's Pragmatic Turn," *New York Times,* July 29, 1996, 1.

59. Y. Ganzach, "Attribute Scatter and Decision Outcome: Judgment versus Choice," *Organizational Behavior and Human Decision Processes* 62 (1995): 113–22.

60. Zur Shapira, "Making Trade-offs between Job Attributes," *Organizational Behavior and Human Performance* 28 (1981): 331–55.

61. George, *Presidential Decisionmaking,* 32–33.

62. Barton J. Bernstein, "The Atomic Bombings Reconsidered," *Foreign Affairs* 74 (January/February 1995): 147.

63. Richard E. Neustadt, "Presidents, Politics, and Analysis," lecture given at the Institute of Public Policy and Management, Graduate School of Public Affairs, University of Washington, Brewster C. Denny lecture series, May 13, 1986.

64. George, *Presidential Decisionmaking,* 34.

· 2 ·

Psychological Sources of Good Judgment in Political Leaders

A Framework for Analysis

Stanley A. Renshon

*T*echnology has shrunk the world, but not its problems. The increasing sophistication of political instrumentalities has made leaders more powerful, but not necessarily more successful. The question seems not to be, as Burns (1978, 1) asked, "Where are the great titans of leadership?" Rather, the real question seems both more prosaic and paradoxically more profound: Where are the effective ones? Having failed to resolve many old problems, it remains an open question whether leaders will be more successful with new ones.

We can see these paradoxes unfold in the United States. We expect our president to manage the domestic economy, ensure domestic tranquility, and keep Americans safe at home and powerful abroad. We give him the technical means to do so—budgets, troops, advisers, and staff—and an almost endless list of resources he can call upon. Yet, few modern presidents have been considered outstanding, and that judgment could be made of many leaders abroad as well.

Immense instrumentalities and modest results are a key paradox of modern political leadership. Are leaders asked to do too much to expect successful decisions? Have the problems become too complex to yield to rigorous analysis? Have the expectations become too high to allow even the best leaders to succeed?

To some degree all of these elements play a role. However, the core of the problem lies elsewhere. Instrumentality is a vehicle of leadership decision making, not its essence.

Graham Allison (1971, emphasis in original) opens his classic book *Essence of Decision* with a quote from John Fitzgerald Kennedy: "The *essence of ultimate decision* remains impenetrable to the observer—often, indeed, to the decider himself. . . . There will always be the dark and tangled stretches in the decision process—mysterious even to those who may be the most intimately involved."

This chapter starts with a different premise. There is nothing mysterious about the "essence of decision." It is the leader's judgment. Our purpose here is not to romanticize but to understand it.

At the heart of leadership lies choice. And at the heart of choice lies judgment. It is here that the leader's character, experience, and vision intersect with political realities to produce the results that are central to assessing any leader's performance.

Judgment is a complex but little studied concept with obvious relevance to leadership performance. Having reached the point of diminishing returns with an emphasis on decision procedures, a focus on judgment offers the possibility of making new advances on a subject that might well result in better decisions. However, such a focus immediately brings us face to face with a set of basic questions.

What is judgment? How can it be analyzed? What differences are there between flawed judgments and those that appear adequate to the circumstances? Is there such a thing as good judgment, and if so, how is it related to circumstances? Can we distinguish a set of characteristics that would support the exercise of good judgment? We clearly have more questions than answers.

THE NATURE OF GOOD JUDGMENT

Any answers to such questions must begin with the nature of judgment itself.[1] We can understand judgment as *the quality of analysis, reflection, and ultimately insight that informs the making of consequential decisions.* Only decisions that pose significant questions and therefore have significant consequences for presidential areas of responsibility raise issues of good or flawed judgment in any fundamental way.

I term these major forks in the decision road *framing judgments.* Framing judgments are crucial because they represent key and sometimes (but not always) starkly contrasting alternatives, each of which will point to different paths, open up some options, close others, and bring about different results. One consequence of emphasizing the relationship of judgment to framing options is that it allows us to distinguish the quality of judgment in the making of framing decisions from those that follow.[2]

Framing judgments are fundamentally important to a leader's capacity to have successful outcomes. They are central to the leader's self-placement in a position where he or she will have the opportunity to exercise good judgment as the decision process proceeds. In short: Wrong framework, bad judgment.

The development of a framework for assessing judgment requires us to focus on four related considerations: the problem itself, the domain(s) within which judgments are made, the actual judgments that were made, and the results of those judgments. In analyzing the problem, we must first know what fundamental issues it raises. In analyzing domains, one can distinguish domestic from foreign policy spheres (Wildavsky 1996) and then further specify an appropriate placement within those domains for a particular problem (e.g., economic interdependence). Some problems, such as terrorism, may transverse domains. In analyzing the decisions themselves, we need to understand what factors were weighed (e.g., the relative weight given to policy and political concerns[3]) and with what results. Lastly, in analyzing outcomes, we need to appreciate the consequences of the judgment.

Judgment Frameworks

Judgment is a joint function of the match between a leader's analytical and reflective abilities, on the one hand, and the nature of the problem to be faced, on the other. Procedural, cognitive, and psychodynamic models of decision making have treated the problem at hand as a given rather than as a variable.[4] Nothing could be farther from the truth. Analyzing judgment without attention to the issue that calls it forth is like taking a picture without the proper lens. You will miss great deal of what you are trying to capture.

The analysis of a leader's judgment is concerned with the problem to be addressed in two distinct ways. First, appreciating the nature of a problem is crucial to deciding what is at issue and what solutions are viable. Additionally, the nature of the problem also has an impact on the understanding and experience that a leader can bring to bear on it.

I use the term *judgment framework* to denote the major conceptual organization that a leader brings to bear on the analysis of a problem. Judgment frameworks can be conceptualized as *appropriate* or *defective*. An appropriate framework places the problem into a frame for analysis that correctly, but not necessarily fully, fits the problem at hand. For example, before the collapse of the Soviet Union, many international problems could be put into the conceptual category "superpower conflict" or "East–West tensions." This does not mean that a problem did not have other dimensions, only that the category selected did fit a major, primary aspect of the problem.

As noted, framing judgments are critically important. Leaders and senior policymakers must be able to place a problem in the correct category. Sometimes, the failure to do so has most momentous consequences. Consider the response of President Kennedy and his chief advisers to the introduction of offensive missiles into Cuba in 1962 by the Soviet Union. At first, the president and his advisers saw the issue primarily as a military one calling for a military response, such as air strikes against the missile sites or an invasion, if that measure failed.

Yet, that view began to turn when Robert McNamara spoke (May and Zelikow 1997, 111–13, my emphasis):

> **Bundy**: I would like to throw one [suggestion] in that I do not think the Army and Chiefs of Staff would normally consider. And that is the possibility of genuinely making a quite large scale [air] strike followed by [paratrooper] drop. . . .
>
> **McNamara**: It seems to me that there are some major alternatives here that I don't think we discussed here today . . . the first is what I call a political approach. . . . I'll be quite frank. *I don't think there is a military problem here . . .* and therefore, and I've gone on through this today, and I asked myself, "Well, what is it then, if it isn't a military problem?" Well, it's just exactly this problem: that if Cuba should possess a capacity to carry out offensive actions against the U.S., the U.S. would act.
>
> **Unidentified**: That's right.
>
> **Unidentified**: That's right. You can get around that one.
>
> **McNamara**: Now it's that problem. *This is a domestic political problem.*

Somewhat later (1997, 114, emphasis mine; see also 134), he returns to his reframing:

> **McNamara**: [W]hat I tried to do was develop a little package, that meets the action requirements of the paragraph that I read. Because, as I suggested, *I don't believe that it's primarily a military problem. It's primarily a domestic political problem.*

It is now clear in retrospect that McNamara's reframing of the problem away from a military one was instrumental in bringing the group around to the political solution that had the threat of force in the background but not as the primary thrust of the American response.

A defective framework on the other hand, represents an inappropriate assignment of a problem to a framework whose lessons are not generally applicable and that, therefore, does not provide adequate historical or personal experience that can serve as a reliable guide to judgment. Placing U.S.-Japanese economic competition into the framework of "trade wars" may correctly reflect their competitive economic nature but inappropriately add the model of "war" to what is essentially an alliance and developing partnership.

One pressing need for developing a theory of judgment is a greater understanding of the ways in which judgments can go awry from the inappropriate categorical placement of a problem. Here, we can offer several suggestions. One is that frameworks may simply be insufficiently inclusive to contain the important aspects of the problem. The problem here is not that the framework is wrong but rather that it is incomplete.

This can more easily occur if the available framework is both sensible and dominant. When that happens, it tends to overshadow the consideration of other possible, even complementary, frameworks. One example of this occurred during the Cuban missile crisis. A reading of the National Security Council (NSC) transcripts (Welch and Blight 1987/88; Tractenberg 1985) reveals that little thought was given to the Cuban view of this crisis at the time it was unfolding.

At a conference that brought together crisis participants held in 1991 (Blight, Lewis, and Welch 1991), General Smith pointed out that "at that time people . . . dealing with military matters—those at the civilian level and at the military level—*looked at everything primarily through a U.S.-Soviet prism*" (emphasis mine). Arthur Schlesinger, another participant in the events themselves and at the conference, pointed out that "the reduction of a complex triangular crisis to a bilateral conflict between the two super powers . . . reflected . . . unconscious Great Power attitudes towards small states" (197). The use of the great-power conflict lens was not wrong as a judgment framework. However, its power tended to obscure other important considerations.

One question regarding judgment frameworks is the role of analogies (Khong 1993; Neustadt and May 1998). These may be references to specific historical circumstances (e.g., Munich for the dangers of appeasement) or historical experiences that give clues to how leaders think history operates (e.g., the domino theory). Some analogies, though, provide multiple messages. America's war in Vietnam has been viewed as a cautionary tale of (1) fighting only those wars you are prepared to win, (2) committing immediate and overwhelming power to the purpose of winning, (3) not entering a war without public explanation and support, and so on.

Both frameworks and analogies are cognitive repositories and cuing devices that help orient, or disorient, a leader to important aspects of the parallels or concerns that are relevant to his or her judgments. Sometimes analogies are simply minor partners with the more dominant frameworks that truly frame a leader's judgments. Sometimes they are the framework itself.

At the start of the Cuban missile crisis, Dean Rusk (May and Zelikow 1997, 129) reminded Kennedy's senior advisers of several historical analogies including World War I, World War II, and the Korean War to make the point that the support of the American people was central and that consideration "would militate in favor of a consultation with Khrushchev" before decisive action was taken. Yet, this was offered more in the nature of one possible element to consider and not a firm recommendation based on historical analogy of what should be done. On the other hand, the Munich analogy and the dangers of "appeasing aggression" appear to have been very much on George Bush's mind after Saddam Hussein invaded Kuwait. He repeated several times on the day of the invasion, "This will not stand." And it didn't.

A strong framing judgment can act as a barrier to seriously considering alternative frameworks. On the other hand, it can also help to fend off the less adequately framing judgments of others. At the onset of the Gulf War, one top Bush adviser began a presentation of how the United States might adapt to a world in which Iraq controlled Kuwait oil production. The president cut him off with the curt comment that we would not "adapt," period.

Or, consider Adlai Stevenson's first suggestion to Kennedy on the eve of the unfolding Cuban missile crisis. He wrote (May and Zelikow 1997, 118–19, emphasis in original; see also 201), "*the means adapted have such incalculable consequences you should have made it clear that the existence of nuclear missiles anywhere is negotiable anywhere before we start anything.*" There were two major problems with this idea. First, it offered up a major possible bargaining chip that the president had—the willingness to discuss other missile sites, without getting anything in return. Second, as phrased, it appeared to suggest that the nuclear shield that had provided rough stability between two superpowers would be open to abandonment. The president ignored this recommendation.

Later, Stevenson proposed that the president offer to abandon Guantanamo base and withdraw U.S. missiles from Turkey to induce the Russians to withdraw their missiles from Cuba. The president (May and Zelikow 1997, 199) "sharply rejected the thought of surrendering our base at Guantanamo in the present situation. He felt that such action would convey to the world that we had been frightened into abandoning our position. He was not opposed to discussing the withdrawal of our missiles from Turkey and Greece [sic] but he was firm in saying we should only make such a proposal later."

May and Zelikow (1997, 700) report the provocative finding that the use of historical analogies declined over the unfolding of the Cuban missile crisis. This suggests that while analogies may provide an initial set of more or less helpful cues, good judgment lies elsewhere. It may lie not so much in the appropriateness of this or that historical experience but in the ability to see and understand *this particular* historical one.

PSYCHOLOGICAL ELEMENTS OF GOOD JUDGMENT

While good judgment is, to some degree, contextually specific, I argue that poor judgment tends to be systematic. Good judgment, as noted, is related to the qualities of both analysis and reflection. This distinction is meant to underscore the point that good judgment is only partially cognitive.

The model of judgment developed here distinguishes among analysis, reflection, and enactment. *Analysis* refers to the capacity to discern the essential nature of problems, the potential avenues of response and their implications, and a sense of the method(s) by which these might be accomplished. Of course, this requires the ability to comprehend and process information, as well as to compare information elements with each other and with other frames of reference. These are ordinarily considered cognitive skills, and, to some extent, they are. However, they are substantially affected by other elements of a person's psychology.

Reflection refers to the capacity to consider and evaluate analytical information from a series of perspectives. Good judgment also requires the ability to place information in a framework that makes intellectual, experiential, and emotional sense, not only to the leader but also to those whom the decisions affect. The reflective dimension of good judgment, therefore, rests not only on cognitive skills but on the capacity to anchor analysis by frameworks of understanding, evaluation, and action. These include the leader's own ideals, values, and views; the values and views of other actors involved; and both long- and short-term political/strategic considerations.

Finally, *enactment* refers to the ability to find and utilize means to implement the results of judgment. The focus here is on the means that are chosen. Are they adequate and appropriate to the task? Does a leader choose to talk, to threaten, to fight? Does a leader concentrate on one or choose a mix? Could other, less costly means accomplish the same ends? These questions are important not only because they bear on the issue of the quality of a leader's thought and judgment but because they also reveal something about his leadership.

Psychologically then, good judgment reflects a set of composite skills. Among them are the ability to:

1. see the framing judgment for the crucial choice point that it represents;
2. understand the essential elements of a problem and their significance, and place it within an appropriate judgment framework;
3. consider and reflect on the range of issues and values raised by the situation in order to deal adequately with the various interests (political, social, and psychological) involved;
4. consider and reflect on information that is frequently limited and often discordant;
5. make use of, but not be subservient to, feeling or impulse,[5] including the anxiety generated by uncertainty and high risk;
6. place these considerations in a framework of understanding that ade-

quately assesses the basic nature of the problem and points to a range
of responses that preserve, and even perhaps advance, the values and
interests at risk to develop a fitting solution;

7. draw on the understanding of the past and present (point 1) to consider
how alternative choices will shape the future (the extrapolation of
implications);

8. develop, set in motion, and maintain a series of steps to accomplish
purposes consistent with one's understanding of the issues raised and
values at risk: the steps should accomplish these goals with minimal
possible or necessary harm.

This list includes both analytic and reflective skills. Some of these capacities are clearly cognitive; others are more clearly affective. Some require the leader to translate effective thought into effective policy. All however are, to some degree, shaped by elements of the leader's internal character psychology. The relationships among them, however, are varied and complex. It is to these linkages that we turn in the following sections.

THE PSYCHOLOGICAL SOURCES OF
GOOD JUDGMENT: CHARACTER

A leader's judgment is not primarily an act of cognition or general intelligence, as cognitive models of political decision making suggest. Judgment reflects a blend of intelligence, experience, and insight. It also requires a consolidated set of character elements to withstand the rigors of the decision process.

I have defined character (Renshon 1998b, 185–96) as an individual's basic psychological stance, along with the capacities and resultant style that he or she brings to bear toward experience. Character, at its best, reflects a leader's sense of him- or herself as an able, honest, and related person. It includes the style that the leader has developed to engage the world and his or her beliefs in doing so. The leader's feelings of capacity and worth, and the psychological structures that support them, are linked to good judgment in a number of ways. So, too, feelings of inadequacy (or hyperadequacy) or low (or high) self-regard and the psychological structures in which they are embedded are linked with poor judgment. We shall explore both of these sets of relationships shortly.

In examining character, we must also be interested in the extent to which a leader's character structure has evolved, consolidated, and integrated the diverse demands with which it must deal.[6] Among these are the capacity both to modulate and to satisfy basic (developmentally normal and appropriate) wishes for accomplishment and recognition. Mature character consolidation also reflects having satisfactorily resolved the sometimes conflicting needs and resulting dilemmas; for interpersonal connectedness and personal autonomy, for approval and independence, and for self-interest and a concern for others. While poor judgment can result from a failure to respond adequately to threat, it can also occur when a leader realizes the risks but because of overconfidence is not deterred. Unbridled ambition and rage (Renshon 1993) are two other characterological sources of poor judgment. Lastly, good judgment reflects having developed and consolidated a personal and professional identity (including a set of ideals and values that provide the leader with an internal compass for evaluation), which provides a vehicle for the expression of oneself in the world, which is in turn voluntarily recognized and validated by others.

Character consolidation reflects relative success in another crucial developmental and functional task— that of making and developing a range of interpersonal relationships. Being able to make emotional connections to others reflects a number of important psychological accomplishments. It reflects a capacity to go beyond self-interest and provides direct emotional and cognitive experience with the concerns and feelings that others have. This experience is crucial to empathetic understanding, and this capacity is a fundamental element of political empathy and, I will argue, good policy judgment as well.

JUDGMENT FRAMEWORKS: THREE CHARACTEROLOGICAL QUESTIONS

Can characterological strengths overcome the operation of incomplete judgment frameworks? Preliminary evidence suggests the answer is a qualified yes. The NSC tapes reveal that on the first day of the Cuban missile crisis, Kennedy was not only surprised but stunned and enraged by what he saw as the audacity and duplicity of Khrushchev's move of missiles into Cuba. The first NSC session was given over to Kennedy's assertion that the missiles must go, most likely by military force in the form of an air strike.

It is one reflection of Kennedy's characterological strength that he was able to recover from his shock and anger and harness his determination to respond carefully as well as forcefully. It is also evident in his openness to information and argument during the process. The level of give-and-take that characterizes the meetings is evident, even if the progression of the argument is not always systematic or sequential.

Complex judgment frameworks usually involve the integration of one or more frameworks into which the problem might productively fit. It is now clear, for example, that a more complex framework for judgment and analysis during the Cuban missile crisis would have been one that included U.S.–Cuba (large power–small state) relationships. Had Excomm committee members had that model in their minds, they might have been better able to answer the question "Why would the Soviet Union put missiles in Cuba?" and perhaps had the basis for a settlement of the crisis, a "no-invasion pledge."[7]

Do complex judgment frameworks require an equally complex mind? The ability to hold and synthesize alternative frameworks is partially a reflection of cognitive capacity. Some leaders are able to integrate and hold more information, what Suedfeld (1976; see also Tetlock 1984) has termed *cognitive complexity*. However, it is not clear that cognitive complexity is necessary for high-quality decisions, an issue that Tetlock raises.

Complex thinking does not necessarily lead to better policy judgment. Obsessive thinkers, for example, usually exhibit highly complex and differentiated thinking. However, such individuals do not as a rule have good judgment. While their thinking may be complex, it often lacks depth, flexibility, and sophistication. It is the latter three qualities, not the first, that help define the quality of good judgment.

What is crucial to good judgment is *understanding*, not complexity per se. The capacity to see a problem clearly, for what it is and what it represents, is absolutely crucial. The amount of reflective insight that a leader brings to bear on a problem may prove more important than the degree of complexity in his or her thinking. Reflective insight, a crucial element of good judgment is, itself, only partially related to cognitive complexity.

Is good judgment situational? Character is enacted in patterns. The psychological structures that underlie these enactment patterns do so because they have become consolidated and therefore continue over time. This would seem to argue in favor of a general characteristic of good (or poor) judgment in leaders. While accurate to some degree, the problem with that view is that good judgment is also connected to particular domains, problems, and the frameworks of understanding that are a by-product of experience. A leader's range and depth of understanding of a problem is related to his or her experience with (and understanding) of problems of this particular sort.[8]

A president, for example, could have good judgment on domestic issues and politics but lack the experiential frame to have equally good judgment on national security or foreign policy issues, and vice versa. Even within one domain, say, international relations, it seems possible for different problems to result in different levels of judgment in response. A president, for example, might be very well positioned to exercise good judgment in the areas of international political competition and conflict, but not be well prepared if the major international challenge were, say, primarily economic.[9] This is not to contend that good judgments cannot be reached in unfamiliar areas, only that it is facilitated by understanding that has been refined by experience.

The extent to which good judgment is possible in the absence of accumulated experience in a major area (e.g., domestic politics or foreign policy) is an open question. Certainly experience is no guarantee of good judgment or of successful presidential performance. For example, in the 1992 presidential election, Ross Perot argued that his experience running large corporations and "getting things done" was a sufficient qualification for him to be seriously considered for president.

Perhaps. But what experience provides are judgment frameworks developed and refined in the same contexts in which they will be applied. Perot's experience was head of a business of which he was undisputed boss. Yet, politics in the United States are more clearly a matter of "persuade and convince" than of "command and control." Moreover, Perot's business experience, however successful and whatever the lessons he learned there, would not necessarily prepare him for the political and military complexities of possible military intervention in Bosnia. When experience is lacking, sophisticated judgment frameworks are difficult to develop.

Policy Framing and Analysis: The Role of Character

Good judgment begins with understanding the nature of the problem. Of course, to understand the essential elements of a problem, one must first recognize there is one. Not all leaders are able to do this. Some cannot discern the facts, others discern the facts but decline to accept them, while others feel that there are special reasons they can afford to ignore them.

At the level of character, the reasons for not being able to grapple with problems can be complex and varied. It can originate in either a meager or inflated sense of capacity and self-regard. Leaders who suffer from the first can either be too inhibited to respond boldly and directly to an issue or prefer optimism over realism. Similarly, the optimistic weighing of sobering information (wishful thinking), a dislike of conflict, a strong sensitivity to criticism, and a strong need to be liked all inhibit the capacity to meet difficulties directly.

On the other hand, an inflated sense of capacity and self-regard can lead to equally damaging results. The sense that "it can't happen here" can inhibit the accurate appreciation and diagnosis of problems. So, too, can feelings in the president that he possesses unusual competence, invulnerability, and entitlement.[10] These beliefs arise from feelings that the leader is special, powerful, and beyond the reach of ordinary circumstances. In such cases, a leader may discern the facts but discount their significance because of his or her special accomplishments and circumstances.

A second analytic requirement is the capacity to diagnose a problem. This is not a matter just of being smart in the IQ sense of intelligence but of being able to discern and appreciate the essential issues raised by a problem. This requires the ability to appreciate implications and to extract significance from an incomplete set of facts.

The capacity to understand and diagnose a problem often reflects a leader's range of experiences and what he or she has learned from them. Learning from experience requires that mistakes not be viewed or felt as intolerable indictments of self-competence and respect. Leaders with low self-regard have trouble learning from mistakes precisely because it is so difficult for them to acknowledge having made them without further damaging their feelings of self-worth. One basic problem that dictators have in this regard is that they are often shielded from the results of their mistakes. Therefore, experiences that might have an ameliorating effect on the leader's policy- and decision making cannot play that role.

Character and Reflective Skills

Reflective abilities require more of leaders than the capacity to analyze discrete elements. Ultimately, skillful judgment leads to higher-quality decisions because information is assembled into an understanding that both correctly diagnoses the situation and points toward adequate responses. Information alone, however abundant, is not enough.

Good judgments require a leader to weigh, evaluate, and place into a framework many elements of information, assumption, and analysis. A leader must be able to see the ways that parts relate to one another and to larger frames of reference that help give meaning to discrete events. So, too, a leader must be able to extrapolate implications from limited data and to anticipate some possible results of various situational elements and actions.

The ability to reflect, to draw on past and present, and to extrapolate from them to possible future scenarios involves several psychological processes. Among the most important is the capacity to hold onto and work with incomplete and often unsettling information while shifting among perspectives. A leader must be able to endure uncertainty without overcoming anxiety by action.

A leader must also enter into a weighing process by which the various factors are accorded importance and then put together into some overall assessment. That obviously includes the leader's own views but also requires him or her to do that with others' (discussed later). This requires more than a listing of pros and cons. It is not only the facts that must be weighed but also the frames of analysis. Does a leader give more or less weight to his or her own policy ambitions, the policy concerns of others, his or her standing with the public, calculations for reelection, or other considerations?

Individuals with tenuously held personal or political identities, or an identity that has not yet resolved and incorporated consolidated ideals, would seem to be particularly vulnerable in this process. Why? First, because a firmly rooted personal and political identity can help anchor and shape this part of the decision process. Second, because a lack of a consolidated personal and political identity also has implications for the individual's level of consolidated self-esteem. Those without such an anchor run the risks associated with having either too high, too low, or too labile a sense of themselves, which in turn has implications for learning.

Individuals with low or labile self-esteem and who lack a consolidated sense of personal effectiveness often avoid new information.[11] It may present too much of a challenge to existing views, may challenge the individual's ability to make sense of it or to act on it. Inflated esteem, on the other hands, runs the risk of leading the individual to ignore or downplay important information because it does not fit in with what the person already knows to be true or because he or she overestimates their capacity to overcome its implications.

Last, good judgment rests on the leader's ability to consider the facts and understandings from the vantage point of his or her own and others' perspectives. Judgment requires evaluation, but the question is from what perspective. Facts rarely speak for themselves, and complex situations can be addressed in numerous ways.

Ultimately, myriad facts and alternatives must be filtered to be evaluated, and the most important filter is the leader's own set of ideals, values, and personal and political ambitions. A leader without a coherent, well-informed, and consolidated personal and political identity is like a ship without a rudder. Such a leader runs the danger of drift and being subject to the strongest current.

We can see this element at work in the Cuban missile crisis. The subject of debate is a surprise attack on the missile sites before they become fully operational. The joint chiefs and other advisers support such an attack as a way of lessening the immediate danger to the United States should the sites become operational and well defended. For them, the security of the United States trumped whatever ethical concerns might, in other circumstances, be appropriate. Other advisers, chief among them Bobby Kennedy, raise the analogy of Pearl Harbor and how foreign that is to American tradition. For them, the violation of American tradition is paramount. From October 16 to October 22 that debate raged; finally, on the afternoon of the 22nd, the president spoke on the issue. His judgment did not rely wholly on the moral argument, nor was he was swayed by the immediacy argument. He decided against a surprise attack, yet his judgment blended the moral value position with the pragmatism of anticipated results (May and Zelikow 1997, 230): "After talking to General Sweeny and then after talking to others, it looked like we would have all the difficulties of Pearl Harbor and not have finished the job. The job can only be finished by invasion."

May and Zelikow (1997, 696) ask the question of whether the outcome of the missile crisis would have been different with someone other than Kennedy. They think so, but prefer not to "speculate." Yet, the evidence here, in this one very central decision, suggests that a Bobby Kennedy or a Dean Rusk in the White House would have come to that question and others with a very different mix of morality, values, and pragmatism and the associated understanding of what policy decisions would best enact them.

Character and Empathy in Good Judgment

A consolidated sense of self, including the ambitions, ideals, and values that inform it, is an important anchor for exercising good judgment in a complex decision field. But a leader acts in a world of others, many of whom do not share the same values or perspectives. An effective leader, it is said, must be able to "take the role of other."

Empathy is one of those "virtues" that bears closer examination. It has been put forward (mistakenly, in my view) as a foolproof cure for misunderstanding and conflict. In reality, there are strong limits to what empathy can accomplish along these lines. And while leadership empathy with the position of others is an important aspect of good judgment, it does not require of a leader that he or she adapt the others' view.

What is empathy? *Empathic attunement* refers to the capacity to understand another by entering into an appreciation of the other's experiences, feelings, expectations, and perspectives. It is a function of at least partially shared, in the sense of understood and appreciated, perspectives. It is a reflection of a person's ability to make real connections with others.

Why is empathetic attunement important to a leader's performance? One set of reasons has to do with the limitations of other alternatives. When weighing policy alternatives and their implications, simple or selfish national or individual self-interest is ultimately a poor criterion for adequate policy. The obvious reason is that both are frequently self-defeating. Treating general policymaking as a zero-sum game in which one's gains must necessarily be at another's expense and every compromise a substantial loss guarantees high levels of conflict, some of it unnecessary and counterproductive.

There are other reasons as well, one set political and the other more psychological, to focus on the uses of empathy. The political reason derives from the fact that considering the concerns and feelings of others is an important element of political authority in democracies. The voluntary ceding of power to a leader is based on the expectation that he or she will consider other points of view even if an ultimate decision is adverse to the leader's interests.

Leaders whose ambitions and sense of entitlement lead them to view their actions as inherently justified don't worry much about the effects of their acts on others. Doing so might require them to reconsider their sense of entitlement or moderate their ambition. They are more concerned with assessing what others feel for their own purposes. The result is "strategic empathy."

Strategic empathy[12] is clearly distinguishable from empathetic attunement. Its basic purpose is advantage rather than understanding. There are several motivational variations of this strategy; each is related to the advantages that accrue to an individual. Each reflects a different level of interpersonal connectedness.

One motivation for strategic empathy is to use understanding to get others to do what you want and what they might not necessarily wish to do. Strategic empathy in this instance is a sophisticated form of manipulation. The leader who makes use of this form sees others as objects whose primary function is to provide what he wants or needs. There is no real consideration of the other since to do so might interfere with his or her use.

A second form of strategic empathy shares some aspects of the first but is based on a different set of relationships with others. The leader using this form of strategic empathy begins from narcissistically projected feelings of self-identification with "the people." In these cases, a leader has no real empathetic connection with others apart from his or her own belief that somehow his or her rule embodies their aspirations and needs.[13] This form of strategic empathy reflects the most severe absence of interpersonal connectedness. In this case, individuals are not even considered for what they *might* provide since the leader already assumes that he or she has a right to expect that what others have is the leader's.

A last motivational source of strategic empathy is the attempt to please others. Here empathy is put in the service of knowing what others want so that the leader can please them and be liked or appreciated in return. The primary motivation in this instance is not so much to take as to receive. There is a level of connection with others in this case, but it runs counter to good judgment. The reason is that the leader becomes too attuned to what others say they need (want) without being able to distance him- or herself and perhaps make a decision others may find adverse. Here, the need to be accepted or appreciated interferes with the ability to make decisions that may be necessary but disliked.

A leader who wants to make effective and feasible policy must be able to enter into the experience of others. How does the leader accomplish this task? It requires more than political calculation or strategic empathy.

Real empathy begins with the capacity to make real interpersonal connections. This is not, it should be stressed, a matter of appreciating what "I would do or feel if I were in this situation." That approach presupposes that the other is fundamentally similar to oneself. Rather, realistic empathy involves an attempt to enter into a different frame, one that starts from different assumptions and that may lead to different conclusions.

Realistic empathy is a difficult psychological task for several reasons. It requires a leader to "suspend self" and self-interest, if possible, if only for a short period. It also requires that the leader enter into a perspective that can frequently be approached by analogy and extrapolation, and not by directly similar past experience.[14]

Realistic empathy does not require a leader be bound by the concerns, expectations, experiences, and perspectives of others, only that the leader really consider them. Ultimately, a leader must be guided by his or her values, policy aspirations, and feelings regarding a policy issue; these are appropriate and legitimate tools of policy choice.

However, for these tools to be effective, they must be present. Ultimately the ability to follow these analyses to some conclusion requires a coherent political and personal view, if not vision. These come primarily from a strong sense of purpose, direction, and identity.

While the capacity for empathy is related to good judgment, the two are not synonymous. Empathy, like other psychological characteristics, is not without its dangers. Strong empathetic attunement with others can combine with other characterological elements that can produce effects that run counter to good judgment.

A leader can become pulled too much by the emotional weight of an empathetic experience. By many accounts, President Jimmy Carter was extremely preoccupied and distracted by his concerns for the fate of the American hostages taken from the American embassy in Iran. While such concern is personally laudable, a preoccupation can have troubling consequences to presidential performance.

A leader whose characterological foundation includes low self-esteem or who lacks a consolidated sense of personal effectiveness can be overly dependent on others. Having less confidence in themselves, they may become too adept at ascertaining what others think or want. Finally, too much empathy may lead to overvaluation of some concerns and the underevaluations of others. Too much focus on the concerns of one person or group may leave other groups relatively underrepresented in the leader's thoughts.

Finally, the relentless pursuit of empathy by a leader may indicate a defensive reaction to less altruistic feelings such as anger and entitlement. Empathy requires the ability to temporarily suppress feelings of competition and the wish for personal advantage, which are a part of ordinary life. A feeling that one must suppress these feelings in favor of always being in attunement with the needs of others is not necessarily a desirable psychological trait for any leader.

Character and the Capacity to Endure Anxiety and Uncertainty

Major political decisions generate intense emotions as well as calculations. Especially in times of crisis, but other times, too, a leader must control and delay whatever impulses toward premature closure or action may be activated by the circumstances.[15] In the 1990 Gulf War, these pressures on President Bush included the potential costs of delay, which might have placed the situation beyond even difficult solutions.

The capacity to persist in trying to find solutions in the face of personal and public anxiety, policy criticism, and demands for action is crucial to being able to carry out effective policy search procedures. From day 1 of the Cuban missile crisis, there was great pressure to launch a surprise attack to take out the sites. This raised complex issues of enormous consequence. Time was passing. Missiles were becoming operational. Sites were being hardened and protected. Yet, it wasn't until the afternoon of October 22, a full week into the crisis, that Kennedy made his monumental decision not to order a surprise attack, and he did so with these words: "I've attempted to communicate why we took the course of action we did, even though, as I've said from the beginning, the idea of a quick strike was very tempting, and I really didn't give up on that until yesterday morning" (May and Zelikow 1997, 230). The capacity to resist temptation in the form of aggressive impulse was clearly important to successful avoidance of a wider, more deadly conflict.

Why is it preferable to have political leaders with a strong, stable[16] sense of effective capacity and personal confidence in office during times of crisis? One reason, as Janis and Mann (1977) have argued, is that even the best-designed information-producing procedures will not be adequately used in the absence of optimism that a solution can be found. Without hope, purpose falters.

Janis and Mann argue that a strong sense of hope in the ultimate ability to accomplish one's goals is crucial for vigilant decision making. Hope, of course, reflects a belief that accomplishment is not only possible but plausible. In the absence of a sense of effective capacity, of having had substantial positive experience in realizing one's values and ambitions, there is little likelihood that hope can be maintained in the face of deep policy dilemmas and their attendant anxiety.

In a decision context characterized by high stakes and conflicting information, the lack of personal confidence can lead to paralysis. Leaders are frequently faced with conflicting views. Often they are strongly held. The ability to preserve one's options in the face of strong views (i.e., to resist pressure) requires either strong views of one's own or the ability to tolerate the pressure of intense persuasion efforts (or both). The latter rests on those same two character elements.

Consider the case of President Warren Harding who, when faced with an important economic decision, confided to a friend (Fenno 1959, quoted in George 1974, 187):

> John, I can't make a damn thing out of this tax problem. I listen to one side and they seem right, and then God! I talk to the other side and they seem just as right, and there I am where I started. I know somewhere there is a book that would give me the truth, but hell, I couldn't read the book. I know somewhere there is an economist that knows the truth, but I don't know where to find him and haven't the sense to trust him when I do find him. God, what a job.

A leader whose basic character beliefs reflect the assumption that hard effort is worthwhile, and whose confidence in his abilities rests on solid ground, is not likely to experience the deep doubt and inadequacy reflected in Harding's lament.

Character by itself shapes but does not guarantee positive policy outcomes. A leader's skill, judgment, and character are, after all, parts of a complex causal process that includes a number of factors that cannot be fully controlled. Still, other things being equal, I would argue that substantially developed character capacities are instrumental, if not necessary, correlates to good judgment. It is also clear that good judgment is a necessary but insufficient element in presidential performance. Presidents must still put their judgments into action. It is to the last part of the presidential performance equation, political leadership, that we turn to in the following sections.

DOES ASKING GOOD QUESTIONS EQUAL USING GOOD JUDGMENT?

It would be a mistake to treat good judgment as a fully ready and available dimension of a leader's skills or capacities, which only needs the right circumstance to bring it forth in full bloom. By saying this I am not repeating my general argument that good judgment is related to circumstances. Rather, I am making a more specific claim: Leaders may well have more or less capacity for

good judgment, but the actual quality of the judgments in specific circumstances depends on the actions they take. What actions are these?

Asking good questions is a key to developing a good judgment in particular circumstances. Asking good questions is not a simple matter. First, you must
know you don't know. Second, you must not be afraid to say you don't know.
And third, you have to ask questions that allow you to fill in the information
that you need to make a good judgment.

Most studies, even case-oriented studies of judgment, depend on characterizations of a leader's judgment, and we rarely are able to follow the process
of their actual thinking in any deep or extended way to see how the leader
arrived as them. One exception to this is the recently published transcripts of
the meetings between President Kennedy and his advisers during the Cuban
missile crisis (May and Zelikow 1997). They are not perfect. There are some
questions about aspects of the transcriptions (Stern 2000a, 2000b; Sullivan
2000a, 2000b; Zelikow and May 2000). And, of course, Kennedy was the one
who turned the taping system on and off. Yet, it is the most ongoing comprehensive unfolding of a critical decision set that we have available.

So, what do we learn there about asking questions? The first thing we
learn is that Kennedy was not afraid to ask them, even when it might betray a
lack of basic information that other leaders more concerned with how they
appear might allow to pass by. Midway into an October 22 meeting with his
advisers, the talk turns to American missiles, and the following exchange takes
place:

> **Nitze**: They did come back with another point: NATO strategic contact
> [Soviet nuclear attack] requires an immediate execution of EDP in such events.
> **President Kennedy**: What's EDP?
> **Nitze**: European Defense Plan, which is nuclear war. (223)

A little later, discussing the difference between U.S. missiles in Turkey
pointed at the Soviet Union and Russian missiles in Cuba pointed at the
United States, the following exchange takes place:

> **Rusk**: On that, in 1957 there was a decision by NATO [that] it's fairly
> certain that these weapons are imminently in Europe. This was in the face of a
> announcement by the Soviet Union. . . .
> **President Kennedy**: At the time we sent missiles to Turkey and to Italy,
> did we have intercontinental missiles ourselves? Or did the Soviets? (235)

Later, the group is talking about possible Soviet reinforcements and the
following exchange takes place:

> **President Kennedy**: The only place they can come in by air, as I understand it, [2 seconds excised from tape as classified information]. Is that correct?
> **President Kennedy:** They can do that? (241)

Nor is Kennedy inhibited about expressing his doubts, puzzlement, and owning up to possible previous errors. Early in the crisis, discussion turns to the motivations of the Soviet Union. The president says, "Well, it's a goddamn mystery to me. I don't know enough about the Soviet Union, but if anyone can tell me any other time since the Berlin blockade that the Russians have given so clear a provocation. . . . Now, maybe our mistake was in not saying, sometime before this summer" (107).

In all of these examples, and there are many more, Kennedy did not need to prove himself the smartest person in the room. Indeed, he seemed quite comfortable in asking some fairly basic questions. There is no evidence of elevated sensitivity to his own status or reputation and how it might suffer by asking questions he didn't know the answer to but needed to understand. Nor does he shy away from asking whether his past errors had some role in the onset of the crisis.

The capacity to ask good questions, of course, goes farther than simply filling in acronyms. On October 16 at the 11:00 A.M. meeting, attitudes had hardened, and the president was presented with a detailed briefing of the new intelligence that had led there (May and Zelikow 1997, 122). The following excerpts (122–25) suggest how important questions became.

> **McCone**: Based on photography from Sunday October 14 and two [flights] from Monday October 15 . . . we expect the initial readout to start later tonight. . . .
> **President Kennedy:** They don't know how much coverage they got, do they?
> **Lundahl**: The total picture has not emerged yet. We're flying in the clouds.

Lundahl finishes his briefing and the following exchange takes place:

> **Lundahl**: That's all I have at the moment, Sir.
> **President Kennedy**: What percentage of the islands do we have covered up there?
> **Lundahl**: These separate missions . . . represent a considerable percentage . . . but the business of plotting the [areas obscured by the] clouds has not been completely done, so I can't give you a good figure.
> **President Kennedy**: But, in other words, from the information we have prior to the development of these new films you would say that there are how

many new missile sites? As well as how many different launch pads on each site? (125)

Later in that same session, Dean Rusk briefs the president on his views and some unfolding information. At the end, he says that he has become increasing convinced that limited strikes won't do.

> **Rusk**: [A]nd therefore, the chiefs and I would have certainly recommended last night, and I would recommend more strongly today . . . that we would consider nothing short of a full invasion as a military action. . . .
> **President Kennedy**: Why does this information change the recommendation? (131)

Here the president is receiving a very strong recommendation from a senior and trusted adviser. Yet, his response is to ask for the logic by which the information made a difference in Rusk's recommendation. Indeed, he is trying to get some understanding of the processes that resulted in Rusk's judgment.

President Kennedy's questions also reveal an attempt to enter into Khrushchev's circumstances to gain advantage and understanding. This is an example of strategic empathy. The group is discussing whether to notify the Soviet leader of our intentions, and the president asks, "What do we ask him to do under that notification? What is it we'd be trying to get out of him?" (151).

It seems clear that asking good questions facilities, but does not guarantee, good judgment. It also seems clear that the capacity to ask good question is related to analytical abilities but is not synonymous with them. To be able to ask good questions requires in part that you not be inhibited by your psychology in doing so. That means, no inhibiting concerns with status, how smart or not you appear, how much you think you need to know or ought to know, and above all the sense that it is all right and even important to acknowledge that you have something to learn.

THE CONSEQUENCES OF GOOD JUDGMENT

It is difficult enough to reach a good judgment, but the trials of doing so don't end there. Good judgments by individual leaders and their advisory groups take place in a rather insular context. That is, they are internal to the outside world and meant to decide how to deal with it. Once a judgment has been reached, it ceases to be an matter internal to the group and those who comprise it, and it begins to become a matter of enactment in the real world beyond the interior borders of the group. How that judgment is enacted is the second and equally important dimension of the judgment process.

Leadership: The Bridge from Good Judgment to Successful Enactment

Political leadership can be understood in relation to the capacity to act on the implications of one's judgments and achieve results. In that respect, both leadership and power share a definition that includes the ability to accomplish purposes. However, political leadership in a democracy requires, where power does not, that a leader's judgments not only lead to "fitting solutions" but also be publicly understandable and defensible.

Political leadership also requires skills that affect whether judgment can be translated into effective policy. Political leadership does not take place in a behavioral vacuum. The personal and political means that a leader has at his or her disposal, and chooses to use, will weigh heavily on the policy ends.

It is important to underscore the means selected to exercise leadership. That in itself represents another important judgment. Even good judgments can be frustrated if the means of their implementations are not productive and appropriate.

I have (Renshon 1998a, 226–29) proposed three distinct aspects of political leadership: mobilization, orchestration, and consolidation. Although they are related, each requires different skills. The first, *mobilization*, refers to the leader's ability to arouse the public. It requires that a leader be invested in solving the problem, communicate that to the public, and awaken their willingness to join in solving it. The second component of political leadership, *orchestration*, refers to the bringing together and directing the various elements that will be instrumental in addressing and resolving the problem. The effective use of arousal requires that it be applied to the achievement of goals. It refers to the ability to shape mobilization in specific, policy-relevant ways. Lastly, *consolidation* refers to the skills and tasks necessary to develop and preserve a set of supportive relationships and institutionalizing the results of one's policy judgments.

Consolidation also involves setting up and putting into motion policy structures or procedural regimes that solidify the results of the leader's policy judgments. They may involve the creation of new agencies, working groups, or other institutional forms. Or, it might combine these with refocusing the functions or direction of existing policy structures. These methods of consolidation also represent a way in which a leader's policy decisions can have an enduring effect. They are, in essence, a legacy of a leader's judgment.

Does Good Judgment Guarantee Good Outcomes?

An important question to be considered is this: Does good judgment necessarily lead to good outcomes? The answer to that question seems clear: no. Good judgment improves the chances of good outcomes, just as bad judgment improves the possibilities of poor outcomes.

Yet good judgment alone cannot guarantee either policy progress or successful leadership. There are at least three important reasons why this is the case:

1. A framing decision may reflect good judgment, but some of the subsequent decisions that flow from it may be flawed. In making an overall assessment, one would have to balance the judgments that went into making an appropriate framing decision and the nature of the flaws in any decisions that followed from that initial decision during implementation.[17]
2. Judgment is only one part of the process that leads from decisions to results. Good judgments alone, if they are not accompanied by a set of capacities to realize the fruits of one's judgments, will not result in high-quality outcomes. The bridging link between high-quality judgments and (the potential for) high-quality outcomes is political skill, the most important of which revolves around political leadership.
3. The complex process that leads from presidential judgments to outcomes is not carried out in a contextual vacuum. That process involves other actors, some of whom have considerable resources of their own. Their actions may deflect or even thwart the impact of leaders' judgments. The assessment of a judgment's impact, therefore, has to include not a static world in which judgment proceeds without interference but a world in which others are actively striving to modify or reverse the effects of a leader's judgments.

Does Good Judgment Lead to Better Predictions?

The importance of anticipating consequences raises the question of the degree of foresight that one should expect to inform evaluations of judgment. Tetlock (1992) argues that the ability to *predict* outcomes is a crucial element of good judgment. This may be too strong a requirement.

Consequences, sometimes unintended and at other times unforeseen, do play a role in assessments of judgment. Good judgment, though, does not require that a leader foresee specific or even most consequences that unfold from making a framing decision. To do so would require that a leader be able either to read minds or to predict the future. Neither our current theories, the complexity of events, nor past experience provide much confidence that we (or any leader) can count on this. In reality, the issue may not be so much the ability of a leader to predict outcomes as it is the capacity to understand and anticipate a *range* of possible or likely ones.

May and Zelikow (1997) underscore that point in their analysis of Kennedy's performance. They write:

> Saturday, October 27, may have been the finest hours of John F. Kennedy's public life. To us he seems *more alive to the possibilities and consequences of each new development* than anyone else. He remains calm, lucid, and *is consistently a step, or several steps ahead of his advisors*. He is the only one in the room determined not to go to war over obsolete missiles in Turkey. Yet, he fully understands and is trying to work around the consequences of appearing to sell out the Turks. (690–91)

We can expect that a leader will have appreciated the possible major consequences that flow from a framing decision and act accordingly. Indeed, one way we can distinguish good from poor judgment is that in the latter case a leader will fail to appreciate what clearly could and should have been known, or else realize it but fail to act accordingly. Good judgment entails the capacity to appreciate and act on *probable* consequences.

Evaluating the Consequences of Judgment

Evaluating the consequences of judgment in policy decision making is perhaps the most controversial and difficult task connected with developing a theory of good policy judgment. This task has proved so conceptually difficult that it has led political psychology theorists to focus on the quality of the decision process[18] rather than attempting to assess outcomes.[19] But attempting to assess outcomes, while very difficult, is worth the effort. Decisions and the judgments that support them are important because of their effects, not because they were arrived at by proceeding through a process.

The ultimate test of any judgment is how well it addresses the issue at hand. Of course, most problems raise more than one issue. George (1980, 1) has pointed out the trade-offs that occur frequently between decision quality and (political) acceptability. The "best" decision may not be politically possible. Often a leader is forced to choose between a better and worse decision, rather than a good or bad one. Some policy problems appear to have no good solutions (Calabresi and Bobbitt 1979).

Still, an analysis of the quality of decision making that focused on political feasibility alone would still leave important, unanswered questions. Was the quality of the decision regarding substance compromised by too much concern with feasibility? Could the commitment of leadership resources and skills make a different decision more politically feasible? These are difficult questions to answer since they are, to some degree, counterfactual.

Evaluating the quality of a leader's judgment is difficult and always complex given that policy choices are often so varied. Evaluating a leader's judgment is difficult after he or she is in office, but increasingly attempts are made to do so before the leader gets there. Yet candidates don't make real policy judgments. They are running for office and not already in it.

Deprived of real case data on a candidate's policy judgments, the press and public focus, not unreasonably, on his or her personal and political judgment during the campaign. While many complexities are involved in appraising the judgment of others, it sometimes quite possible to do so. (See chapter 3.) Thomas Eagleton's failure to disclose his psychiatric hospitalizations was clearly a case of poor judgment. The same can be said for Gary Hart's judgment in connection with his failed campaign for the Democratic Party's presidential nomination in 1988, carrying on an affair while inviting reporters to follow him around if they didn't believe he was happily married.

GOOD JUDGMENT: SOME BASIC QUESTIONS

Developing theory begins with asking questions, and there are many in analyzing good judgment. Few of them are easily answerable, and certainly this chapter and those that follow cannot lay claim to having done more than provide some suggestions, hopefully solid, as to how they might be adequately answered.

Nonetheless, since asking questions is central to developing good theories, and since one purpose of this book is to stimulate a focus on this central force in successful decision making and leadership, I offer here a series of questions about good judgment. I begin with a series of general questions and then proceed to ask more specific ones.

The Basic Nature of Good Judgment

1. What is good judgment?
2. What qualities exemplify good judgment?
3. How, if it all, is it related to decision procedures?
4. Is good judgment synonymous with good political judgment? If not, in what ways might they differ?
5. Is good judgment synonymous with rationality? If not, how are the two related?
6. Is good judgment synonymous with intelligence or expertise? If so, just how are they related?
7. What role do "community norms" play in evaluating judgments? How is the problem of multiple communities to be handled?

8. What is the relationship, if any, between good judgment and the ability to predict outcomes?
9. Is the "ideal" policy a good starting place from which to reach good judgment?
10. Does the concept of "good judgment" apply equally to all levels and ranges of decisions, or do we reserve that term for particular kinds of decisions?
11. What is the relationship between good judgment and political leadership?

The Circumstances of Good Judgment

1. Is good judgment situational? To what extent is a leader's range and depth of understanding of a problem related to his experience with and understanding of problems of a *particular* sort?
2. We use the term *judgment framework* to denote the major conceptual organization that a leader brings to bear on the analysis of a problem. What specific role does *adequate, defective, incomplete,* or *complex* judgment play in arriving at good judgments?
3. Do firmly established and frequently used frameworks distort or aid judgments?
4. Is the specific judgment being analyzed a difficult one to analyze or understand? Was the situation characterized by unusual uncertainty, high risk, value conflict, time pressure, or domestic political pressure? With what effects?
5. What effect does making judgments within a *group* context have on the quality of the judgments?

The Interior Psychology of Good Judgment

Viewed from one perspective, a leader's judgment is ultimately a result of his or her views, understanding, and capacity to make use of skills the leader can bring to bear on the problem at hand. From this perspective, a number of questions arise about a leader trying to reach a good judgment:

1. Since judgments involve the ability to handle complexity, is good judgment always a matter of intelligence or the capacity for complexity?
2. How are ambition and the leader's core values related to good judgment?

3. What personal characteristics facilitate or inhibit a leader from seeing or acting on crucial information?
4. What personal characteristics facilitate or inhibit the leader from understanding the essential elements of a problem and their significance?
5. What personal characteristics facilitate or inhibit a leader from placing his or her understandings within an appropriate judgment framework that points to a range of responses that preserve, and even perhaps advance, the values and interests at stake?
6. What personal characteristics facilitate or inhibit a leader from reflecting on the range of issues and values raised by the situation to deal adequately with the various interests (political, social, and psychological) involved?
7. What personal characteristics facilitate or inhibit a leader from considering or reflecting information that is frequently limited and often discordant?
8. What personal characteristics facilitate or inhibit a leader from using, without being subservient to, feeling or impulse, including the anxiety generated by uncertainty, high risk, and value conflict?
9. What personal stylistic techniques does the leader use to handle the above issues—fact gathering, procrastination, action as a release of tension, rules of thumb, or historical analogies?
10. How does a leader adequately draw on the understanding of the past and present to consider how alternative choices will shape the future (the extrapolation of implications)?
11. What personal characteristics facilitate or inhibit a leader from developing, setting in motion, and maintaining a series of steps to accomplish purposes consistent with one's values and ideals.

The Process of Good Judgment

1. What are the trade-offs between the *quality* of a foreign policy decision, the *time and resources* spent in formulating a solution, and its political *acceptability* in reaching a good judgment?
2. What is the relationship between costs and risks, on the one hand, and good judgment, on the other?
3. Is good judgment synonymous with prudence?
4. How is good judgment influenced by the number and nature of other decisions with which a leader or president must contend?
5. What is the relationship of good judgment to short-term or long-

term goals? Is good judgment more clearly associated with a leader's emphasis on one or the other?

6. How does value complexity, the presence of multiple competing values embedded in a situation, affect good judgment? What strategies are available for resolving these issues?

7. What is the relationship of good judgment to implementation?

The Consequences of Good Judgment

1. Does good judgment always lead to favorable outcomes? Under what circumstances does it do so, and under what circumstances, and why, does it not?

2. What are the measurement issues involved in reaching judgments about good judgments? Are there any ways to help minimize the "subjective" aspects of such evaluations?

3. Is good judgment always flawless? Or, can good judgment be "good enough"?

CONCLUSION

None of the chapters that follow take up all these questions. Nor were they meant to do so. The model of character and judgment put forward in this chapter and the questions I raised at its conclusion were meant to help develop a framework by which judgment can be understood and assessed. A focus on judgment suggests that answering the question of *what* the leader decided is not the end of an analysis but its beginning. *How* a leader arrived at his or her judgment is a critical element in understanding judgment itself and perhaps improving it.

An important parallel appears between Neustadt's (1990) insight about the importance of self-help for presidential leadership and good judgment. In both cases, the leader cannot depend on others but must make use of his or her own skills and resources. In working toward a good judgment, the leader is likely to encounter many barriers. There is what is unknown and unknowable. There are the limits to the leader's own information and understanding. There are also the views and psychologies of the others on whom they partially depend to navigate often difficult, sometimes treacherous, decision currents.

If successful political leadership provides a critical compass for effective governance, then surely good judgment is its indisputable anchor.

NOTES

1. This analysis that follows in this essay builds upon and extends my previous published analyses of good judgment (Renshon 1992, 1993, 1998a, 1998b).

2. All decisions, of course, reflect judgment to some degree. However, minor or routine decisions do not ordinarily raise issues of good or poor judgment. In the case of framing decisions, it is the major judgment and those connected with carrying it out that are the focus of our theoretical attention.

3. George (1980, 1–3) has discussed the trade-offs that often occurs between the quality of a decision and its acceptability. A decision might be sound but not feasible or, alternatively, feasible but not sound. Reconciling these two is a critical task of any president or decision maker. A similar trade-off may be seen to operate between judgment and politics. During the 1992 check-cashing scandal in Congress, some House members faulted the Speaker "for being thoughtful and judicious but not political enough" (Clymer 1991).

4. Decision-making theorists have not looked carefully at the impact of the problem itself but have discussed the leader's definition of the problem. How the leader defines the problem has implications for both decision making and political processes. It is also true that perception operates within historical and personal frames that have some factual (e.g., real-life) basis.

5. The importance of affect in decision making is becoming more widely recognized, but its exact roles are not clear. Some years ago, Abelson (1959) introduced the concept of "hot cognition" to account for the finding that in some areas cognition became suffused with affect, and in doing so it became more salient and powerful in shaping behavior. Janis and Mann's (1977) emphasis on the importance of feelings of hope in being able to reach optimal political decisions represents a further attempt to integrate the two domains.

Traditional "rational actor" theorists of decision making view affect as interfering with calculations of "value maximizing," which is, in their view, the essence of rational decision making. Affect can interfere in two ways. First, it can result in people giving inappropriate weight to some consideration; second, feelings of empathy, for example, would appear to undercut a totally self-interested calculation.

Full rational actor models have given way to "bounded rationality" models (Kinder and Weiss 1978), which place a number of constraints on the assumptions of the "rational actor." Most of these constraints have to do with the cognitive requirements of the full rational actor model. The role of affect in these models is somewhat unclear.

In some models of "self-interest," feelings are viewed as simply another datum to be factored into the overall self-interest evaluation. This solves the problem of accounting for affect in some way and thus preserving the (self-interest) model, but whether it provides a useful theory of the relationships of affect to decision is another issue.

Psychoanalytically inclined theorists tend to emphasize affect, especially as it presents itself in the form of impulse. This has the virtue of examining how and why affect impacts decisions, but it appears to limit the role to affect primarily to the expression of unconscious wishes.

6. Describing persons as having some degree of psychological maturity does not mean such persons are conflict-free. Psychologically developed persons have areas of conflict,

emotional and interpersonal difficulties like everyone else. However, their difficulties take place in the more general context of psychological accomplishment, rather than vice versa.

7. The exact reasons that the Russians put missiles into Cuba has been a subject of strong debate (Allison 1971). Khrushchev's son, Sergei, states flatly, "The reason for installing missiles was a single one: the defense of Cuba" (Allyn, Blight, and Welch 1992, 38). My point here is not that the reasons given by the Russians are necessarily the correct ones but rather that the members of the Kennedy decision-making group never seriously considered this possibility as an alternative, at least in the portions of the meeting transcripts then available. We have now the complete transcript of those meetings (May and Zelikow 1997), which is an enormously important resource for the study of judgment and decision making.

8. As the aphorism says, "Good judgment comes from experience. Experience comes from bad judgment." The thrust of this adage is that mistaken but corrected judgment is the basis of better judgment. So too, the concept of skillful judgment suggests that skills in making judgment, like other skills, can be developed and refined.

9. This possibility is raised by Gelb's (1992) analysis of President George H. Bush's mishandling of his trip to Japan in January 1992 with executives of the major automobile manufacturers.

10. A leader's grandiosity and accompanying sense of invulnerability and entitlement can often reflect an underlying masked anxiety and/or an insufficiently consolidated sense of self-esteem. This anxiety may arise from the direct personal and political implications of events themselves or may be related to the steps that may need to be taken if events are viewed clearly and seriously.

11. Support for the view that individuals with a strongly consolidated sense of self-worth tend to be better learners is found in a number of studies. For example, Barber (1992) argues on the basis of his extensive case studies that active-positive presidents (those characterized by high self-esteem) are better able to learn from experience. This relationship also received strong support in a study by Sniderman (1972) of several nationally representative samples of adults including one of party and political leaders. His intensive study of the impact of self-esteem to political orientations suggested that "low self-esteem clearly inhibits the acquisition of political knowledge" (161). In both studies, low self-esteem is associated with inhibitions to learning.

12. For an example of strategic empathy in the context of the rational actor model of international conflict management, see Allison (1971, 256). White (1983, 1991) has examined the impact of empathetic identifications with the Soviet Union and Iraq, respectively, and their implications for American foreign policy.

13. The unshakable belief that one embodies a large collectivity in all of its important respects is, of course, grandiose. It is also difficult to sustain in democracies (with their traditions of opposition and critical dissent). It is for this reason that this form of strategic empathy is more likely to be found in dictatorships where there are no institutional or informational alternatives to the leader's beliefs.

14. This is very difficult even when the other shares a similar culture. It is extremely difficult when leaders face each other across cultures as well as being in conflict over policy interests.

15. This does not mean that immediate feelings are necessarily wrong, only that there needs to be the capacity to supplement the information they supply.

16. Consistency of character functioning can be as important as its level. A labile sense of self-esteem, for example, can result in episodic performance. Leaders who do well so long as they are amassing power may do less well when they have to share it.

Tucker (1965) suggests that Woodrow Wilson's difficulties as president of Princeton, governor of New Jersey, and president of the United States resulted not from low self-esteem but from swings in his sense of esteem (for another view of the origins of Wilson's difficulties, see George and George 1956).

Thomas Eagleton's history of clinical depressions that were revealed during the 1972 presidential election provides another illustration. While there was much discussion of Eagleton's depression and its treatment, there was much less discussion of his periods of high activity preceding the depressions. These periods of high tension, great anticipation, and activity led to a decline in judgment in at least one documented case—his handling of the questions posed to him at the time of his selection as a vice presidential candidate regarding the existence of any "skeletons in his closet."

In the 2000 presidential campaign, Vice President Al Gore's three very different per-formances during his three nationally televised debates with George W. Bush raised the same kind of questions. In the first, Gore was very aggressive, at one point invading Bush's personal space and glowering at him. In the next, criticized for his overly assertive style, the vice president refrained from any behavior that suggested assertiveness. In the third, he returned to a much more confrontational style, though not as assertive as he had been in the first debate.

17. An individual might make one or several misjudgments on small matters because they were not consequential enough to engage concern or for others reasons. Good judg-ment does not require perfect judgment. However, numerous instances of misjudgment, especially in connection with the sequelae of framing decisions, would raise questions about overall judgment.

18. See Renshon (1993, 68–71; 1998b) for an examination of the contributions and limitations of the procedural model of decision making.

19. In a rare exception, Herek, Janis, and Muth (1987; see also Janis 1989, 119–35) studied nineteen major crises since World War II to determine whether good decision pro-cedures resulted in high-quality outcomes. Using content analysis of bibliographic sources, they rated the decision procedures used (211). Experts then rated the outcomes on two dimensions, increased (or decreased) international tension, and favorable (or unfavorable) outcomes for U.S. interests. They found that "quality of decision-making process is related to the decision's outcome" (218).

Two other interesting findings of the Herek et al. study are also worth noting. Interest-ingly, they also found that raters of decision outcomes agreed much more about short-term than long-term effects, which were considered so unreliable that they were omitted from the analysis (213, n.3). Herek et al. also found that in judging outcomes (increased world tension, advances for U.S. interests), "the conservative expert was inclined to see more of the outcomes as favorable or neutral, while the liberal saw more of them as negative" (215). This point suggests how political views may frame the evaluation of outcomes, even for scholarly observers.

REFERENCES

Abelson, Robert P. 1959. "Models of Resolutions of Belief Dilemmas." *Journal of Conflict Resolution* 3: 342–52.

Allison, Graham T. 1971. *Essence of decision: Explaining the Cuban Missile Crisis.* Boston: Little, Brown.

Allyn, Bruce J., James G. Blight, and David A. Welch. 1992. *Back to the Brink: Proceedings of the Moscow Conference of the Cuban Missile Crisis, January 27–28, 1989.* Cambridge, Mass.: Harvard University Center for Science and International Affairs.

Barber, James David. 1992. *Presidential Character: Predicting Performance in the White House.* 4th ed. Englewood Cliffs, N.J. Prentice Hall.

Blight, James G., David Lewis, and David A. Welch. 1991. *Cuba between the Superpowers.* Providence, R.I.: Center for Foreign Policy Development, Brown University.

Burns, James McGregor. 1978. *Leadership.* New York: Harper and Row.

Calabresi, G., and P. Bobbitt. 1979. *Tragic Choices.* New York: Norton.

Clymer, Adam. 1987. "The Momentous Decision Not to Run for President." *New York Times,* February 22, C2.

———. 1991. "Leadership and Its Limits." *New York Times,* May 1, A1.

Fenno, Richard F. 1959. *The President's Cabinet.* Cambridge, Mass.: Harvard University Press.

Gelb, Lawrence. 1992. "Three Wine Mice." *New York Times,* January 12, A15.

George, Alexander L. 1974. "Adaptation to Stress in Political Decision Making: The Individual, Small Group, and Organizational Contexts." In *Coping and Adaptation,* ed. G. V. Coelho, D. A. Hamberg, and J. E. Adams. New York: Basic.

———. 1980. *Presidential Decision Making in Foreign Policy: The Effective Use of Information and Advice.* Boulder, Colo.: Westview.

George, Alexander L., and Juliette George. 1956. *Woodrow Wilson and Colonel House: A Personality Study.* New York: Day.

Herek, Greg, Irving Janis, and Paul Muth. 1987. "Decision Making during International Crises: Is the Quality of Process Related to Outcome?" *Journal of Conflict Resolution* 31: 203–26.

Janis, I. 1989. *Crucial Decisions: Leadership in Policy Making and Crisis Management.* New York: Free Press.

Janis, I., and L. Mann. 1977. *Decision Making: A Psychological Analysis of Conflict, Choice, and Commitment.* New York Free Press.

Khong, Yuen Foong. 1993. *Analogies at War.* Princeton, N.J. Princeton University Press.

Kinder, Donald R., and J. A. Weiss. 1978. "In Lieu of Rationality: Psychological Perspectives on Foreign Policy Decision Making." *Journal of Conflict Resolution* 22: 707–35.

May, Ernest R., and Philip D. Zelikow, eds. 1997. *The Kennedy Tapes: Inside the White House during the Cuban Missile Crisis.* Cambridge, Mass.: Belknap.

Neustadt, Richard E. 1990. *Presidential Power and the Modern Presidents: The Politics of Leadership from Roosevelt to Reagan.* New York: Free Press.

Neustadt, Richard E., and Ernest R. May. 1986. *Thinking in Time.* New York: Free Press.

———. 1998. *Thinking in Time: The Uses of History for Decision Makers.* New York: Free Press.

Renshon, Stanley A. 1992. "The Psychology of Good Judgment: A Preliminary Model." *Political Psychology* 13, no. 3: 477–95.

———. 1993. "Good Judgment and the Lack Thereof, in the Gulf War: A Model with Some Implications." In *The Political Psychology of the Gulf War: Leaders, Publics and the Process of Conflict,* ed. Stanley A. Renshon (pp. 67–105). Pittsburgh: University of Pittsburgh Press.

———. 1998a. *High Hopes: The Clinton Presidency and the Politics of Ambition.* New York: Routledge.

———. 1998b. *The Psychological Assessment of Presidential Candidates.* New York: Routledge.

———. 2001. "The Comparative Psychoanalytic Study of Political Leaders: John McCain and the Limits of Trait Psychology." In *Profiling Political Leaders and the Analysis of Political Leadership: Methods and Cross-Cultural Applications,* ed. Ofer Feldman and Linda O. Valenty. Westport, Conn.: Greenwood.

Sniderman, Paul M. 1972. *Personality and Democratic Politics.* Berkeley: University of California Press.

Stern, Sheldon M. 2000a. "Source Material: The 1997 Published Transcripts of the JFK Cuban Missile Crisis Tapes: Too Good to Be True?" *Presidential Studies Quarterly* 30, no. 3: 586–93.

———. 2000b. "Response to Zelikow and May." *Presidential Studies Quarterly* 30, no. 4: 797–99.

Suedfeld, Peter and A. D. Rank. 1976. "Revolutionary Leaders: Long-term Success as a Function of Changes in Cognitive Complexity." *Journal of Personality and Social Psychology* 34, 169–78.

Sullivan, Terry. 2000a. "Confronting the Kennedy Tapes: The May–Zelikow Transcripts and the Stern Assessment." *Presidential Studies Quarterly* 30, no. 3: 594–97.

———. 2000b. "Reacting to Zelikow and May." *Presidential Studies Quarterly* 30, no. 4: 800–802.

Tetlock, Philip E. 1984. "Cognitive Style and Political Belief Systems in the British House of Commons." *Journal of Personality and Social Psychology* 45: 118–26.

———. 1992. "Good Judgment in International Politics: Three Psychological Perspectives." *Political Psychology* 13: 517–40.

Tractenberg, Mark. 1985. "White House Tapes and the Cuban Missile Crisis." *International Security* 10: 164–203.

Tucker, Robert. 1965. "The Dictator and Totalitarianism." *World Politics* 17: 555–83.

Welch, David A. and James G. Blight. 1987/88. "The Eleventh Hour of the Cuban Missile Crisis: An Introduction to the Excomm Tapes." *International Security,* Winter: 5–92.

White, Ralph K. 1983. "Empathizing with the U.S.S.R." *Political Psychology* 4: 121–37.

———. 1991. "Empathizing with Saddam Hussein." *Political Psychology* 12: 291–308.

Wildavsky, Aaron. 1996. "The Two Presidencies." *Transaction,* December 7.

Zelikow, Philip D., and Ernest R. May. 2000. "Source Material: Controversy: The Kennedy Tapes: Past and Future." *Presidential Studies Quarterly* 30, no. 4: 791–96.

Part II

THE DYNAMICS OF GOOD JUDGMENT: APPRAISALS AND IMAGES

· 3 ·

Appraising Good Judgment Before It Matters

Al Gore, George W. Bush, and the 2000 Presidential Campaign

Stanley A. Renshon

> The Presidency is basically a place of decision; it's important that you work hard. . . . But in the end hard work is not enough. You also have to make good decisions, and that requires a certain level of experience, a certain level of judgment, a certain instinct.
>
> —William J. Clinton (2000, 2585)

*W*hom would you prefer serve in the White House making life-and-death decisions about matters of war and peace? Would you prefer a president with a well-deserved reputation for good judgment, or would you prefer someone who has demonstrated in his public life that his judgment is open to serious question? What about making important decisions regarding domestic policy that could have serious implications? Would you prefer someone with good judgment or someone whose judgment you found questionable?

If you answered both questions "Good judgment, of course," you validated in a personal way the premise of this chapter. Perhaps not surprisingly, you share that view with a large majority of the American public. In 1995, 76 percent of Americans thought that "sound judgment in a crisis" for a president was "absolutely essential."[1] Twelve percent thought it "essential." By 1999, 78 percent thought "sound judgment" an "absolutely essential" trait for a president, and 12 percent more thought it "essential" (see table 3.1).

On that basis, you might have expected that judgment, sound or otherwise, would have received substantial and direct attention during recent presidential campaigns. It hasn't. Judgment, when it comes up at all, ordinarily does so indirectly, through surrogate issues such as "temper," "experience," and even intelligence. Just how much surrogate terms and discussions really clarify the judgment issues raised by each candidate's psychology is questionable.

Table 3.1   Public Views of Most Important Presidential Qualities

	Percentage considered "absolutely essential"	
	1995	1999
Sound judgment	76	78
High ethical standards	67	63
Compassion	64	63
Saying what one believes	59	57
Consistent positions	51	50
Forcefulness & decisiveness	50	46
Experience in public office	30	38
Willingness to compromise	34	33
Party loyalty	25	33
Experience in Washington	21	27

In this chapter, I explore the question of whether it is possible to reach any understandings of a presidential candidate's judgment before he enters office. If it is possible, on what basis might it proceed? What are the most promising frames of analysis through which to view these issues, and what cautions might be observed in doing so? In another work (Renshon 2000a), I examine the issues surrounding Republican Party presidential hopeful John McCain's temper and psychology in relation to his judgment. Here, I focus on the two major party nominees in the 2000 presidential campaign, George W. Bush and Albert Gore Jr. Bush went on to become president, and Gore seems likely to run against him in the 2004 presidential campaign. Although my focus here is on American presidents and candidates, I hope that the analysis that follows will provide useful perspectives to those whose interest in these issues lies in other geographical, political, and cultural areas.

Is the issue of judgment in the presidency important to the American public? I present data that answer that question with an emphatic yes. Is it possible to make use of an unfolding presidential campaign process to draw some inferences about a candidate's judgment? I present material drawn from recent elections that suggests it is. Before turning to those issues, however, a central theoretical question involving the possible dual nature of the office and the judgments of the person who occupies it must be raised.

TWO PRESIDENCIES OR ONE?
THE DUAL JUDGMENT PROBLEM

Aaron Wildavsky (1966) begins his well-known paper on the presidency with the following statement: "The United States has one president, but two presidencies; one presidency is for domestic affairs, and the other is concerned with defense and foreign policy" (7). His point is that the president has more control over his foreign policies than his domestic ones. This is a result of having to share institutional and political power domestically and having less need to do so internationally.

Wildavsky's argument in favor of two presidencies raises the issue of whether there is a parallel dualism in presidential judgment. I term this *the dual judgment problem*. The most basic formulation of the questions involved are these: Do presidents use different judgment frameworks in these two areas? Do they make substantially different kinds of calculations in domestic and foreign policy decisions? Do they weigh evidence in different ways in these two contexts? Finally, do they make different use of their advisers and advisory systems in the two contexts?

Perhaps foreign policy operates by a wholly different judgment calculus. Perhaps, paralleling Wildavsky's two presidencies argument, presidents have two sets of judgment frameworks, one for domestic and one for foreign policy. Perhaps the lack of constraint on presidents in foreign policy, again momentarily accepting Wildavsky's argument, means that we get to see the president's "real" judgment in foreign affairs because he doesn't have other centers of power to inhibit or otherwise temper them. Or perhaps foreign policy judgments, especially those dealing with armed conflict, provide their own inhibitions on poor judgment because of the consequences of making errors. Wildavsky (1966) quotes President Kennedy as saying, "[D]omestic policy . . . can only defeat us; foreign policy can kill us" (13).

Obviously, it is not possible to settle these issues here. But they are important questions to address, even if preliminarily, for reasons having to do with one purpose of this chapter. If foreign policy judgments are of a substantially different sort than domestic or personal political judgments, then there is not much substantive traction on the issues of good judgment to be gained by looking at presidential election campaigns.

Why is it that the questions that public opinion polls ask regarding candidate "experience" are not a reliable substitute and guide for answering such questions? Primarily because most recent modern presidential candidates have not served in positions where their judgments about foreign policy have been put to the acid test of command. Examples include Georgia Governor Jimmy Carter, Arkansas Governor Bill Clinton, Colorado Senator Gary Hart, Massachusetts Governor Michael Dukakis, Minnesota Senator Walter Mondale, Texas Governor George W. Bush, and California Governor Ronald Reagan.

Even in cases in which an incumbent is running for reelection, as was the case with Clinton in 1996, Reagan in 1980, and to some degree Gore in 2000, foreign policy may be crowded out of the public discussion by domestic concerns. In an October 1999 poll, Americans rated Social Security/Medicare (17 percent), the economy (16 percent), education (15 percent), moral breakdown (13 percent), and health care (12 percent) as the top five double-digit problems facing the country. Only one foreign policy issue, nuclear proliferation, was mentioned at all in the top tier of ten issues, and this by only 7 percent of respondents.[2]

Needless to say, trying to gauge candidates' judgment by their answers to hypothetical circumstances is little better than reading tea leaves. Moreover, any discussion of foreign policy differences between two candidates, even when they do arise, is not the same as direct inquiry about the qualities of judgment that a candidate might bring to bear on foreign policy questions. Does it show good judgment to be for more aid to the United Nations? Perhaps—however, that depends on your view of that organization's purpose, effectiveness, and responsiveness to reform. What about continuing American aid to the Soviet Union? Is being in favor of that an illustration of good judgment? Perhaps, but that depends on your views of American interests in the area, the purposes for which the aid is given and spent, and the nature and monitoring of the expected results.

Trying to divine judgment from policy positions is a difficult undertaking often shaped by partisan politics, or personal and professional investments in the specific policies themselves. Working backward from policy preferences to qualities of judgment runs the further risk of confounding legitimate policy disagreements with a different, more basic set of psychological skills and capacities that enter into making good judgments *in unfolding circumstances*. One can be for or against allowing China to join the World Trade Organization (WTO), without necessarily revealing anything very much about one's policy judgments about whether to build an antiballistic missile (ABM) system regardless of Chinese opposition. And neither of these are necessarily helpful in anticipating how a president might handle a spy plane forced down by a Chinese air force fighter.

The dual judgment problem associated with the "two presidencies" thesis represents one possible framing of the issues, but there is another. It is found in the seminal work of Richard Neustadt (1990). Neustadt's paradigm-changing insight was that while the president might wear many hats, they were all worn on the same head. Rather than standing on the outside looking in at the president, Neustadt suggests that it is better to look over his shoulder. Doing that, Neustadt believes, leaves one inescapable conclusion: Whatever roles the president plays, his purposes are unitary. They are to preserve his policy prerogatives and enlist others to act on behalf of them.

From the perspective of Neustadt's framework, you can no more easily separate the "two presidencies" than you can argue the president becomes a different person when he ends a discussion with the secretary of state and leaves for a fund-raising event at which he puts on his party leader hat. The argument is not that the two activities the same, only that they are carried out by the same person in the service of the same general purposes.

Neustadt has been criticized for focusing too much on power and bargaining, but no one has suggested that his insight about the singularity of the person occupying the office is wrong. Similar arguments occupied psychology at one time: Is it the person or the circumstance that determines behavior? The answer is obviously both, with the additional caveat that the latter can have no effect without the former. Another version of this time-consuming, but not enlightening, debate asks, Are we different people with different people? Well, yes. We don't often treat our children like our spouses, and most adults can discern some difference between their parents and their coworkers. However, that doesn't mean there can't be, or is not, an underlying set of psychological patterns clearly evident in almost all people, if you were able to see them over time and across circumstances.

The person at the center of all these relations remains who he or she is, with her own core ambitions, ideals, and ways of relating with others—even as these are and must be somewhat adjusted to circumstance. It is the same person who is parent to his child and child to his parent. Little substantive or theoretical traction is gained by positing an ever-expanding multiplicity of selves, as postmodern theorists have done. The person unencumbered by either the consistent and effective functioning of his own character psychology or the consolidated psychological lessons drawn from experience is, in a very elemental way, psychologically adrift—not adroit.

IS PRESIDENTIAL JUDGMENT IMPORTANT? THE PUBLIC'S VIEW

There are a number of ways to establish the importance of good judgment in presidential candidates. We can rely on our own or others' experiences regarding the benefits of good judgments or the costs of not exercising it. We can also look to literatures in psychology and political science that establish judgment as an important element to consider. We can look to historical experience to appreciate that judgment plays a role, on occasion an absolutely critical one, in the making of decisions with the most profound consequences. Certainly, the process of judgment in the Cuban missile crisis (see chapter 2) would appear to qualify as evidence there. Finally, given that democracies take citizen concerns seriously, we can examine public sentiment for signs of judgment's relevance.

Of course, the fact that the public believes that judgment should be considered and is important does not establish that in any particular case it *is* important. On the other had, if the public does believe judgment is important, two issues would be immediately raised: (1) to what extent, and in what circumstances, does judgment enter into the voting calculus, and (2) to what extent do campaigns provide information about it to the voters who think it important?

How important is the good judgment of candidates to the American electorate? Apparently, it's very important. As noted earlier, 76 percent of Americans in 1995 thought that "sound judgment in a crisis" for a president was "absolutely essential," and, by 1999, 78 percent thought "sound judgment" an "absolutely essential" trait for a president. In each of those two years, 12 percent more thought it "essential."

Sound judgment in a president was more important to Americans than high ethical standards (67 percent) or compassion (64 percent), saying what one believes in (59 percent), having consistent positions (51 percent), being forceful and decisive (50 percent), having experience in public office (30 percent), being willing to compromise (34 percent), having party loyalty (25 percent), and having experience in Washington (21 percent). Indeed, from 1995 to 1999, of the top six personal attributes wanted by the American public in a president, only "sound judgment" registered an increase in the percentage of people who thought it important. The other five declined.

Does this hold for groups across the ideological spectrum? Yes. In a series of studies leading to the development of new categories of stable public opinion group placement, the Pew Research Center identified nine separable groups[3]: Staunch Conservatives, Moderate Republicans, Populist Republicans, New Prosperity Independents, The Disaffecteds, Liberal Democrats, Socially Conservative Democrats, New Democrats, and the Partisan Poor (see table 3.2).[4]

Table 3.2   **Important Presidential Qualities by Political Viewpoints, in percentages**

	Staunch Conservs	Moderate Reps	Populist Reps	New Prosperity Indeps	Disaffecteds
Sound judgment	85	81	78	82	82
High ethical standards	84	81	75	61	67
Compassion	44	62	67	53	67

	Liberal Dems	Socially Conserv Dems	New Dems	Partisan Poor
Sound judgment	79	82	77	64
High ethical standards	46	58	56	53
Compassion	66	70	61	76

The importance of sound judgment was evident across all ideological groups. Staunch Conservatives, Moderate Republicans, Populist Republicans, New Prosperity Independents, Disaffecteds, Liberal Democrats, Socially Conservative Democrats, and New Democrats all thought sound judgment in a president more important than high ethical standards and compassion, often by a substantial margins. Across all groups but one, "sound judgment" was, on the average, twenty-three percentage points more important than compassion. The only exception to his rule was found among the Partisan Poor who, perhaps not surprisingly given their precarious state, saw compassion as more important than sound judgment. Yet, even in this group, 64 percent thought sound judgment extremely important. Somewhat surprisingly, "sound judgment" just beat out high ethical standards among Staunch Conservatives.

FROM IMPORTANCE TO APPRAISAL: NO EASY MATTER

The fact that the public thinks a candidate's quality of judgment important is no guarantee that it will be adequately covered during the campaign. This was the case in the 2000 presidential election. Even when the campaign coverage focused on the personal attributes of the candidates, a concern with qualities of judgment was nowhere to be found.

The evidence for this comes from an unusual study conducted by the Pew Research Center for the People and the Press and the Project for Excellence in Journalism and the Committee of Concerned Journalists. The study, entitled "A Question of Character,"[5] examined five weeks of stories in newspapers, television, radio, and the Internet that spanned the five months between February and June 2000. The study identified six lines of character analysis in the articles, three each for George Bush and Al Gore. For Bush they were (1) Bush is a different kind of Republican, (2) Bush lacks the intelligence or knowledge for the job, and (3) Bush has relied heavily on family connections to get where he is. For Gore the three were (1) Gore is experienced and knowledgeable, (2) Gore is scandal tainted, and (3) Gore exaggerates or lies.

Of these six major story lines, four appear to be possibly related to good judgment. They are Bush's intelligence, Gore's experience/knowledge, Gore being scandal tainted, and Gore's exaggerations or lies. These major stories lines refer only to the frames that journalists repetitively used to cast their stories. They do not constitute the universe of possible stories frames related to judgment that might have been used. With that caveat in mind, let us briefly examine how they might possibly be related.

Is George Bush Smart Enough to Have Good Judgment?

The argument could be made that high intelligence facilitates good judgment. That argument might even be put in the form of a contingent relationship: The higher the candidate's intelligence, the greater his capacity for (or actual) good judgment. The first requirement for having substantive confidence in this argument is to be more precise about what one means by "intelligence." Is the conventional general intelligence factor said to be reflected in standard intelligence tests?[6] Or, does it refer to the newer theories of multiple intelligence argued for in the work of Steinberg (1979) and Gardner (1993a, 1993b, 2000; see also Goleman 1997).

If we take the route of multiple intelligences, we are immediately drawn into the conceptual and evidentiary morass of the many measures' validity. Gardner (1993a, 1993b) started with seven such "intelligences": music, math, language, social practice, naturalism, insight into others, and self-insight. While the idea is educationally and political appealing (everyone their own prodigy, in some area), evidence for them is scant. In his latest book, Gardner (2000) adds at least one and possibly three new "intelligences" (naturalist, spiritual, and existential). However, since he's not yet sure, he talks in his lectures of $7^{1}/_{2}$ intelligences. One is reminded here of the early trait theorists who, in their enthusiasm for the idea, posited a separate one for each behavior.

If we adapt the more conventional understanding of intelligence, we are by no means free of difficulty. Candidates may have taken IQ tests sometime in their past; however, no presidential candidate has ever been asked, or volunteered, to release them. We are then left to search for proxies of judgment, among which intelligence is a possible—but not necessarily accurate— indicator. What had heretofore been a *possible* correlate of judgment has now become its equivalent.

Saying that intelligence is what IQ measures, without having a test result to guide us forces us back to our understanding of judgment and how the two might be related. Earlier (chapter 2), I defined judgment as the quality of analysis, reflection, and ultimately insight that informs the making of consequential decisions. Clearly the analysis part of the definition is related to what is generally understood as intelligence. Individuals with poor analytical abilities, unable to see the constituent elements of an issue and how they fit together, would seem to start out with substantial barriers to reaching a good judgment. On the other hand, how much analytical ability is enough? Do people with high IQ scores always make good judgments? Bill Clinton, Thomas Eagleton, and Gary Hart are three of many possible illustrations of highly intelligent people who made serious mistakes of judgment, sometimes serially, for reasons having much more to do with their psychology than their reasoning abilities. Indeed, in these cases, their psychologies undercut their judgment and trump their intelligence.

In 1988 Democratic presidential candidate Gary Hart invited reporters to follow him if they disbelieved his assertions of an affair-free marriage as he flew to Washington to spend a weekend with his girlfriend, Donna Rice. Vice presidential candidate Thomas Eagleton failed to disclose to Walter Mondale that he had been hospitalized three times for a major clinical depression and helped defeat his running mate's attempt to gain the presidency. Clinton's history is filled with questionable personal and political judgments, in spite of his extraordinary ability to survive the difficulties he creates for himself. [7] So, while the ability to analyze is clearly related to good judgment, it obviously doesn't guarantee it.

There is a further issue as well. Suggesting that good judgment is a result of analytic ability, reflection, and insight raises the question of how intelligence is related to the latter two elements. Can we assume that intelligence is instrumental in reflection or that it more frequently leads to insight? We simply do not yet know the answers to these questions.

The capacity for reflection seems more closely associated with the capacity to gain appreciation and understanding of the various elements of an issue and their significance. And what does that take? Certainly it takes a capacity to first *suspend* judgment, resist the pressure for action that may arise from many quarters—not the least of which is one's own psychology and an ability to weigh the alternatives in a way that does justice to both the issue at hand and those that might arise. Moreover, good judgment entails the capacity to make these evaluations not only on the pragmatic calculus of net gain but in a way that allows real voice—and some realization—of key personal values and ideals. Intelligence may well be a necessary instrument for making good judgments, but it is clearly not sufficient.

Let us now focus on the question at hand. If intelligence is, to some degree related to the capacity for good judgment, is George Bush smart enough to have it? Let us return to the Pew study. Its analysis found that a full 30 percent of all the media stories on Bush, during the five months they collected data, were about this issue. Charges that Bush lacked intelligence accounted for 26 percent of the stories, and only 3 percent of them reported he had the requisite intelligence.[8]

Does that point settle the issue? Not really. Contrary to the "you know" theory in which like-minded people repeat to each other what they already know to be true, the Pew study was interested in the nature of the evidence introduced on behalf of these assertions. What was the evidence? Not much. The Pew study found:

Usually, this ticklish subject would come in a thinly veiled but unmistakable form . . . journalists would write about Bush's intellect by talking about how a rival candidate would exploit it. Often, the route was amazingly circuitous. "By invoking the name of Dan Quayle, who as vice president was not known for his experience or substance, and linking it with the presidency of Governor Bush's father, Mr. Gore is trying to conjure up the image of a candidate who is neither ready for the presidency nor capable of sound economic decisions," wrote Katherine Q. Seelye in *The New York Times* in mid March.

During the period studied, doubts about Bush's intelligence were more like to come from journalists themselves (57 percent). Only 4 percent came from voters, and only 6 percent came from "experts." Even Gore and his surrogates accounted for only 25 percent of such accusations. Gore and his allies clearly had a motivation to make such charges; the news media in theory did not.

So, what evidence did they use? Often none. The study notes, "Journalists were also more likely than average people to simply express an opinion that Bush lacked intelligence rather than cite evidence. . . . Indeed, nearly a third of all the statements about Bush's intellect were unsupported."

When evidence was cited, it came from a variety of sources. However, the most frequent sources of evidence were Bush's campaign platform (12 percent) and analysis of his tactics/strategy (14 percent). How one would be able to infer a lack of intelligence from Bush's policy proposals in unclear. They may have been wrong, but they were not unintelligent. As to strategy/tactics, it is hard to credit stupidity to a candidate and campaign that challenged an incumbent vice president, presiding over a robust economy during a period of no major foreign conflicts and enjoying the active support of a popular president, who still managed to lose the election.

The study concluded its analysis by noting, "Perhaps because the evidence is so soft, the idea that Bush may lack intellectual firepower has not been embraced by the public. Indeed, a slightly greater percentage of Americans actually attribute not being a serious person to Gore than to Bush."

The poll findings on this matter were quite striking. The *Washington Post's* director of polling reported:

Throughout the primary campaign, the Texas governor was criticized as lacking the maturity or intelligence to be president. The *Post*–ABC News survey finds that Americans strongly reject both claims. Seven in 10 voters—including six in 10 Democrats—agree that Bush is "mature enough to take on the responsibilities of the presidency." And three in four believe he is "very intelligent," a view shared by more than two out of three Democrats and independents as well as nine in 10 Republicans. (Morin and Balz 2000)

These findings do not mean there were not important questions to be answered about Bush's level of knowledge. Bush had come to politics late in his life. He clearly did not have the decades of immersion in policy debate that Gore had acquired over the course of his long political career. Moreover, Bush, unlike Gore, did not relish or make use of the mastery of a wide variety of policy details as an important source of self-validation.

Bush's leadership style appeared to be one of finding the right people, setting the goals and letting them follow through. Gore's style, on the other hand, was to keep his own counsel, rely on a few close advisers, and continue to be minutely involved in making and enacting decisions. Keeping in mind the importance of self-help for exercising political leadership that Neustadt emphasized, and my earlier suggestion that this point applies as well to presidential decision making, Gore's style might appear at first to be an advantage and Bush's a disadvantage.

However, Greenstein (2000) has recently pointed out the distinction between Ronald Reagan's very active stance in setting the tone and agenda of his presidency and in communicating its basic elements to the American public, and his more hands-off manner in the workings of the office. Greenstein notes, "As the spokesman in chief and principle negotiator of his presidency, Reagan was unsparing in his efforts. He was more than its star performer however. *He was its producer, setting the tone and direction of his administration's policies"* (150, emphasis mine).

An "active" *and* a "passive" president! The question that arises here is whether a leadership style that delegates responsibility to others can't be very active in the formulation of goals by that very same leader. Greenstein's analysis provides a caution to a simple equation of a leadership and decision style that delegates, like Bush's, and a lack of interest in deciding or leading.

Bush himself, in commenting on his decision-making style, has appeared to endorse a relationship between how he thinks and how he leads. Asked in an interview how he would decide among conflicting advice on economic policy, he replied, "It's just a matter of judgment. It's a matter of a person in my position sorting out, amongst all the voices, who's got the best judgment, who's got the best common sense" (quoted in Shapiro 1999).

The issue of Bush's intelligence was raised by his opponents and the press as part of their story line for covering the candidates. However, it was also fueled by Bush's periodic mangling of syntax, mispronouncing of words (e.g., *subliminable*), confusing words (e.g., *presumptive* and *presumptuous*) and geography (Slovakia for Slovenia), and his most famous misstep: failing to correctly identify the leaders of several countries during a pop quiz by a reporter early in the campaign.

None of these slips appeared to have much impact on the public's perception of Bush as smart enough and qualified enough for the office. Presenting the results of a national ABC News poll, Gary Langer (1999), head of that unit, reported:

> Nearly six in 10 Americans think George W. Bush knows enough about world affairs to serve effectively as president—whoever Pervaiz Musharraf is. Bush failed in a pop quiz two weeks ago to name the leaders of three foreign nations or republics—Pakistan, India, and Chechnya. He got just one answer right: the leader of Taiwan. He also said Musharraf, who seized power in Pakistan in a military coup, "is going to bring stability to the country and I think that's good news for the subcontinent." While critics pounced, most Americans don't share their concern. In a new ABCNEWS.com poll, 59 percent of respondents think the Texas governor does have sufficient knowledge of foreign affairs to serve effectively as president; 36 percent think not.

In the end, the public did make specific judgments about Bush's intelligence and his judgment. In a Pew poll[9] taken in early September 2000, 38 percent thought that Bush would have good judgment in a crisis (the comparable figure for Al Gore was 44 percent). By October 2000, that figure had risen to 43 percent, slightly surpassing the percentage (42 percent) of people who thought so of Gore.

Bush, in the words of George Will (1999), is "no intellectual," but then Will asks, "So what?" Gardner, whose theories of multiple intelligence were noted earlier, said that Bush had great "people intelligence." However, his greatest weakness was what Gardner called "existential intelligence, "meaning the capacity to ask and consider big questions. Who are we? What are good and evil? Will we survive or falter? What should we want from our lives?" So far, Gardner says, "W. seems to be clueless" in this mode of thinking" (quoted in Merida 2000). Gardner's remarks raise the question of whether we should prefer as president a person who is a good judge of people or one who can have an interesting discussion about the meaning of life.

One of Bush's suite mates at Yale said of him, "He is not the kind of guy you would go back to the dorms and talk about the Reformation with. . . . It would have been a total surprise if he had turned out to be an English professor" (quoted in Merida 2000). On the other hand, however, one reporter (Merida 2000) inquiring into Bush's intelligence noted that while Bush often does, more often than many, mangle syntax and so on,

> he had the most interesting answer of all at a recent GOP debate. The question was: Which two things would you put in a time capsule to best represent America as it begins the 21st century? Most of his rivals felt compelled to include the Constitution or the Declaration of Independence. Bush's answer: Martin

Luther King Jr.'s "I Have a Dream" speech and the microchip—something to "show the heart of America" and something "to show the entrepreneurial spirit of the country."

Another important question needs to be raised about Bush's judgment, and that is his interest and involvement in the issues he might be called upon to decide. This issue has been raised by allies of Gore (McGrory 2000) under the heading of "curiosity." Does Bush have the intellectual curiosity that leads to asking questions that result in the acquisition of knowledge that can facilitate good judgment?

Many strong opinions on this matter have been expressed, but there are little reliable data or indeed much data of any kind. One of the few attempts to gauge Bush's decision-making style (Berke 2000; see also Merida 2000 for an independent confirmation of many of these points) confirmed that Bush carefully selected his advisers, worked with them to develop confidence in their loyalty and judgment, and then relied on them. Among his findings drawn from wide-ranging discussions with Bush advisers were the following: Bush prefers to speed through meetings to get to the heart of the matter. Both candidates (Gore and Bush) tend to be stubborn, often not yielding to their advisers' suggestions. Bush is not inclined to alter a speech sharply or a schedule on the fly. When he was beaten by John McCain in the New Hampshire primary, he told his aides that the campaign had to become more aggressive and not be passive as McCain claimed the reformer mantel. He then asked his aides to come up with suggestions, which they did, and he accepted a number and rejected some. He does not hesitate to overrule his advisers, and when he does, he is often guided more by instinct than policy. At staff meetings, Gore is more like a sometimes overbearing teacher, while Bush often plays the impatient student. "I've seen the governor say, 'Why don't you close the book and tell me what you think is most important?'" "His classic question is 'Have you told me everything I need to know?'" "If he doesn't know, he'll say, 'Hold it.'" "If somebody uses an acronym he doesn't know, he'll stop him or her and say, 'What does that mean?' Sometimes he says, 'Use plain English.'" Bush made no excuses for his gaps in knowledge, saying:

> I don't think anybody knows everything about every subject, and anyone who pretends they do is someone I don't want to be the president, because this is a complicated world. . . . The key to the presidency is to set divisions, to lay out the parameters by which decisions will be made and to encourage really good, competent people to serve the country for the right reasons and to build a team.

Perhaps the clearest instance of questionable judgment exhibited by Bush occurred very late in the campaign and has never been adequately explained.

On November 2, just five days before the election, Bush was forced to admit that he had once been arrested in 1976 for driving while intoxicated (Mitchell 2000a). That information was disclosed by a man with long ties to the Democratic Party. However, a reporter from the *Portland Press Herald* had actually uncovered the story three months before it broke, and he and the assignment editor thought it too far in the past to have any relevance to Bush's candidacy (Associated Press 2000a, 2000b).

Why hadn't Bush disclosed it before? He said he wanted to serve as a role model to his daughters "and made the decision as a dad that I didn't want my daughters to do the kinds of things that I did" (quoted in Mitchell 2000a; see also Allen and Balz 2000). Bush preferred to focus on the fact that the report was leaked by a Democrat with strong, documented anti-Bush views (Harkavy 2000; Associated Press 2000a).

That incident causes concern for several reasons. Candor is the first issue. In 1998, a reporter asked Bush whether he had ever been arrested after 1968, the year of a fraternity prank that he had already acknowledged. The reporter recalls Bush saying no. Bush disputes that. He recalls having replied, "I don't have a perfect record." That disagreement is unlikely to be satisfactorily resolved because Bush's principal adviser, Karen Hughes, was apparently the only other person in the room.

Bush took a substantial and unnecessary risk in not disclosing the incident much earlier. He ran on a platform of restoring honor and integrity to the White House. This incident appeared to be inconsistent with that. Moreover, the excuse he offered was flimsy since presumably both his daughters already knew he had had an alcohol problem. He would have been on firmer ground simply to say, again, that he had already admitted an alcohol problem and did not feel it relevant or appropriate to get into the details of a manifestation of it that occurred twenty-four years ago.

Such a response would have certainly resulted in a surge of questions about other such incidents. However, in the absence of other fuel to feed the fire, the incident would have burned out. Moreover, by bringing up the incident himself, Bush could have added to his reputation for candor, not subtracted from it.

Surely, given the level of opposition research in past elections and the past experiences of Gary Hart, Bill Clinton, and others, it was very likely that such information would come out, especially since it involved court records that are public. Bush therefore took a substantial risk, one made larger by it being unnecessary, with his own candidacy and all that it stood for. The costs to Bush were considerable, but not as catastrophic as they might have been.[10]

Is Al Gore Too Smart to Have Good Judgment?

The flip side of questions about Bush's intelligence is the general agreement that Gore is the "smarter" of the two. This view is not easily supported by the academic accomplishments of the two. Gore went to Harvard and received so-so grades overall, and Bush did the same at Yale.[11] Bush completed a post-undergraduate degree at the Harvard Business School, and Gore finished neither of his two graduate school degree attempts (one at Vanderbilt Divinity School, the other at Vanderbilt Law School).

The attribution of intelligence to Gore is built on his mastery of and immersion in the details of policy, his ability to provide long, detailed answers to policy questions on the stump and during the campaign debates, and Bush's missteps. These are not "perceptions" with little substantive foundation. On the basis of experience and knowledge, Gore is obviously qualified to be president.

However, a question should be raised in connection with Gore's obvious experience and knowledge. It is exactly the opposite of questions raised about Bush. The concern with Bush is whether he is smart enough. The issue for Gore is whether he isn't too smart.

Too smart? What could possibly be wrong with being well versed or knowledgeable? The issue I want to raise here is the psychology within which the knowledge and experience are encased. During the campaign, aides to Gore told *New York Times* reporter Richard Berke (2000) that Gore "sometimes sees himself as the smartest person in the room, and often he is right."

The implications of this view were suggested in a large number of interviews conducted with Gore and White House staff members by David Maraniss and Ellen Nakashima of the *Washington Post* for their book *The Prince of Tennessee* (2000c). These interviews are a form of primary data and are striking in the extent to which those interviewed, a diverse group, came to similar conclusions: "Mr. Gore could be both bold and very hesitant. Mr. Gore took a bold stand on the Administration's response to the Kyoto Conference on Global Warming, but called up his aide Carter Eskew to ask if it would look bad if he baby-sat for his grandson instead of joining his wife and daughter at the Million Mom March in Washington" (*New York Times* 2000). Maraniss and Nakashima write,[12] "Those first words of self-doubt that Gore uttered during his 1976 congressional campaign—How'm I doin'? How'm I doin'?—became the private mantra of his political career."

Variations on the theme were recounted by people who worked for him and admired him yet could recall scenes like this one offered by a former aide: " 'There was a situation where he was asking me how he did, how he did, how he did, and I guess I was getting annoyed,' and he said, 'Don't you know how insecure I am?'" One former adviser reached the conclusion that insecurity was "the seminal force that motivates Gore," a trait, this adviser said, that tended to obscure his better side—"an insightful, intelligent, subtle and well-intentioned person."

So which was it? Gore the leader or Gore the staffer; the bold Gore or the subservient Gore? Those questions go to the struggle within Al Gore that has long been evident—a duality that he brought with him into the vice president's job, that became more pronounced once he was there, and that remained unresolved as he sought to move up to the Oval Office. "He was at once competent and self-confident about anything that he could translate into what he considered a question of fact, yet often insecure and plagued by self-doubt when it came to perceptions and emotions and aspects of life that could not be established with mathematical certainty."

This split between high self-confidence alternating with substantial self-doubt creates difficulties for Gore's decision-making style and the quality of his judgments. As one aide comparing Gore and Clinton noted, "Gore is inductive. Once the facts take him to a position, he tends to frame an issue in black and white, at least in his public expressions of it. Clinton is more intuitive, always allowing for more shades of grey" (quoted in Maraniss and Nakashima 2000a).

Facts may be the starting point of judgment, but they are not synonymous with it. The ability to put facts into perspective is a key element of good judgment. Gore's certainty when he has what he believes are "the facts" and his view that they lead to inescapable conclusions can led him to take somewhat rigid positions and also to disparage those who don't happen to hold his view. Several staffers told Maraniss and Nakashima (2000a):

> While the president and vice president agreed that the White House should offer its own balanced budget in 1995 in the decisive battle with the Republican Congress, once that was done, it was Gore who showed the most resolve, according to aides. Clinton was constantly luring the Republicans with hints of possible compromise, while Gore held an unyielding position from which he hectored his opponents about the waywardness of their reasoning. For Gore it was really kind of simple: "The Republicans were just wrong, so there was no reason to give in to them," said one former top aide. "He really believed it as a matter of fact, not as a matter of faith." Clinton is prepared to compromise off ideology. Gore is less willing to compromise because he thinks his views are fact-based.

The question arises here: Isn't Gore's position simply a matter of having principles on which he stands? Yes, to some degree; however, there is an important distinction to be drawn here. Strong adherence to the principle "I'm certain I'm right" is not the same as standing for a principle with the understanding that others may legitimately differ. Humility leavens hubris.

One of the dangers of high self-certainty is that it is hard to admit when you're wrong. Maraniss and Nakashima's interviews with his advisers after Gore's much criticized remarks on the Joint Chiefs of Staff and policies toward gays in the military suggested

> a stubborn refusal to acknowledge that he had articulated a damaging position— that such military leaders as Colin L. Powell or H. Norman Schwarzkopf would be ineligible for command in a Gore administration since they believe that allowing gays to serve openly hurts military effectiveness. After two days of internal deliberation, Democratic sources said, Gore grudgingly agreed to state that his original answer had been misinterpreted.

Not surprisingly, Gore's insistence on being correct leads him to be closed off at times to good advice. The reality is that Gore is the driving force behind virtually every big decision of his campaign, and many small ones, even in logistical matters. Berke (2000) notes, "[W]hen he was in a rush to travel from New York to Washington, Gore announced that he was scuttling Air Force Two because he would make better time on the US Airways shuttle. His stunned military and Secret Service aides knew not to try to talk him out of it."

Joe Biden, the Delaware Democratic senator who supported Gore in the primaries, had this to say about Gore's open-mindedness:

> Gore comes off to me as a guy who has absolute confidence in what should be done and really isn't all that interested in what you think substantively. . . . Al is interested in getting briefed, forming an opinion and then it's settled. That reflects a political certitude: a guy who will make decisions à la Harry Truman and go home and go to sleep. Except Truman operated on a gut assessment based on a historical context. Al operates on an intellectual assessment that doesn't accommodate much input. (Quoted in Berke 2000)

Another analysis in the *New York Times* (2000) details the ways in which Gore often asks his chief aides for advice, but it ended by noting,

> Mr. Gore's aides could not come up with a major example in which they had persuaded the governor to change his mind. After weeks, the Gore campaign offered only one: The vice president was adamant that he go to the Super Bowl last January to see the Tennessee Titans. The problem was that the game was on the Sunday before the New Hampshire primary. It took Eskew and Charles

Burson, the chief of staff who is also a Titans fan, to tell Mr. Gore that "it was not the best use of his time," said Chris Lehane, a Gore spokesman. Indeed, the Titans lost the game.

Gore's tendency to self-certainty when he believes he has "the facts" has another, more troubling side. You can see the results if you examine the transcript of the meeting between Gore and Clinton and critics of his initiative on race relations that took place at the White House on Christmas Eve in 1997. In it, he used moral reproach as a means of discrediting opponents of affirmation action. His opponents were "profoundly wrong" and "denied the obvious," and he ended by giving those assembled the following glimpse into his view of human nature: "It is naive in the extreme to assert that there is no persistent vulnerability to prejudice rooted in human nature." "That evil," he continued, "lies coiled in the human soul," and to deny that is "just wrong."

Or, consider his speech to Atlanta's Ebenezer Baptist Church on Martin Luther King Day in 1998. In it, he railed against "modern apostles of apathy" who "roll [King's] words off their tongues, even as they try to roll back equal opportunity" and

> invoke the phrase "content of our characters" . . . to pretend that all we need is to establish a color-blind society. They use their color-blind, the way duck hunters use a duck blind. They hide behind the phrase and just hope that we, like the ducks, won't be able to see through it. They're in favor of affirmative action if you can dunk the basketball. But they're not in favor of it if you merely have the potential to be a leader of your community. (Quoted in Sleeper 1998, 20)

There is no doubt this position is politically congenial to some, but embedded in it is a harsh tone of moral stridency. Gore's opponents are not merely mistaken; they are devious, hypocritical, wholly opposed to racial progress and increasing opportunity—in short, thoroughly despicable people. Being able to adhere to boundaries of respect and legitimacy for one's opponents might well be an element of good judgment in political leaders, regardless of your experience and knowledge.

Does Gore's Experience and Knowledge Lead to Good Judgment?

Gore's experience and knowledge present a somewhat different frame though which to analyze a set of factors often seen to be related to good judgment. The Gore competency themes—experience coupled with knowledge—are an obvious outgrowth of his long career in government service. He was elected to the Congress and to the Senate, where he developed an expertise in military and environmental policy. Moreover, he had been a two-term, highly involved, and very influential vice president under Clinton.

Gore's competence was an obvious and legitimate theme for news stories about his candidacy. Surprisingly, those themes accounted for only 14 percent of the news coverage themes of him during that period. The Pew study notes:

> Gore's competence was a central message being promoted by his campaign. Sometimes this thread came up in the form of reporters simply summarizing Gore's mindset. "The vice president has great faith in his own national security experience and instincts. . . . The vice president has participated in every major national security debate over the past decade and has access to intelligence and foreign policy expertise throughout the government," noted reporter John Broder in the *New York Times*. Often the praise of Gore came through the coverage of Clinton.

Who raised the theme of Gore's competence? Gore campaign surrogates were more than twice as likely to plug Gore's competence than journalists.

What is the relationship of experience and knowledge to judgment? Experience in government and in high decision-making circles, as Gore had, provides a front-row seat and an opportunity to participate in the debates that shape an administration. By all accounts, Gore made it his business to be involved and was. He was thus present at most of the administration's policy debates when policy options were suggested and weighed, and when participants sorted through the mix of policy and political considerations that frame most executive decisions. A seat at such high levels gives one the opportunity to asses other styles of decision making and the judgments that result. For a person given to reflection, they can provide some insight into one's own decision-making style and the ways in which one reaches a judgment. These can be valuable experiences.

What Gore did not have in his experience, which Bush did, was the final authority, and the responsibility that followed, for making decisions. That experience would be different in important ways from being *part* of decision processes. Quite obviously, as part of the decision group, you are one of the advisers. As the president or governor, you are the person with ultimate responsibility. Your role is not to be a skillful advocate of a position (yours) but to be a skillful and thoughtful appraiser of others' arguments and their implications.

The two positions are, in important ways, inconsistent with each other. An advocate/adviser's general stance is to discount other options and bolster his or her preferred one. The leader charged with ultimate responsibility reaches a better judgment by weighing the various advocacies presented before reaching his or her own position.

There is one final important aspect of experience and the acquisition of knowledge that bears mention. Experience provides not only knowledge but lessons. I am not referring here to the broad historical kinds that underlie the use of analogy at suitable moments. Nor am I referring to the insights into one's own decision and leadership style that political experience can provide. The lessons I have in mind here are of a more personal, characterological nature.

It is well known that immersion in the routines of an institution or a profession's life can have important consequences. The idealism of young medical students, teachers, and police officers, for example, have all been shown to be responsive to experience in those professions that accumulate over time. There is no reason to think political life is an exception.

Gore has been in political life much longer than Bush and had more time to acquire and internalize those kinds of lessons. What kinds of lessons might these be? Both Al Gore and George Bush had fathers whom they loved and (perhaps especially for Bush) idealized and who had lost elections. Both young men took these losses hard. What lessons might they learn here?

Both had personal experiences with losing races. Bush lost his first political campaign for a congressional seat, and Gore lost in his run for his party's presidential nomination in 1988. Also, Gore was an instrumental partner for eight years in an administration marked by erratic fortunes and uneven performance. What lessons in leadership and decision making did Gore learn in that capacity? And both were engaged in a brutal, few-holds- (if any) barred fight to secure the presidency after the vote on November 7, 2000. What lessons did this experience confirm or teach?

What of knowledge? How is that related to good judgment? Obviously experience increases knowledge. However, knowledge is not a unitary concept. There are different kinds of knowledge, and they often get confounded in discussions of experience.

It is important to distinguish between policy *knowledge* and policy *understanding*. We can define the first as a basic building block of understanding. What is missile throw weight? Who is Viktor Chernomyrdin?[13] What are the advantages and disadvantages of allowing people, on a voluntary basis, to invest some of their Social Security funds in the stock market (Kessler 2000a, 2000b)?

There is no doubt that knowledge can be an important ingredient in reaching good judgments. Yet, how much knowledge is necessary, and in conjunction with what other elements, remains an open question. Familiarity with policy details *may* facilitate good judgment, but that it must necessarily do so is far from clear. Recall that numerous times during the tense debates of the Cuban missile crisis, President Kennedy asked for explanations of terms or historical precedents (see chapter 2). Keep in mind as well that a concern with details can often be at the expense of being able to step back and see their larger implications. That is one reason, and there are others, why highly obsessive people are not necessarily good decision makers.

Gore's immersion in the details of the areas that he has selected for specialization is well documented. Indeed, he has been characterized as having "nearly an obsessive hands-on approach" (Allen and Connolly 2000). When he was searching for an issue to make him a player in the Senate, he selected arms control and went about acquiring mastery in a characteristic way (Turque 2000, 142–50). He asked a colleague, Edward Boland, chair of the House Select Committee on Intelligence, to recommend someone to help him acquire that knowledge. Boland recommended Leon Furth, who remains a senior Gore adviser.

Gore biographer Bill Turque (2000; see also Zelnick 1999, 117–18) describes the tutorial thus: "for more than a year . . . Furth tutored Gore in the bleak arcana of throw weights, hard-target kill capacities, and war-head to silos ratios. They met at least once a week, sometimes for four or five hours at a time" (144). One of those invited to make a presentation to Gore, then Undersecretary of the Navy James Woolsey (later to head the CIA under President Clinton), said "that he had never had such a detailed technical discussion with a member of Congress."

Gore's technical mastery of the subject made him a player in the debates on the basing of the MX (multiple-warhead) missile system and the deployment of the so-called "Midgetman" missiles, singe-warhead missiles on mobile launchers (Turque 2000, 142–50; Zelnick 1999, 117–36). His major speech on March 22, 1982, laid out his proposal, which was to convert all the MX missiles to Midgetman missiles. Zelnick (1999) says, "[T]here was nothing particularly new about Gore's idea, it had been kicked around for years at Livermore and other Western think tanks" (122). Turque (2000) agrees: "The centerpiece of Gore's proposal was not an original idea. It had been kicking around the arms control community for years and was certainly well known to Furth" (145).

At first, Gore's idea was greeted with silence, but a series of events over the next year stimulated by the congressional cutoff for funds for the MX missile system revived the idea of the Midgetman. A commission chaired by former air force general Brent Scowcroft recommended the Midgetman option but coupled it with a recommendation to build one hundred MX missiles in hardened silos to prevent U.S. vulnerability in the event of a Soviet first strike. It was this plan that was adopted. In the end, the MX missile was revived by a Senate vote, but the Midgetman program never was developed and ultimately was canceled. Fifty MX missiles were built and housed.

Turque (2000) calls Gore's strategy of supporting a revival of the MX as a carrot to get the Reagan administration to take arms control seriously "wishful on two fundamental levels" (147). First, it substantially underestimated the opposition of Reagan senior advisers such as Caspar Weinberger and Richard Perle. Second, it substantially underestimated President Reagan's preference for a more powerful missile defense, a view that eventually resulted in the push for the Strategic Defense Initiative. Some thought that Reagan and his advisers had made use of Gore's personal and policy ambitions to revive the MX missile system (Turque 2000, 148; Zelnick 1999, 123), which they did. Reviews of Gore's performance over this debate were mixed:

> Gore's defenders say he stepped into a debate in which few people were making sense and developed a clear workable approach to nuclear stability. . . . The less enamored saw a hyper-ambitious young man who let his penchant for self promotion and zeal for a place at the table outrun his judgment. (Turque 2000, 149–50)

Zelnick notes that Gore saw the Soviet Union as a permanent partner in managing nuclear arms and great power rivalry, but Reagan saw the weakness in the Soviet system and was determined to exploit it to change it profoundly. His endorsement of SDI helped drive the Soviet Union toward perestroika (restructuring) and glasnost (openness). Once liberalization started, it could not be stopped or controlled, and the Soviet Union as we knew it collapsed.

Zelnick (1999) makes a more profound assertion given our interest in the relationship of knowledge to good judgment. He underscores:

> [T]he irony for Gore is that on nuclear arms control, the issue that turned him from a mildly interesting and promising Tennessee representative to one of his party's premier voices on national security, he was brilliantly, imaginatively, responsibly and valiantly wrong. To Gore, the nuclear issue was part of a rela-tionship with the Soviet Union that had to be managed. To Reagan, it was part of a struggle that had to be won. (125)

Scandal and Good Judgment

The issue of scandal in relation to the presidential candidates came up early in the 2000 primary season. John McCain, Republican presidential hopeful, admitted that campaign contributions to him as head of an important Senate committee had influenced his willingness to grant access. Appearing with Democratic presidential hopeful Senator Bill Bradley to discuss campaign finance reform, he said, "I believe I probably have been influenced because the big donor buys access to my office and we know that access is influence" (quoted in Kuntz 1999). He took the step of confessing his ethical boundary transgression and then made his admitted lapse the basis of a personal crusade to do away the influence of soft money contributions.

Gore's reported lapses were of a different sort and handled in a different way. While a number of possible issues might have been raised in connection with this story line, the Pew study found, "Usually, the discussion of Gore as scandal tainted came in the form of reminders of Gore's questionable fundraising." When you combined statements that Gore had scandal problems with those that said he really didn't, the total made up almost half of the statements (46 percent) of the three themes that the Pew study found being used to characterize the vice president.

The scandal theme was established early in the campaign. Over half, 57 percent, of these assertions appeared in March 1999 and another 21 percent in February 2000. Less than a quarter of the assertions of Gore's problems with scandal came in the last three months, between April and June.

What was the factual basis of such assertions? According to the Pew study, "The scandal issue was also notable in that there was more evidence for it than any other. Fully 90 percent of the references offered some form of evidence. Usually—64 percent of the time—that evidence was interpreting Gore's public record." Only 8 percent of the scandal assertions were made by an opponent.

Did those raising the issue of scandal link it to judgment? No. The Pew study notes:

> Usually they were tied to how he was running his campaign rather than how he might govern the country. Half of the statements about Gore and scandal were tied to his tactics and strategy. Not quite a third (31 percent) concerned his leadership and just 3 percent had to do with his relations with voters, or whether it would affect his chances of winning.

On its face, the association of a presidential candidate with scandal would not appear to be an encouraging sign in the search for good judgment. An involvement in political or personal improprieties is itself an indication that something in the process of making a good judgment has faltered or failed. That something is often the triumph of self-interest over more ethical norms, whether they are those of the community or person. Perhaps the person rationalizes his or her misstep by saying that it will just be this one time. Or, perhaps the person believes that the stakes are important enough to justify the ethical lapse as an "exception." Perhaps the person is subjected to pressures that compete with his or her moral sense and is unable to resist being pulled off course. Or, perhaps the person's ethical standards had always been more forceful in the abstract than in practice. Whatever the reason for it, taking steps away from one's core ethical standards always runs the risk they will more easily be compromised the next time.

Gore's personal and political circumstances were complex. Few hints of scandal were associated with his career or politics before he assumed the vice presidency. He was known as an ambitious, smart, and somewhat inhibited ("wooden") senator, with a reputation for hard work, attention to detail, and self-promotion. In short, Gore had, before he became vice president under Clinton, a not very out of the ordinary profile that could fit a number of well-thought-of senators or political leaders.

That changed with the complexities of his relationship to Clinton. Gore was unusual in laying out to Clinton his demands that if they were elected, he be given substantial access and policy responsibility. Clinton was unusual in agreeing to do so. As a result, Gore was not only a uniquely influential vice president but was for all intents and purposes president in the areas that Clinton ceded to him. According to Maraniss and Nakashima (2000b, see also Maraniss and Nakashima 2000a; Broder and Henneberger 2000):

> Al Gore's relationship with Bill Clinton was defined in an agreement they worked out in Little Rock after the 1992 election and before the inauguration. . . . Gore would be a managing partner. He would have an office in the West Wing. Members of his staff would be integrated into the president's staff. The president and vice president would meet for lunch once each week and the meeting would be inviolate, held no matter what else was preoccupying them. And Gore would have what he called spheres of interest in which Clinton would defer to him and let him take the lead for the administration. Though it was not stated in those terms, within the White House it became understood that Gore was essentially president of the subjects within his spheres of interest. The list grew over time, as Clinton gave him new assignments at their weekly lunches, eventually including all environmental issues, science, high-tech, the Internet, communications, space, reinventing government, voluntary ratings for network television, the tobacco industry and nuclear disarmament of the former Soviet states. Clinton was willing to cede these spheres of interest to Gore because there were other policy matters that he was more interested in, and because he implicitly trusted Gore to handle them with skill and discretion.

Aside from the unique historical nature of the relationship, their arrangement had a number of obvious psychological results. First, from Gore's standpoint, it satisfied his personal and political desire to be influential. It satisfied his ambitions and provided a clear basis for leveraging them further. It also created a level of connectedness that was certainly advantageous to Gore so long as Clinton had anything resembling a normal presidency.

In exploring the toll that Clinton's dishonesty about his affair with Monica Lewinsky took on the Clinton–Gore relationship, Broder (2000) writes:

Friends and associates say he was angered by Clinton's deceit, repulsed by his behavior and appalled at his recklessness. Gore brooded then and afterward about what the episode might mean for his own presidential ambitions. His sense of loyalty struggled against an offended morality, a conflict that, his friends say, has not yet been resolved.

Apparently those feelings had been resolved to some degree by December 19, 1998. It was on that day after Clinton was impeached that Gore, standing with members of the Democratic Congress, said that the vote "does a great disservice to a man I believe will be regarded in the history books as *one of our greatest presidents*. There is no doubt in my mind that the verdict of history will undo the unworthy judgment rendered a short while ago in the United States Capital" (Harris 1998, emphasis mine).

Given a number of chances thereafter to modify his glowing assessment of Clinton, Gore declined. In an interview on *Face the Nation* (transcript 5), the following exchange occurred:

> **Schieffer:** Let's talk about your friend, Bill Clinton. A lot of people remember that Saturday afternoon—I remember it very well—when the House voted to impeach the president. You went to the White House Lawn and said, "This president will be remembered as one of the greatest presidents in history." Do you still believe that?
>
> **Vice President Gore**: Look at the economic record, Bob. We've gone from the biggest deficits to the biggest surpluses. We've gone from a triple dip recession to tripling the stock market. Instead of quadrupling the debt, we've seen the creation of 20 million new jobs.
>
> **Schieffer**: So you still stand by the statement.

The president's impeachment was not the only problem Clinton's behavior presented to Gore. Neustadt (1990) argues, "The first eighteen months or more [of a president's term] becomes a learning time for the new President" (169). Certainly Clinton's first two years in office are consistent with the view. However, his uneven performance during this period raised more questions about the president than about Gore. Also, Clinton did recover his political footing facing a newly elected Republican Congress.

What put Gore in his predicament was not Clinton's somewhat erratic political leadership during his first two years of office but the means by which he carried through his determination to reverse his losses. That entailed winning back Congress as well as his own reelection. And that in turn required raising unprecedented amounts of money to begin an early campaign. That effort was critical to Clinton's reelection chances and therefore to Gore's as well, but the president's reelection was also critical to whatever ambitions Gore had to succeed Clinton.

It was that effort that ensnared Gore. Bob Woodward (1997a) reports,

> In his zeal to raise money and do President Clinton's bidding, Gore took the unusual step of requesting large contributions for the Democratic National Committee—often in private phone calls—with an urgency and directness that several large Democratic donors said they found heavy-handed and inappropriate for an incumbent vice president. Gore became known at the DNC as the administration's "solicitor-in-chief" after Clinton adamantly refused to make direct requests for contributions, according to two senior Democratic officials.

From fall 1995 to spring 1996, Gore made fund-raising phone calls from the White House using a Clinton–Gore campaign credit card. At first, Gore acknowledged making "a few calls" from the White House for soft money contributions. However, when detailed notes of the solicitations emerged, he acknowledged that he had made eighty-six calls and reached forty-six potential donors (Woodward 1997b). Criticized for doing so, Gore responded in a hastily called news conference on March 3, 1997, that there is "no controlling legal authority" that prohibited him from making fund-raising phone calls from the White House.

Gore also got in trouble by attending a high-level meeting at which the money coming into the Clinton–Gore campaign was allocated to hard money/soft money categories.[14] In early August 1997 when the details of Gore fund-raising became a matter of public knowledge, a spokesperson for the Democratic National Committee, Amy Weiss Tobe, said that "the vice president was not aware that money was being designated for the federal [hard money] account" (quoted in Woodward, 1997b). However, a short while later, a memo turned up that contradicted Gore.[15]

At first, Gore said he wasn't paying that much attention to the discussions in the meeting. However, that statement was inconsistent with Gore's generally detailed approach to matters and was also contradicted by aides who were present. Then, in an August 8, 1998, FBI interview, Gore said that because he drank a lot of iced tea and might have needed a restroom break, he could have been absent during key parts of a meeting on fund-raising attended by the president and campaign aides (Lardner 2000). However, former White House chief of staff Leon Panetta said in a deposition that he remembers Gore "attentively listening" to the hard-money conversations, and former White House deputy chief of staff Harold Ickes testified that whenever the vice president left the room, he, Ickes, stopped the meetings. In light of the evidence, FBI general counsel Larry Parkinson wrote to the assistant attorney general that there was "sufficient evidence" to prove that the vice president made a false statement to investigators on this matter.

On April 29, 1996, Gore attended a Buddhist temple fund-raiser where $60,000 in illegal donations were raised and for which he gave several different understandings (Fineman, Breslau, and Isikoff 1997; see also Lewis 2000). On October 22, Gore said he thought the Buddhist temple event was for "community outreach," not a fund-raiser. Then, in the spring, the vice president conceded that it was "finance-related." Somewhat later his aides describes it as an exercise in "donor maintenance." They noted—accurately—that no solicitation was made at the event.

In all those instances, Republicans called for Attorney General Janet Reno to investigate whether the facts warranted an independent counsel investigation. On three different occasions, she concluded that they didn't. Some senior members of her staff, notably FBI Director Louis J. Freeh and others, disagreed. However, Gore did not escape unharmed politically.

There is evidence that all these allegations and Gore's responses to them did affect him and his candidacy. Harris and Connolly (2000) write that questions like whether Gore lied to FBI investigators

> strike at places where Gore is already vulnerable. Independent voters who think the Clinton administration has set a low ethical tone, who think Gore is emblematic of Washington politics and its money-chase culture, or who think Gore is not a straight shooter—all their concerns could be exacerbated by the controversy.

The evidence appears to support the view that Gore's association with questionable fund-raising practices did adversely affect him. At the time the Pew survey was being conducted, the campaign had not really commanded the attention of large numbers of voters. Nonetheless, the scandal theme did have some resonance with voters. Another Pew study[16] designed to assess whether voters were responding to the themes raised in the media found "Approximately half the public says they would be less likely to vote for the vice president if they heard charges that Gore panders or stretches the truth. Messages that emphasize scandals involving President Clinton or allegations about Gore's own role in illegal fund-raising would turn off about four-in-ten Americans."

"Clinton fatigue" was a real fact throughout the campaign. It was almost certainly an important factor in Gore's selection of Senator Joseph Lieberman, a man who had publicly criticized the president for his "immoral behavior." However, it had a more direct effect on the public's voting as well.

Morin and Deane (2000), poll directors for the *Washington Post* writing about Clinton fatigue, note:

The majority of voters—about seven in 10—said their vote had nothing to do with the First Bubba. But among those who were trying to send a message to 1600 Pennsylvania Ave., the edge went to those who didn't have anything nice to say. In all, about two in 10 said their vote was meant to express opposition to Clinton, and about one in 10 said their vote was meant to express support. We were watching those voters who like Clinton's work but not his persona. As predicted, one in three of these voters defected to Bush. *Moreover, "honest" ranked as the single most important trait voters this year were seeking in the next president*—and eight in 10 of these voters supported Bush. (emphasis mine)

Exaggerations, Lies, and Good Judgment

The fourth and final area that arose in the Pew study with relevance for assessing judgment is the question that arose regarding Gore's truthfulness. These concerns took two separate but related forms. One asked whether Gore had a tendency to embellish or exaggerate. The other asked whether at times he would "say anything" to get elected.

The Pew study found that

more than third of the Gore assertions studied (34 percent) were about his tendency to lie or exaggerate. . . . Once again, Gore's record was often what did him in. More than third of the statements about Gore's tendency to stretch the truth referred to his public record, slightly higher than for all other themes. . . . Like his ties to scandal, Gore's honesty problem was hammered at during the key primary battle. In all, 43 percent of the assertions came in March.

Did the press explore the implications of their story frame for Gore's judgment? Here, paralleling the failure to do so in the case of the scandal story line, the answer is no. The Pew study reported that

the press was less likely to explore the implications of this problem on a Gore Administration than to tie the issue to some more immediate concern, such as Gore's campaign. Nearly two-thirds (64 percent) of the time the assertion was related to how it would affect Gore's tactics and strategy. The press put Gore's exaggerations into the context of his potential leadership just 23 percent of the time.

It should be clear that exaggeration is related to judgment in a different way than it is to leadership, and it is primarily judgment that is my focus here. What is the relationship, if any, between exaggeration and judgment? The first step in delineating the relationship is to ask what an exaggeration represents both psychologically and politically.

When someone exaggerates, that person takes a step or more beyond what one can reasonably or truthfully claim. The consequence is to put the exaggerator in a more advantageous position than he or she would be in were the person to stick with a wholly accurate accounting. Exaggeration, therefore, is a deception with a purpose: to present the person in a way that gives him or her unwarranted or unearned credit.

An exaggeration is often considered a "harmless" overstatement to which many political leaders are prone (Perry and Cummings 2000).[17] For example, Lyndon Johnson's great-grandfather did not die at the Alamo but peacefully in bed. Ronald Reagan told Israeli Prime Minister Yitzhak Shamir during Shamir's 1983 visit to the White House that he had been one of the first photographers to take pictures of emaciated inmates of Nazi concentration camps. Reagan, an Army Air Corps captain attached to the First Motion Picture Unit in Culver City, California, never left the United States during World War II. The incident was reported by Reagan biographer Lou Cannon, who speculated that when Reagan told that story, he probably believed it. The actor had seen films of the death camps, and, Cannon wrote, films were "real" to him.

In 1988, Senator Joseph Biden of Delaware was running for the Democratic presidential nomination. He gave a very moving speech about how he was the first member of his family to go to college. However, much of his speech was lifted word for word from a political commercial broadcast by Labour Party leader Neil Kinnock in Britain. Later, Biden claimed that he had graduated in the top half of his law school class; he hadn't.

Richard Nixon lied when he told the nation he couldn't disclose Watergate details because "national security" was involved. It wasn't. Candidate Lyndon Johnson promised to never send "American boys to fight in an Asian war," at precisely the same time as he was seriously planning to do just that. President Clinton lied when he told the nation he had never had sexual relations in the White House with Monica Lewinsky. He also committed perjury in the same matter before a trial judge and a federal grand jury.

Obviously gross deceptions with large policy or political consequences like those of Presidents Johnson, Nixon, and Clinton are different than padding a résumé. In the case of each of these larger lies, the motivation is clear: to escape from the negative consequences of one's behavior (Nixon, Clinton) or avoid the negative voting judgments that are likely to occur if you tell the truth (Johnson).

In each of these cases, the president knows that he is lying but puts his own self-interest before the public's. There are as many ways to rationalize this kind of deception as there are reasons for a leader to think that his self-interest should trump the public's. However, what is basic to all these cases is that the deceiver never tests his rationalization to anyone other than himself (Bok

1978), who, of course, thoroughly understands and approves of the deceptive steps that had to be taken.

The rationale for smaller lies and exaggerations is precisely the same: to gain unwarranted benefits and/or avoid unwanted consequences. The magnitude of the consequences differs, of course, but not their underlying dynamic.

It also seems obvious on its face why lies and exaggerations would be troublesome for political leaders and their leadership. Leadership capital (Renshon 2000b) depends on expectation and the experiential confirmation of trust between the leader and the public. And that, in turn, rests on a history of honesty.

However, what of judgment? The key question that is raised about judgment from the standpoint of exaggeration, lying, and other forms of misrepresentations is the relationship of ambition and self-interest, on one hand, and a person's ethical ideals and standards, on the other. Does self-interest and personal or political ambition trump ethical ideals and standards? Or do ethical ideals and standards provide a stable framework that places limits on self-interest and ambition?[18]

An exaggeration, lie, or other misrepresentation represents the crossing of an ethical boundary. At the same time, it represents a judgment that one's personal self-interest is more important than the normal expectation for honesty and accuracy that others have and to which most people at least say they subscribe themselves.

One might characterize the relationship between ambition/self-interest and personal ethics/community interests as *the* basic judgment-framing issue in every important decision a leader makes. Every leader must balance his or her own personal and political interests with a robust consideration of what's in the public's best interest. Sometimes the two are synonymous. However, most often they are not.

A leader who repeatedly puts a psychological finger on the scales to tip the balance toward his or her own self-interest has at minimum a weighing bias. Such a leader cannot adequately give each element in a decision the weight it might deserve because his or her self-interest already tipped the scales. The judgment error in this instance consists in the weighing of the evidence elements. However, that is not the only error.

Starting out with a psychologically unbalanced scale is a much more fundamental than the plain description earlier suggests for three reasons. First, it is a primary framing error. That is, it takes place at the very start of the judgment processes and influences what follows. Second, it persists throughout the judgment process. It is not an error that is committed just once but rather each and every time evidence must be considered. Third, it is a systematic, motivated error rather than one that might arise from time to time.

Gore's exaggerations were not at the level of those of Presidents Johnson, Nixon, and Clinton already noted. So, it is not their magnitude that requires our attention but their frequency. They include the following: Gore said he and his wife, Tipper, were the models for Erich Segal's novel *Love Story*. The author repeatedly corrected Gore by pointing out that the male character was a composite and Tipper Gore was never used (Powers 1997; Associated Press 1997). In November 1999, Gore claimed to be a cosponsor of the McCain–Feingold campaign finance reform legislation. However, that bill was not introduced until three years after Gore had left the Senate (Bennett 2000). During the same month the vice president claimed to be the author of the Earned Income Tax Credit (EITC; *Time* 1999).[19] In fact, the EITC law was enacted in 1975—two years before Gore entered Congress. Gore claimed credit for providing major phrases for Hubert Humphrey's acceptance speech at the Democratic National Convention in 1968 through his talks with Charles Bartlett, whom Gore described as a major Humphrey speech writer. In subsequent interviews, Barlett said Gore had no role in helping Humphrey write his convention speech (Maraniss and Nakashima 1999). Gore claimed at a news conference that "he had been involved in discussions about the strategic oil reserve in its early stages" (Mitchell 2000b). Yet the Strategic Petroleum Reserve was established in 1975, two years before Gore arrived in Congress.[20]

There are other such incidents as well. A claim that his mother-in-law's arthritis medicine cost three times what Gore paid for the same drugs for his dog turned out to be both inaccurate and untrue. The information had come not from his mother-in-law, as Gore had claimed, but from a Democratic briefing paper, and it played loosely with the comparative figures (Robinson 2000). There was artful ambiguity about Gore's Vietnam experience that left the impression that he had seen combat in the participant sense, rather than having seen the aftermath of it, once (Zelnick 1999). Bill Bradley complained that Gore had lied repeatedly about his record (Allen 1999).[21]

Some have argued that Gore's exaggerations were taken out of context (Parry 2000). However, a closer inspection of the many assertions (e.g., that he had "taken the lead in developing the Internet") all were correctly understood at the time for what they were presented to be: a claim for credit where less was warranted.[22] Gore's tendency to exaggerate is not a creation of his enemies or itself an exaggeration. The *New York Times* published a memo from Gore's press secretary in 1988, Arlie Schardt (2000), warning him "that his main pitfall was exaggeration," and it noted an earlier memo that had warned Gore of making "remarks that may be impossible to back up." Schardt protested the publication of the memo, but not its content.

Establishing a pattern of embellishments is not the same as psychologically accounting for them. That task is certainly possible but takes us beyond the purposes of this chapter. Rather, I want to turn here to another question, that of consequence.

Did these exaggerations hurt Gore? Some evidence indicates that they did. The Pew survey found that

> Gore's veracity did seem to penetrate to some degree with the public, though not overwhelmingly. The public was noticeably more likely to attribute saying anything to get elected to Gore than to Bush, by a margin of 36 percent to 25 percent. And it seems to matter to people. About half of Americans said that Gore's tendency to lie or exaggerate would make them "less likely" to vote for him, compared with 40 percent who said it wouldn't make much difference.

Did it make an actual difference in the way the public cast its votes? Apparently, it did. In an analysis of exit polling data reported by the *New York Times*, Toner and Elder (2000) write:

> Voters were generally in a contented mood as they cast their ballots, but there were also signs of Clinton fatigue: in their negative judgment of the president's character and in the priority many put on straight talk and honesty. When given a choice, a plurality of voters—about a fourth—rated honesty a more important consideration than experience or an understanding of the complex issues of the day, according to the voter polls. And those people tended to vote for Bush, who also had an edge among those who considered strong leadership most important . . . two-thirds of respondents said the country, enjoying a record economic boom, was going in the right direction over all. But 6 in 10 said it was on the wrong track morally. Clinton's job approval rating stayed fairly high, but his personal unfavorability rating was equally high in the surveys. . . . Most voters said they would remember Clinton more for the scandals of his presidency than for any leadership he provided.

CONCLUSION: GOOD JUDGMENT, FOREIGN POLICY, AND ELECTION CAMPAIGNS

It seems fair to conclude that it is possible to tell a fair amount about candidates' judgment from their behavior during the unfolding campaign and a focused look back over their record. It also seems fair to say that this is not often done. We are thus faced with a paradox.

A candidate's judgment is very important to most voters, but they are not helped in reaching their own good judgment about these matters by the reporting that covers important campaign issues. This is one more area in which there appears to be a disconnection between voters and media reporters. Voters, of course, are able to reach their own conclusions on these matters in egregious cases of poor judgment, like Gary Hart's. However, it is probably ill advised to depend on such flamboyant episodes since poor judgment does not always advertise itself so blatantly.

One way to address this problem is have media analysts become more aware of the links they need to explore and report. This in turn will require a step back from the "horse race" aspect of the campaign to a more substantively oriented focus on the things that matter to governing. A focus on candidates' judgment may well be in the same position as "character issues" were ten years ago—recognized as important, but technically difficult to translate in concrete behavioral or career terms for nonclinicians.

What of the questions with which we began this essay? Is there evidence of dual judgment? The evidence we have examined herein points to the unitary nature of the personal aspects of the judgment process. Ambition, ethics, and their relationship to political career choices appear to reflect the balances or imbalances that exist in a person's interior character psychology. Gore's dilemmas with Clinton amply demonstrate their importance.

There is also evidence that such considerations can play an important role in more strictly policy judgments. John McCain's personal ethical lapses as the basis for his emerging as a champion of campaign finance reform, and Gore's support for this issue as well, suggest a role here. So do the suggestions of an intersection between Gore's leadership aspirations and this support of the Midgetman missile system.

Yet, as suggestive as such evidence might be, it is an error to try to reduce policy judgments to characterological psychology. Yes, it is probably true that the historical analogies one selects reflect the lessons that are most personally salient to the person doing so, and they are therefore personal in that sense. However, it is also true that analogies and the history they rest upon have their own independent factual weight. Reality in the form of the current circumstances that exist and are unfolding does, and ought to have, enormous weight in the calculations of foreign policy judgments. What to do in the Middle East may have a lot to do with Clinton's search for a historic legacy, but the immediate facts exert their own inexorable presence as well. Can we analyze the failed Camp David summit in 2000 without asking about the impact of Clinton's historical and political ambitions on his judgments? I think not. Can we assign them primacy? Perhaps. Can we then say that because of this we can therefore safely disregard the facts and the knowledge of how these parties acted in the past? Absolutely not.

NOTES

1. All figures in this and the following paragraphs on sound judgment are drawn from the Pew Research Center for the People and the Press, The Political Typology—Version 3.0, Section V: The Clinton Legacy and the Next President, www.people-press.org/typo99rpt.htm (accessed November 11, 2000).

2. Pew Research Center for the People and the Press, "Candidate Qualities May Trump Issues in 1999," www.people-press.org/oct99mor.htm, October 18, 1999 (accessed November 1, 2000).

3. Using factor and cluster analysis to place individuals, respondents were asked a series of questions in eight areas: environmentalism, religion and morality, social tolerance, social justice, business sentiment, financial security, antigovernment sentiment, and patriotism/militarism. More specific descriptions of the methodology and of the groups may be found at www.people-press.org/typo99sec.1.htm (accessed March 1, 2000).

4. The groups and their descriptions are as follows:

Staunch Conservatives: Probusiness, promilitary, prolife, antigay, and anti–social welfare with a strong faith in America. Antienvironmental. Self-defined patriot. Distrustful of government. Little concern for the poor. Unsupportive of the women's movement. Predominately white (93 percent), male (62 percent), and older. Married (74 percent). Extremely satisfied financially (54 percent make at least $50,000). Fifty-seven percent are white Protestants.

Moderate Republicans: Probusiness, promilitary, but also progovernment. Strong environmentalists. Highly religious. Self-defined patriots. Little compassion for poor. More satisfied than Staunch Conservatives with state of the nation. White, relatively well educated, and very satisfied financially.

Populist Republicans: Religious, nationalistic, and prolife. Negative attitudes toward gays and elected officials. Sympathetic toward the poor. Most think corporations have too much power and money. Tend to favor environmental protection. Roughly six in ten are dissatisfied with the state of the nation. Heavily female (61 percent) and less educated. Fully 31 percent are white evangelical Protestants compared to 15 percent overall.

New Prosperity Independents: Probusiness, proenvironment; many are prochoice, sympathetic toward immigrants, but not as understanding toward black Americans and the poor. Somewhat critical of government. Tolerant on social issues. Well educated (40 percent have a college degree), affluent (almost four in ten earn at least $75,000), young (70 percent under the age of fifty), and male (64 percent). Less religious (only 15 percent go to church weekly).

The Disaffecteds: Distrustful of government, politicians, and business corporations. Favor creation of third major political party. Also, anti-immigrant and intolerant of homosexuality. Very unsatisfied financially. Less educated (only 8 percent have a college degree) and lower income (84 percent make less than $50,000). Half are between the ages of thirty and forty-nine. Second only to Partisan Poor in number of single parents.

Liberal Democrats: Prochoice and supporters of civil rights, gay rights, and the environment. Critical of big business. Very low expression of religious faith. Most sympathetic of any group to the poor, African Americans, and immigrants. Highly supportive of the women's movement. Most highly educated group (48 percent have a college degree). Least religious of all typology groups. One-third never married.

Socially Conservative Democrats: Patriotic, yet disenchanted with the government. Intolerant on social issues. Positive attitude toward the military. Think big business has too much power and money. Highly religious. Not affluent but satisfied financially. Slightly less educated, older (32 percent are women over age fifty).

New Democrats: Favorable view of government. Probusiness, yet think government regulation is necessary. Concerned about environmental issues and think government should take strong measures in this area. Accepting of gays. Somewhat less sympathetic toward the poor, black Americans, and immigrants than Liberal Democrats. Many are reasonably well educated and fall into the middle-income bracket. Nearly six in ten (59 percent) are women, and 17 percent are black.

Partisan Poor: Nationalistic and anti–big business. Disenchanted with government. Think the government should do even more to help the poor. Very religious. Support civil rights and the women's movement. Have very low incomes (39 percent make under $20,000), and nearly two-thirds (63 percent) are female. Thirty-six percent are African American, and 13 percent are Hispanic. Not very well educated. Largest group of single parents.

Bystanders: Somewhat sympathetic toward poor. Uninterested in what goes on in politics. Rarely vote. Young (46 percent are under thirty), less educated, and not very religious.

5. Available at www.journalism.org/publ_research/character1.html, July 27, 2000 (accessed October 3, 2000).

6. For a review of the evidence for a generalized intelligence (G) factor, see Jensen (1998).

7. I analyze judgment in each case elsewhere in some detail (Renshon 1996a, chap. 6, 9–11).

8. Such charges were routinely made by Gore indirectly and by his surrogates directly. For example, in an interview with the *Washington Post* (Balz and Connolly 2000), the following exchange took place:

> **Post:** Do you think Bush is smart enough to be president?
>
> **Gore:** I have not questioned his intelligence. And I don't think anyone should question his intelligence. I don't have any doubt about his intelligence.

Yet, here is a quote from one of Gore's supporters (Friedman 2000) on a foreign policy speech Gore made: "Gore delivered a provocative foreign policy speech Sunday that raised an important question: Does George W. Bush have the experience, the gravitas and, by implication, the brains to run U.S. foreign policy?"

This incident parallels another when Gore denied that he had said that Bush was not ready to assume the presidency when he clearly had said so. The headline in the *New York Times* accompanying the story read "Gore Describes Texan as Not Up to the Job" (Seelye

2000). An earlier Gore campaign ad had pointedly asked of Bush (Marks 2000), "Is he ready to lead America?" Actually Gore had questioned Bush's lack of basic knowledge about foreign affairs after he wasn't able to identify several leaders in a pop quiz sprung on him (Neal 1999).

9. The Pew Center for the People and the Press, "Bush Gains on Personal Qualities," http://www.people-press.org/july00rpt.htm, November 1, 2000 (accessed November 20, 2000).

10. Early polling reports suggested that few would change their vote because of the discovery of a twenty-four-year-old arrest for driving while under the influence. Several polls suggested (Associated Press 2000c) the late revelation that Bush was arrested in 1976 for driving under the influence of alcohol would not be much of a factor in the election. More than eight in ten said the news did not raise doubts for them about Bush as a candidate. Those who found it influencing their decision were about evenly split between doubting their support for Bush and their support for Gore (because a Democrat had leaked the arrest record), according to the Pew poll. About half in the NBC–*Wall Street Journal* poll thought Bush should have disclosed the information previously, but 85 percent in that poll said it made no difference anyway. Only 17 percent in an ABC News poll said the arrest was relevant, and most of them were Gore supporters.

After the election, Karl Rove (2001, 210), senior Bush campaign manager, was not so sanguine. He estimated that Bush lost the state of Maine, with its five electoral votes, because of it. Others estimated that Bush lost about several hundred thousand votes nationwide.

11. *NBC Nightly News* anchor Tom Brokaw (2000) had this to say about the college careers of both men:

> All of this comes to mind as more stories emerge about the undergraduate years of George W. Bush at Yale and Al Gore at Harvard. For a time, apparently, both men barely kept their heads above water, hovering just at C level. We're told Governor Bush was much more interested in intramural sports and fraternity social life than the classroom. Classmates of Vice President Gore remember he shot a lot of pool, reportedly smoked a little marijuana, played sports and managed to get a D in one course and not one A during his sophomore year.

12. The quotes that follow are drawn from Maraniss and Nakashima (2000b).

13. He is the former Russian prime minister with whom Gore negotiated and signed a secret arms agreement that became controversial during the campaign (Vita 2000). It was also a name that Bush dropped "causally" during one of the presidential debates to demonstrate that he was familiar in an easy way with this important official with a somewhat difficult-to-pronounce name.

14. *Soft money* is defined as contributions not intended to support individual candidates but to promote "party building" and other general campaign activities such as television advertising. While it must be reported, it can be given in unlimited amounts. Hard money contributions are highly valued by campaigns because they can be used directly to benefit individual candidates. But federal law places specific restrictions on the solicitation, amount,

and use of such contributions. Among those restrictions, the law says that such regulated contributions cannot be solicited on federal property.

15. Grunwald (1998), who reported on the memo, says:

> The memo is potentially damaging to Gore, who has insisted that in making calls to 45 donors during the campaign he only asked for "soft money" that would go to the Democratic Party's general campaign efforts, and not "hard money" specifically for the Clinton campaign. David Strauss, then Gore's deputy chief of staff, scribbled on the Nov. 21, 1995, memo "65 percent soft/35 percent hard." The notation is followed by a scrawled definition of soft money: "corporate or anything over $20K from an individual." Those notes, made during a DNC finance meeting attended by Gore, could cast doubt on Gore's protestations that he never intended to solicit hard money, but are not necessarily conclusive, investigators said.

16. The Pew Research Center for the People and the Press, "Voters Unmoved by Media Characterizations of Bush and Gore," www.people-press.org/july00rpt.htm, July 27, 2000 (accessed November 20, 2000).

17. The examples that follow, unless otherwise noted, are drawn from this article.

18. I have discussed these matters in details elsewhere (1996a, 1996b) and put forward a theoretical framework with which to analyze them.

19. The transcript reads in part (emphasis mine):

> **Time**: Given how critical Senator Bradley has been of welfare reform, what do you think of the poverty proposals he put forward this week?
>
> **Gore**: [Bradley's proposals were] an old-style approach that spends a lot of money but doesn't have any new ideas. [He proposes] the expansion of the Earned Income Tax Credit. *I was the author of that proposal. I wrote that,* so I say, welcome aboard. That is something for which I have been the principal proponent for a long time.

20. On ABC's *This Week* the following exchange (transcript, 2000) on the subject took place between Cokie Roberts (moderator) and Dick Cheney, Republican vice presidential nominee:

> **Roberts:** You've been making the same kinds of charges. What are you really saying here? Are you saying this man's not fit to be president?
>
> **Cheney:** I think it raises questions about his—his character. I think he consistently over the years has a pattern of exaggeration. Turns out he's made statements that are not true, in everything from the Internet to "Love Story," most recently the question of prescription drugs for his mother-in-law and his dog. This week we've had the statement that he was there when the decisions were made on setting up the Strategic Petroleum Reserve; he wasn't.
>
> **Roberts:** But he was in Congress. . . .
>
> **Cheney**: He was not in Congress.

Roberts: He was in Congress when the oil was actually put into the reserve.

Cheney: The decisions were made in the Ford Administration. I was there as White House chief of staff; Al Gore wasn't. He wasn't even in Congress yet.

21. Allen (1999) quotes Bradley as saying, " 'But I'm afraid he didn't tell you the whole truth about my record—or even half of it,' Bradley began. 'He said that I proposed raising the eligibility age of Social Security. Not true—he knows it's not true. He suggested I'd cut Social Security benefits and increase Social Security taxes. Not true—he knows it's not true.' "

22. As an example of the press misunderstanding Gore, Parry (2000) gives the example of his claims about Love Canal. Parry says that the reporter quoted him saying, "That was the one that started it all," which became transformed to "I started it all." The only problem is that Gore is really quoted as saying that his hearings on Love Canal "started it all" when in fact President Carter had declared Love Canal a disaster area months before Gore's hearings.

In fact that original story was clear in its quote and in the inference to be drawn from it (Connolly 1999a, emphasis mine):

> Speaking later at Concord High School, Gore boasted about his efforts in Congress 20 years ago to publicize the dangers of toxic waste. "I found a little place in upstate New York called Love Canal," he said, referring to the Niagara homes evacuated in August 1978 because of chemical contamination. "I had the first hearing on that issue." Gore said he first became aware of the problem when a young girl in Tennessee wrote to him about a mysterious illness that had befallen her father and grandfather. Although few remember his hearings on that site in Toone, Tennessee, Gore said his efforts made a lasting impact. *"I was the one that started it all,"* he said. Gore's shorthand description of Love Canal—and his failure to note that the hearings he chaired came a few months after President Jimmy Carter declared the neighborhood a disaster area—were reminiscent of earlier attempts to embellish his role in major events.

REFERENCES

Allen, Mike. 1999. "Gore Lies Repeatedly, Bradley Says." *Washington Post*, December 3, A1.

Allen, Mike, and Dan Balz. 2000. "Bush Seeks to Minimize DUI Fallout." *Washington Post*, November 4, A1.

Allen, Mike, and Ceci Connolly. 2000. "Glimpses Show Candidates Cool as Cucumbers." *Washington Post,* November 26, A12.

Associated Press. 1997. "Gore Concedes 'Miscommunication' about 'Love Story' Role." December 14.

———. 2000a. "Campaign 2000: Candidates Spar on Issues as Bush's Past Is Addressed." November 3.

———. 2000b. "Portland Paper Ignored Bush DWI." November 4.

———. 2000c. "Presidential Polls Glance." November 4.

Balz, Dan, and Ceci Connolly. 2000. "Excerpts: *Post* Interview with Gore." *Washington Post,* May 13.

Bennett, William J. 2000. "A Lifetime of Lies." *Wall Street Journal,* October 11.

Berke, Richard L. 2000. "Gore Dots the i's That Bush Leaves to Others." *New York Times,* June 9, A1.

Bok, Sissela. 1978. *Lying: Moral Choice in Public and Private Life.* New York: Pantheon.

Broder, John. 2000. "Clinton's Affair Took a Toll on Relationship with Gore." *New York Times,* March 3, A1.

Broder, John, and Melinda Henneberger. 2000. "Few in No. 2 Spot Have Been as Involved as Gore." *Washington Post,* October 31, A1.

Brokaw, Tom. 2000. "The Gentlemen and Their C's." *New York Times,* April 3.

Clinton, William J. 2000. "Remarks at a Reception for Representative Maurice D. Hinkley in Kingston, New York (October 22, 2000)." *Weekly Compilation of Presidential Papers* 36, no. 43 (October 30): 2582–89.

Connolly, Ceci. 1999a. "Gore Paints Himself as No Beltway Baby." *Washington Post,* December 1, A10.

———. 1999b. "'New' Gore Bears Striking Resemblance to '88's." *Washington Post,* December 11, A8.

Face the Nation. Transcript, October 3, 1999.

Fineman, Howard, Karen Breslau, and Michael Isikoff. 1997. "You Can Call Him Caught." *Newsweek,* September 15, 77.

Friedman, Thomas L. 2000. "Foreign Affairs: Yellow Brick Geopolitics." *New York Times,* May 5.

Gardner, Howard. 1993a. *Multiple Intelligences: The Theory in Practice.* New York: Basic Books.

———. 1993b. *Frames of Mind: The Theory of Multiple Intelligences.* New York: Basic Books.

———. 2000. *Intelligence Reframed: Multiple Intelligences for the 21st Century.* New York: Basic Books.

Goleman, Daniel P. 1997. *Emotional Intelligence.* New York: Bantam.

Greenstein, Fred I. 2000. *The Presidential Difference: Leadership Style from FDR to Clinton.* New York: Free Press.

Grunwald, Michael. 1998. "Justice Department Looks Again at Gore Fund-raising Role: Aide's Notes Hint at Calls Seeking 'Hard Money.'" *Washington Post,* August 21, A1.

Harkavy, Jerry. 2000. "Maine Lawyer Discovered Bush DUI." Associated Press, November 3.

Harris, John F. 1998. "Clinton Vows to Finish Out Term; President Says He Will Keep Working to 'the Last Hour of the Last Day.'" *Washington Post,* December 20, A1.

Harris, John F., and Ceci Connolly. 2000. "Analysis: Vice President Finds Past Still Perilous." *Washington Post,* June 24, A1.

Jensen, Arthur R. 1998. *The G Factor.* New York: Praeger.

Kessler, Glenn. 2000a. "Between Bush, Gore Claims Is Reality of Social Security." *Washington Post*, November 5, A25.

———. 2000b. "Two Visions, Both Quiet on Tough Choices." *Washington Post*, October 24, A10.

Kuntz, Phil. 1999. "McCain's Financing Stance Recalls Keating-Five Role." *Wall Street Journal*, December 17, A16.

Langer, Gary. 1999. "Public Says Bush Has Smarts to Lead Nation." ABCNEWS.com, November 15.

Lardner, George, Jr. 2000. "Public Integrity Chief, GOP Clash on Probes." *Washington Post*, May 25, A35.

Lewis, Neil. 2000. "Gore Fund-Raiser Convicted for Arranging Illegal Gifts." *New York Times*, March 3.

Maraniss, David, and Ellen Nakashima. 1999. "Senator's Son Feels Pull of Political Life in Caldron of Chicago '68, a Mix of Caution, Ambition." *Washington Post*, December 27, A1.

———. 2000a. "After Careful Courtship, a Natural Affinity." *Washington Post*, August 11, A1.

———. 2000b. "The Bureaucrat vs. the Risk-Taker." *Washington Post*, August 12, A1.

———. 2000c. *The Prince of Tennessee: The Rise of Al Gore.* New York: Simon & Schuster.

Marks, Peter. 2000. "The Ad Campaign: Commercial Attacking Bush Is Most Hostile of Campaign." *New York Times*, November 3.

McGrory, Mary. 2000. "Caught in the Switch." *Washington Post*, February 27, B1.

Merida, Kevin. 2000. "George W. Bush: Is He or Isn't He Smart Enough?" *Washington Post*, January 19, C1.

Mitchell, Allison. 2000a. "Bush Acknowledges an Arrest for Drunken Driving in 1976." *New York Times*, November 3.

———. 2000b. "Bush Attacks Gore, Citing 'Pattern of Embellishments.'" *New York Times*, September 24.

Morin, Richard, and Dan Balz. 2000. "Poll: Bush's Lead over Gore Is Gone." *Washington Post*, March 12, A18.

Morin, Richard, and Claudia Deane. 2000. "Why the Fla. Exit Polls Were Wrong." *Washington Post*, November 8.

Neal, Terry M. 1999. "Gore Blasts Bush Quiz Answer, Vice President Questions GOP Leader's Foreign Expertise." *Washington Post*, November 6, A9.

Neustadt, Richard E. 1990. *Presidential Power and the Modern Presidents: The Politics of Leadership from Roosevelt to Reagan.* New York, Free Press.

New York Times. 2000. "Where the Candidates Turn for Some Advice." June 9.

Parry, Robert. 2000. "He's No Pinocchio: How the Press Has Exaggerated Al Gore's Exaggerations." *The Washington Monthly* (April).

Perry, James, and Jeanne Cummings. 2000. "History Has Shown Politicians Can't Resist a Little Embroidery." *Wall Street Journal*, October 11, A1.

Powers, William. 1997. "For Gore, It Was No Love Story." *The National Journal*, December 20, 2568.

Renshon, Stanley A. 1996a. *High Hopes: The Clinton Presidency and the Politics of Ambition.* New York: Routledge.

————. 1996b. *The Psychological Assessment of Presidential Candidates*. New York: Routledge.

————. 2000a. "The Comparative Psychoanalytic Study of Political Leaders: John McCain and the Limits of Trait Psychology." In *Profiling Political Leaders and the Analysis of Political Leadership: Methods and Cross-Cultural Applications*, ed. Ofer Feldman and Linda O. Valenty. Westport, Conn.: Greenwood.

————. 2000b. "Political Leadership as Social Capital: Governing in a Fragmenting Culture." *Political Psychology* 21, no. 1: 199–226.

Robinson, Walter V. 2000. "Democrat Is Faulted Anew over Drug Costs." *Boston Globe*, September 22.

Rove, Karl. 2001. "Karl Rove." In *Electing the President 2000: The Insiders' View*, ed. Kathleen Hall Jamieson and Paul Waldman. Philadelphia: University of Pennsylvania Press.

Schardt, Arlie. 2000. "My Memo Said What?" *New York Times*, February 16.

Seelye, Katherine Q. 2000. "Gore Describes Texan as Not Up to the Job." *New York Times*, November 4.

Shapiro, Walter. 1999. "Apt Student Bush Making the Grade." *USA Today*, November 11.

Sleeper, Jim. 1998. "Color Bind." *New Republic*, March 2, 18–20.

Steinberg, Robert J. 1979. "The Nature of Mental Abilities." *American Psychologist* 34: 214–30.

This Week. 2000. Transcript, September 24.

Time. 1999. "Nation/Interview," November 1, 154:18, 1–2.

Toner, Robin, and Janet Elder. 2000. "An Electorate Largely Split Reflects a Race So Very Tight." *New York Times*, November 14.

Turque, Bill. 2000. *Inventing Al Gore: A Biography*. Boston: Houghton Mifflin.

Vita, Matthew. 2000. "GOP Uses 1995 Arms Pact to Turn Up Heat on Gore." *Washington Post*, October 26, A25.

Wildavsky, Aaron. 1966. "The Two Presidencies." *Transaction* (December): 7–14.

Will, George F. 1999. "He's No Intellectual—And So What?" *Washington Post*, September 23, A29.

Woodward, Bob. 1997a. "Gore Was 'Solicitor-in-Chief.' " *Washington Post*, March 2, A1.

————. 1997b. "Gore Donors' Funds Used as 'Hard Money.' " *Washington Post*, September 3, A1.

Zelnick, Bob. 1999. *Gore: A Political Life*. Washington, D.C.: Regnery.

· 4 ·

Bad Guys and Bad Judgments

Stephen J. Wayne

$\mathscr{P}$residents have them, use them, and consistently invoke their image. They serve as political foils, unifying figures, and fodder for the exercise of presidential power, and they provide at least the appearance of strong presidential leadership. They are part and parcel of the public dimension of the office. They are the enemies that every president has and needs, the people who allegedly cause the problems that presidents and their advisers are forced to address and to which their decisions and actions are directed. They are the "bad guys."

For presidents, invoking the image of a bad guy serves a number of useful purposes. It helps focus people's attention, simplifies policy explanations, and helps the public determine right from wrong. It allows presidents to claim the moral high ground in political conflicts as well as justify the necessity for saying or doing something potentially controversial. Blaming the problem on a bad guy can make a complex issue more understandable to more people more quickly, thereby reducing or removing nuance. Take George Bush's justification for opposing Iraq's invasion of Kuwait, for example: "you have such a clear case of . . . good versus evil. We have such a clear moral case. . . . It's that big. It's that important. Nothing like this since World War II."[1]

His son evoked similar sentiments as he rallied Americans behind his administration's diplomatic and military responses to the 9/11 terrorist attacks against the World Trade Center and the Pentagon. "Al Qaeda is to terror what the mafia is to crime," Bush stated in his speech before a joint session of Congress on September 20, 2001. He went on to describe the terrorists and those who support them as "the heirs of all the murderous ideologies of the twentieth century. By sacrificing human life to serve their radical visions—by abandoning every value except the will to power—they follow in the path of fascism, and Nazism, and totalitarianism. And they will follow that path all the way, to where it ends: in history's unmarked grave of discarded lies."[2]

As his father had done a decade earlier, Bush continued to present the challenge as one of good versus evil.

We value life; terrorists ruthlessly destroy it. We value education; the terrorists do not believe women should be educated or should have health care, or should leave their homes. We value the right to speak our minds; for the terrorists, free expression can be grounds for execution. We respect people of all faiths and welcome the free practice of religion; our enemy wants to dictate how to think and how to worship even to their fellow Muslims.[3]

He voiced utter amazement that there could be vitriolic hatred for America in some Islamic countries: "I'm amazed that there is such misunderstanding of what our country is about, that people would hate us . . . like most Americans, I just can't believe it. Because I know how good we are. . . . We are fighting evil. And these murderers have hijacked a great religion in order to justify their evil deeds. And we cannot let it stand."[4]

Nor are bad guys necessarily a creature of presidential imagination. They do exist in real life. They may threaten those who oppose them and try to impose their goals on those who resist. They test presidential leadership by challenging it. If these enemies did not exist, however, presidents would have to create them. They have become an vital component of the contemporary office, a target toward which blame and hostile emotions may be directed and from which political support can be generated.

But bad guys can also be dangerous to presidents who invoke their "evil" images. Their presence and perceived malevolent actions can serve to restrict vision, limit options, shorten time frames, expose decisional processes to public view, unleash emotions, impair analysis, and bind and inhibit future decisions and actions, consequences that will be explored later in this chapter.

Good judgments require sensitivity and understanding. At the very least, decision makers need to be aware of their own biases, how their mind-set and those of their advisers affect perceptions of the problem and of the environment in which it exists. Alexander and Juliette George's depiction of Woodrow Wilson's unyielding position on the Versailles Treaty and his campaign to convince the American public of the correctness and righteousness of his view illustrates the extent to which psychological needs and the behavioral responses to them can impair the judgment of even the most intelligent people.[5]

Decision makers must also be conscious of the adequacy and currency of the information they receive, the range of viable options they have from those that are minimally feasible to those that are maximally optimal, and the likely reactions of others, individually and collectively, to the judgments they make, including their methods for implementing those judgments. Too narrow a vision, too superficial an understanding, too emotional a reaction can adversely affect judgments, as can unconscious desires, unexamined priorities, and unchallenged assumptions.

A good judgment is one in which realism, reflection, and rationality dominate the decisional process. It is also one in which experience is a guide but not a straitjacket and consistency is an attribute, not a liability.

This is a chapter about presidential rhetoric and judgments, about how the use of bad guys as symbols of negativity contribute to good public relations but potentially to bad policy judgments. It is not a case study; it is not a normative argument for deciding what is good or bad; nor is it an empirical analysis that applies certain criteria to place public figures on a good to bad continuum. Rather, it is a theoretical discussion with some contemporary, real-world examples about image making by presidents and its impact on their policy judgments.

The chapter begins by examining how bad-guy depictions help presidents reinforce their claims of leadership in the public arena; it then turns to the heightened effect of news media coverage on the ability of presidents to achieve their policy goals in situations in which bad guys are designated as the raison d'être for that policy. The final sections explore the potential constraints that bad guys impose on presidential decision making in the foreign and domestic spheres.

BAD GUYS AS HELPERS

The need for enemies stems from public expectations of strong presidential leadership in a political system and constitutional structure designed to inhibit such leadership. "Separate institutions sharing powers,"[6] internal checks and balances, the federal system of government, and decentralized political parties all work to prevent power from accumulating in any one institution, such as the presidency. The need for bad guys also results from presidents having to make and implement policy decisions in a venue in which external pressures activate and shape the "when, how, and what" of governmental decision making. Going public is no longer a presidential option; it has become a practical necessity on major issues for which there is no obvious consensus. Constant campaigning from behind the bully pulpit for public approval and political support is the rule, not the exception, today, particularly for those policy actions that require a cooperative legislative response.

Bad guys provide a lot of good things for presidents. They help them achieve their policy and political objectives. They contribute to the president's good-guy image. Bad guys are a unifying figure to dislike, a personification of evil, a reason for action, a point around which support can rally. They also contribute to stature by elevating presidential actions, sometimes to heroic proportions. When taking on their enemies, presidents become valiant warriors, fighting against the forces of evil (a term that they frequently employ) and, in the process, demonstrating their own leadership skills.

The list of people demonized by presidents is long and growing. It consists of many different types and gradations of political and personal enemies whose actions presidents have found to be objectionable, embarrassing, threatening, or in other ways antithetical to their interests, to their party's, and to their judgment of what is good for the United States. For John F. Kennedy, it began with Nikita Khrushchev and his decision to place missiles in Cuba, and Roger Blough, chairman of the board of U.S. Steel, and other giants of the industry who tried to raise prices in the spring of 1962. Lyndon Johnson had the "nervous Nellies" who questioned and later actively opposed the Vietnam War. He also had to contend with his private nemeses, the Harvard crowd, left over in the government from the Kennedy years, especially Bobby Kennedy, the heir apparent. President Johnson also had to deal with his "friends" from the South, Democrats who opposed his civil rights initiatives, and increasingly vocal Republican opponents who took issue with his conduct of the war and his social welfare programs.

Richard Nixon saw practically everyone as his enemy: liberal Democrats; Jews; journalists; Russians and other communists; Daniel Ellsberg and his psychiatrist; the "bums" (as he referred to them) on college campuses who precipitated the antiwar protests; Democratic Party officials who were headquartered in the Watergate office complex; his 1972 election opponent, George McGovern; his own White House special counsel, John Dean, after the latter confirmed the president's cover-up of the burglary; Senator Sam Ervin, chairman of the committee investigating the dirty tricks of Nixon's reelection campaign; and all those members of Congress who would have voted for his impeachment had they been given the opportunity to do so. Nixon was careful, however, only to demonize in public those who had railed against him in public. He also used his cabinet, White House aides, and especially Vice President Spiro T. Agnew in this task of public condemnation.

For Gerald Ford, it was those responsible for the poisonous political climate he inherited and tried to dissipate with his pardon of Richard Nixon; Cambodians who seized the American merchant ship, the *Mayaguez;* conservative Republicans who sabotaged the moderate domestic policy agenda that Vice President Nelson Rockefeller had fashioned and who later supported his primary opponent, Ronald Reagan; and a news and entertainment media intent on caricaturing the president as a bumbler and stumbler.

Jimmy Carter began as Saint Jimmy but soon, instead of turning the other cheek, he turned on all those Washington politicians who put their own political interests above his good government intentions and policies: members of Congress whose myopic view of their representational responsibilities obscured the obvious wisdom of the president's proposals; oil lobbyists paid to protect the industry's interests at the expense of the country's; Ayatollah Khomeini, whose fundamentalist religious beliefs, fanatical political views, and irrational hatred of the United States led him to reject Carter's overtures to free American diplomats held hostage in Iran; and, finally, the general public whose perception of malaise precluded the president from exercising strong leadership and gaining a larger-than-life image in the last years of his presidency.

Ronald Reagan initially confronted "the evil empire"[7] (the Soviet Union), U.S. air traffic controllers, Muammar al-Qadaffi, big government, tax-and-spend Democrats, and welfare queens and their liberal "do-gooder" allies. Later he had to contend with his own overzealous cold warriors, national security aides John Poindexter and Oliver North, who carried the president's anticommunist crusade to new heights in Nicaragua by providing money, obtained from secret arms sales to Iran, to the *contras* who opposed the Marxist Sandinista government.[8]

George Bush's principal protagonists were Manuel Noriega, Saddam Hussein, Pat Buchanan, and other Republicans who crucified their president after his repudiation of a much publicized pledge not to raise taxes.

For Bill Clinton, the list is almost as long as Nixon's. He began with the press, always a favorite target among "thin-skinned" politicians, first the tabloids, which reported Gennifer Flowers's allegation of her twelve-year sexual liaison with the then-governor of Arkansas, and quickly extended his wrath to the entire establishment media, which covered her news conference, the stories that followed, and later the draft-dodging and marijuana accusations that plagued him on the campaign trail and in government. Practically all of the White House press corps were soon placed in the unfriendly, combative, avoid-at-all-costs category. Next came his partisan opponents, Republicans who filibustered his economic stimulus package in the Senate and who, along with their counterparts in the House, voted unanimously to oppose his deficit reduction bill, plus southern Democratic Senators Richard Shelby, David Boren, and others who opposed his proposed BTU tax. Business and issue groups, particularly the pharmaceutical industry, gun advocates, and cigarette manufacturers, were all categorized as self-interested rather than public interested. By 1995, Newt Gingrich and his army of "true believers," including most of the talk radio crowd, especially Rush Limbaugh, enlarged the already bloated group of Clinton foes. The vitriolic rhetoric, abrasive style, and extremist views of these Clinton haters made them into easy targets for the administration and provided the president with beneficial contrasts for his newly found moderation and popularism. The Republican Congress's inept legislative record and Senator Bob Dole's anticharismatic candidacy, which Democratic image makers combined into their 1996 Dole–Gingrich campaign monster, completed the bad-guy catalogue for the first term—an impressive group of adversaries, to be sure!

But it was in the second four years that Clinton and his friends turned demonizing into a fine art. Hillary Clinton referred to the conspiracy against her husband when accusations of his on-the-job womanizing first surfaced. Other Clinton supporters, both inside and outside the government, questioned the impartiality and credibility of the independent counsel investigating these charges, Kenneth Starr. Not only did they criticize Starr's report to Congress as unnecessarily salacious, overly invasive, and blatantly biased, but they alluded to the House Judiciary chair, Henry Hyde, and his gang of ten impeachment managers, in equally negative terms. The picture they presented was that of a much victimized president trying valiantly to pursue the nation's policy agenda while his enemies engaged in a personal and political vendetta against him. And if that wasn't enough, two foreign despots, Saddam Hussein and Slobodan Milosevic, and one international terrorist, Osama bin Laden, were also literally added to the administration's "hit" list.[9]

Although George W. Bush was careful to cultivate a good-guy image in his domestic political relationships and fulfill his promise of returning civility to Washington politics, he did unload emotional, vitriolic rhetoric against terrorist foes Osama bin Laden and, later, Iraqi leader Saddam Hussein. Referring to both as evil men, Bush described bin Laden as "one of the worst [terrorists]," adding, "We published the twenty-two Most Wanted; he's one of the twenty-two we're after. In terms of Mr. bin Laden himself, we'll get him running. We'll smoke him out of his cave, and we'll get him eventually."[10] As for Hussein, Bush said, "There is no question that the leader of Iraq is an evil man. After all, he gassed his own people. We know he's been developing weapons of mass destruction."[11]

The impact bad guys can have on public relations and presidential judgments relates in part to the extent and success of their demonization. All bad guys are not equally bad. Some are worse than others. Those who support U.S. interests are seen as less malevolent than those who oppose them. In general, foreigners are described as more sinister and evil than domestic foes. Foreign rulers are also more likely to be categorized in era-laden terms: the World War II *totalitarian rulers* such as Hitler, Mussolini, and Franco; the *communist despots* such as Stalin and Mao; the *religious fanatics* such as Khomeini; and those who harbor and abate *international terrorists* such as Muammar al-Qadaffi, Saddam Hussein, and Osama bin Laden. In contrast, the language for domestic adversaries tends to be more muted.[12]

Bad guys contribute to presidential politics, especially the politics of public relations, although they do so in different ways. Their beliefs and actions are frequently cited as explanations for and justifications of presidential decisions and actions. In many respects, bad guys have become more valuable to presidents than their so-called friends because adversaries can help build and maintain support in a way that friends and partisan allies usually cannot. Not only do political and personal enemies solidify the president's sympathizers, but they can also attract others within the body politic, people who may not be attuned to partisan politics, or even those who side with the opposition party but who are repelled by the bad guys and the threats they pose. Domestic bad guys are also great assets in fund-raising.

MEDIA AS HYPERS

Flaming public passions is an essential component of a successful bad-guy strategy. Presidents need to provide political cover for politicians at home and demonstrate their credibility to friends and foes abroad. This strategy is pursued by going public. By virtue of their bully pulpit, their public relations infrastructure, and the capacity of their aides to stage and orchestrate events, presidents can usually present the initial bad-guy story in a manner that works to their political advantage. They cannot, however, control that story indefinitely, as Lyndon Johnson found out with the war in Vietnam.

Johnson had gone on television to describe North Vietnam's aggression against U.S. naval forces in the Tonkin Gulf, information that later turned out to be inaccurate. The speech helped galvanize popular backing for the president's actions in the Gulf, including a congressional resolution that gave the president carte blanche to do what was necessary to repel and prevent further aggression against the United States and assist in the defense of South Vietnam. Public backing of Johnson's policy of retaliation and escalation began to splinter, however, the following summer when news of a deepening conflict, increasing casualties, and inconclusive results blanketed the airways.[13] The pictures and commentary enlarged the debate, extending it from the simple story of a blatant communist aggression that had to be contained to a much more complex situation in which the legitimacy of the South Vietnamese government, its military will and capacity, the validity of the domino theory,[14] American national interests in Southeast Asia, and the morality of the war itself were all called into question. Unable to keep the media's focus on the North Vietnamese invasion, Johnson lost control of the public debate and soon lost the public's confidence as well.

Whereas television broadcasts of the Vietnam War, the Iranian hostage crisis, and the events surrounding the Iran-*contra* affair, especially the congressional hearings into the matter, adversely affected the administrations on whose watch these events occurred, television coverage of the war in the Persian

Gulf, the civil strife in Bosnia and Kosovo, and the U.S. military action against the Taliban in Afghanistan helped Presidents George Bush, Bill Clinton, and George W. Bush in gaining support for themselves and their policies.

Media coverage cuts both ways. It can heighten or weaken a president's claim to leadership depending on how the coverage, the pictures, words, and overall story, conform to the administration's stated goals, factual claims, and desired outcomes. In the short run, "the rally round the flag effect" gives advantage to the president. In the long run, it may not if the public tires of the issue, especially if the president fails to resolve it satisfactorily.

Regardless of the overall effect of news media coverage on public opinion, adding to or subtracting from presidential support, the amount of that coverage, particularly at the onset of the problem, will up the president's ante, raise the stakes, shorten the time frame for decisions, and, frequently, require a demonstrative (tangible) response. Pictures of American hostages in Iran, burning oil wells in Kuwait, U.S. soldiers dragged through the streets of Mogadishu, bloody pilots captured and interrogated by the Serbian military, starving children, raped women, homeless and desperate people in Kosovo, and of course the collapse of the towers at the World Trade Center in New York all produced emotions that heightened demands for a quick and unambiguous action to end the horror. Under these circumstances, the one thing that presidents could not do was nothing.

On the other hand, the absence of extensive, everyday coverage, such as in the civil strife in Rwanda, Ethiopia, East Timor, or Sierra Leone, makes doing something demonstrative, such as providing economic or military aid or a contingent of American peacekeepers, much more difficult, even if presidents desire to do so. The constraints against foreign intervention—constitutional, political, and psychological—necessitate an educational effort to overcome them and sustain a policy response. Presidential speeches can contribute to this end, but they are rarely sufficient in and of themselves. Besides, the impact of speeches has a very short duration. Unless the threat is perceived as real and direct such as the loss of a significant number of American lives, military aggression against an ally, or the possession, testing, and potential use of nuclear, chemical, or biological weapons, media coverage is necessary to bring the point home, to stir up emotions, to show the malevolence. Seeing is believing, as far as most people are concerned; hearing about the problem secondhand is much less compelling, especially if the source is a public official promoting a policy in which that official has an interest and may be an advocate.

Part of the difficulty with tackling a distant, less visible problem are the constraints under which all contemporary presidents labor. Some of these constraints are constitutional and political: the separation of powers, divided party control of government, the onset of elections, ideological differences, turf fights, even personal political vendettas that pit one powerful figure against another. In a system designed to prevent institutional dominance, to preclude a plurality from easily and quickly getting its way, consensus building within government requires public persuasion outside it. All of this takes time.

Some of the constraints are material, particularly in the foreign arena. Having sufficient military equipment and personnel available and being able to move them fast enough is obviously necessary to make a threat credible, as is having the resources to follow through on a promise of technical aid, financial assistance, intelligence sharing, or defensive weaponry. But even within the domestic sphere, material, organizational, and strategic resources constitute the capability component of a policy decision. President George Bush and his Federal Emergency Management Agency (FEMA) clearly had problems of this nature when dealing with the aftermath of Hurricane Andrew in South Florida in 1991. In contrast, President Clinton and his FEMA were better organized to confront a series of natural and man-made disasters throughout his eight years in office.

Some of the constraints have their roots in self-interest and are difficult to surmount. If presidents lack the capacity to gain international compliance for an embargo, cooperation for a joint military action, or even political support necessary to enact legislation, ratify a treaty, or mute opposition at home, it naturally limits their options and the actions that follow from their policy decisions.

For international intervention, however, the most amorphous, and perhaps in the long run the most critical constraints are those that lie within the American psyche: the long isolationist tradition, the Vietnam syndrome, and what has followed from that fear, the "war without casualties" mentality evident in Clinton's policy in the Balkans.

At the very least these constraints place a major education burden on a president who wishes to engage in tough talk, make credible threats, or carry out longer-term policy initiatives. Whereas George Bush was able to make his case for involvement in the Persian Gulf, in part because of the oil, the blatant nature of the Iraqi aggression, and the post–World War II history of a continuing U.S. interest in the Middle East, he still encountered significant political opposition at home, a divisive congressional debate, a very close Senate vote for a resolution supporting the administration's policy, and numerous lawsuits against U.S. military involvement. The strength of this opposition in the extended period before the Persian Gulf War testifies to the depth of anti-interventionist feeling in the many other situations in which a direct and immediate threat to the nation's interests and security is not perceived by the public.

Until the terrorist attack on 9/11, presidents had to labor in the public arena to build and maintain support for interventionist policies. The difficulty of doing so with an inattentive and un– or underinformed public created an incentive for reducing complexity to simplicity, abstraction to personalization, and moral dilemmas to judgments of good and evil. Demonizing one's opponent is an easy and quick way to achieve these objectives. It may also be a dangerous way to exercise responsible leadership.

Obtaining sympathetic press coverage is also a critical component of any strategic policy that requires broad-based public support. It saved Clinton in Kosovo. Although he was not nearly as persuasive as his predecessor in convincing the American people of the need to become militarily involved, television news, particularly CNN and the major broadcast networks, came to his rescue with nightly pictures of desperate refugees fleeing their homeland and recounting persistent tales of Serbian horrors committed against the Kosovar Albanians and their families.[15]

Presidents who want to maximize their discretion, about whether to address a problem and, if so, how, need to influence media coverage so as not to place themselves in situations in which the news, especially the pictures, dictate a certain type of response (which they may not want to hear or make) or in which the absence of news (pictures) over time precludes one or several policy options.

Good policy judgments and good public relations go hand and hand, so much so that they have become inextricably tied to one another in all but the most routine situations. Just as policy decisions must take into account information about external conditions, current and anticipated, so, too, must they consider the source, scope, and spin of the news that is likely to impact on the public's reaction to those conditions and the policy response to it. In this sense, the press is the fourth branch of government, and potentially the most dangerous one for presidents, because it is least subject to their political influence, much less to the pursuit of their policy goals. Yet the success of interventionist policy is closely related to the amount of coverage that the problem that precipitated it received and to the dominant spin placed on that coverage by the news media.

Press spin thus becomes an independent variable affecting public policy decisions. As we have noted earlier, government officials must factor in anticipated media coverage and its political effect, but they must also try to influence that coverage to make their case, defend their actions, and mobilize public support. The danger in doing so is that their description and explanation of the situation, the policy options, and the most desirable response may be unbalanced to the point of being untrue. On the other hand, to have a largely private, profit-oriented news media describe the nature of the problem, dictate the parameters of debate, and evaluate various policy solutions would be equally dangerous because it abdicates the responsibility that those in authority have to provide leadership.

FOREIGN DESPOTS AS SATAN

Presidents are prone to blame their international problems on others, particularly foreign leaders, frequently referred to as dictators or despots. This negative characterization highlights the evil intent and immoral behavior of these malevolent figures.[16] But this practice, while it may generate short-term support, also can result in long-term difficulties. This section discusses the pluses and minuses of demonizing foreign leaders.

By placing the blame squarely on the shoulders of the bad guys, rather than on external conditions, unpredictable events, longtime ethnic or racial rivalries, or a collective national mood, presidents try to get themselves off the hook. They thereby deflect criticism from their policy decisions, indecisions, or ambiguities that allowed the situation to develop or may even have encouraged it to happen. Not wanting the policy statement that Ambassador April Glaspie communicated to Saddam Hussein on July 25, 1990—"we have no opinion on the Arab-Arab conflicts like your border disagreement with Kuwait"—to be a focus of public attention or an excuse for Hussein's actions, the administration quickly turned its wrath on the Iraqi leader instead, whom, Bush asserted, caused the crisis.[17]

Moreover, by pinpointing responsibility on others, presidents clarify the issue in favorable terms for public consumption as well as justify their demonstrative response. They give a signal that makes their threat more credible. Had the United States not reacted strongly to Saddam's aggression, Bush stated, "it would be a signal to actual and potential despots around the world."[18] He added, "Let me also make clear that the United States has no quarrel with the Iraqi people. Our quarrel is with Iraq's dictator and with his aggression."[19]

A few days later, Bush reiterated his Saddam-is-the-cause, Saddam-is-the-devil theme: "He [Saddam Hussein] had become the epitome of evil in taking hostages and in his treatment of the Kuwaiti people. He himself tried his best to personalize the crisis, pouring out rhetoric that portrayed our efforts to eject him from Kuwait as a matter of the United States picking on Iraq and the Arabs."[20] After demonizing his adversary, Bush noted parenthetically and somewhat ironically, "our policy was based on principle [not letting dictators get away with aggression], not personalities."[21]

But designating an enemy also limits options, raises stakes, and makes a satisfactory result more difficult (and perhaps as a consequence, less likely). So why would presidents consciously paint themselves into a corner? I can think of three principal reasons: (1) They believe it to be true, that a despot is the root cause of their problem; (2) they don't believe it to be true or the whole truth, but they still find it useful for the purposes of fashioning public support for their policy at home or to make their threats more credible to those abroad; (3) they may not perceive that they have other viable alternatives, especially if the situation caught them by surprise and they need to react quickly.

Some presidents believe their bad-guy rhetoric to be a real description, not simply an image designed for public consumption. In his memoirs, Carter describes Khomeini as "fanatical,"[22] "insane,"[23] and "deranged."[24] Bush frequently employed the "Hitler" analogy in describing Hussein's aggression and the need to stand firm against it.[25] For Clinton, Milosevic was perceived increasingly as an irascible and irrational dictator, a war criminal:

> He unleashed wars in Bosnia and Croatia, creating 2 million refugees and leaving a quarter of a million people dead. A decade ago, he stripped Kosovo of its constitutional self-government, and began harassing and oppressing its people. He has also rejected brave calls among his own Serb people for greater liberty. Today, he uses repression and censorship at home to stifle dissent and to conceal what he is doing in Kosovo.
>
> Though his ethnic cleansing is not the same as the ethnic extermination of the Holocaust, the two are related—both vicious, premeditated, systematic oppression fueled by religious and ethnic hatred.[26]

But even when presidents can distinguish their rhetoric from a more complex reality, they still run the risk of getting caught up in their own words. That risk can result in serious oversimplification of the problem and unwarranted assumptions about motives and behavior of the adversary, both of which may lead to a overly demonstrative response that becomes in effect a self-fulfilling prophecy. In other words, presidents can box themselves in by adopting a Satan-oriented mentality *even when they are aware of the danger of doing so.* George Bush admits that he may have put himself in such a position in the months following Iraq's invasion of Kuwait: "I became very emotional about the atrocities. . . . I know there was a danger I might overreact. . . . Yet at some point it came through to me that this was not a matter of shades of gray . . . it was good versus evil, right versus wrong. . . . This was how I worked it out in my mind, which made the choice before me clearer."[27]

Bush had reacted in a similar way to Panamanian dictator Manuel Noriega's drug trafficking and to the anti-American incidents that his forces perpetrated, the killing of an American marine, the beating of a navy lieutenant, and threats of sexual abuse to his wife.[28]

But even if a president does not take his enemy designation to be literal truth, the public may do so, thereby creating much the same danger for the president. By targeting the bad guy in the public arena as the principal cause of the problem, presidents often place themselves in a zero-sum game with that bad guy, a game they must win decisively or lose support and credibility. Moreover, they have also eliminated or at least reduced the political feasibility of backing off and doing nothing, which might have been possible under other characterizations of the problem and its causes. Bush had to act firmly with Noriega and Hussein after he had demonized them. Similarly, Clinton had to do something demonstrative against Milosevic once he and others in his administration had described the Serbian leader in dictatorial terms and held him responsible for Serbian atrocities in Kosovo. George W. Bush has placed himself in a similar predicament with his strident anti–Saddam Hussein rhetoric.

Attributing all that is undesirable to a bad guy makes it much more difficult to seek a diplomatic solution. Almost by definition, bad guys cannot be trusted. Once their motives have been imputed and their behavior attributed to personal ambition, self-aggrandizement, and/or unlimited territorial goals, then bargaining and negotiation become a naive and pointless exercise, a hunt for fool's gold. The analogy of British Prime Minister Neville Chamberlain at Munich is ritualistically trumpeted by opponents of temporizing with the enemy.

Moreover, if the demonizing is extensive and successful, it can bind one's successors and/or increase the costs of rehabilitation. Not only was it much more difficult for George Bush to find a peaceful solution to the Gulf crisis once he repeatedly lashed out at Saddam Hussein, but Bill Clinton was also constrained in his policy toward Iraq by the general acceptance of Bush's depiction. When Iraq refused to permit United Nations weapons inspectors to conduct unannounced searches for biological and chemical weapons, Clinton acted as if the experience of his predecessor compelled him to respond in a similarly forceful manner although he may very well have manipulated himself into that position precisely because he wanted to respond in that way. It is difficult to know whether demonization is perceived as a proximate cause or a rationalization for actions that in and of themselves may have made strategic sense, pursued a national interest, or achieved a political objective.

For many years, the demonizing of Cuban leader Fidel Castro also constricted the options of American presidents. As years passed and the situation changed, as the Soviets withdrew and Cuba's economy worsened, Castro's persona, which had been presented in a highly negative way by both Republican and Democratic presidents, could have softened and faded were it not for the memory and political clout of the Cuban refugee community in southern Florida that has exploited the incidents and events that reinforced Castro's malevolent, dictatorial image.

Ronald Reagan's characterization of the Soviet leaders as immoral and the Soviet Union as an "evil empire" in his first term helped justify his administration's strong anti-Soviet posture, its defense buildup, and the president's Strategic Defense Initiative. But Reagan in his second term, with his unimpeachable anti-Soviet credentials, confident that he had successfully upped the ante with the enemy by using his strong rhetoric and defense muscle as bargaining chips, changed his tune, not his goals, and in the end was able to use both carrots and sticks to hasten the end of the cold war. Nixon's initiative with China and his détente policy with the Soviets are also examples that a president, having established himself clearly as a foe of communism, could then deal with the enemy without engendering the charge of "selling out." Although these instances demonstrate that it is possible to reverse policy with a country whose leader or officialdom has been demonized, they are also exceptions to the proposition that demonizing makes changing policy more difficult.

Take Nelson Mandela and Yasir Arafat, for example. As the head of insurrectionist movements against established authority, both were initially portrayed as terrorists by U.S. officials whose policy supported the legitimacy of the white South African government and the state of Israel. As each of these governments began to moderate its position and accommodate the claims of its nativist opponents, the negative images of these leaders had to be transformed into more positive profiles to justify a change in U.S. policy.

Exit strategies are also made more difficult by personalizing the problem and demonizing the opponent. George Bush found this out the hard way when he ordered an end to the fighting in the Gulf War. Even though the administration had carefully defined its goal as the removal of Iraqi forces from Kuwait, even though there were good humanitarian and public relations reasons for not killing defenseless Iraqi troops who were struggling to return home, even though there was reason to fear extensive American casualties if coalition forces continued to Baghdad, Bush's decision to end the war without successfully removing Saddam Hussein from power hurt the president politically, particularly after Hussein's forces put down internal rebellions in the northern and southern parts of the country that Bush's rhetoric had encouraged and his administration (specifically, the Central Intelligence Agency) had actively aided. In reflecting on his decision to end the fighting with Saddam still in control, Bush noted:

> I worried he would emerge from the war weakened but as a "hero" still in charge. We discussed again whether to go after him. None of us minded if he was killed in the course of an air attack. Yet it was extremely difficult to target Saddam, who was known to move frequently and under tight security. The best we could do was strike command and control points where he may have been.[29]

Bill Clinton faced much the same problem in Kosovo, which may be why Milosevic's residences were high on the list of approved NATO targets during the air strikes.[30] It is also why the president, compelled by his rhetoric, his beliefs, and his need to maintain a consistent policy, stood firm against providing a Milosevic-led Serbia with economic aid (except for heating oil and other petroleum products) after the fighting ended until the Serbian leader agreed to hold free and fair elections.

It was not only from Bush's experience in the Gulf that Clinton learned about the dangers of permitting the bad guy to remain in power after the fighting had ended. In the aftermath of the terrorist bombings of two U.S. embassies in Kenya and Tanzania in 1998, the president found himself in much the same predicament. Clinton had gone out of his way to blame those attacks on Osama bin Laden and the organization he bankrolled. Thus, when the president responded to the anti-American terrorism with bombings of his own, he was trying to kill two birds with one stone by targeting the organization's Afghanistan base at a time when U.S. intelligence sources believed bin Laden would be there. The success of the U.S. retaliation was muted by the failure to hit bin Laden, who remained at large (as well as by the bombing of a Sudanese pharmaceutical factory that the United States claimed had produced ingredients for chemical weapons, a claim that could not be substantiated).

These lessons were not lost on George W. Bush. After castigating Osama bin Laden as the incarnation of evil, the worst of the worst terrorists, he reminded himself and the American people that the war on terrorism was bigger and more important than the capture of any one terrorist. "[S]uccess or failure depends not on bin Laden; success or failure depends upon routing out terrorism where it may exist all around the world. He's just one person, a part of a network. And we're slowly, but surely, with determined fashion, routing that network out and bringing it to justice."[31]

However, he also seemed to paint himself purposely into a corner by his strident criticism of Saddam Hussein's government in Iraq in his State of the Union address of January 29, 2002:

> Iraq continues to flaunt its hostility toward America and to support terror. The Iraqi regime has plotted to develop anthrax, a nerve gas, and nuclear weapons for over a decade. This is a regime that has already used poison gas to murder thousands of its own citizens—leaving the bodies of mothers huddled over their dead children. This is a regime that agreed to international inspections—then kicked out the inspectors. This is a regime that has something to hide from the civilized world.[32]

There is another problem to which demonizing foreign despots contributes. The implicit threat accompanying such demonizing can unite the publics of the enemy behind their leaders, undercutting domestic opposition to them. It can also precipitate bad-guy rhetoric and thinking by the "demon," thereby locking both sides into a confrontation from which they may find it more difficult to escape. Besides, if a multitude of factors were responsible for the undesirable situation, then the elimination of the bad guy naturally, peacefully, or forcefully would not solve the problem. The unstable economic conditions, unequal resource distribution, large-scale corruption, pervasive crime, perceptions of external threats, and/or national humiliation suffered by military defeat, which may have produced the environment in which a bad guy gained power, may still persist. In fact, removal of the bad guy could do more harm than good if a new bad or worse guy emerged or, alternatively, a vacuum was created in which others ruthlessly competed for power. The argument "The devil we know is better than the one we do not" is a difficult sell after extensive demonization has occurred.

Furthermore, the removal of the bad guy may actually worsen the situation if it produces civil strife that results in economic destabilization or social upheaval. Add to that the reaction of one's own public that has just witnessed the expenditure of considerable time, money, and effort to remove the despot. Assuming that the problem is over, the public may tire of the situation or simply not want to devote more resources to it. Each of these circumstances potentially constrains presidential policy more than dealing with a complex set of international problems with a variety of political, economic, and noninterventionist military options would.

DOMESTIC CRITICS AS ENEMIES

Unlike their foreign counterparts, domestic adversaries are foes of a different kind although they tend to serve similar purposes. They are not usually described as evil but merely as wrong-headed, single-minded, and self-serving people who would stop or roll back progress.[33] Adjectives such as *ruthless, extreme,* and *driven* are frequently employed to convey their no-holds-barred approach to politics, their unyielding policy positions that brook little or no dissent, and their emotionally laden rhetoric that impedes rational discourse and eventual compromise.

Harsh domestic critics may be stereotyped as partisan and ideological extremists, overly zealous, righteous, and intense, even renegades who oppose for the sake of opposing. They may be presented as political fundamentalists, a depiction that is intended to be upsetting, even scary, to many people and serves as a magnet for unifying and activating partisan opponents.

The portrayal of Franklin Roosevelt during the 1930s by conservative

Republicans; the presentation of Senate Joseph McCarthy in the 1950s by those opposed to his "red-baiting" tactics; the not-so-subtle depiction of what might happen if Barry Goldwater were elected in 1964 in that infamous "Daisy Girl" advertisement; Carter's description of Ronald Reagan's opposition to popular social programs in their 1980 debate (which precipitated the latter's famous "There you go again" response); to a lesser extent, Bush's stereotyping of Michael Dukakis in 1988; and the Clinton administration's criticism of Newt Gingrich, Kenneth Starr, and the House impeachment managers are examples of domestic demonizing. Most partisan opponents, however, are presented in less vitriolic and extreme language than are foreign policy adversaries.

Despite the harsh rhetoric, it is difficult to make the case to the public that hostile domestic opponents are as bad as foreign despots, nor do the domestic foes seem to constrain presidential judgment and decision making as much as do the enemies abroad. So long as the conflict remains within the accepted bounds of political competition, domestic adversaries, even when they are demonized (e.g., the Dole–Gingrich monster), are not usually considered permanent enemies. They can't be. There will always be other issues to consider, other battles to fight, and other support that will be needed. Shifting alliances are part and parcel of American politics today. Because candidate–driven elections, constituency-based representation, and special interest groups have undercut the influence of parties as unifying forces across policy areas, coalitions have to be built and rebuilt along issue lines.

Moreover, Americans have become increasingly dissatisfied by the negativism that pervades contemporary politics, particularly electoral politics. The emphasis on bad news by the press, the negative stereotyping by and of the candidates, and the large amount of negative advertising by the candidate organizations and special interest groups are regularly cited as sources of public cynicism and apathy.[34]

The preference for dispensing carrots rather than wielding sticks within the American political system also limits and mutes the designation of domestic adversaries and the permanency of that designation. Although friends and enemies are more interchangeable in domestic politics than in the international arena, the increasingly public context in which contemporary policymaking occurs has had the effect of hardening positions, reducing options, and making negotiation more difficult.

Two principal judgmental dangers result from domestic demonizing. One relates to judgments that are politics driven; the other to those that become personal vendettas.

When partisan and/or ideological politics becomes the dominant issue, other judgmental factors may be suspended. Not only does the scope of the decision narrow, but the time frame shortens; the future becomes the present, with the next election the finish line. The anticipated political fallout of the decision becomes a principal criterion for making a judgment as well as for evaluating the merits of the decision down the road. Politics begets politics. A decision that seems on its surface to be motivated by political factors is likely to engender a similar type of political response by one's partisan opponents.

Clinton's initial reaction to the allegations that he had a sexual relationship with a White House intern is a case in point. Fearful that public knowledge of the affair would have jeopardized his reelection, the president choose to be coy about his behavior. He denied that he had engaged in a sexual relationship with Monica Lewinsky while the White House leaked stories to impeach the impartiality and credibility of the independent counsel who was investigating the allegations. The president's deceit prolonged the issue and ultimately encouraged leaks by the independent counsel's office and a political reaction by the Republicans, culminating in Clinton's impeachment by the House of Representatives.

It is easy for elected officials to fall into the conceptual blinders that frame policy decisions as essentially political judgments. For one thing, the mind-set of a politician is naturally attuned to thinking about social issues within a political context in which the winners and losers align along a partisan spectrum. Additionally, many politicians have personalities that thrive on playing the game of politics.[35] In Washington, in fact, politics is described as the only game in town with the result that political perceptions and behavior are reinforced.

Politics can affect personal relationships as well. One of the by-products of the ideological and partisan cleavages in the 1970s was a loss of civility and trust within government among elected officials and a growing public cynicism outside it about the rhetoric, motives, and judgments of those officials who make policy decisions.[36] The perception that self-interests and special interests dominate national public policymaking has contributed to the public apathy and disillusionment with government and those who serve within it, and it became a major issue trumpeted by Senator John McCain in his campaign for the 2000 Republican presidential nomination and his successful push for campaign finance legislation.

When a political adversarial relationship also turns into a personal confrontation, such as the impeachment issue did between Clinton and Starr and Clinton and some of his Republican detractors, the judgmental trap for both sides intensifies and becomes even harder to surmount. Political and personal goals interact to strengthen emotions, which may not easily dissipate, even when the issue that precipitated the conflict has lessened or passed. Mutual mistrust between Clinton and his Republican opponents extended well beyond the impeachment calendar and initially affected even their willingness to sit down together to discuss public policy issues in the spring of 1999, much less find a basis for reaching compromises on them. Little substantive legislation was enacted during the session of Congress in which the president was impeached and acquitted.

George W. Bush made much of this dysfunctional rhetoric and behavior in his 2000 presidential campaign, promising to return civility to political discourse and bipartisanship to government. To make good on his promises, he avoided demonizing Clinton over the way he left office and members of Congress who opposed his issue positions. He was particularly careful to avoid hostile language in public statements concerning the U.S. reconnaissance aircraft that collided with a Chinese fighter and was forced to land in the People's Republic of China.

Personal vendettas convert policy matters into ego battles. The public interest takes a back seat to personal, competitive needs. Even the rules of institutional procedures and processes cannot contain the emotions that pervade and often overwhelm personal judgment. Policymaking becomes public relations in a fight to the finish.

CONCLUSION

Politics is a struggle among people and groups for competing and sometimes contradictory interests and goals. It is fought primarily among governing elites but within an increasingly public arena. That arena encourages insiders to look outside for support. Here is where the bad guys come in. Presidents use them to justify their judgments and enhance their own perceived leadership skills. Bad guys become a rationale for action and a rallying point around which to sustain that action. But they also raise the political stakes by virtue of the attention they receive, the imperative they present, and the successful confrontation that is required to eliminate, reduce, or contain their malevolent effects. Using their bully pulpit, presidents are in the best and perhaps only position within the American political system to take them on and get credit for doing so.

The problem with bad guys is that they can and do affect judgments. In essence, they constrain vision, simplify (and perhaps change) problems by personalizing them, limit viable options, infuse emotion into decision making, and require more decisive and demonstrative actions that involve a tangible response than might otherwise be advisable. They can even affect the termination of the problem and the claims and perceptions of victory. Although presidents may be conscious of these judgmental dangers, and most of them or their advisers seem to be, they can still be trapped by them, by their own rhetoric and mind-set, by their personification of the problem and implicitly the solution, and by the increasingly public arena in which such decision making occurs. For these reasons, presidents should think twice before pursuing a bad-guy "PR" strategy.

Here are some recommendations for making good judgments and avoiding the temptations of demonizing:

- Think clearly not only about what to do but how best to explain it. Realize that the explanation itself can become part of the problem even as it attempts to build support for the current policy.
- Be careful of oversimplification. Presenting a situation in black and white terms may help engage an inattentive public and generate a quick, emotive response, but over time, as other factors become evident, the emotion may fade, the explanation may look increasingly shallow, but the policy options may still be constrained by it.
- Maximize flexibility. Political leaders need to pursue realistic opportunities if they are to be successful. They may also need to take unpopular positions and let the electoral chips fall where they may. They should remember that it is conditions, not rhetoric, and results, not rationalizations or promises, that usually have the greater impact on incumbent reelectability at the presidential level.

The paradox of democratic leadership today is how to lead without appearing to follow, how to gain support without seeming to manipulate public opinion, how to make good judgments within a partisan political environment, often in full public view, and how to factor in long-term considerations into the here and now. This task is not easy, especially for those for whom political success and public adulation are pursued to satisfy deeply imbedded psychological needs.

The leadership dilemma is compounded by the nature of the constitutional system in which power is divided but decisional responsibility is shared. It is also heightened by a political system that reflects and represents diversity more easily than it builds and maintains an issue consensus. These institutional and political variables contribute to the temptation to make a hard sell easier by demonizing and spinning rather than informing, educating, and persuading. To the extent that these public responses mirror or constrict contemporary policy judgments and/or constrain or complicate future ones, they are potentially dangerous and may be dysfunctional.

NOTES

I wish to thank my Georgetown colleagues, Andrew Bennett and Yossi Shain, and the editors of this book, Deborah Welch Larson and Stanley A. Renshon, for their helpful criticism and suggestions for improving this chapter.

1. Bob Woodward, *The Commanders* (New York: Simon & Schuster, 1991), 344.

2. George W. Bush, news conference, October 11, 2001, www.whitehouse.gov/news/releases/2001/10/2001/1011-7.html.

3. George W. Bush, "The Global War on Terrorism: The First 100 Days," October 2001, www.whitehouse.gov/news/releases/2001/12/100dayreport.html.

4. Bush, news conference.

5. Alexander L. George and Juliette L. George, *Woodrow Wilson and Colonel House: A Personality Study* (New York: Dover, 1964), 118–21.

6. Richard E. Neustadt, *Presidential Power and the Modern Presidents* (New York: Free Press, 1990), 29.

7. Edmund Morris, *Dutch* (New York: Random House, 1999), 473.

8. Providing this money violated the law, revealed the administration's arms-for-hostages deal with Iran, and illustrated the dangers of the president's laissez-faire management style.

9. On the other hand, the president muted his criticism of those individuals and groups, primarily Democrats, who opposed normalizing trade relations with China in 2000. Clinton needed their support for other issues on his legislative agenda.

10. Bush, news conference.

11. Bush, news conference.

12. Different rhetoric must be used in describing domestic foes in part because they are U.S. citizens, may hold elective positions, usually have a cadre of loyal supporters, and may be future allies in subsequent political battles.

13. A Gallup poll conducted in June 1965 reported 20 percent wanted to continue the military action, 21 percent wanted to increase it, 26 percent wanted to end it, and 28 percent had no opinion. George H. Gallup, *The Gallup Poll: Public Opinion 1935–1971*, vol. 3 (New York: Random House, 1972), 193.

14. The domino theory held that the spread of communism in Southeast Asia could generate a chain reaction among countries similar to falling dominoes. If one fell, others would follow.

15. According to a national poll, conducted after the NATO bombing by the Pew Research Center for the People and the Press, interest in the Kosovo crisis, even at its height, did not rival that of the Persian Gulf War. Whereas two-thirds of the public paid very close attention to the Gulf War, interest in the Serbian conflict did not exceed 47 percent. The Pew Research Center for the People and the Press, "Muted and Mixed Public Response to Peace in Kosovo," www.people-press.org./nato99rpt.htm.

16. During the cold war, all dictators were not evil from the perspective of U.S. foreign policy. Anticommunist dictators such as Ferdinand Marcos, Augusto Pinochet, and Mohammed Reza Pahlavi (the shah of Iran) were deemed friends and allies, whereas communist rulers such as Kim Il Sung, Erich Honecker, Ho Chi Min, and, initially, Mao Zedong were not. Since the end of the cold war, however, human rights and democratic principles have become more important criteria for evaluating the merits of foreign leaders, particularly those in smaller countries over which the United States might be able to exercise some control. As a consequence, those authoritarian leaders who outlived their usefulness such as Manuel Noriega and General Suharto were recast as bad guys, but the leaders of the so-

called moderate Arab countries of Egypt, Jordan, and Saudi Arabia were not. Neither was General Pervez Musharraf of Pakistan after he supported U.S. efforts in Afghanistan.

17. Woodward, *The Commanders,* 212.

18. George Bush and Brent Scowcroft, *A World Transformed* (New York: Vintage, 1998), 370–71.

19. Bush and Scowcroft, *A World Transformed,* 371.

20. Bush and Scowcroft, *A World Transformed,* 375.

21. Bush and Scowcroft, *A World Transformed,* 375.

22. Jimmy Carter, *Keeping Faith* (New York: Bantam, 1982), 440.

23. Carter, *Keeping Faith,* 459.

24. Carter, *Keeping Faith,* 499.

25. Bush and Scowcroft, *A World Transformed,* 375.

26. William Jefferson Clinton, "Remarks to Veteran Groups on Kosovo," May 13, 1999, www.whitehouse.gov/uri-res/12R...:pdi://oma.eop.gov.us/1999/5/19/13.text.

27. Bush and Scowcroft, *A World Transformed,* 374–75.

28. Woodward. *The Commanders,* 171.

29. Bush and Scowcroft, *A World Transformed,* 463.

30. A presidential directive currently prohibits a policy of assassinating foreign leaders, although the directive is not applicable in time of war.

31. Bush, news conference.

32. George W. Bush, "State of the Union Address," January 29, 2002, www.white house.gov/news/release/2002/01/2002/0129-11.htm.

33. Actually, Republican candidate John McCain did refer to Protestant fundamentalist ministers Jerry Falwell and Pat Robertson as "agents of intolerance" and "forces of evil," terms that he later conceded were ill advised and improper.

34. See Thomas E. Patterson, *Out of Order* (New York: Knopf, 1993); Stephen Ansola-behere and Shanto Iyengar, *Going Negative* (New York: Free Press, 1995).

35. Stanley A. Renshon, *The Psychological Assessment of Presidential Candidates* (New York: Routledge, 1998), 25–48, 205–30.

36. A good source for data on public attitudes toward government and public officials is the national surveys conducted by the Pew Research Center for the People and the Press. See its November 1999 publication, *Retropolitics,* 139, for data on trends from the mid-1980s through the 1990s. See also the Gallup Poll (www.gallup.com).

Part III

JUDGMENTS AND MISJUDGMENTS IN FOREIGN POLICY DECISIONS

· 5 ·

Truman and the Berlin Blockade

The Role of Intuition and Experience in Good Foreign Policy Judgment

Deborah Welch Larson

*C*onventional wisdom holds that decision makers will follow a rational, considered, deliberative process when the stakes are high. But presidents sometimes make highly consequential decisions for war and peace with very little consideration of alternatives, and they do so, moreover, to good effect.

President Harry S. Truman's decision making in the 1948 Berlin crisis is such a case. In June 1948, the Soviet Union restricted ground access to West Berlin. The stakes were very high. Paul Nitze recalls that the Berlin crisis of 1948 came closer to "drawing us into conflict with the Soviet Union than the later Cuban missile crisis."[1] A withdrawal from West Berlin might have cost the United States the support of West Germans and endangered the success of the Marshall Plan. Incidents on the ground might have inadvertently escalated into armed conflict between the United States and the Soviet Union. The Soviets could have kept up the traffic restrictions indefinitely, forcing the United States to spend millions of dollars to keep Berlin supplied, an effort that sucked up available military air transport. The Soviets could have rendered the airlift ineffective by jamming U.S. radio communications, forcing the United States to withdraw in humiliation.

Truman's decision to "stay in Berlin come what may" is an exemplar of good intuitive political judgment. He had received very little information about the situation on the ground and only a sketchy analysis of a few broad options, each of which had substantial disadvantages. His advisers were divided and could not reach a recommendation. Truman had little choice in this situation but to rely on his intuition and experience.

Truman was attuned to the fears of the American people and avoided any actions that risked war with the Soviet Union. To maintain a united front in negotiating with the Soviet Union, he subordinated his own reelection concerns to maintaining bipartisan support for his course in Berlin. He made a swift decision to stay in Berlin but retained other options if the airlift proved to be ineffective. Truman patiently waited for a diplomatic breakthrough, although the expense, risks, and uncertainty of the airlift caused his military advisers to exert pressure for a decision to break the blockade by force or disengage the United States from a dangerous situation. Truman intuitively knew when to act and when to wait. He successfully balanced foreign policy with domestic political concerns and chose a policy that achieved U.S. objectives while maintaining public support.

THE BREAKDOWN OF ALLIED
COOPERATION IN GERMANY

The Soviets' blockade of West Berlin from 1948 to 1949 exploited the anomalies of the postwar occupation set up in Germany, aiming to coerce the West into accepting their position on Germany. The 1945 Potsdam Agreement had divided Germany into four zones occupied by the United States, Britain, France, and the Soviet Union pending a peace conference and establishment of a unified German government. The Allied occupying powers, though, could not agree on the regime for a postwar government or on reparations for the Soviet Union. The November–December 1947 London foreign ministers conference merely reaffirmed the disagreements between the Soviet Union and its Western allies. Secretary of State George C. Marshall adjourned the London Conference without setting a date for another session.[2]

After the United States decided that Germany would be divided, the Western military presence in West Berlin became an exposed salient. Located 110 miles inside Soviet-occupied East Germany, West Berlin was strategically vulnerable and indefensible. The United States had a written commitment from the Soviets for one air corridor and a verbal agreement for one road and two railway lines. The United States did not need to maintain an authority in West Berlin to administer the Western occupation zones. Officials in France, Britain, and the United States assumed that the Western powers would eventually withdraw from Berlin after a West German government was set up and the country was no longer governed by four powers.[3]

The Soviet military governor, Marshal Vassily Danilovitch Sokolovsky, gave lengthy speeches charging that the United States and the United Kingdom intended to transform their zones into a separate German government, that they were abandoning quadripartite rule of Berlin, and that they intended to use their presence in Berlin to interfere with the Soviet occupation zone.[4] In January, Soviet military began to harass Western rail traffic into Berlin by attempting to board and inspect trains. The U.S. military governor, General Lucius D. Clay, stationed armed guards with instructions to block any Soviet soldiers from entering the trains.[5]

Despite these harassments, representatives from Britain, France, and the United States, joined a week later by ones from Belgium, Netherlands, and Luxembourg, met in London in late February 1948 to discuss political and economic reorganization of the Western occupation zones. They instructed their military governors to call an assembly of the ministers president of the German Lander to draw up a constitution for West Germany. After adjourning the conference on March 6, the Western countries issued a communiqué stating that they had decided to coordinate the economic policies of their zones and to establish a federal government for West Germany.[6]

At the March 20 Allied Control Council meeting, Marshal Sokolovsky demanded information about the London Conference decisions. The Western military governors replied that his request was reasonable, but they could not give him the information he requested until they had heard from their governments. Reading a prepared statement, Sokolovsky charged that the London Conference was considering questions that ought to be decided by the Control Council. Since the other delegates had broken away from the Control Council machinery on Germany, it no longer existed. Sokolovsky adjourned the meeting, and the Soviet delegation abruptly walked out.[7]

On March 31, the Soviets imposed new requirements for inspection and permission for Western rail traffic through the Soviet zone to Berlin that would have interfered with Western supply of its garrison and the two million German civilians in West Berlin. Clay proposed to Washington that he give the train commandant a list of passengers and a manifest for freight shipments but "instruct our guards to open fire if Soviet soldiers attempt to enter our trains."[8] Army Chief of Staff Omar Bradley recalled that if he had enough hair on his head to react, "this cable would probably have stood it on end." Bradley said that he could sympathize with Clay's "instinctive gut reaction" but that this was neither the time nor the place to open fire on the Soviets.[9]

Military officials in Washington, aware of the weakness and lack of preparedness of U.S. military forces, were far more risk-averse than Clay. In Washington, high-level state, defense, and military officials discussed a reply to the Soviet restrictions. Since Clay's request might result in armed conflict with the Soviets, Truman was also consulted.[10] On his own, Truman decided not to call on congressional leaders because it would leak and contribute to "war hysteria."[11] In a teleconference later that evening, Bradley instructed Clay to take no action that was different from what had been the practice and that "our guards not fire unless fired upon."[12]

When Clay tried to send a few trains through Soviet lines as a test case, the Soviets shunted them off the main track to a siding, where they remained until dawn before ignominiously retreating.[13] With the military supply trains stopped, Clay began a small airlift on April 2 to supply the U.S. garrison in West Berlin.

In an April 10 teleconference with Clay, Bradley predicted that Soviets would continue to add restrictions one by one until the U.S. position in Berlin was untenable, unless the United States was prepared to initiate war to remove the restrictions. "Here we doubt whether our people are prepared to start a war in order to maintain our position in Berlin and Vienna." Bradley suggested that the United States announce its own withdrawal to "minimize loss of prestige," rather than be forced out by threats.[14]

Clay replied that the United States should not leave West Berlin short of a Soviet ultimatum to drive the Americans out by force. Departure from Berlin would result in "a tremendous loss of prestige."[15] Washington did not have to make this decision, because the Soviets withdrew the new regulations on April 12, ending the "baby blockade."[16]

INCREASING SOVIET RESTRICTIONS AND PRESSURES FOR U.S. WITHDRAWAL

The United States reconvened the London Conference with France, Britain, and the Benelux countries from April 20 until June 2 for more detailed discussions on establishing a West German government. After notifying the Soviets, the Western countries issued a communiqué on June 7 that sketched out the procedures to establish a West German government, including convening a constitutional assembly to draw up a constitution.[17]

Soviet military personnel began to hold up freight trains bound for Berlin on various pretexts; sometimes railroad cars disappeared from the trains. On June 10, Soviet representatives tried to hijack switching locomotives and railroad cars in West Berlin until Clay stationed armed guards on the trains. On June 18, Soviet armed guards began to stop freight trains bound for West Berlin on the pretext that the cars were "out of order."[18]

Clay then initiated a much-needed currency reform to curb inflation and encourage West German production. On June 18, he sent a letter to Sokolovsky informing him that the Western countries were issuing a new currency for their zones in Germany, excluding West Berlin.[19] Clay treated Berlin differently because it would not be practical to have two different currencies circulating in the city.

The Soviets immediately responded to the currency reform by closing passenger traffic to Berlin on both the autobahn and the railways; freight was allowed to proceed with delays for inspections. On June 19, Sokolovsky addressed a letter to the German population of Berlin announcing that banknotes issued in the Western occupation zones of Germany would not be accepted in the Soviet zone of Germany or "in Berlin, which is part of the Soviet occupation zone." Clay replied publicly that Berlin was an international city.[20] In his June 20 reply to Clay, Sokolovsky charged that the currency reform was illegal and completed the division of Germany. He warned that Soviet occupation authorities would have to protect the economy of the Soviet occupation zone.[21]

On June 22, Soviet authorities ordered their own currency reform for the Soviet occupation zone, including Berlin.[22] Soviet authorities shut down their power plant, which supplied electricity to the Western sectors. The following day, Clay informed Sokolovsky that he would join with his colleagues in placing the new Western banknotes into circulation in West Berlin. The three Western powers introduced their banknotes, stamped "B," into their sectors of Berlin on June 24. As Clay later explained to Secretary of the Army Kenneth Royall, to have accepted the Soviet mark under Soviet control "would have placed Berlin financially completely in Soviet hands."[23] The army had instructed Clay in April that he should not accept a new Soviet mark as legal tender in Berlin: "currency issuance is a sovereign power."[24]

The Soviets then shut off West Berlin's last link to the Western zones of Germany by barring trains carrying food and supplies to the population of Berlin. At the U.S. Army Headquarters in Heidelberg, General Clay declared publicly that the Soviets "can't drive us out by any actions short of war." The *New York Times* story observed, though, that the United States might have to withdraw from Berlin for humanitarian reasons if the suffering of the German population became too great.[25]

Indeed, Washington military officials had not authorized and did not approve Clay's statement. Some officials wondered whether Clay's position was sound and, even if sound, whether he should make such a statement.[26] A June 18 staff study prepared by the army's Plans and Operations Division (P& O) observed, "Soviet intentions and determination to force our withdrawal by means and methods short of war are reasonably within their capability." If the Soviet government decided to force Western withdrawal at the risk of war, any counteraction by the West would precipitate war. "The psychological advantage to the U.S. of remaining in Berlin is not worth doing so *at all costs*." Since it would be impossible to supply the two million German civilians in West Berlin by air if the Soviets restricted ground access, the United States might have to withdraw for "purely humanitarian reasons."[27] A June 26 Army P&O staff study suggested that the United States negotiate a withdrawal from Berlin in exchange for Soviet occupied territory. The Soviets had the physical capacity to make the Western position in Berlin untenable through the effects of their actions on the German population. If "the sufferings imposed on the German people by Soviet action" became severe, the United States should consider whether "humanitarian grounds" overrode "the major political and prestige reverse involved in withdrawal in the face of Soviet pressure."[28]

Clay proposed to march trucks of supplies guarded by U.S. soldiers down the autobahn to establish U.S. rights of access. "I am still convinced that a determined movement of convoys with troop protection would reach Berlin and that such a showing might well prevent rather than build up Soviet pressures which could lead to war."[29]

"I would not want any action taken in Berlin which might lead to possible armed conflict," Royall cautioned Clay in a teleconference the same day. Clay reassured the army secretary that "I do not expect armed conflict." On the other hand, "we cannot be run over and a firm position always induces some risk." Royall felt "strongly" that the limited issue of Berlin's currency was "not a good question" on which to go to war. Clay assured him that "[i]f Soviets go to war, it will not be because of Berlin currency issue but only because they believe this the right time."[30]

At a June 25 cabinet meeting, Royall outlined the difficulties facing the Berliners. Since Thomas Dewey had received the Republican Party nomination for president yesterday, however, much time was spent discussing domestic politics. Truman noted with satisfaction the coolness of the reception given to Dewey at the convention.[31]

Secretary of Defense James Forrestal, Royall, and Undersecretary of State Robert Lovett stayed behind for a meeting with Truman on Berlin. They agreed that General Clay should be advised not to make any more statements referring to war. Royall emphasized that if war were inevitable, it should not take place over separate currencies in Berlin.[32]

The British military governor, General Brian Robertson, persuaded Clay to try an airlift of food and supplies to the Berlin population. The British government had already authorized such an operation. Without consulting Washington, by scraping together every available C-47, Clay began an airlift of food and coal to the beleaguered German residents of Berlin.[33] On June 26, food was delivered to the West Berliners. Initially Clay intended to use the airlift mainly to supply the Western garrisons and boost the morale of West Berlin's German population, rather than trying to meet their requirements for food and coal. The first airlift was only supposed to ship about two hundred tons, a minuscule amount given estimates that the daily food supply required for Berlin's German population was about two thousand tons. The airlift was a temporary measure to buy time; no one believed that a city of two million inhabitants could be fed and supplied by air.[34] *New York Times* correspondent Drew Middleton reported that the airlift food shipments were not intended to meet any immediate need but to augment existing stocks so that the Germans could maintain a balanced diet. The official view was that the people of West Berlin could be fed for thirty days "on the existing stocks plus the goods flown in by air."[35]

Against the recommendations of his closet advisers, on June 26 Truman directed that Clay's improvised airlift be organized on a full-scale basis and that it be augmented with every plane in the European Command.[36] Both Truman and Clay had to decide what to do in Berlin without the benefit of an agreed staff recommendation. If Truman and Clay had waited for more detailed analyses or a consensus to emerge before launching the airlift, their options would have been severely narrowed, and there would have been no U.S. position in Berlin left to defend.[37]

"WE STAY IN BERLIN. PERIOD."

An emergency meeting was held on Sunday, June 27, at Secretary Royall's office in the Pentagon. Attending the Pentagon meeting were Royall, Forrestal, Lovett, Secretary of the Navy John Sullivan, Bradley, Assistant Chief of Air Staff Lauris Norstad, and other state and defense officials. Available estimates suggested that food supplies for the Germans would last for at least thirty and perhaps as long as sixty days, if dried food was used.[38]

The officials considered three broad options: (1) withdraw from Berlin at an appropriate time, presumably when the constituent assembly for West Germany met on September 1; (2) defend the U.S. position in Berlin by all possible means, including supplying Berlin by armed convoy or using force if all other diplomatic means had failed, but accepting the possibility of war if necessary; or (3) maintain an unprovocative but firm stand in Berlin by local means and later diplomatic means while postponing the ultimate decision.[39]

Each alternative had substantial disadvantages. Withdrawal from Berlin might endanger the U.S. position in Europe and promote the spread of communism. On the other hand, remaining in Berlin would subject the United States to the stress of consistently recurring crises and frequent humiliation. Efforts to supply the city by force risked provoking a war with the Soviet Union.

Army Chief of Staff Bradley argued that an armed convoy should be used only as a last resort and only if the United States was prepared for war. If there were an exchange of gunfire between U.S. and Soviet soldiers, whoever lost the first round would escalate. Sooner or later there would be "all-out war" between the United States and the Soviet Union.[40]

There was no consensus around any alternative. Unable to agree on a rec-ommendation, the officials decided that Forrestal, Lovett, and Royall should present the options to Truman the next day to see what he wanted to do.[41] The officials also recommended that the British be consulted about their will-ingness to accept two groups of B-29s, a nuclear-capable bomber.[42]

In a June 28 meeting with Truman, also attended by Forrestal and Royall, Lovett summarized the previous day's meeting, including advantages and dis-advantages of the three options. First, the United States could make an imme-diate decision to withdraw from West Berlin at an appropriate time, presumably when a constituent assembly for a West German government was called on September 1. If they were not prepared to use force in Berlin, the United States would have to withdraw anyway. The humiliation of remaining in Berlin under existing conditions was worse than getting out. Even if the current crisis passed, there would be recurring frictions over the U.S. position in Berlin. On the other hand, if the U.S. voluntarily withdrew from Berlin, "we would never be able to find out whether withdrawal was in fact really necessary." Withdrawal might cause Western Europeans to lose confidence in the United States in light of repeated bold statements of the U.S. intent to remain in Berlin. West German leaders' fear of Soviet retaliation might make it impossible to establish an effective government. The loss of German confi-dence would have highly detrimental effects on the European Recovery Pro-gram.

Second, the United States could decide to retain its position in Berlin by all possible means, including supplying Berlin by convoy or using force in some other manner as a last resort after having exhausted all diplomatic means to stay in Berlin, but accepting the possibility of war if necessary. Military leaders would discuss the currency situation with the Soviets, and the United States would utilize all diplomatic means to make a case for the necessity of military action. The Soviets might back down if force were used, as in an armed con-voy. If war were inevitable, this was as good an issue as any. Use of force in Berlin would avoid the loss of prestige accompanying withdrawal. On the other hand, this option would require the United States to initiate military action in a situation in which it was uncertain whether the American people would understand the issues involved and it was doubtful whether the advan-tages to be gained by remaining in Berlin were worth a war.

Third, the United States could maintain an unprovocative but firm stand in Berlin, using first every local means and subsequently diplomatic means to obtain recognition of U.S. rights while postponing the ultimate decision to stay in Berlin or withdraw. The United States could use the time gained by discus-sion to plan for the use of force or withdrawal should either course be chosen. They could probe Russia's intentions. The main argument against this option was that it avoided a definitive decision and would subject the United States to charges of uncertainty and vacillation. In addition, the more forcefully they asserted U.S. rights to remain in Berlin, the greater the prestige that would be lost if the United States was then forced to withdraw.[43]

When Lovett asked Truman what the U.S. future policy in Germany should be—should we stay in Berlin or not?—Truman interrupted by saying, "There was no discussion on that point; we were going to stay, period."

Royall tactfully questioned whether Truman had thought through the problem fully. Royall said that he did not want the United States committed to a position where we might have "to fight our way into Berlin" unless Truman recognized this possibility and accepted the consequences. Truman retorted that "they would have to deal with the situation as it developed" but the essential issue was that "we were in Berlin by terms of an agreement and . . . the Russians had no right to get us out by direct or indirect pressure."[44] Truman's "spot" decision to stay in Berlin was prompted by his firm belief, dating back to Missouri machine politics, that agreements should be kept.[45]

Truman then explained that he intended to stay in Berlin "at all costs" but that this was not final. He would review the two papers given to him and discuss the matter further.[46] Truman did not respond to the suggestion that nuclear-capable B-29 bombers be sent to Britain, but Lovett construed his silence to mean tacit approval.[47] Truman had decided to stay in Berlin while trying for a diplomatic solution. He avoided the risks of either withdrawal or the use of force.

To arrive at this decision, Truman had to use his own best judgment of what was feasible. Available policy analyses conducted by the army suggested that the United States should withdraw from West Berlin. The Department of Defense viewed the airlift as militarily unsound. The airlift tied up all available American transport planes, which the Soviets could easily destroy on the ground, leaving the United States unable to transport or supply its troops overseas.[48] Army staff members regarded U.S. withdrawal as inevitable. On June 30, 1948, Brigadier General T. S. Timberman of P&O wrote that he felt that "certain preliminary action should be taken to divest our eventual withdrawal of the appearance of rout." While the United States should strongly reaffirm its rights of free access to Berlin, the U.S. garrison should in the meantime be "reduced to a tactical force" and that they should withdraw U.S. troops "when, in the opinion of General Clay, the majority of Germans in the Western Sectors are convinced that the only hope of ameliorating their condition lies in our withdrawal."[49]

Truman had to decide whether to make a speech dramatizing the plight of Berlin to mobilize public support for maintaining the U.S. presence. Alarm bells, however, risked setting off war hysteria, endangering Republican support for a bipartisan foreign policy, and provoking Soviet reactions. Truman decided to keep Berlin out of the news as much as possible. Thus, in contrast to British Foreign Minister Ernest Bevin's June 30 impassioned statement to the House of Commons that Britain would stay even if a "grave situation" should arise,[50] Truman did not address Congress or explain why the United States was in West Berlin. Marshall was in Walter Reed Hospital for tests when Truman made the decision to stay in Berlin. Truman had Marshall make a statement from the hospital: "We are in Berlin as a result of agreements between the Governments on the areas of occupation in Germany and we intend to stay."[51] Truman, however, said nothing but would only confirm that he had approved Marshall's statement when asked at a press conference. Truman refused further comment.[52]

SEARCH FOR A DIPLOMATIC SOLUTION

The Soviets made clear that they would lift the blockade if the United States postponed the London Conference program for a West German government. At a July 3 meeting with the Western military governors, Marshal Sokolovsky claimed that traffic on the railway was held up for "technical reasons." Economic disorders in the Soviet zone caused by the London Conference decisions, he said, made it impossible for the Soviet Union to provide alternative routes. Sokolovsky refused to discuss removing traffic barriers unless they considered the London Conference decisions. The Western military governors concluded that Germany, not Berlin, was the real issue.[53]

On July 6, the three Western governments sent similar notes to the Soviet ambassadors in Paris, London, and Washington asserting their rights of conquest to be in Berlin. The United States would not be induced by "threats, pressures, or other actions" to abandon its rights as an occupying power. The United States would be willing to negotiate to resolve differences over administration of Berlin but only if transport restrictions were first lifted.[54]

The Soviet July 14 reply dropped any remaining pretense to "technical difficulties" and made clear that the London Conference decisions and the currency reform had precipitated the blockade. The Soviets took a hard line. The United States had forfeited its right to be in Berlin by the separate currency reform and its dismemberment of Germany. The Soviets would negotiate, but only on the German question as a whole and without lifting the blockade.[55]

Clay advocated sending an armed convoy through East Germany to West Berlin. Clay did not believe that the Soviets would go to war in response to U.S. action to relieve the blockade unless they already planned to do so, in which case the Soviets would keep pushing until the Western Allies were provoked into war. Consequently, the United States had nothing to lose by trying to break the blockade by a show of force.[56]

Army officials in Washington were firmly opposed to Clay's proposal for an armed convoy. The plan involved sending a convoy of two hundred trucks supported by a rifle troop and an engineer battalion equipped with bridge, train, and road repair equipment. According to a staff memorandum, the Soviets might allow a single convoy to get through to Berlin, permitting the United States to enjoy a brief "moral victory," after which it would become apparent that Berlin could not be supplied by motor convoy over the autobahn. The Soviets could also use passive resistance and bottle up the convoy by destroying bridges in front and behind, further embarrassing the United States. Finally, the Soviets could interpret U.S. actions as a justifiable cause for initiating a war. The army P&O dismissed General Clay's proposal because it depended on "an imponderable psychological factor for success against the risk of an embarrassing failure."[57] Army Secretary Royall regarded armed convoys as a "last resort."[58] In a July 22 memorandum, the Joint Chiefs observed that Soviet passive interference could make the armed convoy method abortive, while Soviet interference by military action would shift the problem from local friction to major war involvement. They recommended that armed convoys not be used unless every other solution had been tried or discarded; the operation appeared likely to succeed; the United States government had decided that it would go to war if necessary to maintain its position in Berlin; and the airlift was used to gain all possible time for war preparations.[59]

State and Defense Department officials did not view the airlift as a long-term solution, either. A July 17 memorandum from Army Chief of Staff Bradley judged that "continued air supply for Berlin as a long-term operation is not feasible." The airlift was failing to meet minimum requirements by one-third. At this rate of depletion, all fuel and food stocks would be exhausted in approximately three months.[60] The Joint Chiefs stated that Berlin could be supplied for a considerable period by air, at the cost of reduced capabilities for air transport in the event of war. Therefore, the airlift should be augmented and used to provide a "cushion of time" during which some other solution to the Berlin problem might be found. The chiefs requested that the political leadership consider "the possibility that some justification might be found for withdrawal of our occupation forces from Berlin without undue loss of prestige."[61]

The arrival of cold weather around October 15 would increase the minimum requirements for fuel, further widening the gap between the minimum requirements of the German population and the capacity of the United States to supply Berlin by air. Secretary of Defense Forrestal and Undersecretary Lovett regarded October 15 as an implicit deadline, after which the United States would have to take some other action to bring the crisis to an end.

Lovett termed the airlift an "unsatisfactory expedient." Assistant Secretary of the Air Force Cornelius V. Whitney said that the "Air Staff was firmly convinced that the air operation was doomed to failure."[62] *U.S. News & World Report* predicted that the real crisis would come in the winter, when the United States would not be able to fly in enough coal.[63]

The air force was against expanding the airlift any further, because they would be dipping into planes required for emergency war plans. Secretary Marshall was concerned about having so many U.S. planes in a concentrated area where 25 percent might be destroyed at the first blow. Then there was the expense. The cost of the airlift at $1.25 per mile, using 139 C-54s, was a minimum of $165,000 per day.[64] *Newsweek* magazine raised the question "How long could and would the Western powers maintain the ultra-expensive airlift?"[65]

RISK OF WAR

On July 19, a series of high-level meetings on Berlin were held at which Truman reiterated his decision to stay in Berlin, at the risk of war. At 11:45, Truman met with Secretary of Defense Forrestal and Secretary of State Marshall. Marshall declared that they could either remain firm in Berlin or accept the consequences of failure of the rest of their European policy. He felt there was some chance of containing the Russians in Western Europe. Forrestal objected that the United States had total reserves of about two and one-third divisions, of which only one division was ready to commit. At the end of the discussion, Truman announced that the policy would remain fixed: the United States would stay in Berlin until all diplomatic means had been exhausted in order to come to some kind of accommodation to avoid war.[66] As Truman later recorded in his diary, "I'd made the decision ten days ago to *stay in Berlin*." He wrote, "We'll stay in Berlin—come what may."[67]

At a later meeting also attended by Royall, Lovett, and Forrestal, Undersecretary of the Army William Draper conveyed to Truman the recommendations of Averell Harriman, special U.S. representative for the European Cooperation Administration, who was in Paris. Harriman recommended that Truman decide that the United States would not be forced out of Berlin by any measures short of armed conflict and that it was prepared to fight on this issue. Truman replied that the decision to stay in Berlin even at the risk of war had already been made.[68] Truman later complained in his diary that he had "to listen to a rehash of what I know already and reiterate my 'Stay in Berlin' decision. I don't pass the buck, nor do I alibi out of any decision I make."[69]

Harriman advised Truman to make a speech before Congress and the nation that would lay out "the full significance of the Berlin crisis." Truman objected that a statement about Berlin at the opening of Congress "might unnecessarily disturb the present delicate international situation." He would cover the present crisis with the Congress at the appropriate time.[70] Truman later declined an invitation from Representative Charles A. Eaton, chairman of the House Foreign Affairs Committee, to use his opening speech to a special session of Congress to address the Berlin situation and the possibility of war.[71]

TRUMAN'S EXPANSION OF THE AIRLIFT

Leaks of Clay's armed convoy proposal and the close proximity of U.S and Soviet planes in the crowded Berlin air corridors prompted a brief war scare. *Newsweek* warned that war could break out in Berlin over a "chain-reaction accident," brought about by an incident such as the Soviets' shooting down a U.S. plane. The U.S. authorities in Berlin reported that the chances of war were now one out of four.[72] Columnist James Reston reassured the public that Washington would not try to push through any "armed trains" or make any other rash moves. He reported that there was little evidence of Russian preparations for war in Europe. U.S. and British military experts doubted that the Soviets could ready themselves for a major push against the West in the remaining six weeks or two months of good weather.[73]

Clay again requested permission to send an armored column down the autobahn. He complained that diplomatic measures such as exchange of notes or taking the issue to the United Nations would take time, during which the U.S. position could deteriorate. He assured the army that the Soviet Union would only attack U.S. forces if it had already decided on war. Their lack of real readiness or preparations for war in Europe suggested that the Soviets were bluffing.[74]

The army recalled Clay and Murphy to Washington to present their views to Truman and the National Security Council. In a letter to his wife, Bess, Truman complained that "my muttonhead Secretary of the Army ordered Clay home from Germany and stirred up a terrific how-dy-do for no good reason. Marshall and I decided it was not necessary for him to come and so told Forrestal—but you know how smart that Defense set up thinks it is."[75]

When asked at a press conference whether there was any justification for the widespread fear of war, Secretary Marshall replied that the United States would use every resource of negotiation and diplomatic procedure to reach an acceptable solution of the Berlin crisis without war, but that this country would not be "coerced or intimidated in any way."[76]

At his press conference, Truman refused to comment on the Berlin situation. He did say that the chances for world peace were good, just as they had always been. In fact, he added, he thought they were excellent.[77] That same day, Soviet Yak fighters harassed three British pilots, in violation of the quadripartite rules for administration of the air space.[78]

Given the prevailing political climate, it should have been a surprise to no one that Clay's armed convoy idea did not receive serious consideration. At the July 22 National Security Council (NSC) meeting, Truman approved an expansion of the airlift over air force opposition. General Clay said that abandonment of Berlin would have a disastrous effect on U.S. plans for West Germany and slow down European recovery, which depended on more production, particularly from West Germany. The United States should be prepared to go to any lengths to find a peaceful solution but should be determined to remain in Berlin.

General Clay reported that the airlift was averaging about 2,400 to 2,500 tons per day, which was more than enough to handle food requirements but was inadequate to meet the need for coal. The minimum necessary to sustain Berlin without extreme hardship was 4,500 tons per day. He requested seventy-five additional C-54s, which together with the British contribution would enable the airlift to reach a daily tonnage of 4,500. He admitted that because the "use of armed convoys obviously could create an act which might lead to war," the United States should not resort to this step until all other means had been tried and failed.

Air Force Chief of Staff Hoyt S. Vandenberg objected that any additional planes for the airlift would disrupt the Military Air Transport Service. The maximum airlift would require using planes intended for emergency use, many of which might be destroyed if there were hostilities, adversely affecting U.S. capabilities to wage strategic warfare. If the majority of U.S. planes were caught and destroyed, this would make it difficult to supply U.S. troops and hold outlying bases. Another risk was that the Soviets shared the air corridors and might object that they could not use their airports on the corridor.

In answer to a question from President Truman, Clay said that he did not think that the Soviets intended to go to war. They were operating with greater care than they had in March. There had been no troop movements or other signs to indicate preparations for war. General Clay estimated that the Soviets had about 360,000 ground and air troops in Germany, compared with a Western force of about 210,000.

Clay said that "if we move out of Berlin we have lost everything we are fighting for." President Truman said that this was his opinion also.[79]

The NSC approved Clay's request for an additional seventy-five C-54s and reaffirmed the decision to "stay in Berlin at any event," a euphemism for war.[80]

Clay conducted a news conference at the Pentagon, at which he expressed confidence that a vastly expanded airlift of supplies into Berlin would sustain the city until negotiations "we will be and are carrying on" broke the deadlock with the Soviet Union. Clay said that he doubted that anyone, including the Soviets, wanted war. Responding to reports that he had advocated testing the blockade with an armed convoy, the general declared that it was not his duty as a soldier "to carry us into war." That decision would have to be made by the government, if necessary.[81]

Secretary of State Marshall asked Lovett, a Republican, to keep John Foster Dulles, Dewey's chief foreign policy adviser, informed about developments in Berlin. The Truman administration's careful cultivation of Dulles was rewarded on July 24, when Dewey announced his support for the U.S. policy of staying in Berlin while seeking a peaceful settlement. He also affirmed his commitment to bipartisanship in foreign policy.[82]

High-level reassurances from Washington and the NSC meeting with Clay quieted domestic political fears of war. "Peace is 'busting out all over,' " Reston wrote. Last week the talk was of war, but this week, although nothing tangible had changed, "the lady with the olive branch is getting a big official rush."[83]

COLLAPSE OF NEGOTIATIONS AND
RENEWED FEARS OF WAR

Truman decided to have Ambassador to Moscow Walter Bedell Smith seek a private interview with Joseph Stalin before sending a formal reply to the July 14 Soviet diplomatic note. A formal diplomatic note refuting Soviet charges would engage Soviet prestige and make it more difficult for the Soviets to back down.[84] Many people, including Truman, believed that the Politburo was divided and that Stalin was more reasonable than Molotov. On June 11, during his whistle-stop tour, Truman, speaking off the cuff, recalled the Potsdam Conference:

> I got very well acquainted with Joe Stalin, and I like old Joe. He is a decent fellow. But Joe is a prisoner of the Politburo. He can't do what he wants to. He makes agreements, and if he could he would keep them. But the people who run the government are very specific in saying that he can't keep them.[85]

When the three Western representatives met with Stalin on August 2, the Soviet leader appeared affable and relaxed. Stalin explained that the Western powers had forfeited their juridical rights to occupy Berlin by their decision to set up a West German government at Frankfurt. He admitted that the "real issue" was the "formation in the Western zones of a German Government." He offered to lift the blockade if the Soviet mark was the sole medium of currency in Berlin, on condition that the Western countries record the Soviet government's "insistent wish" for delay in implementing the London Conference program.[86]

From the Western countries' willingness to approach him personally and the evasive replies of their diplomatic representatives, Stalin inferred that the Truman administration was weakening and would agree to postpone implementation of the London Conference decisions until the four powers had a chance to negotiate.[87] Despite Stalin's promise, Soviet Foreign Minister Vyacheslav Molotov several times tried to make delay in establishing a West German government a condition for ending the blockade.[88]

The United States hardened its position as well. Clay advised the State Department to insist on quadripartite control over Berlin's currency to prevent the Soviet Union from controlling Berlin's banking and credit systems.[89] By August 30, the Western powers had agreed to accept the eastern mark throughout Berlin in return for the Soviets' lifting traffic restrictions. In due course, the four powers would hold a foreign ministers conference to discuss Berlin and Germany.[90] Smith failed to get into the directive Stalin's private assurance that the four-power financial commission would have authority over Berlin's currency.[91] If they couldn't get the West to postpone its program for establishing a West German government, as a fallback position, Stalin and Soviet Foreign Minister Molotov wanted to gain control over Berlin's currency to link West Berlin to the financial and economic system of the Soviet occupation zone.[92]

The Moscow agreement instructed the military governors in Moscow to agree on the details for introducing the Soviet mark and lifting the traffic restrictions and to report back to their governments in a week.[93] The convening of the Parliamentary Council on September 1 to write a constitution for a West German government disappointed the Soviets because it showed that the West would not delay carrying out the London Conference decisions.[94] Reflecting the Soviets' displeasure, Sokolovsky imposed new conditions for lifting the blockade. He refused to allow the four-power commission to oversee circulation of the Soviet mark in Berlin and even tried to impose new restrictions on civil aviation.[95] Lovett concluded that the Soviets did not want an agreement, complaining that the Soviets' heads were "full of bubbles."[96]

At a September 7 NSC meeting, Marshall reported that the state of the Berlin negotiations was "discouraging and serious." Sokolovsky had ignored the Moscow agreements. In addition, the Soviet government was permitting and probably encouraging mass disturbances in Berlin. A communist mob had prevented Berlin's City Assembly from meeting in city hall and drove them to the British zone. Lovett proposed to make one last approach to Molotov asking whether the Soviets intended to observe the Moscow agreements, then put the issue before the United Nations Security Council. Marshall warned that time was on the side of the Russians. They could think of ever-new ways to try our patience.[97] On September 9, a mass demonstration of 250,000 West Berliners gathered in front of the Reichstag to protest the communist violence. A few demonstrators tore down the Soviet flag and burned it. Others stoned Soviet soldiers. Soviet soldiers fired into the crowd, killing a young man.[98] When pressed by a journalist at his regular news conference, Truman said that the United States would stand up for its rights in Berlin and continue to negotiate.[99]

AN ABORTIVE PEACE MISSION

As the Berlin crisis continued, Truman traveled by train across the United States campaigning for president, making an average of ten speeches per day. His grueling schedule affected Truman's judgment so that he nearly made a serious political blunder. Concerned that the Progressive candidate Henry Wallace was stealing votes away from Truman by accusing him of being a warmonger, two of Truman's speech writers, David Noyes and Albert Z. Carr, persuaded the president that he should send a special emissary to Stalin to reassure him about U.S. intentions. Truman recalled that he had sent Harry Hopkins to Moscow in 1945 to persuade Stalin to resolve differences over the Polish government that threatened the success of the United Nations Conference in San Francisco. Without consulting the State Department, on October 3 Truman asked Supreme Court Justice Fred Vinson whether he would be willing to meet with Stalin for an informal exchange of views. Truman believed that Stalin would open up if approached honestly. "If we could only get Stalin to unburden himself to someone on our side he felt he could trust fully, I thought perhaps we could get somewhere."[100] Vinson agreed, and on October 5, Truman's press secretary Charlie Ross asked the radio networks for free air time at 10 or 10:30 P.M. so that Truman could make a speech announcing the mission. When the networks asked for assurances that the speech would be "nonpolitical," Ross briefed them off the record about the Vinson mission.[101]

Truman then had a teleconference with Marshall, who was in Paris to place the Soviet blockade before the UN Security Council as a threat to the peace. Marshall objected strongly. To send an emissary to Stalin would convey an image of weakness, undermine his presentation at the UN, and betray Britain and France, which had agreed on a unified approach to the Security Council. Disappointed, Truman returned to the cabinet room where he told his political advisers to rescind the request for radio time. When some White House aides tried to persuade him to go ahead with the plan, Truman replied simply, "I have heard enough. We won't do it."[102] White House staff member George Elsey recorded in his diary that "there is much confusion and taut nerves, due to the political campaign and the belief that the president is going to be defeated."[103]

Three days later, as Truman was traveling by train through upstate New York, news of the aborted mission leaked to the national press. Truman was accused of incompetence, disorganization, and playing politics with the nation's foreign policy. A government official complained, "Just as we got things rolling, some politician had to give the boss this 'brilliant' idea." Truman returned to Washington on October 9 to meet with Marshall, who had been recalled from Paris to assuage the secretary's indignation. His campaign adviser Clark Clifford called the Vinson mission the "worst mistake" of the Truman presidential campaign and expressed astonishment that Dewey did not take advantage of it. [104]

Dewey, however, trying to convey an image of statesmanship and convinced that he had already won the election, chose to make oblique references to Truman's mistake. By this time, Dewey was already committed to bipartisanship on foreign policy. Dewey's political advisers believed that Truman had committed an error of such proportions that it alone could determine the election, if that were in doubt. As it was, the aborted Moscow mission would only increase Dewey's margin of victory.[105]

Truman's campaign aides were dejected at the impact this fiasco would have on his already slim chances for reelection, but the president replied, "I don't think it's so bad." Truman later speculated that although it "would have been better for the mission to have been consummated, still there was a meaning that was implicit in this undertaking that said for all to hear and to know that we would do anything that was honorable and practicable to pursue peaceful negotiations."[106] White House staff member George Elsey later commented, "I think that people said to themselves, 'Harry Truman is trying to do something for peace, but the State Department has blocked him again.'"[107] While Truman erred in failing to consult with Marshall, he instinctively knew that the public would approve of a special peace mission.

CIVIL-MILITARY DIFFERENCES OVER ACCEPTANCE OF RISK

Truman reached decisions through intuitive rather than analytical methods. He refused to state clearly whether maintaining the U.S. presence in West Berlin was worth a war, which greatly frustrated the military. On October 4, Clay requested an additional sixty-six C-54 aircraft so that he could meet Berlin's needs in the approaching winter.[108] The NSC asked the Joint Chiefs to give their views on the military implications of continuing the airlift through the winter and possible military actions in response to Soviet interference with the airlift.

In an October 13 memorandum, the Joint Chiefs acknowledged that the airlift could be continued indefinitely, at great cost, in terms of both money and readiness for war emergency. In view of Truman's July 22 decision "to remain in Berlin in any event," the Joint Chiefs recommended that the airlift be increased by sixty-six aircraft. Some might interpret "at any event" to mean war, but it was possible that this was not the original intention. This issue should be clarified "beyond all doubt." If the United States was willing to go to war over Berlin, the military needed to make plans and acquire the necessary forces. Soviet interference with the airlift, though, raised the risk that the United States would be faced with a decision whether Berlin was worth a war. The Joint Chiefs wanted an immediate decision whether the added risk of war in Berlin inherent in the airlift was acceptable. If so, then all-out preparations for war should be begun immediately. If not, plans should be made and action taken leading to U.S. withdrawal from Berlin.[109] In the military view, to start a war "in our present state of readiness and for the Berlin issue would be neither militarily prudent nor strategically sound."[110]

The Joint Chiefs were soundly rebuffed at a special October 14 meeting of the NSC, which Truman did not attend. Lovett emphasized that the United States faced the "risk of war" last July when the NSC had agreed that we were determined to stay in Berlin. Public opinion polls at the time showed that 80 percent of the American people said that the United States should stay in Berlin and fight if necessary. "We are, therefore, in Berlin with a full knowledge of the risks involved. It is our policy that we do not intend to be forced out of Berlin."[111] Lovett did not say, however, whether maintaining the U.S. presence in Berlin was worth a war. The "risk of war" was something entirely different. The Joint Chiefs withdrew their objections and recommended that Truman approve the sixty-six additional C-54s requested by Clay.[112]

As a political leader, Truman was willing to take a calculated risk that the Soviets would not provoke a war. Mobilization risked creating a war scare and provoking the Soviets. Given antitax sentiment in the Congress, there was little hope for increased military appropriations. The military had a fundamentally different outlook. The Joint Chiefs were responsible for planning for operations should war break out. They wanted to avoid military operations in an area where the Soviets seemingly had vast superiority.[113] Army Chief of Staff Bradley later complained that Truman's postponement of the decision was "outrageous." During the Berlin blockade, when the United States was "nose to nose with massive Soviet military power, the JCS [Joint Chiefs of Staff] were so poorly advised that we could not draw contingency war plans."[114]

Bad weather and fog reduced the number of flights in November and December. Then in late January, the weather lifted and the airlift delivered increasing amounts of food and supplies.[115] On January 31, 1949, Stalin hinted that he was ready to settle the Berlin issue by omitting any reference to the currency issue when asked by a journalist to give his conditions for ending the blockade.[116] On May 5, the four occupying powers issued a communiqué by which the Soviets would lift traffic restrictions on May 12. The West would participate in a council of foreign ministers conference on May 23 to discuss questions relating to Germany and the situation in Berlin.

CONCLUSION

Decision making during the 1948–49 Berlin blockade was much messier, politicized, and disorganized than conveyed by rational choice models. Truman intuitively decided that the U.S. should remain in West Berlin despite the risks and expense of the airlift. When he decided to stay, he had received only a brief sketch of broad policy options, without a recommendation. He had received no analyses of the Berliner's needs for food and coal or whether those needs could be met by an airlift. Part of good political judgment is knowing when to act and when to wait for events to settle. Truman refused to be panicked into making a precipitous decision to withdraw or fight, although either course would have removed the uncertainty and stress. He was willing to postpone an ultimate decision whether to go to war over Berlin.

Did Truman exercise good judgment, or was he just fortunate? Bradley later stated, "I have always felt that we were very, very lucky in the Berlin Blockade."[117] The Soviets could very easily have rendered the airlift ineffective by buzzing U.S. airplanes, filling the air corridors with their own planes, jamming radar, and so on. Stalin could have maintained restrictions on traffic indefinitely, until the expense and wear and tear on planes forced the United States to give up the airlift. Truman's decision to stay did not foreclose other possibilities, however, should the airlift prove ineffective. He could have agreed to postpone implementation of the London Conference decisions to establish a West German government pending negotiations with the Soviets. He could have agreed to exchange the U.S. presence in West Berlin for Soviet occupied territory in East Germany. The United States tested Soviet intentions by offering to accept the east mark in Berlin, a concession that was not reciprocated.

Truman maintained public support for a costly operation without resorting to alarmist rhetoric. By avoiding public statements on Berlin, he kept the U.S. presence from becoming a partisan political issue. The Soviets were following the U.S. press coverage very closely.[118] Stalin might have interpreted division within the United States over Berlin as an indication that it would be safe to interfere with the airlift. Truman gave priority to foreign policy interests over his personal political fortunes, even though he was far behind in the polls. In his sense of timing, balancing of foreign policy and domestic political concerns, and knowledge of what was politically feasible, Truman showed good political judgment.

NOTES

1. Paul Nitze, "Foreword," in W. R. Smyser, *From Yalta to Berlin: The Cold War Struggle over Germany* (New York: St. Martin's, 1999), xiv.

2. Avi Shlaim, *The United States and the Berlin Blockade, 1948–1949* (Berkeley: University of California, 1983), 31–32; Jean Edward Smith, *Lucius D. Clay: An American Life* (New York: Holt, 1990), 416, 450.

3. Marc Trachtenberg, *A Constructed Peace: The Making of the European Settlement 1945–1963* (Princeton, N.J.: Princeton University Press, 1999), 81–82.

4. Political Adviser for Germany Murphy to the Secretary of State, March 3, 1948, *Foreign Relations of the United States* [hereafter cited as *FRUS*], *1948*, II (Washington, D.C.: Government Printing Office, 1973), 878–79.

5. Robert Murphy, *Diplomat among Warriors* (Garden City, N.Y.: Doubleday, 1964), 313.

6. Communiqué Issued at the Recess of the London Conference on Germany, March 6, 1948, *FRUS, 1948*, II, 141–43.

7. Lucius D. Clay, *Decision in Germany* (Garden City, N.Y.: Doubleday, 1950), 356; *FRUS* 1948, II, 884, 141.

8. Clay to Bradley, March 31, 1948, Clark Clifford Papers, Subject File 1945–1954, "Russia [5 of 8]," Harry S. Truman Library (HSTL), Independence, Mo.

9. Omar N. Bradley and Clay Blair, *A General's Life: An Autobiography by General of the Army* (New York: Simon & Schuster, 1983), 478.

10. Forrestal Diary, March 30, 1948, in Walter Millis, *The Forrestal Diaries* (New York: Viking, 1951), 407–8.

11. Forrestal diaries, March 31, 1948, in Millis, *Forrestal Diaries*, 408.

12. Teleconference TT-9287, Bradley, Wedemeyer, Royall, March 31, 1948, in *The Papers of General Lucius D. Clay, Germany 1945–1949*, vol. 2, ed. Jean Edward Smith (Bloomington: Indiana University Press, 1974), 604–6.

13. Clay, *Decision in Germany*, 359; Shlaim, *The United States and the Berlin Blockade*, 128.

14. Smith, *Lucius D. Clay*, 476; Teleconference TT-9341, Bradley to Clay, April 10, 1948, in Smith, *Clay Papers*, 622, 624–25.

15. Smith, *Clay Papers,* 623.

16. Shlaim, *The United States and the Berlin Blockade,* 167–68.

17. Communiqué of the London Conference on Germany, June 7, 1948, *FRUS,* 1948, II, 313–17.

18. Clay, *Decision in Germany,* 362.

19. *FRUS, 1948,* II, 870–75, 879–82.

20. W. Phillips Davison, *The Berlin Blockade: A Study in Cold War Politics* (Santa Monica, Calif.: RAND Corporation, 1957), 91–92.

21. *FRUS 1948,* II, 909–10.

22. *FRUS, 1948,* II, 912–14; Clay, *Decision in Germany,* 363–64; Kenneth W. Condit, *The History of the Joint Chiefs of Staff: The Joint Chiefs of Staff and National Policy,* vol. II, *1947–1949* (Wilmington, Del.: Glazier, 1996), 127; Shlaim, *The U.S. and the Berlin Blockade,* 156, 158.

23. From Clay Personal to Royall, June 25, 1948, in *Clay Papers,* 698.

24. Department of the Army to U.S. Military Governor for Germany Clay, April 28, 1948, *FRUS,* 1948, II, 897–98.

25. Jack Raymond, "Clay Declares U.S. Won't Quit Berlin Short of Warfare," *New York Times,* June 25, 1948, 1.

26. John H. Ohly, June 24, 1948, Memorandum for the Secretary of Defense, RG 330 (Secretary of Defense), CD 6–2-9, National Archives (NA), College Park, Md.

27. Colonel Henry A. Byroade to General Wedemeyer, June 18, 1948, P&O 092 Sec. 1A, Box 36, "General Wedemeyer's Black Book," RG 319, NA, College Park, Md.

28. Memorandum, June 26, 1948, P&O 381 TS, P&O Hot Files, RG 319, NA, College Park, Md.

29. Clay to Royall, June 25, 1948, *FRUS, 1948,* II, 917–18.

30. Clay, *Decision in Germany,* 366.

31. Cabinet meeting, June 25, 1958, Matthew J. Connelly Papers, HSTL, Independence, Mo.

32. Memorandum by the Chief of the Division of Central European Affairs Beam, June 28, 1948 [minutes of June 25 meeting], *FRUS,* 1948, II, 928–29.

33. Smith, *Lucius D. Clay,* 497–99; Murphy to Marshall, June 26, 1948, *FRUS: 1948,* II, 918–19.

34. Clay, *Decision in Germany,* 365–66.

35. "U.S. Will Mobilize Planes in Europe to Supply Berlin," *New York Times,* June 27, 1948, 1.

36. Margaret Truman, *Harry S. Truman* (New York: Morrow, 1973), 12; Truman, *Memoirs: Years of Trial and Hope* (Garden City, N.Y.: Doubleday, 1956), II, 123.

37. Davison, *The Berlin Blockade,* 149–50.

38. Bradley and Blair, *A General's Life,* 479.

39. Bradley and Blair, *A General's Life,* 479.

40. Millis, *Forrestal Diaries,* 453.

41. Millis, *Forrestal Diaries,* 452–54; Bradley and Blair, *A General's Life,* 479–80.

42. Condit, *The History of the Joint Chiefs of Staff,* 134.

43. State-National Defense Meeting of 27 June 1948 Held for the Purpose of Deter-

mining the U.S. Position Regarding the Continued Occupation of Berlin, RG 330 (Secretary of Defense), CD 6-2-9, NA, College Park, Md.

44. Millis, *Forrestal Diaries*, 455.

45. Deborah Welch Larson, *Origins of Containment: A Psychological Explanation* (Princeton, N.J.: Princeton University Press, 1985), 132–37, 319.

46. Millis, *Forrestal Diaries*, 455.

47. Bradley and Blair, *A General's Life*, 480.

48. Davison, *The Berlin Blockade*, 150.

49. T. S. Timberman, Memorandum for General Schuyler, June 30, 1948, Notes on the Berlin Situation (Army View), P&O 381 TS (June 28, 48), RG 319, P&O Division Decimal File 1946–1948, 381 Sec. V-A, Part II, NA, College Park, Md.

50. Herbert L. Matthews, "British Accept Risk of War; U.S. Also Is Firm on Berlin," *New York Times*, July 1, 1948, 1.

51. W. H. Lawrence, "Marshall Asserts U.S. Will 'Deal Promptly' With Any Issues—More B-29s Sent," *New York Times*, July 1, 1948, 1.

52. "Stand on Germany Backed by Truman," *New York Times*, July 2, 1948, 1.

53. *FRUS*, 1948, II, 929–30; Condit, *The History of the Joint Chiefs of Staff*, 137–38; Clay, *Decision in Germany*, 367.

54. Secretary of State to Soviet Ambassador Panyushkin, July 6, 1948, *FRUS 1948*, II, 950–51.

55. Soviet Ambassador Panyushkin to Marshall, July 14, 1948, *FRUS: 1948*, II, 960–64; Condit, *The History of the Joint Chiefs of Staff*, 138; Truman, *Memoirs*, 123.

56. Clay to the Department of the Army, July 10, 1948, *FRUS: 1948, II*, 955–56; from Clay to Bradley, July 15, 1948, in *Clay Papers*, II, 740.

57. Lt. Col. Osmanski, July 13, 1948, P&O 381 TS, sec. B-A (Part II), RG 319, NA, College Park, Md.; Smith, *Clay Papers*, II, 735–38.

58. Memorandum for the President, July 16, 1948, National Security Council Files—Meetings, "Memoranda for the President—Meeting discussions (1948)," Box 220, HSTL, Independence, Mo.

59. Memorandum for the National Security Council, July 22, 1948, Records of the JCS, 381 (4–20–43), sec. 17, RG 218, NA, College Park, Md.

60. Memorandum by the Chief of Staff, U.S. Army to the Joint Chiefs of Staff on "U.S. Military Courses of Action with Respect to Berlin," July 17, 1948, Records of the JCS, 381 (8–20–43), sec. 17, RG 218, NA, College Park, Md.

61. Forrestal did not forward these views to the NSC until July 26. Memorandum for the National Security Council, July 22, 1948, Records of the JCS, 381 (4–20–43), sec. 17, RG 218, NA, College Park, Md.; Condit, *The History of the Joint Chiefs of Staff*, 141, 143–44.

62. Memorandum to the President, July 16, 1948, PSF, National Security Council Files—Meetings, "Memoranda for the President—Meeting Discussions (1948)," Box 220, HSTL.

63. "Is Pressure at Berlin a Bluff? Prospect of Squeeze by Soviet," *U.S. News & World Report*, July 9, 1948, 11.

64. Memorandum for Chief of Staff, U.S. Army, Maj. Gen. Ray T. Maddocks, July 13,

1948, P&O 381, sec. 6-A, part II, RG 319, NA, College Park, Md.; Memorandum to the President, July 16, 1948, PSF, National Security Council Files—Meetings, "Memoranda for the President—Meeting Discussions (1948)," Box 220, HSTL, Independence, Mo.

65. "Push-Button Marked 'Obliteration'," *Newsweek*, July 19, 1948, 25.

66. Millis, *Forrestal Diaries*, 459.

67. Truman diary, July 19, 1948, Robert Ferrell, *Off the Record* (New York: Harper & Row, 1980), 145.

68. Memorandum of Conversation with Mr. Averell Harriman, July 17, 1948, RG 335 Under Secretary of the Army, Draper/Voorhees Germany 000.1, "Berlin Crises, Book 1"; Memorandum for Record by William H. Draper, July 19, 1948, Records of the Under Secretary of the Army (Draper/Voorhees), RG 335, NA, College Park, Md.

69. Truman diary, July 19, 1948, in Ferrell, *Off the Record*, 145.

70. Memorandum of Conversation with Mr. Averell Harriman, July 17, 1948, RG 335 Under Secretary of the Army, Draper/Voorhees Germany 000.1, "Berlin Crises, Book 1"; Memorandum for Record by William H. Draper, July 19, 1948, Records of the Under Secretary of the Army (Draper/Voorhees), RG 335, NA, College Park, Md.

71. Anthony Leviero, "Truman to Deliver Congress Message in Person Today," *New York Times*, July 22, 1948, 1.

72. "Berlin: The Squeeze on the Corridors," *Newsweek*, July 26, 1948, 30.

73. James Reston, "West Bars Any Rash Moves in Solving Berlin Impasse," *New York Times*, July 22, 1948.

74. From Clay for Draper, July 19, 1948, in *Clay Papers*, II, 744–46.

75. Truman to Bess, July 23, 1948, in *Dear Bess: The Letters from Harry to Bess Truman, 1910–1959* (New York: Norton, 1983), 555.

76. Herbert I. Matthews, "West Willing to Discuss All Germany if Russians Recognize Berlin Rights," *New York Times*, July 22, 1948, 1.

77. Bertram D. Hulen, "Truman Asserts Chances for Peace Are Excellent," *New York Times*, July 23, 1948, 1.

78. "Soviet Planes Peril British; Russians Seize 3 Americans," *New York Times*, July 23, 1948, 1.

79. Memorandum for the President, July 23, 1948, President's Secretary File, National Security Files—Meetings, "Memoranda for the President, Meeting Discussions (1948)," Box 220, HSTL, Independence, Mo; Truman, *Memoirs*, II, 124–26. In his memoirs, Truman has an account of an exchange where he replies to Vandenberg that the airlift involves less risk of war, but this conversation does not appear in the minutes of the meeting.

80. Minutes of the 167th meeting, National Security Council, July 22, 1948, President's Secretary File, National Security Council Files, Meetings, "Meeting 16, July 22, 1948," Box 204, HSTL, Independence, Mo.

81. Walter H. Waggoner, "Clay Is Confident of Berlin Supply till Impasse Ends," *New York Times*, July 24, 1948, 1.

82. Leo Egan, "Dewey Declares We Must Not Yield to Soviet in Berlin," *New York Times,* July 25, 1948, 1; Robert A. Divine, *1940–1948: Foreign Policy and U.S. Presidential Elections* (New York: New Viewpoints: Franklin Watts, 1974), 224–25.

83. James Reston, "U.S.-Soviet Weather: Calmer but Storms Brewing," *New York Times*, July 25, 1948, Sec. IV, 3.

84. Charles E. Bohlen, *Witness to History: 1929–1969* (New York: Norton, 1973), 278–79; Marshall to Douglas, July 20, 1948, *FRUS: 1948*, II, 971; Condit, *The History of the Joint Chiefs of Staff*, 146; Shlaim, *The United States and the Berlin Blockade*, 184–85.

85. Quoted in Donovan, *Conflict and Crisis*, 400.

86. Smith to Marshall, August 3, 1948, *FRUS, 1948*, II, 999–1000, 1005; Walter Bedell Smith, *My Three Years in Moscow* (Philadelphia: Lippincott, 1950), 244–45; Smith, *Clay*, 516–17.

87. Michail M. Narinskii, "The Soviet Union and the Berlin Crisis, 1948–49," in *The Soviet Union and Europe in the Cold War, 1945–53*, ed. Francesca Gori and Silvio Pons (New York: St. Martin's, 1996), 69–70.

88. Davison, *The Berlin Blockade*, 159; Smith to Marshall, August 6, 9, 1948, *FRUS: 1948*, II, 1018, 1024–25; Smith, *My Three Years in Moscow*, 246.

89. Clay to Department of the Army, August 4, 1948, *FRUS: 1948*, II, 1011–12; Carolyn Eisenberg, *Drawing the Line: The American Decision to Divide Germany, 1944–1949* (Cambridge: Cambridge University Press, 1996), 431.

90. Smith to Marshall, August 27, 1948, *FRUS: 1948*, II, 1085–87.

91. Davison, *The Berlin Blockade*, 161–62; Smith to Marshall, August 30, 1948, *FRUS: 1948*, II, 1093–94; Smith, *The Defense of Berlin*, 119; Clay, *Decision in Germany*, 369.

92. Narinskii, "The Soviet Union and the Berlin Crisis," 69.

93. Davison, *The Berlin Blockade*, 183; Smith to Marshall, August 27, 1948, *FRUS: 1948*, 1085–87; Shlaim, *The United States and the Berlin Blockade*, 326.

94. Narinskii, "The Soviet Union and the Berlin Crisis," 70–71.

95. *FRUS: 1948*, II, 1100–12, 1118–22, 1135–40; Davison, *The Berlin* Blockade, 184; Smith, *Clay*, 517–18; Clay, *Decision in Germany*, 370–71.

96. Forrestal diary, September 6, 1948, in Millis, *Forrestal Diaries*, 482.

97. Forrestal diary, September 7, 1948, in Millis, *Forrestal Diaries*, 483–84; Memorandum for the President, September 9, 1948, PSF, National Security Council Files—Meetings, "Memoranda for the President—Meeting Discussions (1948)," HSTL, Independence, Mo.; Truman, *Memoirs*, 128; Clay, *Decision in Germany*, 376. Truman lists the date of the meeting as September 9.

98. Davison, *The Berlin Blockade*, 188–89.

99. Anthony Leviero, "Truman Says U.S. Will Stay in Berlin Despite Pressure," *New York Times*, September 10, 1948, 1.

100. Robert J. Donovan, *Conflict and Crisis: The Presidency of Harry S Truman, 1945–1948* (New York: Norton, 1977), 423; David McCullough, *Truman* (New York: Simon & Schuster, 1992), 685; Alonzo L. Hamby, *Man of the People: A Life of Harry S. Truman* (New York: Oxford University Press, 1995), 460; Truman, *Memoirs*, II, 213, 215 (quotation), 219.

101. James Reston, "Truman Blocked in Move to Send Vinson to Stalin," *New York Times*, October 9, 1948, 1; Eben Ayers diary, October 5, 1948, in *Truman in the White House: The Diary of Eben A. Ayers*, ed. Robert H. Ferrell (Columbia: University of Missouri Press, 1991), 276. Ayers recorded in his diary that James Reston had been accurately briefed in some detail about the Vinson mission. Ayers diary, October 9, 1948, in *Truman in the White House*, 278.

102. Ayers diary, October 5, 1948, in *Truman in the White House*, 276; Donovan, *Conflict*

and Crisis, 424; Jonathan Daniels, *The Man of Independence* (Philadelphia: Lippincott, 1950), 28.

103. Ayers diary, October 6, 1948, in *Truman in the White House*, 277.

104. Donovan, *Conflict and Crisis,* 425; Reston, "Truman Blocked (quotation)"; Clark Clifford with Richard Holbrooke, *Counsel to the President: A Memoir* (New York: Random House, 1991), 233.

105. Douglas Dales, "Dewey Reassures World Our Policy Has Not Changed," *New York Times*, October 11, 1948, 1.

106. Irwin Ross, *The Loneliest Campaign: The Truman Victory of 1948* (New York: 1968), 214; Divine, *1940/1948,* 259; Truman, *Memoirs*, II, 219.

107. Hamby, *Man of the People*, 461.

108. Smith, *Clay Papers*, 878–79; Shlaim, *The United States and the Berlin Blockade, 1948–1949* (Berkeley: University of California Press, 1983), 359.

109. Condit, *The History of the Joint Chiefs of Staff*, 150–52.

110. Condit, *The History of the Joint Chiefs of Staff*, 153.

111. Memorandum for the President, October 15, 1948, President's Secretary File, National Security Council Files—Meetings, "Memoranda for the President—Meeting Discussions (1948)," HSTL, Independence, Mo.

112. Condit, *The History of the Joint Chiefs of Staff*, 155.

113. Condit, *The History of the Joint Chiefs of Staff*, 164.

114. Bradley and Blair, *A General's Life*, 481.

115. Jean Edward Smith, *The Defense of Berlin* (Baltimore, Md.: Johns Hopkins University Press, 1963), 126.

116. Bohlen, *Witness to History*, 283.

117. Bradley and Blair, *A General's Life*, 481.

118. Narinskii, "The Soviet Union and the Berlin Crisis," 67.

· 6 ·

Perceiving the End of Threat

Ronald Reagan and the Gorbachev Revolution

Barbara Farnham

*J*udgments about the source and nature of external threat constitute a crucial first step in the process of decision making related to security and are thus central to the development of foreign policy. The ability to revise such judgments, when appropriate, is equally vital.

The Reagan administration came into office in 1981 "with the most avowed anticommunist crusading policy in two decades."[1] For President Ronald Reagan, this policy reflected a profound sense of threat that was deeply rooted in his firm convictions about the nature of communism in general and the Soviet Union in particular. Yet by the end of his second term, Reagan had substantially revised his view of this threat and accepted the possibility of working with the Soviet Union in the interests of peace. He had been transformed from an "essentialist" who believed that the Soviet Union was governed by an ideology that put no limits on what it could justifiably do to gain its ends of "absolute power and a communist world," to an "interactionist" who saw the conflict between the Soviet Union and the United States in terms of mutual misperception and was hopeful about the possibility of substantial change.[2]

This presents us with a puzzle because the psychological literature strongly suggests that central beliefs are altered only with great difficulty, if at all.[3] Since people tend to interpret new information in the light of what they already believe, they are likely to be slow to change their views, and those most committed to their beliefs will have the most difficulty revising them.[4] This suggests that decision makers may not always be responsive to changes in the nature or level of threat. Yet, as Reagan's behavior demonstrates, they do sometimes overcome their cognitive limitations to make fairly accurate assessments of threat. What enables these decision makers to reevaluate threat successfully while others remain prisoners of their predispositions?

The question is particularly intriguing in view of the numerous criticisms that have been leveled at Reagan's cognitive abilities. According to one observer, for example, he was intellectually shallow and inconsistent, superficially attached to different, and not necessarily compatible, beliefs.[5] Moreover, David Stockman gives us a picture of the president as both ignorant of the complexities of policy and profoundly muddled,[6] while others note his lack of analytical ability, lack of curiosity, and legendary dislike of detail, which, combined with his ignorance of many issues, put him at the mercy of his advisers.[7] Thus, Richard Neustadt has remarked on Reagan's unfortunate habit of "combining ignorance and insistence" (incuriosity about details together with deep commitment to his convictions),[8] which provided fertile soil for such fiascos as the Iran-*contra* scandal.[9] Clearly, Reagan's success in perceiving and responding to the changes in Soviet policy, especially when many others did not, needs to be explained.

I propose to explore the role of judgment in overcoming cognitive biases by examining the responses of President Reagan to the changes proposed and implemented by Mikhail Gorbachev. At what point did Reagan assess the changes in Soviet policy as significant, and for what reasons, and how does his response compare to those of others in his administration?

BASELINE 1981–84: REAGAN'S INITIAL PERCEPTION OF THE THREAT

Showing that President Reagan's understanding of the threat to American security changed in response to the changes in Soviet policy instituted by Mikhail Gorbachev requires establishing a baseline. How did Reagan perceive the threat initially? What were his beliefs about its source and nature, and what evidence did he use to support them?

Somewhat surprisingly, an analysis of these factors shows that Reagan's conception of the threat to American security was more complex than is often supposed, encompassing from the outset not only the threat posed by the "evil empire"[10] of the Soviet Union but also the specter raised by the existence of nuclear weapons.

The Soviet Threat

From the beginning of his presidency, and indeed long before, Ronald Reagan believed that the Soviet Union was the prime source of threat to American security, a threat so pervasive and limitless that it was almost existential.[11] For Reagan, the Soviets threatened all the basic values of the United States and was behind "all the unrest that is going on" in the world.[12] Moreover, these beliefs were long-standing and deeply rooted.[13] The only mitigating factor in Reagan's analysis of the Soviet Union was a tendency to distinguish the Soviet people from their leaders,[14] plus an occasional reference to mutual suspicion fueling the arms race and U.S.-Soviet conflict, along with intermittent suggestions that this might be mitigated by increased communication.[15]

Reagan's sense of threat was compounded by fundamental mistrust based on what he saw as the Soviet Union's "record of deceit and its long history of betrayal of international treaties." This he claimed "could be found in the writings of Soviet leaders: It had always been their philosophy that it was moral to lie or cheat for the purpose of advancing Communism. . . . [T]hey had told us, without meaning to, that they couldn't be trusted."[16]

Reagan saw the threat posed by the Soviet Union as broad and all-encompassing, political as well as military. "[G]uided by a policy of immoral and unbridled expansionism" and following a pattern set by Lenin,[17] the Soviet Union was advancing "all over the world" with the goal of promoting revolution.[18] It was thus a threat to the security of the free world on all fronts.[19] Not only was it the malign force behind all national liberation movements; it was also the sponsor of international terrorism and a significant threat to human rights.[20]

As evidence of the Soviet threat, Reagan pointed to both intentions and capabilities. His interpretation of Soviet intentions was highly ideological. In January 1981, he told reporters that he did not " 'have to think of an answer as to what their intentions are' because all Soviet leaders since the Revolution had 'more than once repeated . . . their determination that their goal must be the promotion of world revolution and a one-world socialist or Communist state.' "[21]

Reagan's view of the capability side of the equation had two aspects: his perception of Soviet strength and his fears about American weakness. His overall assessment of Soviet capabilities was, again, heavily ideological, combining the conviction that the Soviets held a short-run advantage over the United States with a belief in their inevitable failure over the long term owing to their ideological blinders.

Reagan began his presidency convinced that, due to a massive offensive military buildup the 1970s ("the largest and costliest military buildup in the history of man"), the Soviet Union enjoyed "a definite margin of superiority over the United States," with all the ominous consequences this entailed.[22] However, this superiority was not to endure. Not only could the United States correct the imbalance with a military buildup of its own, but also the Soviet system itself was inherently weak. Briefings during the campaign and once in office had convinced Reagan that

> the Soviet economy was in even worse shape than I'd realized. I had always believed that, as an economic system, Communism was doomed. . . . Now, the economic statistics and intelligence reports I was getting . . . were revealing tangible evidence that Communism as we knew it was approaching the brink of collapse. . . . The Soviet economy was . . . a basket case, partly because of massive spending on armaments.[23]

In the short run, however, the Soviet Union was exceedingly dangerous—in part because of *American* shortcomings. That is, the Soviet threat was magnified by U.S. military weakness and a loss of resolve that could only be cured by an American military buildup.[24] Reagan began such a buildup almost immediately after taking office by requesting a huge increase in the defense budget.[25]

As to the loss of American resolve, Reagan believed that in the late 1970s, the United States "had begun to abdicate [its] historical role as the spiritual leader of the Free World and its foremost defender of democracy. Some of our resolve was gone, along with a part of our commitment to uphold the values we cherished." In line with their malevolent intentions, the Soviets "had tried to exploit [this weakness] to the fullest."[26]

The Nuclear Threat

As serious as the Soviet threat was, it was far from being the only one. Reagan believed that the mere existence of nuclear weapons put Americans equally at risk. He was dismayed that American defense policy placed "our entire faith in a weapon whose *fundamental target was the civilian population*" and appalled by the possible consequences, observing, "Even if a nuclear war did not mean the extinction of mankind, it would certainly mean the end of civilization as we knew it. . . . [A]s long as nuclear weapons were in existence, there would always be risks they would be used, and once the first nuclear weapon was unleashed, who knew where it would end?"[27]

Reagan had adopted these beliefs well before he became president.[28] They accorded with his religious ideas about the coming of Armageddon, and they were exacerbated by his realization in 1979 after a visit to NORAD (North American Aerospace Defense Command) that no defense against nuclear missiles existed.[29] Moreover, his nuclear fears were only reinforced by the briefings he received after he became president.[30]

Reagan's plan for dealing with the nuclear threat was two-pronged. First, his "dream . . . became a world free of nuclear weapons." However, recognizing that this goal would not be easily achieved, he also dreamed of creating "a defense against nuclear missiles, so we could change from a policy of assured destruction to one of assured survival."[31] This dream, of course, was transformed into the (in)famous Strategic Defense Initiative (SDI), a policy to which Reagan clung tenaciously throughout his presidency.[32]

Reagan's commitment to both dreams is clearly shown in the discussion of his negotiations with Gorbachev. However, even before Gorbachev came to power in the Soviet Union, Reagan's apprehension about nuclear weapons was reflected in his attempts in 1983–84 to negotiate with the Russians.

PRE-GORBACHEV CHANGES IN TONE AND POLICY

Toward the end of President Reagan's first term, a shift occurred in his tone and policies that had little to do with Soviet behavior.[33] This shift represented a change in emphasis from the Soviet side of Reagan's sense of threat to the nuclear side; it did not, however, signal a substantive change in his core beliefs about the Soviet Union.

Early in 1983, Reagan began to show an interest in improving relations with the Soviet Union. In February, despite the anticipated (and later openly expressed) opposition of his National Security staff, Secretary of Defense Caspar Weinberger, and the head of the Central Intelligence Agency (CIA), William Casey,[34] Reagan agreed to Secretary of State George Shultz's suggestion that he meet with Soviet Ambassador Anatoly Dobrynin. After the meeting, Secretary Shultz was sufficiently "impressed and reassured" by Reagan's performance to push ahead with his plan to "design a broader and longer-term approach to U.S.-Soviet relations to put before the president," and to get him "heavily engaged."[35] Reagan expressed his own view of the matter in a diary entry on April 6: "Some of the N.S.C. staff are too hard line and don't think any approach should be made to the Soviets. I think I'm hardline and will never appease. But I do want to try to let them see there is a better world if they'll show *by deed* they want to get along with the free world."[36]

The culmination of the president's inclinations and the secretary's efforts was a speech on January 16, 1984, in which Reagan stressed negotiation and dialogue, rather than confrontation, and a common interest in avoiding war and reducing "the level of arms. There is no rational alternative but to steer a course which I would call credible deterrence and peaceful competition."[37] In a another major change, Reagan acknowledged for the first time that "most [third world] conflicts have their origins in local problems" and emphasized the need to "reduce the risk of U.S.-Soviet confrontation in these areas."[38]

While these conciliatory gestures were clearly a departure from his previous stance, however, the president was far from abandoning the negative themes he had sounded earlier. Throughout 1984, both Reagan and members of his administration continued to refer to the Soviet Union as a threat. In a June 2 speech in Ireland, for example, he warned that "the free world faces an enormously powerful adversary, . . . a strong and aggressive military machine."[39] As Garthoff points out, "[I]n his January speech and on most such occasions, Reagan chose to complement his offer of a hand in dialogue with a slap by the other hand."[40]

How can we explain this combination of conciliatory gestures and negative rhetoric? Possibly it was simply an expression of what Oberdorfer has called the "dichotomous nature of Reagan's views" about the Soviet Union.[41] However, while there is considerable evidence of Reagan's dichotomous thinking, we need to understand why in 1984 he chose increasingly to stress the cooperative side.

Heightened Sense of Nuclear Threat

In fact, a number of factors came together for the president in late 1983 that may have triggered this shift in emphasis. To begin with, a series of events occurred highlighting the danger of nuclear weapons.[42] The first of these was the Soviet downing in September 1983 of a Korean airliner that had strayed into Soviet airspace (KAL 007). While Reagan ultimately came to believe that the shooting down of KAL 007 had been a mistake, he was extremely troubled by it, believing that it "demonstrated how close the world had come to the precipice and how much we needed nuclear arms control."[43]

Alarming as the thought of an inadvertently triggered nuclear war was, Reagan's distress was compounded by other events that autumn that made him "aware of the need for the world to step back from the nuclear precipice." The first of these was a television movie (*The Day After*), which graphically depicted the effects of a nuclear war and left the president "greatly depressed."[44]

Following hard on the heels of this distressing cinematic event, Reagan underwent another "most sobering experience," a briefing from the military on the SIOP (Single Integrated Operational Plan) for U.S. strategy to deal with a nuclear attack. He later characterized this briefing as a "scenario for a sequence of events that could lead to the end of civilization as we knew it. In several ways, the sequence of events described in the briefings paralleled those in the ABC movie."[45]

The final episode in this series of nuclear-related incidents was the aftermath of the extensive military exercise carried out by American and NATO forces in November 1983 (Able Archer 83) to test procedures for using nuclear weapons in the event of war. Although the exercise was ultimately scaled down, it remained large enough to alarm the Soviets, causing some to think that the United States was actually preparing a nuclear attack. First dismissed as "Soviet scare tactics," the intelligence reports eventually began to be taken seriously within the administration, especially by the president.[46] For the first time Reagan realized, to his great surprise, that the Soviet Union might actually feel threatened by the *United States*. Thus, in November 1983, he determined to communicate "outside the normal diplomatic channels" with Yuri Andropov, the Soviet general secretary, confiding in his diary that he felt that "the Soviets are so defense minded, so paranoid about being attacked that without being in any way soft on them, we ought to tell them no one here has any intention of doing anything like that."[47]

Impact of the U.S. Military Buildup

A heightened sense of nuclear danger was not the only factor encouraging Reagan's move toward cooperation with the Soviet Union in 1983 and 1984. Another was his perception that the success of the military buildup he had initiated now allowed him to deal with the Soviets from a position of strength.[48] In that sense, the buildup was at least a permissive, and probably a necessary, condition of his willingness to negotiate.[49]

Reagan himself testified to this in his memoirs. While declaring that the Soviets had not changed in their "addiction" to "Lenin's secular religion of expansionism and world domination," he observed that "something *else* had changed: I felt we could now go to the summit, for the first time in years, from a position of strength."[50] This sense of renewed strength was also reflected in Reagan's speeches on January 16 and at the United Nations on September 24, 1984.[51]

Secretary Shultz and the 1984 Election

From the start, George Shultz believed that while it was necessary to be wary of the Soviet Union, "we should also be ready to deal with the Soviets more constructively if the opportunity arose."[52] Throughout 1983 and 1984, Shultz persisted in his endeavor to get the president involved in such an approach, peppering Reagan with memos on the subject and promoting opportunities for dialogue between the president and, among others, Dobrynin and Gromyko. Despite the determined opposition of Weinberger, Casey, and most of the NSC staff, Shultz ultimately prevailed, winning Reagan's support.[53]

We should remember, however, that Reagan, at least, believed the secretary had been effective precisely because his views accorded with the president's own, while those of Shultz's opponents (Cap Weinberger, William Casey, and Edwin Meese) did not. As he confided in his diary in November

1984, "[the dispute] is so out of hand George sounds like he wants out. I can't let that happen. Actually George is carrying out my policy. . . . I didn't disagree with Weinberger that the Russians were an evil force in the world and untrustworthy, but I didn't think that meant we shouldn't talk to them."[54]

Finally, some, although of course not Reagan himself, point to the impending 1984 presidential election as a motivating factor in his willingness to negotiate with the Soviets on nuclear arms. According to Oberdorfer, Reagan was told by his pollster, Richard Wirthlin, that his "most serious political vulnerability" was the public's fear that he would bring America into "an unnecessary war."[55] Moreover, Garthoff contends (on the basis of a "well-informed administration source") that as early as the end of 1982, Reagan was thinking about the need to improve relations with the Soviet Union in terms of the coming campaign and that this impulse continued to play a role in administration planning through the 1984 election.[56] However, while the campaign may have influenced Reagan's approach to the Soviet Union in 1984, it does not seem to have been as important as the other factors, especially given the counterpressures from the right against any such negotiations.[57]

How are we to understand Reagan's rhetorical and policy shifts toward the Soviet Union in 1983 and 1984? Given his persistently negative view of the Soviet Union, it is hard to see them as a serious alteration in his perception of the Soviet threat, especially since the Soviets had not, in fact, changed their behavior. Rather, it represented a change in emphasis from the Soviet threat to the nuclear threat,[58] triggered by a series of nuclear-related incidents and combined with a more confident self-assessment of U.S. military power, Secretary Shultz's initiatives, and the political needs growing out of the forthcoming election campaign, all of which made him more receptive to negotiating with the Soviets.[59] There was, however, no radical change in Reagan's core beliefs about the nature of the Soviet Union and the threat that it posed to the United States. Further change would, as even Jack Matlock (who was considered a moderate within the administration) believed, have to wait until the Soviet Union itself changed: "If the Soviet Union stayed as it was, we could hope only to manage the mutual hostility, not to harmonize policies."[60] Fortunately, as it turned out, such change was not as distant as most believed at the time.

Initial Overtures

The year 1985 began with a continuation of the "unsteady, gradual normalization" of U.S.-Soviet relations of the previous years[61] and when Mikhail Gorbachev came to power as general secretary of the Communist Party on March 11, 1985, the reaction of the Reagan administration was subdued. Although

Secretary Shultz and Vice President George H. Bush had been favorably impressed by Gorbachev at their first meeting,[62] and although Reagan had proposed a summit meeting and Gorbachev had responded positively, the president retained his long-standing suspicion of anything Soviet.[63] Five weeks after Gorbachev's accession to power, Reagan noted in his diary that "Gorbachev will be as tough as any of their leaders. If he wasn't a confirmed ideologue, he never would have been chosen by the Politburo." This meant "We'd have to be as tough as ever in dealing with the Soviets." Reagan also noted, however, that "we should work hard to establish channels directly between Gorbachev and me through quiet diplomacy," and in his public statements he expressed the hope for "more constructive relations."[64]

The Geneva Summit, November 19–21, 1985

Although he was not often acclaimed for his dedication to the briefing book, Reagan's preparations for the summit were extensive. As National Security Adviser Robert McFarlane saw it, he was "clearly determined to be thoroughly prepared for his first meeting with a Soviet head of state. He worked hard, and by the time he reached Geneva, was thoroughly in command of his brief." Moreover, his efforts were, at least in part, motivated by an extremely successful meeting with the new Soviet Foreign Minister, Eduard Shevardnadze, in late September.[65]

These experiences led to a partial change in Reagan's rhetoric. Rather than emphasizing Soviet culpability for problems in the relationship, Reagan pointed to "misunderstandings," and in his speech to the nation just prior to the summit, he stressed his "mission for peace," the need to reduce "suspicion and mistrust," and his belief that nuclear weapons were the real threat. As Reagan himself noted, "once we'd agreed to hold a summit, I made a conscious decision to tone down my rhetoric to avoid goading Gorbachev with remarks about the 'evil empire.'"[66]

Ultimately, the Geneva summit yielded a number of benefits for both sides. Reagan and Gorbachev "had come to like and respect each other," and they were able to establish the basis for a working relationship.[67] Certainly, this was true of the president: "Reagan came out not convinced by Gorbachev's beliefs, but respecting them. And he came out seeing Gorbachev as a person, a fellow politician . . . who had constraints just as he had, and if we could do it, he was willing to try to find a way around [those constraints]. So I think the impact of the personal contact on Reagan was very substantial."[68] Gorbachev had been "humanized" for the president; he had zeroed in on the character of the human being in the other chair, "admitting that the Soviet leader had deep convictions of his own."[69] What is more, the feeling was mutual.[70] Observers sensed a "personal chemistry" between the two leaders.

As an added benefit, according to Matlock, Reagan came away with a renewed sense of "confidence in his ability to convince," which led "him to take chances because he felt that the Soviet system could change."[71] Thus, while the Geneva summit did not alter Reagan's basic view of the Soviet threat, it did represent a considerable step forward. As Reagan himself said on his return to the United States, he and Gorbachev now "understand each other better. . . . I gained a better perspective; I feel he did too."[72] Moreover, while Gorbachev has often been given much of the credit for the success of the summit,[73] it must be acknowledged that it was Reagan who insisted on arranging more time for the private discussions that went a long way to producing these positive effects.[74]

Reykjavik Summit, October 11–12, 1986

During the first six months of 1986, negotiations for the next summit failed to prosper, and it was not until June that Reagan responded favorably to Gorbachev's arms control initiatives, though even then he showed no inclination to abandon his dream of strategic defense.[75] Finally, however, in late September an interim meeting between Reagan and Gorbachev was scheduled to prepare for the next summit. It would be held at Reykjavik, Iceland, in October.[76]

At that meeting, the greater part of the discussion, to say nothing of all the drama, centered on arms control. Negotiations took place with respect to the entire arsenal of nuclear forces of both the United States and the Soviet Union. More strikingly, the two leaders seriously discussed eliminating all ballistic missiles and actually considered doing away with all strategic nuclear weapons as well. The sticking point was SDI, with Gorbachev insisting that it be confined to the laboratory and Reagan refusing to give up testing.[77] Thus, the meeting broke up with both sides registering considerable disappointment; many, including most of the participants, considered Reykjavik a failure.

Given such negative sentiments, it is somewhat surprising that almost all the participants assessed Reykjavik retrospectively as, in President Reagan's words, "a major turning point in the quest for a safe and secure world."[78] Secretary Shultz was even more enthusiastic, calling its results "sensational" because it introduced the INF (Intermediate Nuclear Force) Treaty and created, "in an immense amount of detail, the basic structure of the START [Strategic Arms Reduction Treaty] I agreement." In Matlock's view, though the participants failed to appreciate it at the time, "The Reykjavik meeting produced breakthroughs that cleared the way for subsequent treaties."[79] Moreover, it seems to have marked a turning point in the development of Gorbachev's

attitudes that made a number of later agreements possible ("it was at Reykjavik
. . . that Gorbachev put away passion and decided that he could and would
work with Reagan. He saw in him a person capable of taking great decisions,
and Gorbachev himself told me so when we returned to Moscow.") According
to Matlock, "It was only after Reykjavik that [Gorbachev] understood that
relations could be normalized with the United States only if he dealt with the
full agenda of issues, including human rights and raising the iron curtain."[80]

The Washington Summit and the INF Treaty, December 7–10, 1987

These positive retrospective evaluations of the Reykjavik summit notwithstanding, the relationship between United States and the Soviet Union was far
from smooth in its aftermath. As Matlock describes it, "For several months, a
feeling of bitterness and betrayal weighed upon U.S.-Soviet contacts. The
leaders had come tantalizingly close to agreement, and each blamed the other
for failure." As Reagan himself pointed out, during the fourteen months after
Reykjavik, "progress didn't come easily," although he also recognized that
"not all of the obstacles to continuing the momentum started at Geneva origi-
nated in Moscow."[81]

In January, the White House issued a strongly anti-Soviet paper titled the
National Security of the United States that reflected the influence of the hard-
liners in the administration. Moreover, the president continued to see the shifts
in Soviet foreign and military policy as a consequence of U.S. pressure and
renewed military strength.[82] He was cautious about Gorbachev's domestic
changes as well, although he claims to have taken note of them.[83] According
to Matlock, while these changes did begin in 1987, Reagan's caution was not
entirely misplaced.[84] However, after much negotiation, a date for the Washington summit was set for December 1987.[85]

In contrast to the Reykjavik meeting, the Washington summit was generally thought to have represented progress. Unlike previous encounters, this one
began on a note of considerable warmth between the two leaders. Moreover,
they signed the INF Treaty, in which the United States and the Soviet Union
agreed to destroy all intermediate- and shorter-range land-based missiles and
their launchers and which included "remarkably extensive and intrusive veri-
fication inspection and monitoring arrangements." In addition, they discussed
human rights, bilateral relations, and regional conflicts and agreed to hold
another summit in 1988.[86]

Nevertheless, few considered the Washington summit an unqualified success. As Chernyaev noted, "[T]he INF Treaty was signed in an atmosphere
that I would still describe as a rather high level of mutual mistrust." However,
he also observed, "It was right after the INF Treaty . . . that the character of

our relations changed. And of course, in changing the character of our relations, the personal rapport between Shultz and Shevardnadze and between Gorbachev and Reagan was of great importance. . . . [I]t was after the INF Treaty that our relationship began to evolve in the framework of trust."[87]

On the American side, the reviews were also mixed. Attributing the signing of the INF Treaty to Reagan's having restored America's military and political strength, Secretary Weinberger cautioned that "the restoration of the West's security must not be abandoned to an over-optimistic view of East–West relations."[88] President Reagan himself thought that his own policies had ultimately produced the treaty, and Shultz, while differing from Weinberger in his sense "that a profound, historic shift was under way," also believed that "there is nothing in the 'new political thinking' that suggests that the end of the adversarial struggle is at hand."[89]

Despite these mixed feelings, however, the relationship between Reagan and Gorbachev was progressing rapidly. Moreover, according to Matlock, "From late 1987, . . . we began to register significant results in all parts of the U.S.-Soviet agenda. The speed of change was dizzying for those of us who had worked for decades on what had for long seemed the intractable problems of dealing with USSR."[90]

The Moscow Summit, May 29–June 2, 1988

The Moscow summit meeting saw the culmination of the rapprochement between Reagan and Gorbachev, as well as a substantive change in Reagan's view of the Soviet Union. Ambassador Matlock had been greatly impressed by the changes in the Communist Party program issued in May 1988, and he communicated his excitement to Reagan when he briefed him in Helsinki just prior to the Moscow summit. "I told the president that if they turned out to be real, the Soviet Union could never again be what it had been in the past."[91]

As for the meeting itself, the discussions, although without major breakthroughs, were conducted in a friendly manner.[92] However, the real importance of the summit lay in the impact on Reagan of his visit to Moscow. Impressed by the warmth and friendliness of the Soviet people, he even disavowed his characterization of the Soviet Union as an "evil empire" ("I was talking about another time, another era").[93] As Reagan recalled it, "perhaps the deepest impression I had during this experience and other meetings with Soviet citizens was that they were generally indistinguishable from people I had seen all my life on countless streets in America."[94]

This newfound attitude was tested, but not shaken, by Reagan's firsthand observation of the KGB's rough handling of the crowd during his walk on the streets of Moscow.[95] Indeed, the most interesting aspect of this episode is that it did not have a more negative impact on Reagan's feelings about the Soviet Union, though it clearly confirmed his long-held beliefs. Nor did it deflect his "conversion to a belief in friendly relations" and his respect and admiration for Gorbachev.

> Looking back now, it's clear that there was a chemistry between Gorbachev and me that produced something very close to a friendship. He was a tough, hard bargainer. He was a Russian patriot who loved his country. . . . I liked Gorbachev even though he was a dedicated Communist. . . . [H]e was different from the Communists who had preceded him to the top of the Kremlin hierarchy. . . . [H]e was the first not to push Soviet expansionism, the first to agree to destroy nuclear weapons, the first to suggest a free market and to support open elections and freedom of expression.[96]

On his way home from Moscow, Reagan gave a speech in London that suggests the extent of his transformation. He not only had kind words for Gorbachev ("a serious man, seeking serious reform") but also gave his most optimistic assessment of the future to date: "quite possibly, we're beginning to take down the barriers of the postwar era; quite possibly we are entering a new era in history, a time of lasting change in the Soviet Union. We will have to see."[97]

New York Meeting, December 7, 1988

During the months before the New York summit, relations between the two superpowers were "basically uneventful."[98] Gorbachev continued his efforts to reform the Soviet Union, and, on the day of his meeting with Reagan, gave a pathbreaking speech at the United Nations in which he publicly announced many of those changes. Although many people focused on his most striking pronouncement (that he was prepared to cut half a million troops from the Soviet armed forces), as Shultz noted, "If you read that speech carefully, you will see that for the first time Gorbachev publicly renounced Marxism-Leninism as an approach to the analysis of international issues and international processes."[99]

The meeting between Gorbachev and Reagan later that day, which also included Vice President Bush, was "ceremonial" rather than substantive. Marking the final official encounter between the two leaders, it was notable for its cordiality.[100] Moreover, shortly after Gorbachev left the United States, President Reagan gave a radio address to the nation in which he discussed their meeting in positive terms, noting that "this has been a period of important change inside the Soviet Union" and praising Gorbachev's vision.[101] Secretary Shultz's assessment after his participation in the opening of the General Assembly in September was even more enthusiastic: "The world had changed. Margaret Thatcher had it right . . . [when] she said flatly 'We're not in a Cold War now.' Despite this new reality, many in the United States seemed unable or unwilling to grasp this seminal fact. But to me, it was all over but the shouting."[102]

EXPLAINING REAGAN'S CHANGE
IN THREAT PERCEPTION

By 1988, then, many of the beliefs underlying Ronald Reagan's perception of the Soviet Union as a threat to the United States had been considerably altered, shifting in response to Soviet behavior. Reagan did not change his own ideology (especially his belief in the pernicious nature of communism[103]). However, he did perceive changes in theirs.

After the 1985 Geneva summit, Reagan began to establish a working relationship with Gorbachev and to regard him as a fellow politician with constraints similar to his own. He had also been reinforced in his confidence in his own persuasive powers and his conviction that change in the Soviet Union was possible. After the Washington summit and the signing of the INF Treaty in 1987, Reagan entertained the idea of working with Gorbachev within a framework of genuine trust, while still believing that his own policies had made this possible. Finally, after the Moscow summit, Reagan's perception of the Soviet Union as a threat underwent significant change, and he was imbued with optimism for the future.[104]

While Reagan's perception of the Soviet threat had altered, however, not everyone thought that his new beliefs were well grounded. One stumbling block was that these changes had occurred in the absence of any shift in Soviet capabilities.[105] This was enough to prevent a realist such as Defense Secretary Frank Carlucci from seeing a decline in the Soviet threat,[106] but it had no effect whatever on Ronald Reagan. Although he first attributed the changes instituted by Gorbachev to the pressures of his situation (the American military buildup, SDI, and Soviet economic weakness), ultimately the president was persuaded that real dispositional change had occurred as well.

What are we to make of these changes in Reagan's perception of the Soviet threat? Most versions of rational choice theory hold that "beliefs are formed and updated on the basis of all received information."[107] This, however, is contrary to the model presented in the psychological literature. Just as realists do not expect changes in threat perception without changes in capabilities, cognitive psychologists do not expect such changes to occur readily under any circumstances. Whether the question is viewed in terms of learning theory,[108] belief change,[109] schema theory,[110] images,[111]or attitude change,[112] revising beliefs is thought to be slow and difficult, even in the face of disconfirming information. Such change is even more unlikely if the beliefs in question have any, let alone all, of the qualities that characterized Reagan's perception of the Soviet Union as a threat—if, for example, they are particularly important to the person who holds them,[113] central to his or her belief system (and beliefs about the adversary are thought to be particularly central),[114] linked to other beliefs,[115] strongly held or value laden,[116] held with great confidence,[117] or linked to strong emotion,[118] and if the person has made a public commitment to them.[119]

Thus, Reagan's ability to revise his view of the Soviet threat is something of a puzzle.[120] This might not be true for those with less ideological views such as Shultz, but, as we have seen, Reagan initially held essentialist views much like those of Weinberger and Perle, who unquestionably continued to cling to them.[121] Moreover, while learning theory suggests that learning is more likely in the face of failure,[122] Reagan appears to have revised his beliefs in the face of success. What allowed him to make such changes when others with similar views did not? The evidence suggests a combination of Reagan's personal qualities and a belief system that was somewhat more complex than has usually been attributed to him.

Ideology

Ironically, Reagan's democratic, anti-Soviet ideology, which many considered a fault, may in fact have had the virtue of helping him perceive change in the Soviet Union. Reagan's ideology gave him the sense that the tide of history was moving away from the Soviets and toward democratic freedom. As he said in a 1982 speech in London:

> In an ironic sense Karl Marx was right. We are witnessing today a great revolutionary crisis. . . . But the crisis is happening not in the free, non-Marxist West, but in the home of Marxism-Leninism, the Soviet Union. It is the Soviet Union that runs against the tide of history by denying human freedom and human dignity to its citizens. It is also in deep economic difficulty.[123]

This may have been a simple view of the world, but, as Michael Mandelbaum has pointed out, it was not necessarily wrong,[124] and it seems to have made Reagan more receptive to change in the Soviet Union than he might otherwise have been.[125] For one thing, it sensitized him to the role of ideology in the conflict between the United States and the Soviet Union and perhaps to the significance of ideological change for Soviet foreign policy. For another, it made him more open to the possibility of change altogether. That is to say, Reagan was in some sense primed to accept the reality of change because he already believed it possible, even likely.[126] This, in turn, contributed to his "unquenchable optimism" about the future.[127]

Dual Threats/Dual Goals

Reagan's conviction that the Soviet Union was far from being the only serious threat was as relevant as his ideology in helping him revise his thinking about the Soviet threat. The notion that nuclear weapons were also a grave danger provided Reagan with more than one goal in the security field, and he was untroubled by any sense that his goals were in some way incompatible.[128] Rather, he was able to perceive changes in Soviet behavior that a more consistent person might have dismissed as contradictions.[129]

Some who fail to note the dual nature of Reagan's goals have argued that his inconsistent attitudes toward the Soviet Union were actually due to contradictory beliefs: on the one hand, a "simplistic hardline image of the Soviet Union . . . ; and on the other hand, . . . an equally simplistic, even naïve, liberal faith in the existence of an underlying harmony of interests among men and nations."[130] An uncommitted thinker,[131] Reagan oscillated between the two views according to changes in the situation and the pressure of his advisers.[132]

However, Reagan was not only deeply committed to his basic principles and consistently unwilling to listen to any advice intended to diminish his support for them, but also, rather than vacillating between two sets of incompatible views of the Soviet Union, from at least 1984 he was increasingly concerned about serious threats emanating from *both* the Soviet Union and nuclear weapons. He may not have been cognitively complex, but he did see the problem of threat as having more than one dimension.

Nor did he waver between contradictory policies directed at these threats. Rather, he felt able to concentrate on the nuclear danger (which included attempting to negotiate with the Soviet Union) only after he had—in his own mind, at least—neutralized the Soviet threat by rebuilding America's military strength. Thus, Dobrynin, who was always intrigued by "the paradox of Ronald Reagan," seems closer to the mark in directing us to the "fascinating story of how Reagan's vision of nuclear apocalypse and his deeply rooted but almost hidden conviction that nuclear weapons should ultimately be abolished, would ultimately prove more powerful than his visceral anti-communism."[133]

Strong Principles and Determination

Closely connected to Reagan's belief structure about threat were his firm principles and determination to implement them. There is abundant testimony as to the strength of his "unshakable commitment to a limited number of positions,"[134] including his belief about the dangers of nuclear weapons. Reagan treated these as long-term goals and was not deflected from them by apparent setbacks, nor was he concerned that they violated the "conventional wisdom."[135] Moreover, despite criticism that he was often captive to his advisers, when it came to his principles, Reagan remained in control.[136]

This commitment to principle may have contributed to Reagan's ability to appreciate changes in the Soviet Union in the sense that he perceived and responded to a similar quality in Gorbachev. According to Bessmertnykh, Reagan and Gorbachev "each had their own ideals which they tried to follow all through their lives. Their ideals were not similar, but the dedication to those ideals was similar. They both believed in something. . . . This is what they sensed in each other and this is why they made good partners."[137]

Openness, Attitude to the Future, and Intuition

Other aspects of Reagan's personal style also contributed to his ability to perceive change. For a "putative ideologue," he was strikingly open-minded.[138] By all accounts, Reagan was a good listener and willing to do considerable amounts of homework when the subject interested him.[139] He could also accept criticism gracefully[140] and was capable of a certain amount of empathy. For example, while initially Reagan seemed to have difficulty understanding why the Soviets should see the United States as threatening in any way,[141] after the nuclear scares of 1983, he became sensitive to that possibility.[142]

Closely related to Reagan's openness was his sense of optimism about the future and his willingness to put forward original ideas. Although Reagan was often accused of being doctrinaire, he possessed other qualities, such as a willingness to adopt new ways of thinking, that belied that characterization. Some even thought of Reagan as "visionary,"[143] a man whose approach was anything but incremental, who had "a bold approach and a keen intuition, even if he did not understand many of the important details."[144]

Nor was Reagan hidebound. He had a sense of history yet he was oriented toward the future. Although Reagan's reasoning was clearly less sophisticated and his ability to follow through more limited, Oberdorfer's characterization of Secretary Shultz as one of "the rare policymakers who takes a long view, seeing and thinking in 'time streams' beyond the current day," can in some sense be applied to Reagan as well.[145] Moreover, François Mitterrand, at first "taken aback by Reagan's intellectual emptiness," later concluded that "beneath the surface you find someone who isn't stupid, who has great good sense and profoundly good intentions. What he does not perceive with his intelligence, he feels by nature." This view of Reagan as "a man of finer instincts than intelligence" was also shared by those who believed with Dobrynin that he "grasped matters in an instinctive way but not necessarily in a simple one."[146]

Nor were Reagan's intuitions about trivial matters. Rather, they concerned issues like the viability of the Soviet Union and dangers of nuclear weapons.[147] Thus, the author of a Senate Foreign Relations Committee report noted:

> the President has an intuitive feeling for the larger course of history, the roles assigned by history to Great Powers and the freedom of choice available to leaders who will act—a notion of intuitiveness as being a type of assimilative intelligence of the world about him, a distinctive characteristic of leadership not always perceived by critical observers who tended to underrate his ability and insight.[148]

This notion of intuition as a source of insight recalls Howard Gardner's theory of multiple intelligences, which suggests that people have many different types of ability not covered by the traditional definition of intelligence.[149] Reagan, for example, has been said to possess "emotional intelligence" that guides his intuitions.[150] Thus, his strong emotional reaction to the dangers of nuclear weapons led him to press for their reduction when almost everyone else was content to work for limitation. What is more, he sought a defense against them which had, among other things, the consequence of making the Soviets more cooperative "by threatening to impose unacceptable costs on the already strained Soviet economy."[151] The same emotion was also partly responsible for his desire to negotiate with the Soviets in the first place, helping him to overcome his equally strong anti-Soviet feelings. Moreover, it seems likely that Reagan's characteristic devotion to his principles and his determination to see them carried out were also fired by emotion.

Reagan has been praised for political intelligence as well. This quality manifested itself in a number of ways. First, it affected the cues he responded to. For example, in assessing the Soviet threat, Reagan looked not so much at capabilities as at intentions and, in doing so, was able to focus on the impact of political changes in the Soviet Union which others assessing only capabilities missed.[152]

Second, his political sensitivity made him responsive to Gorbachev's political problems. As Matlock has described it, "[W]here Reagan had a real instinct . . . was as a politician. He understood politicians. We could say about Gorbachev, for example, particularly after he got to know him, 'Hey, Gorbachev's got a problem at home. . . .' He would pay attention to that, he would be willing to take it into account."[153]

Finally, Reagan understood his own political constituency. He was he able to use his popularity and conservative credentials to make his moves toward Gorbachev more acceptable to conservatives.[154] Furthermore, he understood the political climate in the United States well enough to be able to parlay the public's nuclear fears into increasing its acceptance of both negotiations and arms control agreements, instinctively trusting that the American people would follow the path that he himself had traveled.

It seems likely, then, that Reagan's openness and intuitive intelligence contributed substantially to his ability to perceive changes in the Soviet threat.[155] Moreover, the same may be said of his capacity to be more flexible and pragmatic than his "rhetoric" would have suggested possible.[156]

Experiential Learning

While the way Reagan came by his knowledge of the world has often been criticized,[157] in terms of the questions we are addressing here, its effect seems to have been positive. His beliefs flowed "from his life, from personal history rather than study."[158] To make sense of the world, Reagan "crave[d] discourse, not briefing papers." Narrative and experience, rather than analysis and deductive logic, were his tools.[159]

The role stories played in Reagan's thinking has often been noted; he learned by them and told them to convey meaning.[160] Some have objected that his "impressionable" belief system resulted in ill-grounded beliefs, easily changed by the next personal experience.[161] It is not, however, universally agreed that the capacity to learn from one's experience is a handicap. Reagan's (and Gorbachev's) ability to learn from and about one another advanced the dialogue between them and moved the relations between their countries to a new plane which many had longed for but few had ever expected to see.

Belief in Personal Contact

Of course, none of these positive results could have occurred without personal contact between Reagan and Gorbachev, and Reagan, believing that such contact could effect change, was determined that it should take place as often as possible. To him "personal experience counted for everything, and strong personalities could change the world." As Reagan explained in an interview at the time of the Moscow summit, "Systems may be brutish, bureaucrats may fail. But men can sometimes transcend all that, transcend even the forces of history that seem destined to keep them apart."[162] If, as is widely believed, a person's own experiences facilitate learning,[163] then in this case Reagan's instincts served him well.

Moreover, Reagan believed in the efficacy of his own powers of persuasion,[164] and this view was linked to his self-confidence—in both the validity of his own convictions and his ability to implement them.[165] If Reagan was able to see change in the Soviet Union, it is at least partly because he firmly believed that he could help make it happen through personal contact and was confident enough to resist the naysayers among his advisers.[166] Ultimately, his faith was justified by the reaction of the one person who really counted. As Gorbachev himself told the Politburo in December 1987:

> In Washington, perhaps for the first time, we understood so clearly how important the human factor is in international politics. . . . For us, Reagan appeared as a representative of and a spokesman for the most conservative part of the most conservative segment of American capitalism and the military-industrial complex. But . . . policy makers . . . also represent purely human qualities, the interests and the aspirations of common people, and that they can be guided by purely normal human feeling and aspirations . . . . This is an important aspect of the new international thinking, and it has now produced results.[167]

REAGAN AND GOOD JUDGMENT

Ronald Reagan was, then, able to perceive change in the Soviet Union and revise his perception of the Soviet threat accordingly. Moreover, his interpretation was supported by contemporary observers such as Shultz and Matlock, as well as the verdict of later analysts. There is, in fact, considerable evidence that Reagan's initial beliefs about the threat[168] and the nature and timing of his revision of those beliefs were reasonably sound. That evidence supports both Reagan's caution before late 1987 and his acceptance of the importance of the changes instituted by Gorbachev thereafter.[169]

Reagan not only recognized Soviet change, however; he also, as he himself believed, contributed to it. His ideology led him to promote such policies as the U.S. military buildup,[170] SDI,[171] negotiating with the Soviet Union,[172] and broadening the discussion to include human rights and other issues,[173] in the belief that the Soviets would respond to changes in *American* behavior. Many former Soviet officials now agree that these steps did often contribute to the result Reagan desired,[174] and their success in turn encouraged him to continue along the path of trying to influence the Soviet Union, convinced that "it could change if subjected to sufficient pressure and his personal negotiating skill."[175]

What, then, does the success of Reagan's approach to the Soviet Union tell us about his abilities as a leader? Since good outcomes can be the result of any number of factors, including luck, it is unwise to infer automatically that they are a consequence of good processes.[176] In addition to the qualities that allowed Reagan to perceive change, therefore, we must briefly explore the other traits that may have contributed to his effectiveness in this case.

The editors of this volume suggest that judgment is "the quality of analysis, reflection, and insight that informs consequential decisions."[177] Ronald Reagan is unlikely to be the first person who springs to mind when we consider these traits. It is generally agreed that he lacked experience, knowledge, and training in foreign policy. He was sometimes passive, incurious, uninterested in detail, ignorant of the nuances of policy, and stubborn, all of which contributed to a hands–off management style that left him vulnerable to his advisers. However, as we have seen, Reagan possessed other qualities of mind that appear to have compensated for at least some of his failings. When the nature of the problem played to Reagan's particular strengths, his performance could be quite good.

Skills and Temperament[178]

Earlier we noted Reagan's strong principles and determination to implement them. What also mattered was his ability to do so. Certainly, there is little doubt about his impressive "people skills." These were what gave Reagan confidence in personal contact and made it an effective tool for him. His powers of persuasion have been widely recognized,[179] as have his negotiating skills.[180] Moreover, Reagan's openness to information and his capacity to be a good listener must also be noted. The qualities that helped him perceive Soviet change often facilitated his efforts to effect change himself.

While Reagan's skill as the "great communicator" has frequently been acknowledged, however, his ability as a politician has been less often remarked. As we have seen, he was more flexible, pragmatic, and willing to compromise than his ideological orientation led many to expect. Moreover, he was able to sell his policies to the public and use his popularity to get them through Congress—an ability of which he was fully aware.[181] As Fred Greenstein points out, "Reagan was far more than a political front man. He was a politically skilled chief executive whose talents were insufficiently recognized because he was cut from a different cloth from most of those who rise to the nation's highest office."[182]

A number of other qualities that enabled Reagan to be effective have been noted earlier. His clearly defined goals allowed him to concentrate his energies on what was important to him, and his consistency in pursuing them left his subordinates in no doubt about his priorities.[183] Reagan was confident about his own judgment and for the most part made decisions easily. Moreover, when his goals were at stake, he could often assert himself and resist the temptation to delegate his responsibilities.[184]

When he was not so engaged, however, there could be trouble, as Reagan, encouraged by his dislike of detail and content to focus on the big picture, left to others the task of bringing his ideas to fruition. His management style was distinctly hands-off. As a former aide described it, "He made no demands, and gave almost no instructions. . . . Rarely did he ask searching questions and demand to know why someone had or had not done something. He just sat back in a supremely calm, relaxed manner and waited until important things were brought to him." This put Reagan at the mercy of his advisers, with the inevitable result that the system worked well when the his aides were competent and loyal,[185] such as Secretary Shultz, who "enabled Reagan to implement the unexpectedly visionary aspect of his world view."[186] When they were not such paragons, "disaster [could] strike." At such times, as in the Iran-*contra* crisis, not even Reagan's "first class temperament" could save him.[187]

What, then, does this singular mix of attributes and skills tell us about Reagan's leadership abilities? What was it that allowed him to recognize and promote change in the Soviet Union yet failed him so badly in the Iran-*contra* situation? In fact, what stands out is how context dependent good judgment can be. When the nature of the problem played to his particular strengths, his judgment was quite good. But in other situations, these skills could not compensate for Reagan's failings, and some of his strengths became weaknesses.

In perceiving and encouraging change in the Soviet Union, Reagan was able to draw on his strengths. He had long-term goals to which he was deeply committed and vision. His temperament allowed him to be confident, decisive, open to the possibility of change, and optimistic about the future. While not strong on analysis and deductive logic, Reagan possessed good instincts and the intuition that comes from emotional and political intelligence. His political and communication skills were superior. His ideology, vision for the future, and optimism led him to expect change, and his openness and ability to learn from personal experience allowed him to recognize it. His strong principles encouraged him to pursue his dream of a nuclear-free world against the conventional wisdom, and despite his suspicion of the Soviet Union, and to recognize the same desire in Gorbachev. Reagan's determination to support nuclear defense in the face of Soviet opposition gave him unexpected strength at the bargaining table that was reinforced by his political and communications skills. His belief in the importance of personal contact was, at least in this case, not misplaced.

In contrast to Iran-*contra,* what the situation demanded of Reagan to bring his policies to fruition was something he could do. The editors of this volume suggest that one component of good judgment is the ability to "develop . . . , set . . . in motion and maintain . . . a series of steps to accomplish purposes consistent with one's understanding of the issues raised and values at risk."[188] When it came to perceiving and encouraging change in the Soviet Union, those steps required openness and insight, persuasion and negotiation. Unlike the abilities demanded by the Iran-*contra* situation (guiding and controlling staff and a detailed understanding of policy), these were skills that Reagan possessed, and he exercised them willingly. Some tasks are easily delegated, but those at the heart of the enterprise, essential to its success, may not be. In this case, persuasion and communication *were* the essential tasks, and Reagan had no need to delegate them.

What this case suggests about good judgment, then, it that it requires ability in at least four areas: insight into the problem and the capacity to translate this into clear goals (the "vision thing"), the determination to achieve those goals (commitment), the ability to relate them to the appropriate means and to transform them into effective policy (policy understanding), and the capacity to carry out those policies (skill). Within each of these areas, different decision makers may have different abilities (e.g., political and emotional intelligence instead of analytical intelligence, as in Reagan's case) and/or differing amounts of the same ability, and it is sometimes possible to compensate for deficiencies in one area with strengths in another. What is critical, however, is that good judgment often seems to depend on the fit between the nature of the problem and the particular talents of the decision maker. Different domains (type of problem or issue area[189]) may require different abilities. As Machiavelli observed long ago, particular combinations of talents may produce success in some situations but failure in others.[190]

Reagan provides a classic example of this, though not all leaders are likely to exhibit such a huge gap between strengths and weaknesses as he did.[191] As Lou Cannon describes it:

> The paradox of the Reagan presidency was that it depended entirely on Reagan for its ideological inspiration while he depended upon others for all aspects of governance except his core ideas and his powerful performances. In the many arenas of the office where ideology did not apply or the performances had no bearing, Reagan was at a loss.[192]

Reagan could lead the nation and influence his counterparts on the world stage yet fail spectacularly at keeping his own house in order.

NOTES

I would like to thank the Institute of War and Peace Studies at Columbia University for supporting this research, and Deborah Welch Larson and Robert Jervis for their helpful comments.

1. Raymond L. Garthoff, *The Great Transition: American-Soviet Relations and the End of the Cold War* (Washington, D.C.: Brookings Institution, 1994), 1.

2. Garthoff, *The Great Transition,* 767–69. As Thomas Banchoff has observed, no postwar U.S. administration has "altered its view of the threat as significantly as the Reagan administration between 1981 and 1988." Thomas Banchoff, "Official Threat Perceptions in the 1980s: The United States" in *The Changing Analysis of the Soviet Threat,* ed. Carl-Christoph Schweitzer (New York: St. Martin's, 1990), 82.

3. As Janice Stein has put it, "Cognitive psychologists suggest that stability is the default position and change the *exception*" (her emphasis). Janice Gross Stein, "Political Learning by Doing: Gorbachev as Uncommitted Thinker and Motivated Learner," *International Organization* 111 (Spring 1994): 163.

4. See Robert Jervis, *Perception and Misperception in International Politics* (Princeton, N.J.: Princeton University Press, 1976): chap. 7; Yaacov Vertzberger, *The World in Their Minds* (Stanford, Calif.: Stanford University Press, 1990), 113–27; and Deborah Larson, *Anatomy of Mistrust* (Ithaca, N.Y.: Cornell University Press), 32–34. For an example of the Eisenhower administration's persistence in a concept of the Soviet threat rooted in expectations based on past beliefs, see Raymond L. Garthoff, *Assessing the Adversary: Estimates by the Eisenhower Administration of Soviet Intentions and Capabilities* (Washington, D.C.: Brookings Occasional Papers, 1991).

5. Keith L. Shimko, *Images and Arms Control: Perceptions of the Soviet Union in the Reagan Administration* (Ann Arbor: University of Michigan Press, 1991), 236–37, 239–41, 246–47.

6. Richard Neustadt has collected a number of the references that convey Stockman's view. Richard E. Neustadt, "Presidents, Politics, and Analysis," Brewster C. Denney Lecture Series, Institute of Public Management, Graduate School of Public Affairs, University of Washington, May 13, 1986, 17. Others who note Reagan's ignorance and lack of curiosity in matters of policy are Shimko, *Images,* 245–46; Lou Cannon, *Reagan* (New York: Putnam's, 1982), 372–73; Lou Cannon, *President Reagan* (New York: Simon & Schuster, 1991), 130; Alexander L. George and Juliette L. George, *Presidential Personality and Performance* (Boulder, Colo.: Westview, 1988), 224; Richard E. Neustadt. *Presidential Power and the Modern Presidents* (New York: Free Press, 1990), 270, 276; Michael Mandelbaum and Strobe Talbott, *Reagan and Gorbachev* (New York: Vintage, 1987), 128–29.

7. George Shultz, *Turmoil and Triumph* (New York: Scribner's, 1993), 1133; Martin Anderson, *Revolution* (New York: Harcourt Brace, 1988), 289–91; Robert C. McFarlane, *Special Trust* (New York: Cadell & Davies, 1994), 106; Larry Speakes, *Speaking Out* (New York: Scribner's, 1988), 67, 304; Cannon, *Reagan,* 375; Fred I. Greenstein, *The Presidential Difference* (New York: Free Press, 2000), 146, 149; Larry Berman, "Looking Back at the Reagan Presidency" in *Looking Back on the Reagan Presidency,* ed. Larry Berman (Baltimore, Md.: Johns Hopkins University Press, 1990), 5; Cannon. *President Reagan,* 55, 181–82, 304. Reagan's ignorance of nuclear matters is particularly striking; Cannon, *President Reagan,* 291–92, 305.

8. Neustadt, *Presidential Power,* 270, 276, 280. See also Garry Wills, *Reagan's America* (New York: Penguin, 1988), 286, 380. According to Wills, this was a life-long trait: Reagan "quickly isolated a symbolic moral, and devoted all his energies to enforcing that. Details were left to others." He attributes this in part to Reagan's dislike of "unpleasant human

encounters," which led him to keep aloof from the disagreement of his aides. *Reagan's America* (New York: Penguin, 1988), 286, 380.

9. Neustadt, *Presidential Power*, 270–71, 287, 290.

10. Speech to National Association of Evangelicals, March 8, 1983; *Presidential Documents* 19 (March 14, 1983): 369. See also Edmund Morris, *Dutch* (New York: Random House, 1999), 642.

11. The term "existential threat" has been used by Daniel Lieberfeld to connote a threat to basic security or national existence. Daniel Lieberfeld, *Talking with the Enemy* (Westport, Conn.: Praeger, 1999). See also Ronald Reagan, *American* (New York: Simon & Schuster, 1900), 265; Frances Fitzgerald, *Way Out in the Blue* (New York: Simon & Schuster, 2000), 30–31; interview with Walter Cronkite, March 3, 1981, cited in Beth A. Fischer, *The Reagan Reversal: Foreign Policy and the End of the Cold War* (Columbia: University of Missouri Press, 1997).

12. Speech, March 1983, cited in Banchoff, "Official Threat," 87–88; campaign speech, June 1980, cited in Garthoff, *Great Transition*, 12. Such beliefs were by no means idiosyncratic. Not only were they held by almost the entire administration, but beliefs about the aggressive nature of the Soviet Union were firmly rooted in American thinking as well. See Garthoff, *Assessing the Adversary*, 1; Don Oberdorfer, *The Turn: From the Cold War to a New Era, the United States and the Soviet Union, 1983–1990* (New York: Poseidon, 1991), 95; and Mandelbaum and Talbott, *Reagan*, 170. Shimko distinguishes between hard-line images that virtually the whole administration held and inherent bad-faith enemy images that only some, like Caspar Weinberger and Richard Perle, shared with Reagan; see Shimko, *Images*, 233.

13. See Reagan, *American*, 14; Garthoff, *The Great Transition*, 12–13; Betty Glad, "Black-and-White Thinking: Ronald Reagan's Approach to Foreign Policy," *Political Psychology* 4 (March 1983): 44–46, 67; Fischer, *Reagan* , 81–82; and Shimko, *Images*, 101, 120.

14. As Shimko points out, however, the Soviet government "was assumed not to reflect the desires of its people." *Images*, 146.

15. Shimko, *Images*, 372, 374.

16. Reagan, *American*, 14, 267. See also Margaret Thatcher, *The Downing Street Years* (New York: HarperCollins, 1993), 159; Garthoff, *Great Transition*, 8; Glad, "Black and White," 45; and Banchoff, "Official Threat," 88.

17. Reagan, *American*, 548, 239. See also 265–68.

18. Cited in Garthoff, *Great Transition*, 14. See also 22. Shimko, *Images*, 103–4; Fischer, *Reagan*, 19–20. On the administration's view of the political and military threat, see Banchoff, "Official Threat," 83–87.

19. Garthoff, *Great Transition*, 20. See also Banchoff, "Official Threat," 88.

20. Reagan, *American*, 238–39; Garthoff, *Great Transition*, 19–20, 24, 26.

21. Cited in Garthoff, *Great Transition*, 8. Shimko notes that "Virtually every statement [by Reagan] about Soviet global ambitions was accompanied by claims that these impulses were the logical outcome of Soviet ideology. According to Reagan, 'that religion of theirs, which is Marxis[m]-Leninism, *requires* them to support and bring about a one-world Communist state'" (italics added). *Images*, 106. See also 235 and Reagan's remarks in his press conference in March 1981, cited in Banchoff, "Official Threat," 87. For more on the ideo-

logical basis of Reagan's views about Soviet intentions, see Gathoff, *Great Transition*, 33, 98; Edwin Meese, *With Reagan* (Washington, D.C.: Regnery Gateway, 1992), 164, 169; Oberdorfer, *Turn*, 90; and Soviet Ambassador Dobrynin's account of Secretary of State George Shultz's description of Reagan as "stubborn and ideologically unprepared for agreements with the Russians." Anatoly Dobrynin, *In Confidence* (New York: Random House, 1995), 81. See also Eduard Shevardnadze, *The Future Belongs to Freedom* (London: Sinclair-Stevenson, 1991), 81.

22. Reagan, *American*, 294; Garthoff, *Great Transition*, 41. See also Fischer, *Reagan*, 20; Shimko, *Image*, 102–3, 108–11; Caspar Weinberger, *Fighting for Peace* (New York: Warner, 1990), 34; Oberdorfer, *Turn*, 32; and McFarlane *Special Trust*, 218.

23. Reagan, *American*, 23738; Meese, *With Reagan*, 164–65, 169. See also Garthoff, *Great Transition*, 11; Shimko, *Image*, 142–44; Fitzgerald, *Way Out*, 175, n. 106.

24. Reagan, *American*, 294–95. See also Weinberger on his first meeting with the president-elect, *Fighting*, 34–35; McFarlane, *Special*, 218–19; Shimko, *Images*, 102, 144; Fischer, *Reagan*, 26.

25. This buildup, according to Garthoff, "had been decided on before obtaining requests from the military services—it was intended to signal the strong resolve of the new administration to build ('rebuild') military strength." Garthoff, *Great Transition*, 33. As Garthoff also notes, despite the fact that in 1983 the Scowcroft Commission report refuted the idea of a "window of vulnerability" for the United States and the CIA found no "spending gap" between the United States and the Soviet Union, the military buildup continued. Moreover, at least some members of the administration (Weinberger, Perle) exaggerated the Soviet threat to gain support for that buildup (33, 504).

26. Reagan, *American*, 266. See also Shimko, *Images*, 103.

27. Reagan, *American*, 549, 550, his italics. See also Shultz, *Turmoil*, 246.

28. See, for example, his speech to the Republican National Convention in 1976. Anderson, *Revolution*, 71–72; Neustadt, *Presidential Power*, 277.

29. Fischer, *Reagan*, 106–8; Anderson, *Revolution*, 80–83; Oberdorfer, *Turn*, 25–26, 67; Shultz, *Turmoil*, 261–62. On Reagan's beliefs about Armageddon, see Morris, *Dutch*, 632–33. Fitzgerald views the NORAD story as a dramatization of Reagan's long-standing horror of nuclear weapons, with Reagan himself at the center of the drama as an "American Everyman." *Way Out*, 20–29.

30. Weinberger, *Fighting*, 341; Reagan, *American*, 550.

31. Reagan, *American*, 550.

32. Shultz, *Turmoil*, 260–64; Garthoff, *Great Transition*, 99. See also Thatcher, *Downing Street*, 463, 466. For Reagan's interest in strategic defense between 1979 and 1983 when he announced his program to the American people, see Anderson, *Revolution*, 75–76, 84–88, 93–97.

33. As Garthoff points out, in the first eight months of 1983, Soviets leaders sought without success to engage the United States in serious arms control negotiation. *Great Transition*, 111. See also Alexander M. Haig Jr., *Caveat: Realism, Reagan, and Foreign Policy* (New York: Macmillan, 1984), 131.

34. Shultz, *Turmoil*, 159, 164–66, 267; Jack F. Matlock, *Autopsy on an Empire* (New York: Random House, 1995), 77; Oberdorfer, *Turn*, 16; Garthoff, *Great Transition*, 104.

35. Shultz, *Turmoil*, 164–65; Oberdorfer, *Turn*, 16–17.

36. Reagan, *American*, 572. For developments in the spring and summer of 1983, see also Matlock, *Autopsy*, 79.

37. "Soviet-American Relations," *Weekly Compilation of Presidential Documents*, January 16, 1984, 20, 41. For references of this sort to common interests in 1983 and 1985, see Keith L. Shimko, "Reagan on the Soviet Union and the Nature of International Conflict," *Political Psychology* 13 (September 1992): 371–72.

38. "Soviet-American Relations," 42. For an analysis of this speech, see also Garthoff, *Great Transition*, 142–44; and Dobrynin, *In Confidence*, 545. For an extremely optimistic view of the speech as the "turning point in his administration's approach to the Kremlin," see Fischer, *Reagan*, 3–4, 32–38. Throughout 1984, Reagan returned to many of the ideas expressed in this speech. In April, he declared that "a nuclear war cannot be won and must never be fought" and emphasized the need to "reduce the risk of nuclear war and to reduce the levels of nuclear armaments." In June and in September (in a speech before the United Nations General Assembly), he reiterated his desire for better relations with the Soviet Union. Cited in Garthoff, *Great Transition*, 152, 156, 161. For other conciliatory moves by Reagan and his administration, see Fischer, *Reagan*, 40–45.

39. Cited in Garthoff, *Great Transition*, 153. For other negative comments, see also 154, 160. These negative references culminated in the Republican Party's 1984 election platform (adopted by a Reagan-controlled convention) that affirmed that "the Soviet Union's globalist ideology and its leadership obsessed with military power make it a threat to freedom and peace on every continent" (157).

40. Garthoff, *Great Transition*, 157.

41. Oberdorfer, *Turn*, 22–23. See also the similar view of Assistant Secretary of European and Canadian Affairs Rozanne Ridgway in *Witnesses to the End of the Cold War*, ed. William C., Wohlforth (Baltimore, Md.: Johns Hopkins University Press, 1996), 18.

42. Fischer, *Reagan*, 109.

43. Reagan, *American*, 584. See also Matlock's view that "there was a serious concern, beginning with President Reagan, about the lack of communication following KAL." Wohlforth, *Witnesses*, 76. Note that despite the fact that this incident had brought the nuclear threat to the fore, it also confirmed Reagan's view of the *Soviet* threat. Reagan, *American,* 585. For a more detailed account of this episode, see Fischer, *Reagan*, 112–14; and Garthoff, *Great Transition*, 118–27, who also discusses Soviet reactions.

44. Reagan, *American*, 585. See also Fischer, *Reagan*, 115–20. Of course this event, as well as the other incidents, took place in the context of the widespread nuclear fears American society as a whole was experiencing at the time, culminating in the nuclear freeze movement, an atmosphere of which the president was undoubtedly aware. My thanks to an anonymous reader for pointing this out.

45. Reagan, *American*, 585–86. Fischer offers a psychological explanation for the impact of these events on Reagan; *Reagan*, 120–22.

46. Garthoff, *Great Transition*, 138–40. See also Oberdorfer, *Turn*, 66–67; and Fischer, *Reagan*, 122–34.

47. Reagan, *American*, 588–89. See also Thatcher, *Downing Street*, 324; Garthoff, *Great Transition*, 139, 142n; Oberdorfer, *Turn*, 67; and Fischer, *Reagan*, 134–38. Some evidence

indicates that Reagan held such beliefs as early as 1982; see Shimko, *Images*, 107; and "Reagan," 365, 369–70. Reagan's renewed sense of nuclear threat also heightened his interest in nuclear defense. Thus, "several weeks" after the October 1983 SIOP briefing, Reagan, "convinced we had to do everything possible to develop a defense against the horrible weapons of mass destruction that the atomic age had produced, . . . gave a go-ahead to speed up research on the Strategic Defense Initiative." Reagan, *American*, 286.

48. Glad points out that Reagan harbored a long-standing belief that if confronted with strength and aware that they could not win, the Soviets would give up and back down. "Black-and-White Thinking," 64.

49. According to Robert Jervis, "behavior is influenced by leader' perceptions and beliefs about their own nations (self-perceptions). A state that sees itself in decline is likely to see others and to behave very differently from one that conceives of itself as continuing to be strong, if not dominant." Robert Jervis, "Perception and Misperception, and the End of the Cold War," in *Witnesses*, 228. The putative success of his military buildup also allowed Reagan's personal confidence in his own abilities to come to the fore. Matlock, *Autopsy*, 77; Oberdorfer, *Turn*, 22.

50. Reagan, *American*, 594, his italics. See also Thatcher, *Downing Street*, 324; and Garthoff, *Great Transition*, 769.

51. "Soviet American Relations," January 16, 1984, 41. For the September UN speech, see Garthoff, *Great Transition*, 161. See also Oberdorfer, *Turn*, 35–36.

52. Shultz, *Turmoil*, 6.

53. Shultz, *Turmoil*, 159–67, 265–70; Garthoff, *Great Transition*, 102–10; Reagan, *American*, 605–6; Matlock, *Autopsy*, 77–78; Oberdorfer, *Turn*, 34–37; McFarlane, *Sacred*, 295.

54. Reagan, *American*, 606. For evidence that Shultz, too, believed that his views accorded with those of the president, see *Turmoil*, 165–66, 270–71. Of course, it probably did not hurt Shultz's case that Nancy Reagan was also in his camp. McFarlane, *Sacred*, 295; and Oberdorfer, who cites Mrs. Reagan's own testimony on the subject, *Turn*, 91.

55. Oberdorfer, *Turn*, 52. See also Shultz, *Turmoil*, 270.

56. Garthoff, *Great Transition*, 102, 152. See also Reagan's own allusion to the campaign and foreign policy; *American*, 605.

57. Garthoff, *Great Transition*, 161, n. 58, and 163–64. Dobrynin notes, "It is now clear that the turn [from confrontation and mutual escalation] began during the presidential election year of 1984. How much the election campaign had to do with it, no one will ever really know." *In Confidence*, 552. For the opposite view that the forthcoming election was "probably the most important" reason for the change, see Banchoff, who also cites pressure from U.S. allies. However, he, too, notes the importance of the U.S. buildup. "Official Threat," 89.

58. On the basis of a psychological analysis, Beth Fischer argues that this shift represented a real change in Reagan's perception of threat. *Reagan*, 2–5, 135, 141, 146–56. The evidence presented earlier shows otherwise. Reagan changed his emphasis and some policies, but his view of the Soviet threat remained the same.

59. Greenstein also notes this combination. "Ronald Reagan," 215.

60. Garthoff, *Great Transition*, 167; Oberdorfer, *Turn*, 23; Matlock, *Autopsy*, 80. See also

Alexander Dallin, "Learning in U.S. Policy toward the Soviet Union in the 1980s," in *Learning in U.S. and Soviet Foreign Policy,* ed. George W. Breslauer and Philip E. Tetlock (Boulder, Colo.: Westview, 1991), 415.

61. Garthoff, *Great Transition,* 197. Nevertheless, Reagan's inaugural and State of the Union speeches still stressed the Soviet threat and the consequent need for a U.S. buildup and SDI. Garthoff, *Great Transition,* 201–2.

62. Shultz, *Turmoil,* 532. See also Garthoff, *Great Transition,* 207, n. 27; and Thatcher's widely quoted assessment of Gorbachev as a "man we can do business with." *Downing Street,* 463.

63. See Mandelbaum and Talbott, *Reagan,* 44.

64. Reagan, *American,* 615; Garthoff, *Great Transition,* 208. Nevertheless, he also "resumed crusading rhetoric, charges of Soviet untrustworthiness, and reaffirmations of SDI" (213).

65. McFarlane, *Sacred,* 308. McFarlane himself remembers working "harder, probably, than I ever had or would again." This included one hundred meetings with Reagan and eleven NSC meetings (312). See also Oberdorfer, *Turn,* 142; and Garthoff, *Great Transition,* 234.

66. Garthoff, *Great Transformation,* 235–37; "United States–Soviet Summit in Geneva, Address to the Nation," November 14, 1985, *Weekly Compilation of Presidential Documents* 21 (November 18, 1985): 1399; Reagan, *American,* 628.

67. Shultz, *Turmoil,* 606. See also the remarks of Ridgway in *Witnesses,* 18; and Dobrynin, *In Confidence,* 596.

68. Matlock in *Witnesses,* 22–23.

69. Shultz, *Turmoil,* 607; Dobrynin, *In Confidence,* 595. See also Shultz in *Witnesses,* 16; and Oberdorfer, *Turn,* 54.

70. Shultz, *Turmoil,* 607, 606; Oberdorfer, *Turn,* 54; Mikhail Gorbachev, *Perestroika* (New York: Harper & Row, 1987), 227; Pavel Palazchenko, *My Years with Gorbachev and Shevardnadze* (University Park: Pennsylvania State University Press, 1997), 43. See also *Witnesses,* 11.

71. Wohlforth, *Witnesses,* 22; Garthoff, *Great Transition,* 239.

72. Garthoff, *Great Transition,* 247.

73. By Garthoff, for example—*Great Transition,* 239.

74. See Garthoff, *Great Transition,* 236. As Shultz has noted, Reagan and Gorbachev "spent almost five of the fifteen hours of official meetings talking together privately." *Turmoil,* 606.

75. Shultz, *Turmoil,* 265–84; Matlock, *Autopsy,* 94.

76. Garthoff, *Great Transition,* 283–84; Matlock, *Autopsy,* 94–95.

77. Wohlforth, *Witnesses,* 163; Matlock, *Autopsy,* 95–96; Garthoff, *Great Transition,* 285–88; Palazchenko, *My Years,* 54–57. For Reagan's own account of Reykjavik, see *American,* 675ff. For Gorbachev's, see *Perestroika,* 236–44. For a contemporary view of Reagan's "acceptance of the notion of total strategic nuclear disarmament" at Reykjavik as a narrowly averted strategic disaster for the United States, see James Schlesinger, "Reykjavik and Revelation." in *The Reagan Foreign Policy,* ed. William G. Hyland (New York: New American Library, 1987), 247.

78. Reagan, *American*, 683.

79. Wohlforth, *Witnesses*, 175, 174; Matlock, *Autopsy*, 96–97. See also Reagan, *American*, 683–84; Palazchenko, *My Years*, 57–58; and Garthoff, *Great Transition*, 291; Gorbachev, *Perestroika*, 240; Speakes, *Speaking*, 143. For a considerably less rosy assessment, see Thatcher, *Downing Street*, 470–71. Reagan himself thought that "Gorbachev was ready to talk the next time we met in Washington because we had walked out on him at Reykjavik and gone ahead with the SDI program." *American*, 684.

80. Dobrynin, *In Confidence*, 610; Matlock, *Autopsy*, 97. See also the testimony on this subject of Gorbachev's personal adviser, Anatoly Chernyaev, in Wohlforth, *Witnesses*, 109.

81. Matlock, *Autopsy*, 98; Reagan, *American*, 684. For a detailed account of this period, see Garthoff, *Great Transition*, 291–99.

82. In late February, Gorbachev proposed eliminating all intermediate-range forces in Europe without any preconditions and began to redefine Soviet military doctrine "to stress the prevention of war and a defensive doctrine should war nonetheless occur." Garthoff, *Great Transition*, 305–6, 308–9, 316.

83. Reagan, *American*, 686–87; Garthoff, *Great Transition*, 315.

84. "Radical and ambitious as [Gorbachev's] thoughts were, his proposals were, to say the least, incomplete. They pointed in the right direction, but contained both false premises and surprising gaps." Matlock, *Autopsy*, 65–66.

85. For these negotiations, see Garthoff, *Great Transition*, 320–25.

86. Garthoff, *Great Transition*, 325–27. For an analysis of these discussions, see 327–32.

87. Wohlforth, *Witnesses*, 49. See also Gorbachev's statement to the Politburo, December 17, 1987, quoted later.

88. Weinberger, *Fighting*, 332.

89. Garthoff, *Great Transition*, 332, 335; see also Shultz, *Turmoil*, 1003.

90. Garthoff, *Great Transition*, 332; see also Matlock, *Autopsy*, 148.

91. Matlock, *Autopsy*, 121–23. For Matlock's impressions of the changes in Soviet ideology, see 142–47.

92. For the substance of the discussions, see Garthoff, *Great Transformation*, 353–56; and U.S. Congress, House, Committee on Foreign Affairs, *Soviet Diplomacy and Negotiating Behavior—1988–90: Gorbachev–Reagan–Bush Meetings at the Summit* (Washington, D.C.: U.S. Government Printing Office, 1991), 71–72.

93. Oberdorfer, *Turn*, 299, 294–95; Reagan, *American*, 709; Garthoff, *Great Transformation*, 352. See also Hugh Sidey, "Good Chemistry," *Time*, June 13, 1988, 14.

94. Reagan, *American*, 709. See also Sidey, "Good Chemistry," 17.

95. "I've never seen such brutal manhandling as they did on their own people who were in no way getting out of hand." Reagan, *American*, 709. See also Thatcher, *Downing Street*, 776; Oberdorfer, *Turn*, 296–97.

96. Garthoff, *Great Transition*, 253; Reagan, *American*, 707. Reagan voiced the same highly positive view of Gorbachev even while he was still in Moscow and not long after his return to Washington, acknowledging that he considered Gorbachev a "real friend." Sidey, "Good Chemistry," 17; *Soviet Diplomacy*, 111. See also Morris, *Dutch*, 647.

97. "Remarks to Members of the Royal Institute of International Affairs in London, United Kingdom," June 3, 1988, *Weekly Compilation of Presidential Documents* 24 (June 6,

1988): 735. See also remarks on June 2 quoted in Banchoff, "Official Threat," 83; and Garthoff, *Great Transition*, 357–58. Reagan struck a similar note after the Soviet Union agreed to withdraw from Afghanistan. Banchoff, "Official Threat," 91. By contrast, Vice President Bush was cautioning the public several weeks later that "the Cold War is not over." Cited in Bancroft, "Official Threat," n. 41. See also Larson, *Anatomy*, 224–225. On his return to Washington, the president described the Moscow meeting as "momentous" and spoke of his " 'sense of hope, powerful hope' for improvement in Soviet-American relations." *Soviet Diplomacy and Negotiating Behavior,* 73.

98. See Garthoff, *Great Transformation,* 368–71.

99. Wohlforth, *Witnesses,* 91. See also Shultz, *Turmoil,* 365–67.

100. Garthoff, *Great Transition,* 371.

101. "Radio Address to the Nation on Soviet–United States Relations," December 10, 1988, *Weekly Compilation of Presidential Documents* 24 (December 19, 1988): 1613–14.

102. Shultz, *Turmoil,* 1131. By contrast, Garthoff stresses the limits "of the new thinking in American policy." *Great Transition,* 372

103. Fischer, *Reagan,* 148–49.

104. Even Shimko, who minimizes Reagan's belief change, acknowledges that his "comments about the 'unchanging' Soviet system virtually disappeared by 1986–87 . . . [and] would soon be replaced by thoughts of 'a new era in history, a time of lasting change in the Soviet Union.' " *Images,* 108. See also 119. On Shimko's views about the minimal nature of Reagan's belief changes, see 107; and Shimko, "Reagan," 363.

105. Jervis, "Perception," 226. Interestingly enough, Janice Stein has pointed out that the changes in Gorbachev's "cognitive constructs" also could not have been caused by changes in Soviet military capabilities which had not, in fact, declined. "Political Learning," 157. As Garthoff observed after reviewing the strategic relationship between the United States and Soviet Union from 1981 to 1991, "The actual strategic balance was not only stable but also had remarkably little impact on developments." Garthoff, *Great Transition,* 538. See also John Mueller, "Quiet Cataclysm," in *The End of the Cold War,* ed. Michael J. Hogan (Cambridge: Cambridge University Press, 1992), 41–42.

106. "[W]e must be guided by realism, not wishful thinking. The West's security preparations must be based not Kremlin declarations, but on actual Soviet military capabilities." Garthoff, *Great Transition,* 533.

107. Dan Reiter, *Crucible of Beliefs* (Ithaca, N.Y.: Cornell University Press, 1996), 38.

108. Reiter, *Crucible,* 34; and "Learning, Realism, and Alliances," *World Politics* 46 (July 1994): 493–94.

109. Philip E. Tetlock, "Social Psychology and World Politics," in *Handbook of Social Psychology,* ed. D. Gilbert, S. Fiske, and G. Lindzey (New York: McGraw-Hill, 1998) 880, and also "Theory-Driven Reasoning about Plausible Pasts and Probable Futures in World Politics: Are We Prisoners of Our Preconceptions?" *American Journal of Political Science* 43 (April 1999): 337–38; J. F. Voss, C. R. Wolfe, J. A. Lawrence, and R. A. Engle, "From Representation to Decision: An Analysis of Problem Solving in International Relations," in *Complex Problem Solving: Principles and Mechanisms,* ed. R. J. Sternberg and P. Frensch (Hillsdale, N.J.: Erlbaum, 1991), 131–33; Yaacov Vertzberger, *The World in their Minds* (Stanford, Calif.: Stanford University Press, 1990), 118–23.

110. Reiter, *Crucible*, 21–24; Stein, "Political Learning, 163–64; Deborah Larson, "The Role of Belief Systems and Schemas in Foreign Policy Decision–Making," *Political Psychology* 15 (March 1994): 29.

111. Martha Cottam and Dorcas E. McCoy, "Image Change and Problem Representation after the Cold War," in *Problem Representation in Foreign Policy Decision Making,* ed. Donald A. Sylvan and James F. Voss (Cambridge: Cambridge University Press, 1998), 117–18, 123.

112. Jervis, *Perception*, chap. 7; Jon A. Krosnick, "Attitude Importance and Attitude Change," *Journal of Experimental and Social Psychology* 24 (1988), 240–55.

113. Krosnick, "Attitude," 240–41; Cottam and McCoy, "Image Change," 118.

114. Vertzberger, *World*, 118–19, 137.

115. Krosnick, "Attitude," 240.

116. Cottam and McCoy, "Image Change," 118.

117. Tetlock, "Social Psychology," 880; Vertzberger, *World*, 120.

118. Vertzberger, *World*, 120, 137; Cottam and McCoy, "Image Change," 123; Stein, "Political Learning," 169.

119. Krosnick, "Attitude," 241.

120. The notion that Reagan would make such changes was also contrary to the expectations of his contemporaries. See, for example, Garthoff, *Great Transition*, 2, 338.

121. For a comparison of Reagan's image of the Soviet Union with that of his advisers, see Shimko, *Images*, 233–37, 224–25. On Weinberger, see Weinberger, *Fighting*, 37, n. 5, 331–32, 347–51; Garthoff, *Great Transformation*, 531–32.

122. Reiter, *Crucible*, 35, 39 and "Learning," 490; Stein, "Political Learning," 173.

123. Cited in Banchoff, "Changing," 88. See also Thatcher, *Downing Street*, 258; Patrick Glynn, *Closing Pandora's Box* (New York: Basic Books, 1992), 327; Shimko, *Images,* 142–44; U.S. Congress. *Soviet Diplomacy*, 69, 115; Michael Mandelbaum, "The Luck of the President," in *Reagan Foreign Policy*, 132; and Shultz's remarks in an interview with Peter Schweizer: "President Reagan just had an innate sense that the Soviet Union would not, or could not, survive. . . . That feeling was not based on a detailed learned knowledge of the Soviet Union; it was just instinct." In *Victory* (New York: Atlantic Monthly Press, 1994), xiii.

124. Mandelbaum, "The Luck of the President," 140–41, 132.

125. For quite a different view, see Arthur Schlesinger Jr., who, writing in 1983, recognizes the ideological basis of Reagan's thought but has nothing good to say about it and does not foresee a capacity for change. "Foreign Policy and the American Character," *Foreign Affairs* 62 (Fall 1983): 5–7. Gary Wills, too, has scant respect for Reagan's ability to think historically: "He has a skill for striking 'historical' attitudes combined with a striking lack of historical attentiveness." *Reagan's America*, 63; see also 446–47. For Reagan's lack of historical understanding during the Bitburg controversy, see Cannon, *President Reagan*, 588.

126. Dobrynin, *In Confidence*, 549; Matlock in *Witnesses*, 22; Dallin, "Learning," 416. Fischer uses the concept of priming somewhat differently to explain how Reagan's reaction to the events of the fall of 1983 "primed" him to take the nuclear threat more seriously. *Reagan*, 110–12.

127. Cannon, *President Reagan*, 179; Cannon, *Reagan*, 319, 337, 347–48; U.S. Congress, *Soviet Diplomacy*, 69, 114.

128. See the remarks of Ambassador Ridgway in *Witnesses*, 18. On Reagan's general trait of harboring contradictory convictions and commitments, see Neustadt, *Presidential Power*, 277–78. Wills, referring to both conservative and liberal elements in Reagan's political belief system, notes that "All these personae were always present in him, and were not felt to be at odds. Like much of America, he contained contradictions, but never experienced them." *Reagan's America*, 307. See also Oberdorfer, *Turn*, 22; Neustadt, "Presidents," 19.

129. Fischer explains this in terms of increased cognitive complexity which allowed him to distinguish the Soviet leaders who shared his "concerns about international security and nuclear war" from communists in general. *Reagan*, 149.

130. Shimko, *Reagan*, 354–57, 359, 374.

131. John D. Steinbruner, *Cybernetic Theory of Decision* (Princeton, N.J.: Princeton University Press, 1974), 129–31.

132. Shimko, *Images*, 240–42; "Reagan," 354–57, 359, 374. For evidence to the contrary, see Cannon, *President Reagan*, 481.

133. Dobrynin, *In Confidence*, 606. See also 607–8.

134. Thatcher, *Downing Street*, 157–58, 257; McFarlane, *Special Trust*, 106; Speakes, *Speaking*, 301; Cannon, *Reagan*, 372–73; George and George, *Presidential Personality*, 225; Greenstein, *Presidential Difference,* 165–57.

135. Shultz in *Witnesses*, 104. See also George and George, *Presidential Personality*, 224. As a former aide observed, "Reagan is one of the toughest men I have ever known. . . . Once [he] has determined what he thinks is right, and what is important to do, then he will pursue that goal relentlessly." Anderson, *Revolution*, 288. See also Shultz, *Turmoil*, 145, 463; Dobrynin, *In Confidence*, 608–9; Cannon, *President Reagan*, 134. On Reagan's determination as a general character trait, see Cannon, *Reagan*, 218. As Secretary Shultz and others have pointed out, this quality also had its downside and was regarded as obstinacy by those who wanted Reagan to change his mind. Shultz, *Turmoil*, 145, and remarks in *Witnesses*, 104. For a striking example of this stubbornness during the Iran-*contra* crisis, see Cannon, *President Reagan*, 630.

136. Fischer, *Reagan*, 155–56; Greenstein, *Presidential Difference*, 154–55.

137. Wohlforth, *Witnesses*, 107. On the importance of this kind of connection between Reagan and Gorbachev, see Fred Greenstein, "Ronald Reagan, Mikhail Gorbachev, and the End of the Cold War." In *Witnesses*, 218–19; remarks of Ridgway and Shultz, 115, 104. Both Greenstein and Ridgway view Secretary Shultz as a kindred spirit of the two leaders in this regard.

138. Greenstein, "Ronald Reagan," 214. See also Matlock's remarks in *Witnesses*, 114.

139. "Ronald Reagan knew what he didn't know, and he was willing to listen." Matlock in *Witnesses*, 114. See also McFarlane's testimony about Reagan's preparations for the Geneva summit, in the section "The Geneva Summit, November 19–21, 1985"; Speakes, *Speaking*, 301; and Cannon, *Reagan*, 372, and *President Reagan*, 748–49, 763.

140. Cannon, *Reagan*, 140, 372. As Matlock put it, "You felt perfectly free to correct him. I quickly learned that you could tell him what you thought. . . . He didn't take it as a personal insult. He knew he didn't know everything. He knew he didn't know much about the Soviet Union." Wohlforth, *Witnesses*, 114.

141. Garthoff, *Great Transition*, 105, 139. See also Fischer, *Reagan*, 21. As Stein and others

have pointed out, decision makers often have difficulty in empathizing with the other side. "Building," 250–51.

142. See the section "Heightened Sense of Nuclear Threat" and Garthoff, *Great Transition*, 139; Oberdorfer, *Turn*, 67. Shimko finds evidence of this attitude even earlier. "Reagan," 365, 369–70, and *Images*, 107. See also Reagan, *American*, 595, 588–89. Garthoff, however, criticizes Reagan for his lack of insight into the impact of his harsh words on the Soviet leaders. *Great Transition*, 105.

143. "Ronald Reagan had visionary ideas. In pursuing them, he displayed some of his strongest qualities: an ability to break through the entrenched thinking of the moment to support his vision of a better future." Shultz, *Turmoil*, 263. See also, Greenstein, *Presidential Difference*, 156–57; Cannon, *Reagan*, 372, *President Reagan*, 281, 740.

144. Soviet journalist Aleksandr Bovin, cited in Oberdorfer, *Turn*, 438, and Greenstein, "Ronald Reagan," 215.

145. Oberdorfer, *Turn*, 439.

146. Morris, *Dutch*, 442, 445, 495; Dobrynin, *In Confidence*, 494. See also Wills, *Reagan's America*, 384; Neustadt, *Presidential Power*, 309, and "Presidents," 16–23; Greenstein, *Presidential Difference*, 157; Cannon, *President Reagan*, 133–36, 140. For evidence of Reagan's intuitive approach earlier in his career, see Cannon, *Reagan*, 155. On the possible virtues of simplicity, see Peter Suedfeld, "Are Simple Decision Always Worse?" *Society* 25 (1988): 25–27.

147. On the former, see Shultz in an interview with Schweitzer, *Victory*, xiii; and Thatcher, *Downing Street*, 467. On the latter, see Jervis, "Perception," 227. See also Senate Foreign Relations Committee, *Soviet Diplomacy*, 115.

148. Senate Foreign Relations Committee, *Soviet Diplomacy*, 115.

149. Cannon, *Reagan*, 137–38. As Cannon describes his own response to learning of this theory:

> [Reagan] understood all manner of things that suggested powers of analysis without possessing any visible analytical ability. The mistake that I and others made was in trying to fit Reagan into a preconception of the way an "intelligent politician" behaves. This made no sense, for anyone who has spent any amount of time with Reagan knows he is unlike other politicians. I knew he was intelligent, but in his own terms. It was only when Gardner's theory helped me throw the mold away that I could say what I had always seen. (138)

Inability to see Reagan's strengths in other areas may in part account for the "contempt" for him inspired in many intellectuals. Thomas Mann, "Thinking about the Reagan Years," in Berman, *Looking Back*, 20.

150. According to Greenstein, emotional intelligence is a person's "ability to manage his emotions and turn them to constructive purposes, rather than being dominated by them and allowing them to diminish his leadership." *Presidential Difference*, 6; as applied to Reagan, see 157; and "Reckoning with Reagan," *Political Science Quarterly* 115 (Spring 2000): 121–22. On the connection between emotion and intuition, see Deborah Larson, "Good Judgment in Foreign Policy," a paper presented to the American Political Science Association, San Francisco, Calif., August 1997, 5–6.

151. Greenstein, *Presidential Difference*, 154.

152. This political sensitivity was also seen in President Franklin Roosevelt's diagnosis of the German threat after he had observed Hitler's behavior during the Munich crisis. Barbara R. Farnham, *Roosevelt and the Munich Crisis* (Princeton, N.J.: Princeton University Press, 1997), chap. 5.

153. Wohlforth, *Witnesses*, 114. See also Thatcher, *Downing Street*, 301.

154. See Shultz's remarks in Wohlforth, *Witnesses*, 104–105. See also Greenstein, *Presidential Difference*, 155. On Reagan's ability to handle his right-wing supporters on the domestic front, see Cannon, *Reagan*, 316. On political decision makers' responses to the problem of acceptability, see Farnham, *Roosevelt*, chap. 2.

155. As Vertzberger has pointed out, the opposite is true for those with closed cognitive systems. The more the system is closed, the more decision makers "are convinced that they do not need additional information, the less intensive is the search for additional information and the less likely is attention to new information and attitude change to occur." *World*, 134.

156. See Dobrynin, *In Confidence*, 610; Anderson, *Revolution*, 284; Speakes, *Speaking*, 301; Cannon, *Reagan*, 186, 309; Mandelbaum, "Luck," 134.

157. Morris, *Dutch*, 414–15; Shimko, *Images*, 120; Neustadt, *Presidential Power*, 290–91.

158. Leslie Gelb, quoted in Shimko, *Images*, 120. See also Cannon, *President Reagan*, 134.

159. Cannon, *President Reagan*, 376, 139; George and George, *Presidential Personality*, 224. As Howard Gardner concluded, "Reagan's good with language, but not logically. . . . He makes sense of the world narratively. Scientists can be deductive and understand logic but often can't tell stories. Stories are not necessarily logical." Cannon, *President Reagan*, 138. Also noted in Greenstein, *Presidential Difference*, 157.

160. Secretary Shultz, at first irritated by Reagan's love of stories, began to see a positive side:

> [H]e used a story to impart a larger message—and sometimes that message was simply more important to him than the facts. He was a gifted storyteller, who could use a story effectively to make his point take on a deeper and more vivid meaning or to defuse a tense situation. People, he felt, believe in and act on the stories they hear and tell about the past. Stories create meaning. (*Turmoil*, 1133)

See also Cannon, *President Reagan*, 120–22; the testimony of Martin Anderson, *Revolution*, 139–40; and Donald T. Reagan, *For the Record* (New York: Harcourt Brace, 1988), 249–50. However, Cannon also notes that on another occasion, Reagan's commitment to his stories inhibited him from seeing change in the Marcos regime. *President Reagan*, 364.

161. Shimko, *Images*, 116, 120.

162. Mandelbaum and Talbott, *Reagan*, 5; Sidey, "Good Chemistry," 17. See also the section "The Geneva Summit, November 19–21, 1985," and Reagan, *American*, 14; Matlock, *Autopsy*, 77; Shultz, *Turmoil*, 145; Carlucci in Wohlforth, *Witnesses*, 46; Dallin, "Learning," 415. On the positive impact of the two leaders' mutual bluntness, see Shultz, *Turmoil*, 8, 16. On the similar impact on Reagan's beliefs of his personal experience of China, see Garthoff, *Great Transition*, 636; Cannon, *President Reagan*, 482.

163. Jervis, *Perception*, 239–49; Reiter, *Crucible*, 34–35, 37, 39.

164. Cannon, *Reagan*, 745.

165. On the former, see Shultz in Wohlforth, *Witnesses*, 103–105; Dobrynin, *In Confidence*, 608; Anderson, *Revolution*, 286; George and George, *Presidential Personality*, 224–25. On the latter, see Thatcher, *Downing Street*, 157; Shultz, *Turmoil*, 262–63; Wills, *Reagan's America*, 383, 392; Mandelbaum and Talbott, *Reagan*, 129.

166. Greenstein, "Reckoning," 121.

167. Quoted by Chernyaev in Wolhforth, *Witnesses*, 49.

168. As described by Samuel F. Wells Jr.,:

> In reassessing the origins and dynamics of the Cold War from the admittedly one–sided evidence that is currently available, several fundamental conclusions emerge. American officials on occasion did exaggerate the magnitude of the Soviet threat and the malignant intent of Soviet leaders, but . . . it is incorrect to contend that there was no serious threat. A Soviet challenge to a stable world and to U.S. interests in democratic political systems and open economies clearly existed.

Samuel F. Wells Jr., "Nuclear Weapons and Nuclear Security during the Cold War," in Hogan, *End*, 64; see also 65–66 and Garthoff, *Great Transition*, 752–57.

169. See Matlock, *Autopsy*; Mandebaum and Talbott, *Reagan*, 86–87; William J. Jackson, "Soviet Reassessment of Ronald Reagan, 1985–1988," *Political Science Quarterly* 113 (Winter 1998–99): 629–42; Philip Zelikow and Condoleezza Rice, *Germany Unified and Europe Transformed* (Cambridge, Mass.: Harvard University Press, 1997), 15–16, 19; Garthoff, *Great Transition*, 753; Mueller, "Quiet Cataclysm," 41. This view is contrary to Glad's analysis of Reagan as a black-and-white thinker who might be able to change his perceptions, but only after an inordinate amount of "negative evidence." "Black-and-White Thinking," 72. For evidence of the contrast between Reagan's ability to perceive change in the Soviet Union and the inability of the CIA to do so, see Philip Taubman, "How the C.I.A.'s Judgments Were Distorted by Cold War Catechisms," *New York Times,* March 18, 2001.

170. U.S. Congress, *Soviet Diplomacy*, 115. See also David A. Stockman, *Triumph of Politics* (New York: Harper & Row, 1986), 274; Garthoff, *Great Transition*, 353.

171. Reagan "emphasized that—in addition to his earlier arguments in favour of SDI—keeping up with the United States would impose an economic strain on the Soviet Union. He argued that there had to be a practical limit as to how far the Soviet Government could push their people down the road of austerity" (Thatcher's report of a conversation in 1982). *Downing Street*, 467. See also 463; and Reagan, *American*, 548. For an appraisal of the relationship of SDI to changes in the Soviet Union, see Condoleezza Rice, "U.S.-Soviet Relations," in Berman. *Looking Back*, 85–86.

172. Garthoff, *Great Transition*, 102; Shultz in Wohlforth, *Witnesses*, 104–5; Mandelbaum and Talbott, *Reagan*, 170–71; Greenstein, *Presidential Difference*, 154.

173. Matlock in Wohlforth, *Witnesses*, 54; Matlock, *Autopsy*, 77, 148–50.

174. Reagan's conciliatory policies toward the Soviet Union enabled Gorbachev to forge ahead in his domestic and international initiatives. As Dobrynin noted, "If Reagan had stuck to his hard-line policies in 1985 and 1986, . . . Gorbachev would have been accused by the rest of the Politburo of giving everything away to a fellow who does not want to negotiate. We would have been forced to tighten our belts and spend even more on defense." Cited

in Greenstein, "Reckoning," 121. See also Dobrynin, *In Confidence*, 609; Jackson, "Soviet Reassessment." In Wohlforth, *Witnesses*, see the testimony of Bessmertnykh on the impact of SDI (47–48) and the pressure of the arms race (164–65); Chernyaev on the U.S. success in broadening the talks beyond arms control to include other areas (166). In the same volume, see also the analyses of Wohlforth (193) and George (244, 249). For the testimony of others on this point, see Mandelbaum, "Luck," 133; Mandelbaum and Talbott, *Reagan*, 153; Thatcher, *Downing Street*, 813; Wells, "End," 65–66, 73; Glynn, *Pandora's Box*, 341–43, 347–48, 351–52, 357–59; Greenstein, *Presidential Difference*, 154–55; Mann, *Thinking*, 25. Garthoff, however, disagrees with this assessment. See, for example, *Great Transition*, 753, 765, 769.

175. Matlock, *Autopsy*, 77. See also Jervis, "Perception and Misperception," n. 14.

176. On the other hand, Renshon, though recognizing the pitfalls, takes the view that "judgments must be assessed, in part, by reference to outcomes." Stanley A. Renshon, "Psychology and Good Judgment," *Political Psychology* (September 1992): 478.

177. Larson, chap. 1 of this volume. See also Renshon. "Psychology of Good Judgment," 483.

178. For the relevance of these qualities to good judgment, see Philip E. Tetlock, "Is It a Bad Idea to Study Good Judgment?" *Political Psychology* (September 1992): 429–34; Renshon. "The Psychology of Good Judgment"; and Etheridge; "Wisdom," *Political Psychology* (September 1992): 497–516.

179. See, for example, Cannon, *Reagan*, 333, 371; Speakes, *Speaking*, 301; Cannon, *President Reagan*, 122. According to Wills, this is no accident: Reagan "is a passionate believer in his cause and one who works very hard to present it well. This means that he studies everything he and his government do very closely, but from a selective angle, looking first and most intently at what can be done to make the action or idea as attractive to as many people as possible. This gives him a focus that is admittedly partial, but extremely effective." Wills, *Reagan's America*, 381. For an example of Reagan's sensitivity to the nuances of communications, see Marlin Fitzwater, *Call the Briefing* (New York: Random House, 1995), 163–64.

180. See Bessmertnykh in Wolhforth, *Witnesses*, 107; Shultz, *Turmoil*, 145. See also Anderson, *Revolution*, 241, 284–86; and Greenstein, *Presidential Difference*, 150–51, 156, and "Ronald Reagan," 122.

181. Greenstein, *Presidential Difference*, 156; Anderson, *Revolution*, 284; Cannon, *Reagan*, 319, and *President Reagan*, 102, 116.

182. Greenstein, "Reckoning," 122. This assessment has been echoed by Russians such as Bessmertnykh and Evgeniy Primakov ("he is a great political leader"). U.S. Congress, *Soviet Diplomacy*, 116; Wohlforth, *Witnesses*, 108. On Reagan's political skill, see also Neustadt, "Presidents," 17–23.

183. Greenstein, "Reckoning," 122, and "Ronald Reagan," 215; Neustadt, "Presidents," 17.

184. Anderson, *Revolution*, 286; Fischer, *Reagan*, 80–81, 155–56.

185. Anderson, *Revolution*, 289–92. See also Regan, *For the Record*, 266–69, 294.

186. Greenstein, "Ronald Reagan," 217. In the case at hand, according to Oberdorfer, "Schultz provided two key ingredients that otherwise were lacking: a persistent and practi-

cal drive toward the goal of improved relations through the accomplishment of tangible objectives, . . . and organizational skills to mobilize at least parts of the fractious U.S. government to interact on a systematic basis with the Soviet government." *Turn*, 439. See also Cannon, *President Reagan*, 309–10, 373.

187. Anderson, *Revolution*, 292. Greenstein notes that Oliver Wendell Holmes's characterization of Franklin Roosevelt could be applied to Reagan as well (from the manuscript for *Presidential Difference*, 243). Elsewhere, Greenstein points to Reagan's emotional stability and lack of anxiety. "Reckoning," 122. See also Cannon, *President Reagan*, 180. As Neustadt points out, FDR also delegated authority, but differed from Reagan in that his "delegations were time-limited and shifting . . . , whereas Reagan, it seems, could delegate blindly year after year. The one man evidently knew what he was delegating and conducted himself accordingly; the other may have had little or no idea." Neustadt, *Presidential Power*, 273. See also 270, 276, 279–91; and Greenstein, "Reckoning," 118–21. Wills compares Reagan's delegations of authority unfavorably to President Eisenhower's. Eisenhower was aware of what was going on in his administration and manipulated it; Reagan did not. *Reagan's America*, 379–81. See also Cannon, *President Reagan*, 308, 339–41, 362, 373–75, 499–500. On the difference between Chiefs of Staff Baker and Regan in their impact on Reagan, see 564*ff.*

188. Larson, chap. 1 of this volume.

189. Renshon mentions this in "Psychology and Good Judgment," 485.

190. Niccolò Machiavelli, *The Prince* (New York: Penguin, 1981), 131–32.

191. Of course, President Carter did exhibit such a gap between his analytical ability, on the one hand, and his lack of political sensitivity, on the other. See Greenstein, *Presidential Difference*, 141–42; Farnham, *Roosevelt*, 240, n. 47.

192. Cited in George and George, *Presidential Personality*, 225.

· 7 ·

Culture and Emotion as Obstacles to Good Judgment

The Case of Argentina's Invasion of the Falklands/Malvinas

David A. Welch

$\mathcal{N}$ico Jacobellis, a movie theater manager in Cleveland Heights, was convicted and fined under Ohio's obscenity laws for showing the 1959 Louis Malle film *Les Amants*. Pleading constitutional protections of free expression, he pursued his case all the way to the Supreme Court. Justice Potter Stewart, concurring in the Court's reversal of his conviction, insisted that the First Amendment protected all but "hard-core pornography." "I shall not today attempt further to define the kinds of material I understand to be embraced within that short-hand description," Stewart wrote, "and perhaps I could never succeed in intelligibly doing so. But I know it when I see it, and the motion picture involved in this case is not that."[1]

Good judgment is a bit like pornography. It is hard to define, but you generally know it when you see it.

One reason why it is hard to define good judgment is that we normally think of it as having two individually necessary but jointly sufficient dimensions. First, we are reluctant to praise someone for exercising good judgment if she hasn't gone through a certain kind of decision-making process. It need not necessarily closely resemble, say, a technically high-quality subjective expected utility maximization, but at the very least we require that she be attentive to the stakes, to her options, to their likely outcomes, and, where relevant, to the interests and likely responses of others. We also require that her decision reflect a sound and subtle understanding of the world. Thus, we do not praise lottery winners for having exercised good judgment in buying tickets, because lotteries are almost always bad gambles that intelligent, well-informed people will avoid. Good luck and good judgment are two different things.

At the same time, we are reluctant to say that someone has exercised good judgment if things don't turn out well. Intuitively, we tend to feel that if things go badly, then there must have been an option that someone with better judgment would have preferred. We do not easily praise the judgment of an investor, for example, who loses money on a venture that, in prospect, looked like a sure thing.

Good judgment is also hard to define because it is a generic quality that manifests itself in rather different ways in different contexts. Exercising good judgment in a casino requires nothing more than a little mathematical savvy and self-control. Exercising good judgment at sea requires much more (e.g., an extensive knowledge of weather and navigation). Exercising good judgment while being mugged, driving a car, or counseling abused children requires different sets of abilities and dispositions.

A "theory" of good judgment, of course, would specify its necessary and sufficient conditions in detail and would somehow take into account the full range of relevant skills and attitudes. It is the purpose of this book as a whole to help bring us closer to a theory of good judgment, at least with respect to foreign policy decision making. My purpose in this chapter is much more limited: to help us better understand good judgment by contrasting it with bad. I am concerned here with exploring a particular set of obstacles to good judgment that I believe may fruitfully be lumped under the labels "culture" and "emotion."

Uncharitable readers will no doubt point out that culture, too, is hard to define, even if we know it when we see it, and that emotion is an enormous conceptual umbrella covering an unwieldy array of psychological phenomena. True enough. But I wish to make the simple case here that good judgment in foreign policymaking can require circumspection and empathy, and that culture and emotion can be obstacles to both. We can see this clearly in a case in which an inability to transcend culture and emotion led to flawed decisions that we cannot imagine someone having chosen who was not thus constrained.

The Argentine decision to invade the Falkland/Malvinas Islands in 1982 is just such a case.[2] By any standard, the Argentine junta exercised poor judgment—at several points along the way. A Third World country with largely dated military equipment, a conscript army, and virtually no power-projection capability took on a technologically sophisticated, nuclear-armed great power with a modern blue-water fleet and an experienced professional army over territorial stakes of negligible strategic and material value. It did so without an operational plan and without the capability to hold the islands in the face of a British attempt to retake them. The Argentine junta completely misjudged the international reaction to its seizure of the islands, and in particular it misjudged the attitude of the United States. The invasion effectively destroyed a tense but otherwise mutually beneficial relationship between Britain and Argentina, two countries that had every incentive to maintain civil ties and to keep channels of communication open. When the dust settled, Argentina stood defeated and humiliated on the world stage, its relations with advanced Western countries were in tatters, and the junta—disgraced—lost power and served jail terms.[3] It is hard to resist the conclusion that they should have known better. And that, I submit, is the quintessence of poor judgment.

Why did the Argentine junta misjudge so badly? Since the relevant history is not common knowledge, it would perhaps be wise to begin with a short narrative.

BACKGROUND

In the 1770s, Samuel Johnson described "Falkland's Island" as

> a bleak and gloomy solitude, an island thrown aside from human use, stormy in winter and barren in summer; an island which not even the southern savages have dignified with habitation; where a garrison must be kept in a state that contemplates with envy the exiles of Siberia; of which the expense will be perpetual and the use only occasional; and which, if fortune smiles upon our labours, may become a nest of smugglers in peace, and in war the refuge of future buccaneers.[4]

Actually a group islands rather than one (two major, more than two hundred minor), Argentina calls them Las Malvinas, after the first permanent settlers from St. Malo, and Britain calls them the Falkland Islands, after an obscure naval official.[5] Both countries claim sovereignty. Argentina bases its claim largely on historical right, arguing that in 1833 Britain violated the colonial title it inherited from Spain when the Royal Navy seized the islands and evicted the then Spanish-speaking inhabitants. Britain bases its claim largely on the islanders' right of self-determination. While various British officials have come close to admitting the injustice of the 1833 occupation from time to time, Whitehall maintains that the controlling fact is that the overwhelming majority of the Falkland Islanders (known colloquially as "Kelpers") are to all intents and purposes British and wish to remain so.[6]

In 1965, the United Nations called upon the two countries to settle their dispute. The British Foreign Office was happy to oblige, since the islands were of negligible strategic and economic value, and since the interests of the islanders (so the bureaucrats believed) depended on closer ties to the mainland. The two countries negotiated a Memorandum of Understanding in August 1968 whose crucial passage stated:

> The Government of the United Kingdom as part of . . . a final settlement will recognise Argentina's sovereignty over the islands from a date to be agreed. This date will be agreed as soon as possible after (i) the two governments have resolved the present divergence between them as to the criteria according to which the United Kingdom Government shall consider whether the interests of the Islanders would be secured by the safeguards and guarantees to be offered by the Argentine Government, and (ii) the Government of the United Kingdom are then satisfied that those interests are so secured.[7]

But the Islanders would have none of it. In a deft display of domestic political prowess, they convinced the British public that the Foreign Office was on the verge of selling them out, forcing the government to pledge that the *wishes* (not "interests") of the Islanders were "an absolute condition" for any deal.[8] Attempts to entice the Islanders by enabling them to sample the benefits of closer links to Argentina—most notably, through the Communications Agreement of 1971, which established air service to the mainland, bringing the Islanders regular supplies of fresh fruit, produce, other goods, and tourists—failed utterly.[9] The 1976 coup that brought a ruthless military dictatorship to Argentina extinguished any flickering ember of willingness to entertain a transfer of sovereignty that even the most mainland-minded Kelper might have harbored. From that point on, the two countries found themselves at a stalemate.

The mere fact of negotiations on sovereignty, however—coupled with professions from the Foreign Office that Britain truly desired to arrange a formal transfer—encouraged Argentine hopes and expectations, and confirmed Argentina's belief in the legitimacy of its claim. Argentine frustrations grew, and Argentine patience wore thin. January 3, 1983, would mark the sesquicentennial of the British occupation, and this date acquired an artificial but powerful significance in the Argentine imagination as a self-imposed deadline for the "recovery" of the islands.

No one felt this more acutely than Admiral Jorge Isaac Anaya (pronounced "Anasha"), commander in chief of the navy, who was the driving force behind Argentina's policy on the Malvinas under the junta that came to power in December 1981. Anaya's lifelong ambition was to recover the Malvinas for Argentina.[10] He made this a condition of his support for his boyhood friend, Leopoldo Galtieri, in the latter's bid for the presidency. Galtieri and the third member of the junta, commander in chief of the air force Brigadier Basilio Lami Dozo, needed no persuading as to the goal, although Lami Dozo—the least influential of the three—was disposed to be more cautious than his colleagues on the question of means. The three ultimately agreed, however, that if necessary, they would use military force in support of diplomacy to achieve their objective by their self-imposed deadline.

Military contingency planning began shortly after the junta took power. Jesús Iglesias Rouco, a journalist with close ties to the regime, warned in *La Prensa* that Argentina would present Britain with a series of "firm and clear" conditions for the continuation of negotiations, including a strict deadline for a resolution. He hinted that Argentina might use military means to recover the islands if Britain proved intransigent.[11] On January 27, the Ministry of Foreign Affairs delivered a *bout de papier* to the British ambassador calling for negotiations concluding "within a reasonable period of time and without procrastination" in the recognition of Argentine sovereignty. Britain agreed to hold a series of talks in New York but refused to accept preconditions on the outcome.

Talks in New York never got beyond a preliminary discussion of the negotiating framework, as they were overtaken by events on South Georgia, one of the "Falkland Islands Dependencies" seven hundred miles southeast of Port Stanley over which—along with the South Sandwich Islands—Argentina also claimed sovereignty (see figure 7.1). Constantino Davidoff, an Argentine scrap metal dealer under contract with a Scottish firm to salvage an abandoned whaling station, arrived at Leith Harbour aboard the Argentine naval transport *Bahía Buen Suceso* without reporting for entry to the British Antarctic Survey station at Grytviken. As this was the second time in four months that Davidoff

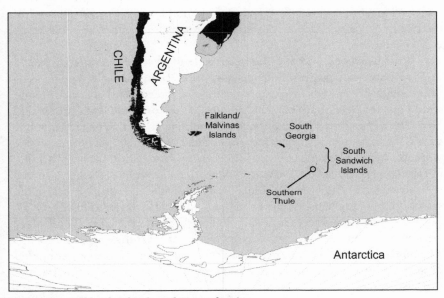

Figure 7.1   Falklands Islands and Dependencies

had failed to observe the necessary formalities on South Georgia, and as his Argentine naval transports observed strict radio silence while in transit on both occasions, British authorities became suspicious that Davidoff's voyages were deliberate challenges to British sovereignty.

These suspicions may have been well founded. The Argentine navy saw Davidoff's contract as an opportunity to assert Argentine sovereignty on South Georgia, and in September 1981, they began planning "Project Alpha," by which Argentine marines would infiltrate Davidoff's team of workers and establish a permanent presence on the island. The aim was to repeat a similar operation that had taken place on Southern Thule, in the South Sandwich Islands, in 1976, where Argentina had covertly established a "scientific station." In that case, Britain had protested but had not insisted on the removal of the Argentine base. However, in February 1982, Argentine Foreign Minister Nicanor Costa Méndez recommended that Project Alpha be postponed, so as not to complicate the forthcoming negotiations in New York. On February 17, the junta agreed. Nevertheless, there is some indication that the navy—without the knowledge either of the junta as a whole or of its own commander in chief—decided to proceed.[12] The British government, informed by the members of the British Antarctic Survey that the Argentine party included military personnel, resolved not to permit a repeat of Southern Thule. The junta, believing that Project Alpha had been shelved and convinced that London had no valid objection to Davidoff's presence on South Georgia (he was there under contract to a British firm and with the full knowledge and approval of the British embassy in Buenos Aires), became suspicious of Britain's unexpectedly vehement reaction.

What happened next is a classic example of how misunderstandings and misperceptions can trigger unintended escalation. Both countries' foreign ministries sought to smooth over the incident, and agreed that *Bahía Buen Suceso* would quietly leave South Georgia, as indeed it did on March 22. The British, however, assumed that Davidoff's party would be aboard and issued a public statement that evening reporting Argentina's agreement to withdraw the workers. When it became clear that Argentine personnel had been left behind, the British press played the event as an Argentine "invasion" of South Georgia. On the advice of Falklands Governor Rex Hunt and other hard-liners on the sovereignty issue, Prime Minister Margaret Thatcher ordered HMS *Endurance*—a lightly armed ice patrol ship and at that time the only Royal Navy vessel in the South Atlantic—to South Georgia to evict the Argentine party.[13] The junta, determined not to permit such a humiliation, ordered a second ship in the vicinity, the ice patrol vessel *Bahía Paraíso,* to land a party of marines at Leith to protect Davidoff's men.

Both countries still sought to avoid a confrontation at this point and searched for a mutually satisfactory face-saving formula. Costa Méndez proposed that the Argentineans on South Georgia present themselves at Grytviken to be issued "white cards." These had served as travel documents for Argentineans in the Malvinas since the Communications Agreement of 1971. Not being passports, they ingeniously finessed the sovereignty issue. Hunt, however, insisted that white cards were not valid on South Georgia, because the Communications Agreement applied only to the Falklands proper, not to the dependencies. He successfully lobbied his government to demand that the Argentineans at Leith have their passports stamped if they wished to remain.

For the junta, this was the last straw. Permitting *Endurance* to evict Davidoff's party, or acquiescing in the British demand that they present their passports, would be tantamount to acknowledging British sovereignty over South Georgia and, by extension (so they believed), over all of the disputed territories, including the Malvinas proper. In Anaya's view, "This was aggression on the part of Britain against the territory of Argentina."[14] It is important to note that the junta believed this quite literally. From their perspective—a perspective certainly not shared by policymakers in Britain or other observers in the West—Britain's actions in the South Georgia incident represented the first attempt to force an end to the sovereignty dispute.

On the evening of March 26, the junta decided to occupy the Malvinas as soon as the necessary military preparations could be completed.[15] Crucial to the timing of the decision was an erroneous intelligence report that a British nuclear submarine had left Gibraltar for the South Atlantic the previous day. The junta believed that with *Endurance* in the vicinity of South Georgia, Argentina had a narrow window of opportunity in which to act without the possibility of the Royal Navy interfering. The plan—code-named "Operation Rosario"—was to land five hundred men to capture and disarm the forty-two-man garrison of Royal Marines at Port Stanley and to evict the British governor, without shedding any British blood. The force would then withdraw, Argentina would place the islands under temporary international administration, and Britain and Argentina would finalize an agreement recognizing formal Argentine sovereignty over the islands and safeguarding the "interests" of the Islanders.

The junta believed that a bloodless touch-and-go operation would signal Argentina's firm resolve on the sovereignty dispute and give the necessary impetus to stalled diplomacy without inflaming international outrage. The junta certainly had no expectation that it would trigger a British military response. Westerners find this difficult to believe—or if they believe it, they take it as evidence of incompetence and naïveté. This reflects an important difference in perspective. Unlike the junta, most Westerners understood the Argentine occupation of the islands as an aggressive act. The British people certainly saw it this way, perhaps none so strongly as Prime Minister Margaret Thatcher.[16] Not only would Britain's historical sensitivity to appeasement rule out acquiescence in such a coup, so also would Thatcher's public commitment to defend the self-determination of the Islanders.[17] To Western eyes, it seemed quite obvious that Britain was very unlikely to accept anything short of a return to the status quo ante, and it seemed preposterous to think that the Argentine occupation would set in train the sequence of events intended by the junta. Thus, it is clear that the junta miscalculated.

Not only did the junta miscalculate; it failed to stick to its script—or, more accurately, Galtieri failed to do so. When news of the occupation broke on April 3, spontaneous wild celebrations erupted in the streets of Buenos Aires. Just a few days earlier, the same crowd had filled the Playa de Mayo to demonstrate *against* the military regime. Now they were cheering, screaming, crying, singing, and waving Argentine flags. Standing on the balcony of the Casa Rosada, basking in his reception as *Libertador de Las Islas Malvinas,* Galtieri was overcome with emotion. Said one senior Argentine official who asked not to be identified, "He did not expect this. He knew that he was unpopular with the people. But the crowds made him feel like a hero, and it went to his head. He decided unilaterally to countermand the withdrawal, and to declare that Argentina would never leave the Malvinas. It was an understandable emotion, but with hindsight it was a big mistake. It tied our hands." Anaya and Lami Dozo, standing behind him, looked at each other, dumbfounded.

Events now began to unfold in ways the junta simply did not anticipate. Far from evincing greater willingness to fast-track a transfer of sovereignty, the British began to gird their loins for battle. Instead of supporting Argentina, the government of the United States first cast itself in the role of neutral mediator (while actually supporting Britain, both morally and materially) and then came off the fence and sided with Britain outright.[18] While governments in Latin America professed their sympathy with Argentina's goal, they were uneasy with Argentina's choice of means, and none offered Argentina any useful support. The Chileans actively supported the British. Diplomacy did go into high gear at the United Nations, and various parties floated various clever formulae to allow both countries to save face and avoid conflict. But since London and Buenos Aires were both entrenched on matters of principle, they failed to avert bloodshed. The war was not a costly one by historical standards, but it certainly shocked everyone—Britain and Argentina included.

WHERE DID ARGENTINA GO WRONG?

The junta's reasons for believing that the occupation would not trigger further escalation are instructive and demonstrate the vital importance of perspective:

- The junta believed that Britain's unexpectedly vehement response to the South Georgia incident constituted the first act of aggression in the conflict. They therefore believed that Argentina—not Britain—was the country forced to choose between appeasement and demonstrating resolve. As Galtieri put it, "Everything has to be put in the larger context of Britain pushing Argentina up against the wall."[19]
- The junta believed that the Argentine cause was just and that the international community was broadly sympathetic. They expected that world leaders would accept (and some even applaud), rather than condemn, a bloodless use of military force in the pursuit of a just end, especially since Argentina was sending troops into what many countries—including virtually all of Latin America—considered to be Argentine territory. Moreover, Argentina was carrying out the operation in pursuit of a principle endorsed by the United Nations—namely, decolonization.
- The junta knew that Britain held a crucial advantage over Argentina at the United Nations, by virtue of its permanent seat on the Security Council. But they believed that either China (because of Hong Kong) or the Soviet Union (because of its geopolitical rivalry with the United States and Britain) would veto a resolution unfavorable to Argentina.
- The junta believed that the United States would restrain Britain and encourage Thatcher to negotiate a final diplomatic settlement, because of (1) Argentina's support for American policy in Central America, (2) Argentina's value to the United States as a bulwark against communism in the Southern Cone, (3) the Monroe Doctrine, and (4) Washington's desire not to be seen supporting a European colonial power against a Latin American country.[20]
- The junta believed that Britain would not be inclined to attempt a military response. First, the physical distance of the Falklands/Malvinas from British bases represented a considerable logistical obstacle. Second, they believed that Margaret Thatcher would be unwilling to make the necessary effort—and pay the necessary political price internationally—to redeem the demands made on her by a mere 1,800 people of British descent. Third, they judged that Thatcher would consider maintaining cordial relations with Argentina more important than fulfilling her pledges to the Islanders. If for any reason Thatcher were inclined to attempt a military response, the junta believed that she would pay heed to American calls to exercise restraint.

On this last point, the junta relied specifically and heavily on the advice of Costa Méndez, an experienced diplomat who, of all senior Argentine officials, should have been most able to anticipate the Western perspective and the Western response. Anaya recalls:

> Costa Méndez's view was that, from [Suez in] 1956, Britain's behavior was always to deal, but not on the basis of force. Rhodesia was the most recent example. There, Britain had abandoned 600,000 British subjects. The sum of perceptions led to the conclusion that Britain would not respond with force. . . . When we met on March 26, Costa Méndez explained the situation and said British actions required military action in order to get them to negotiate seriously. We respected his intellect and his achievements. . . . He had a great deal of experience. He advised us to take military action. How could we doubt his judgment?[21]

Thus, when Argentine commandos stormed ashore in the early morning hours of April 2, decision makers in Buenos Aires did not believe that Argentina was the first to use force to solve the sovereignty dispute, and they did not anticipate further military conflict. Accordingly, Argentine military plans included no provision for defending the islands against a possible British response. As the Argentine military governor of the islands, General Mario Benjamin Menéndez, recalled, "There was nothing in the plans about what would happen after five days. The last entry was, 'D + 5: Menéndez becomes governor.' "[22]

To understand the junta's miscalculations, it is helpful to understand the ideational context in which they arose. Galtieri, Anaya, and Lami Dozo were all strong Argentine nationalists. Generically, Argentine nationalism is probably little different from other forms of nationalism. It reflects an imagined community, in Benedict Anderson's now-famous characterization, and comes with the emotional attachments and symbolic appurtenances typical of other varieties of nationalism.[23] The intensity of nationalist feeling is difficult to gauge rigorously, but Argentine nationalism would appear to be a particularly virulent strain. Foreigners commonly remark on this, often pointing to the example of Argentina's World Cup victory in 1978, which sent the country into paroxysms of national euphoria completely out of proportion to the nature of the achievement.[24]

Argentine nationalism differs from many other nationalisms in one crucial respect: the Argentine imagined community has no ethnic basis. It is a purely civic nationalism. It did not arise naturally from kinship ties but had to be engineered by political elites. In the Argentine case, this was a daunting task. The Argentine population is polyglot and multicultural, composed mainly of various European immigrant communities. In this respect, it differs little from neighboring populations. To cultivate a sense of national identity—and thus a sense of loyalty to the regime—it was necessary, Argentine leaders felt, to find ways of distinguishing "us" from "them" that inflamed a passionate sense of unity and attachment. Playing up what Michael Ignatieff (borrowing from Freud) aptly calls a "narcissism of small differences,"[25] Argentine leaders culti- vated civic nationalism by promoting national myths of loss, defeat, and humil- iation at the hands of Argentina's neighbors. Carlos Escudé has tracked the use of irredentist claims in Argentine schoolbooks and has discovered that bureau- crats in the education ministry deliberately distorted history so as to convince Argentine schoolchildren that various countries had inflicted grievous territo- rial wrongs against the fatherland over the years. At different times, Uruguay, Chile, and Britain have played the role of nemesis.[26] Interestingly, the very junta that ordered the invasion in 1982 was the first cohort to be socialized politically during the period of time in which the textbooks raised the Malvinas to the top of the Argentine irredentist agenda.

Like many other varieties of nationalism, Argentina's also exaggerates the country's international role and importance.[27] This exaggeration interacted synergistically with another key feature of the ideational landscape in 1982: the dominance of realpolitik among Argentina's leaders and foreign policy estab- lishment. When attempting to anticipate the actions of other countries, Argen- tina's leaders assumed that they would be guided largely by considerations of power and narrow material self-interest.

Taken together, this inflated sense of self and the conviction that the world reaction would be shaped by realpolitik had fatal consequences. From a global perspective, of course, Britain was by far the more powerful country. Its popu- lation was almost twice that of Argentina, and its gross domestic product, in purchasing power parity, was almost four times as big. Moreover, Britain was a nuclear power, a member of the European Community, and a member of NATO. More countries had greater material incentive to support Britain than Argentina. Certainly the United States did. And the junta's misreading of American politics stands out as one of its more egregious errors.

It is true that Washington was initially of two minds, because the brewing conflict between Britain and Argentina was a no-win proposition for the United States. But there should have been no question of where American sympathies lay or of where the United States would come down if forced to choose.[28] One group felt from the beginning that the United States should openly support Britain. This was by far the stronger group, not only because of its numbers and seniority but also because its view resonated with public opinion. It included President Ronald Reagan, Secretary of Defense Caspar Weinberger, Secretary of State Alexander Haig, Undersecretary of State for European Affairs Lawrence Eagleburger, and a majority of officials at all levels in the foreign policy establishment. This group shared the British view that the self-determination of the Islanders was the overwhelming moral consideration. They also saw Argentina's occupation of the islands as a use of force that could not be permitted to succeed, because it would set a dangerous global precedent and damage the credibility of British (and Western) deterrence. They also valued Anglo-American relations more highly than Argentine-American relations on virtually every dimension—strategic, economic, ideological, and otherwise. Some—such as Weinberger—were notable anglophiles, and many—including the president—had strong personal relationships with their British counterparts. For these reasons, and because of historical, cultural, and linguistic ties, the weight of American public opinion sympathized with Britain.

A second camp included U.S. Ambassador to the United Nations Jeane Kirkpatrick, Senator Jesse Helms, and Undersecretary of State for Latin American Affairs Thomas Enders. Few among this group sympathized with the Argentine claim on moral or legal grounds, but they felt that American interests would on balance suffer if the United States openly supported Britain. As an ally in the cold war struggle, they felt, Britain could be counted on regardless. But Latin American sympathies were more difficult to cultivate, easier to jeopardize, and vital to the success of the struggle against communism on the front lines, especially in Central America. By openly supporting Britain, the United States would risk untold damage in its hemispheric relations. Additionally, the theater of conflict was out of the NATO area, relieving the United States of any formal collective-security obligation; and since Britain had failed to support the United States in many of the conflicts in which it found itself engaged, Washington had no strict moral obligation based on simple reciprocity. A few rather unrealistically worried that if the United States supported Britain, Argentina would turn toward the Soviet Union.

But no one in Washington advocated siding with Argentina. And it is this that points to the double irony of the junta's realpolitik reading of the United States. On the one hand, if the United States were to be guided solely by realpolitik, it was clearly going to side with Britain. On the other hand, sympathies with Britain were especially strong in the United States for reasons that had nothing to do with realpolitik. American ties to Britain were much thicker and deeper than American ties to Argentina.[29] What is ironic about this is the fact that the Argentine invasion itself was in no sense an act of realpolitik. Argentine leaders understood their *own* motives in terms of right, justice, and national honor. It is curious that they did not appreciate the power of these motivations in Britain and the United States as well.

The claim that Argentine leaders were motivated overwhelmingly by their desire to correct what they sincerely perceived to be a gross historical injustice is one that Westerners (scholars and others) greet with suspicion. The common wisdom in the English-speaking world holds that the Argentine junta ordered the occupation to divert the country's attention from its economic plight and to bolster the public standing of the military regime.[30] Indeed, some political scientists consider the case a classic example of "the diversion hypothesis"—the supposition that wars result from attempts by political elites to externalize domestic frustration and to secure their positions by exploiting the "rally 'round the flag" effect.[31]

The diversion hypothesis is an appealing explanation for Argentine behavior, for three reasons. First, it is logically consistent with the physical act of occupying the islands. If the members of the junta *were* seeking to distract public opinion and to bolster their popularity, they might have opted for an adventure of this kind. Second, Westerners tend to assume that leaders of states—particularly nondemocratic leaders—are motivated overwhelmingly by personal political ambition and that everything they do ultimately flows from this. Third, we naturally dismiss as cynical and instrumental the moral claims made by regimes we do not like, and we do so all the more easily when we regard those claims as having no merit (Britain's claim to sovereignty, which rested on the principle of self-determination, resonates more strongly in the liberal West than does Argentina's historical claim).[32] But while the prevalence of the diversion hypothesis tells us a great deal about foreign policy analysis in the West, it tells us nothing at all about Argentine decision making in 1982. The evidence is overwhelmingly against it. What we know about the beliefs and preferences of the junta members, their personal histories, and the decision-making process leading up to the occupation suggests that their overwhelming desire was to resolve once and for all their sovereignty dispute with Britain.[33]

Of course, even if the junta had been motivated by a desire to bolster their domestic standing, their actions would still be evidence of bad judgment. Things didn't work out in that respect, either. But giving due credit to the role of the justice motive in Argentine decision making does help us better understand the miscalculations and misjudgments to which the junta fell prey.

THE PSYCHOLOGY OF BAD JUDGMENT

To see more clearly why the junta may have stumbled in this case, it may be helpful to ask how a leader's background, life history, and ideational context work their way into and through a decision, purely as a matter of information processing. Macro issues sometimes make more sense when we interpret them through the lens of micro phenomena.

Much in the vast body of knowledge we casually call "the psychology of decision making" enables us to appreciate how and why people make mistakes, particularly how and why they deviate from some "rational" ideal. This is not the place for an extensive survey of the relevant literature.[34] In any case, it is notoriously difficult to diagnose decision-making pathologies in uncontrolled, real-world settings. But as a first cut, it is plausible to argue that many of the mistakes the junta made are precisely the kinds of mistakes we would expect people to make if perfectly normal psychological dynamics were at work.

Among the core insights of cognitive psychology is that people's prior beliefs strongly affect, and often distort, their information processing.[35] Typically, the actions of others are consistent with a number of possible motives and calculations. But our prior beliefs incline us to favor certain interpretations over others. Thus if we believed, as did many during the cold war, that Soviet leaders were inherently opportunistic and expansionistic, we would tend to interpret whatever they did as evidence for the proposition that they were opportunistic and expansionistic, even though their behavior might actually have been motivated by fear or insecurity.[36]

Recent psychological research suggests that culture can have a profound effect on cognition precisely because it so powerfully shapes our prior beliefs. *Culture* as I am using it here is a broad term without a generally agreed-on definition. Indeed, the *Oxford English Dictionary* gives two, both of which seem somewhat lame: (1) "The training, development, and refinement of mind, tastes, and manners; the condition of being thus trained and refined; the intellectual side of civilization"; and (2) "the civilization, customs, artistic achievements, etc., of a people, esp[ecially] at a certain stage of its development or history." Neither of these seems to capture the essence of the term as it is understood by social psychologists. Nevertheless, we *do* know it when we see it, and I believe it is useful to think of it quite simply as a belief and value system into which we are more or less imperfectly socialized as children. We can distinguish cultures very broadly, as we do when we compare and contrast American and Chinese culture, or more narrowly, as we do when we compare midwestern and southern culture within the United States. As long as we can identify differences in beliefs, values, attitudes, dispositions, practices, customs, rituals, and the like, we can distinguish cultures at an arbitrarily fine level of detail.[37]

Because cultures are systems of beliefs and values, they act as lenses and filters on information processing. They can do so in very subtle ways, affecting (for instance) the propensity of people to exhibit certain kinds of information-processing biases of which they are highly unlikely even to be aware.[38] They can affect styles of logical inference.[39] They can affect the substantive contents of judgments—for example, of approval or disapproval,[40] or of relationships between events.[41] They can affect the propensity for people to rely on history or memory when they interpret the world.[42] Psychologists are just beginning to probe the many ways in which our cultural contexts affect our constructions of reality.[43] There is no doubt, however, that they do so quite profoundly.

Motivational psychology explains errors in judgment in terms of human needs—for example, the need to avoid fear, shame, and guilt; the need for self-esteem; the need for social approval; the need for achievement; and the need for effective control. Motivational psychologists would argue that these needs bias information processing and can result in more or less the same kinds of errors that cognitive psychologists describe. However, whereas cognitive errors arise out of the inherent limitations of human information processing and are therefore ubiquitous, people vary in their susceptibility to motivated errors depending on their personality traits and the situational contexts in which they operate.[44] "Push" models explain biases in information processing in terms of individual personality structures and the ways in which they mediate deep-seated, universal human needs.[45] "Pull" models emphasize situations and the needs, fears, and anxieties they arouse in us. A "pull" model of motivation might emphasize the ways in which stress—generated, perhaps, by time pressure, fear of loss, and reluctance to assume responsibility for bad decisions— might lead a decision maker to conduct an inadequate search for information and options, make biased estimates of probability, commit prematurely to a particular course of action, and resist information indicating that his or her decision may have been a poor one.[46]

Finally (for our purposes), there is considerable evidence that people make moral choices differently from other kinds of choices. Human beings have an innate moral faculty.[47] They constantly monitor the behavior of others, and the distribution of benefits, to assess whether it fits with their conception of what is fair or just. When they perceive discrepancies with their moral commitments, they experience a unique sense of outrage that can have a powerful effect on their behavior.[48] If someone views a good as an entitlement, for example, she will value it more highly than its instrumental worth warrants. If someone perceives an injustice, she will be more likely to take risks to correct it; she will be more strident and more categorical in her demands; she will be relatively insensitive to threats; she will be less willing to compromise or to accept compensation in the form of side-payments; and she will be more likely to make errors in judgment about the interests and intentions of those whom she regards as responsible for the injustice or those who stand in her way of correcting it.[49] Motivational and moral psychology highlight the role of emotion in decision making, a subject with which students of international politics are only now beginning to grapple.[50] Invoking culture helps us give content to the substantive issues and considerations that give rise to strong emotional reactions. Culture and emotion, in short, can work synergistically to influence judgment.

All of this helps us make sense of the judgments, inferences, and behavior of Argentine leaders that seem perplexing from a rationalist/realpolitik perspective. First, the moral passion the perceived injustice of the British occupation inflamed helps explains the junta's stridency, sense of urgency, and unwillingness to compromise on the status of the islands to avoid a conflict. Because they understood their own claim as right and just, they naturally understood Britain's contradictory claim as insincere and intended to serve ulterior, narrowly instrumental purposes. Much as British leaders suspected that the junta was using the sovereignty dispute in general, and the South Georgia incident in particular, to divert the attention of the Argentine people from domestic difficulties, the junta suspected that British intransigence was primarily intended to divert public opinion from economic and labor woes then hobbling the Thatcher government. This demonization of British policymakers, quite understandably, carried over into the postconflict period, and it manifests itself today in a bizarre revisionist conspiracy theory whereby Thatcher laid a trap, into which the junta stumbled, designed to secure British hegemony in the South Atlantic.[51] In tone and content, this conspiracy theory reminds one of nothing so strongly as the kaiser's famous marginal comment on the Pourtalès telegram of July 30, 1914:

> So the famous *"encirclement"* of Germany has finally become a complete fact, despite every effort of our politicians and diplomats to prevent it. The net has been suddenly thrown over our head, and England sneeringly reaps the most brilliant success of her persistently prosecuted purely *anti-German world-policy*, against which we have proven ourselves helpless, while she twists the noose of our political and economic destruction out of our fidelity to Austria, as we squirm isolated in the net. A great achievement, which arouses even the admiration of him who is to be destroyed as its result! Edward VII is stronger after his death than I who am still alive![52]

All three members of the junta, in short, believed before the conflict that the British would be guided in the dénouement by the very cold, calculated considerations of narrow material self-interest that they mistakenly believed guided British policy in the drama leading up to it. Since the junta knew that the disputed islands were of negligible instrumental value (Ronald Reagan referred to them as "that little ice-cold bunch of land down there"[53]), they underestimated the likelihood that the British would be willing to fight for them. *After* the conflict, however, the junta explained away Britain's willingness to fight by crediting London with a brilliant but dastardly geopolitically motivated deception. In my interviews, I was completely unable to elicit any acknowledgment from any member of the junta that the British might have been equally sincerely motivated by *their* conception of right or justice.

At several crucial junctures in the unfolding of events, we see the powerful effect of prior beliefs on estimates, of errors stemming from impressionistic judgments, and of the mistaken assumption that one's intentions and perspective will be transparent to others. When estimating the British response to the occupation of the islands, for instance, the junta relied heavily on dubious interpretations of two historical antecedents (Suez and Rhodesia) and Costa Méndez's belief that Britain tended "always to deal, but not on the basis of force."[54] Had the junta thought (as did Thatcher) more in terms of Munich than Suez, they might have made rather different estimates.[55] As I have already noted, the junta also overestimated Argentina's importance to the United States, grossly underestimating the likelihood of American support for Britain. Notably missing from the Argentine calculus was any consideration of the possibility that Westerners would see the occupation of the islands not as a defensive response to a British démarche, but as a proactive, aggressive act; of the moral, cultural, and historical affinities between Britain and the United States; or of Margaret Thatcher's character and reputation for toughness.[56]

Argentine leaders, in short, were (cognitively and emotionally speaking) the prisoners of their history and culture, which so powerfully shaped their beliefs and their goals that they misdiagnosed the nature of the problem they faced and misjudged the consequences of their own actions. In this they were not alone, of course. The most impressive common failure in the strange history of the Falklands/Malvinas war is the failure of *all* parties to appreciate the importance of the cultural and historical contexts in which leaders acquire their basic moral commitments, against the background of which they formulate their conceptions of the national interest, out of which they identify the stakes over which they contend with others, and in terms of which they interpret the actions and intentions of others.[57]

CAN LEADERS TRANSCEND CULTURE AND EMOTION?

Should Argentine leaders have known better? It is tempting to say yes. An ideal observer—someone fully informed and unencumbered by cultural and emotional baggage—would surely have been able to anticipate the broad outlines of the international reaction to the military occupation of the Malvinas. Certainly no ideal observer could have expected that a military occupation of the islands would have promoted the Argentine diplomatic agenda in the way that the junta believed that it would. While there is some possibility that an ideal observer might have concluded that the military occupation itself stood a reasonable chance of success—primarily on the ground that the logistical obstacles Britain faced in attempting to recapture the islands might have proven insurmountable—he or she would surely have known that the truly hard part of the enterprise would only have begun, not ended, at D + 5. It is clear that the junta did not appreciate the very long odds they faced when they rolled the dice on the morning of April 2, 1982.[58]

But to say that the junta *should* have known better logically implies that the junta *could* have known better. Is this plausible? Can people so powerfully shaped and driven by culture and emotion transcend them?

Some with a philosophical bent might be tempted to say no. Intense nationalism and an unshakable faith in the justice of their cause were not incidental to the characters of the members of the Argentine junta but defined who they were. They would have had to have been different people not to be so constrained. The proposition, on this view, seems nonsensical. But we do have before us historical examples of leaders who made serious efforts to put themselves in other people's shoes, who strove to see the world from different perspectives, and who asked themselves hard questions about the accuracy and wisdom of their own beliefs and judgments. We have examples of leaders who found creative ways to keep emotion in check, or at least to let it run its course before committing to a course of action. I would argue that this effort—only partially successful, perhaps, but successful enough—largely accounts for the good judgment President John F. Kennedy showed in his handling of the Cuban missile crisis. The fact that Kennedy was so eminently capable of *bad* judgment, amply on display both in the Bay of Pigs fiasco and in the run-up to the missile crisis itself, demonstrates at least that people are capable of learning from their mistakes and that they can be brought to appreciate the importance of circumspection and an attempt to cultivate empathy.[59]

I suspect this is easier for the worldly than for the parochial. On this score, Kennedy enjoyed an enormous advantage over the members of the Argentine junta, none of whom had any training or experience in world affairs prior to taking office. Nor, for that matter, did the Argentine junta have the opportunity to learn from earlier mistakes. In foreign policy, this was their first—and their last.

But this point merely serves to remind us that different leaders are differentially constrained. Good judgment, in other words, may be a complex function of character and ability, on the one hand, and of context and experience, on the other. Small wonder it is such a difficult notion to wrestle to the ground. But it is important to try to make progress toward that end. It hardly seems more appropriate in politics than in law to be satisfied merely with knowing it when you see it.

NOTES

I would like to thank the editors and an anonymous reviewer for helpful comments on this chapter; Lawrence Freedman, Charles William Maynes, Kim Richard Nossal, and Sir Crispin Tickell for helpful comments on an earlier essay on which this chapter draws (David A. Welch, "Remember the Falklands? Missed Lessons of a Misunderstood War," *International Journal* 52, no. 3 [Summer 1997]: 483–507); the editors of *International Journal* for permission to reproduce portions thereof; Ana Margheritis for expert research assistance; Waleuska Lazo for translation; and the Social Sciences and Humanities Research Council of Canada and the Thomas J. Watson Jr. Institute for International Studies, Brown University, for financial support. The usual disclaimers apply.

1. *Jacobellis v. Ohio*, 378 U.S. 184 (1964) at 197.

2. By far the best and most accurate account of the Falklands/Malvinas war is Lawrence Freedman and Virginia Gamba-Stonehouse, *Signals of War: The Falklands Conflict of 1982* (London: Faber & Faber, 1990). For a helpful review of early works in both English and Spanish, see Joseph S. Tulchin, "Authors Take Sides on the Falklands," *Latin American Research Review* 22, no. 3 (September 1987): 123–39. Useful recent works include Peter Beck, *The Falkland Islands as an International Problem* (London: Routledge, 1988); Michael Charlton, *The Little Platoon: Diplomacy and the Falklands Dispute* (London: Blackwell, 1989); Alex Danchev, ed., *International Perspectives on the Falklands Conflict* (New York: St. Martin's, 1992); G. M. Dillon, *The Falklands, Politics and War* (London: Macmillan, 1989); Douglas Kinney, *National Interest/National Honor: The Diplomacy of the Falklands Crisis* (New York: Praeger, 1989); and David Monaghan, *The Falklands War: Myth and Countermyth* (New York: St. Martin's, 1998).

I draw heavily in this chapter on interviews with current and former Argentine officials, military officers, and analysts, including all three members of the former Argentine junta: President General Leopoldo F. Galtieri; commander in chief of the navy, Admiral Jorge I. Anaya; and commander in chief of the air force, Brigadier Basilio Lami Dozo. Others I interviewed for this study include former military governor of the Malvinas, General Mario Benjamin Menéndez; former chief of military intelligence, Admiral Eduardo Morris Girling; defense minister, Dr. Oscar Camilión; Luis Mendiola, Dirección Malvinas, Ministerio de Relaciones Exteriores y Culto; Dr. Alberto De Vita; Dr. Lucio García del Solar; Commodore Pío Matassi; Admiral Antonio Mozzarelli; Captain Jose Estanislao Cortines; Dr. Roberto Guyer; Oscar Raúl Cardoso; Andrés Fontana; Roberto Russell; and Carlos Escudé.

3. Argentina, Comision Rattenbach, *Informe Rattenbach: El Drama De Malvinas* (Buenos Aires: Espartaco, 1988).

4. "Thoughts on the Late Transactions respecting Falkland's Islands," quoted in Paul Eddy, Magnus Linklater, Peter Gillman, and *The Sunday Times* Insight Team, *The Falklands War* (London: Deutsch, 1982).

5. I shall use both locutions variously, depending on context.

6. The actual dispute is more complicated than this, involving decolonization and acquisitive prescription. Moreover, Britain asserts only the Islanders' right of *internal* self-

determination. For further discussion, see Lowell S. Gustafson, *The Sovereignty Dispute over the Falkland (Malvinas) Islands* (New York: Oxford University Press, 1988); and Fritz L. Hoffmann and Olga Mingo Hoffmann, *Sovereignty Dispute: The Falklands/Malvinas, 1493–1982* (Boulder, Colo.: Westview, 1984).

There were approximately 1,800 Falkland Islanders in 1982, but the population has since grown to more than 2,800, owing in part to an increased British military presence. *CIA World Factbook 2000*, http://www.odci.gov/cia/publications/factbook/geos/fa.html# People.

7. The Right Honorable Lord Franks, Chairman, *Falkland Islands Review: Report of a Committee of Privy Counsellors* (London: Her Majesty's Stationery Office, 1983), 6.

8. See Clive Ellerby, "The Role of the Falkland Lobby," in Danchev, *International Perspectives on the Falklands Conflict*, 85–108.

9. As Undersecretary for Dependent Territories David Scott was fond of saying, Britain would not tolerate the rape of the Falkland Islands but would actively encourage their seduction. Max Hastings and Simon Jenkins, *The Battle for the Falklands* (New York: Norton, 1984), 23.

10. Interview, August 29, 1995, Buenos Aires; see also Charlton, *The Little Platoon*, 116; Jorge I. Anaya, "Malvinas: La Guerra Justa," *Boletin del Centro Naval* 110, no. 766 (April 1992): 252–93. The intensity of Anaya's passion on the issue was evident to U.S. Secretary of State Alexander Haig during his peace mission in April 1982. "My son is ready to die for the Malvinas," Anaya told Haig, "and it is my family's point of view that we would be proud to know his blood had mingled with this sacred soil." Alexander M. Haig Jr., *Caveat: Realism, Reagan, and Foreign Policy* (New York: Macmillan, 1984), 288.

11. *La Prensa* (Buenos Aires), January 24 and February 7, 1982.

12. A circumstantial indication that the navy proceeded with Project Alpha is the fact that it authorized Davidoff's voyage without notifying the Foreign Ministry. Freedman and Gamba-Stonehouse, *Signals of War*, 46. A well-placed Argentine official I interviewed in 1995 who asked specifically not to be identified with respect to this point expressed his conviction that Davidoff's team included marines with orders to carry out the principal elements of Project Alpha.

13. Under the terms of the Thatcher government's 1981 Defence Review, *Endurance* was scheduled to be withdrawn in a matter of months, leaving no permanent British naval presence in the region whatsoever.

14. Interview, August 29, 1995, Buenos Aires. As Lami Dozo put it, "Britain's escalation of the dispute—especially its demand about the passports—came as a complete surprise. . . . [T]here was unanimous agreement that we could not permit that." Interview, August 30, 1995, Buenos Aires.

15. The date agreed on for the occupation was April 1. However, the junta postponed the operation until April 2 because of inclement weather.

16. See generally Margaret Thatcher, *The Downing Street Years* (New York: HarperCollins, 1993), 173–212.

17. See, for example, the statement in the House of Commons by Minister of State Nicholas Ridley on December 2, 1980, 995 House of Commons Debates 5 s., cols. 128–29.

18. American support was crucial to the success of the British military operation. Partic-

ularly valuable were detailed reports on the operational effectiveness of the Argentine navy; signals intelligence; and advanced versions of the *Sidewinder* air-to-air missile, which enabled the Royal Navy's Harrier jets to thwart Argentine bombing runs on British ships. In addition, the United States made available to Britain its facilities on Ascension Island, which proved vital for the staging of British forces. Argentina saw this as a particularly egregious violation of neutrality. However, Washington had no choice in the matter, since Ascension was a British possession and the terms of the American lease required permitting the British military to make use of it in case of "emergency."

19. Interview, August 29, 1995, Buenos Aires.

20. For further discussion, see David Lewis Feldman, "The U.S. Role in the Malvinas Crisis, 1982: Misguidance and Misperception in Argentina's Decision to Go to War," *Journal of Interamerican Studies and World Affairs* 27, no. 2 (Summer 1985): 1–22.

21. Interview, August 29, 1995, Buenos Aires. Several officials interviewed for this study remarked on the importance of the Suez and Rhodesia precedents for the junta, and this stands out as one of the more notable features of the junta's calculations.

22. Interview, August 30, 1995, Buenos Aires.

23. Benedict Anderson, *Imagined Communities: Reflections on the Origin and Spread of Nationalism,* rev. and extended ed. (London: Verso, 1991). See also María Isabel Menéndez, *La "Comunidad Imaginada" en la Guerra de Malvinas,* Estudios de Antropología ([Buenos Aires]: Eudeba Ciclo Básico Común Universidad de Buenos Aires, 1998); and Nora A. Femenia, *National Identity in Times of Crises: The Scripts of the Falklands-Malvinas War* (New York: Nova Science, 1996).

24. See Jimmy Burns, *The Land That Lost Its Heroes: The Falklands, the Post-War, and Alfonsin* (London: Bloomsbury, 1987), 25.

25. Michael Ignatieff, *Blood and Belonging: Journeys into the New Nationalism* (New York: Farrar, Straus & Giroux, 1994).

26. Carlos Escudé, *Education, Political Culture, and Foreign Policy: The Case of Argentina,* Occasional Paper 4 (Durham: Duke–University of North Carolina Program in Latin American Studies, 1992).

27. Escudé notes that this is a common error in Argentina and a byproduct of the effort to cultivate Argentine nationalism. Interview, August 31, 1995; and Escudé, *Education, Political Culture, and Foreign Policy,* passim.

28. See Louise Richardson, *When Allies Differ: Anglo-American Relations during the Suez and Falklands Crises* (New York: St. Martin's, 1996).

29. It is worth noting, too, that the unusually close relationship between U.S. and British military establishments provided additional bureaucratic and affective reasons for the United States to support Britain.

30. In 1981, inflation in Argentina reached 130 percent; the peso fell to one-fifth of its value against the dollar; the gross national product dropped 6 percent; manufacturing output dropped 22.9 percent; real wages fell 19.2 percent; and half a million people out of a total workforce of just under eight million were unemployed. *Economist,* April 10, 1982, 22; Burns, *The Land That Lost Its Heroes,* 29. On March 30, 1982—three days before the occupation of the islands—Argentina's labor unions attempted to stage a massive protest against the regime, which riot police brutally suppressed.

31. Jack S. Levy and Lily I. Vakili, "Diversionary Action by Authoritarian Regimes: Argentina in the Falklands/Malvinas Case," in *The Internationalization of Communal Strife*, ed. Manus I. Midlarsky (London: Routledge, 1992), 118–46.

32. David A. Welch, "Ethics and Foreign Policy," *Georgetown Journal of International Affairs* 1, no. 1 (Winter/Spring 2000): 79–88.

33. In my interviews, I encountered only one remark that tends to support some version of the diversion hypothesis, made to me by an official who spoke only for background. The remark, in full, is as follows: "Admiral Anaya is a very peculiar fellow. He is from Bolivian stock, and is a strong nationalist. This was unusual in the navy, which tended to be pro-British and internationalist. He had a very hard line on Chile. But he felt that the military government was worn out and should go. He worried about the military government being 'fired.' He was obsessed with the military retiring from politics in an orderly fashion. He did not feel that the military was able to rule the country. He developed the idea that only through a spectacular diplomatic triumph was it possible to establish a good bargaining position vis-à-vis the civilians and retreat from politics with honor. He told me this. Galtieri was persuaded, but decided that this was a way to *consolidate* political power. Galtieri was a very unenlightened fellow."

I find it difficult to credit this statement. My interlocutor was not on good terms with the junta in 1982, and the remark presupposes an implausible degree of intimacy. Moreover, the weight of evidence suggests that domestic political considerations did not bear heavily on the decision at any point. I make this argument in greater detail in *Justice and the Genesis of War* (Cambridge: Cambridge University Press, 1993), chap. 6—notably, not on the basis of interviews with Argentine officials, which I conducted later. See also Freedman and Gamba-Stonehouse, *Signals of War*, passim.

All three members of the junta insisted to me in interviews that correcting the historical injustice of the British seizure of the islands in 1833 was their overwhelming motivation. A cynic, of course, will doubt their sincerity. I do not. Having conducted elite interviews all over the world, I flatter myself that I have developed a sensitivity to the subtle (and sometimes not so subtle) clues in tone, expression, and comportment that indicate either sincerity or disingenuousness. Having witnessed firsthand the junta's passion in its full glory, I have no doubts whatsoever of their sincerity on this particular point.

34. For discussion, see Janice Gross Stein and David A. Welch, "Rational and Psychological Approaches to the Study of International Conflict: Comparative Strengths and Weaknesses," in *Decision-Making on War and Peace: The Cognitive-Rational Debate*, ed. Alex Mintz and Nehemia Geva (Boulder, Colo.: Rienner, 1997), 51–77.

35. See, for example, Shelley T. Fiske, "Schema-Based versus Piecemeal Politics: A Patchwork Quilt, but Not a Blanket, of Evidence," in *Political Cognition*, ed. Richard R. Lau and David O. Sears (Hillsdale, N.J.: Erlbaum, 1986), 41–53.

36. See, for example, Ole R. Holsti, "Cognitive Dynamics and Images of the Enemy: Dulles and Russia," in *Enemies in Politics*, ed. David Finlay, Ole Holsti, and Richard Fagen (Chicago: Rand McNally, 1967), 25–96.

37. "Culture" is a concept that has been central to the study of international relations in virtually all times and places, with the notable exception of North America from the behavioral revolution through the decline of structural realism. Since the end of the cold

war, it has enjoyed a resurgence. It is notable, however, that even those who insist that culture is important often seem less concerned with what the concept denotes than with the fact that it is dynamic, multifarious, and constructed. They also seem less interested in its potential first-order explanatory power than in its second-order metatheoretical value. Yosef Lapid, "Culture's Ship: Returns and Departures in International Relations Theory," in *The Return of Culture and Identity in IR Theory*, ed. Yosef Lapid and Friedrich V. Kratochwil (Boulder, Colo.: Rienner, 1996), 3–20; Friedrich V. Kratochwil, "Is the Ship of Culture at Sea or Returning?" in *The Return of Culture and Identity in IR Theory*, 201–22. Notable recent attempts to harness culture to explanation include Alastair I. Johnston, *Cultural Realism: Strategic Culture and Grand Strategy in Chinese History* (Princeton, N.J.: Princeton University Press, 1995); Peter J. Katzenstein, ed., *The Culture of National Security: Norms and Identity in World Politics* (New York: Columbia University Press, 1996); Valerie M. Hudson, ed., *Culture & Foreign Policy* (Boulder, Colo.: Rienner, 1997). See also Fritz Gaenslen, "Culture and Decision Making in China, Japan, Russia, and the United States," *World Politics* 39, no. 1 (October 1986): 78–103; and Roland H. Ebel, Ray Taras, and James D. Cochrane, *Political Culture and Foreign Policy in Latin America: Case Studies from the Circum-Caribbean* (Albany: State University of New York Press, 1991). Since my concern here is with the explication of microlevel judgments, rather than macrolevel policy orientations, I draw primarily on the relevant psychological literature.

38. See, for example, Incheol Choi and Richard E. Nisbett, "Situational Salience and Cultural Differences in the Correspondence Bias and Actor-Observer Bias," *Personality and Social Psychology Bulletin* 24, no. 9 (September 1998): 949–60.

39. Kaiping Peng and Richard E. Nisbett, "Culture, Dialectics, and Reasoning About Contradiction," *American Psychologist* 54, no. 9 (September 1999): 741–54.

40. Richard E. Nisbett and Dov Cohen, *Culture of Honor: The Psychology of Violence in the South* (Boulder, Colo.: Westview, 1996).

41. Li-Jun Ji, Kaiping Peng, and Richard E. Nisbett, "Culture, Control, and Perception of Relationships in the Environment," *Journal of Personality and Social Psychology* 78, no. 5 (May 2000): 943–55.

42. Li-Jun Ji, Norbert Schwarz, and Richard E. Nisbett, "Culture, Autobiographical Memory, and Behavioral Frequency Reports: Measurement Issues in Cross-Cultural Studies," *Personality and Social Psychology Bulletin* 26, no. 5 (May 2000): 585–93.

43. See particularly Alan P. Fiske, Shinobu Kitayama, Hazel Markus, and Richard E. Nisbett, "The Cultural Matrix of Social Psychology," in *The Handbook of Social Psychology*, ed. Daniel T. Gilbert, Susan T. Fiske, and Gardner Lindzey, 4th ed., vol. 2 (Boston: McGraw-Hill, 1998), 915–81.

44. Katharin Blick Hoyenga and Kermit T. Hoyenga, *Motivational Explanations of Behavior: Evolutionary, Physiological and Cognitive Ideas* (Monterey, Calif.: Brooks/Cole, 1984).

45. For example, J. Kuhl, "Motivation and Information Processing: A New Look at Decision Making, Dynamic Change, and Action Control," in *Handbook of Motivation and Cognition: Foundations of Social Behavior*, ed. R. M. Sorrentino and E. T. Higgins (New York: Guilford, 1986), 404–34; J. O. Raynor and D. B. McFarlin, "Motivation and the Self-System," in *Handbook of Motivation and Cognition*, 315–49; A. Tesser, "Some Effects of Self-Evaluation Maintenance on Cognition and Action," in *Handbook of Motivation and Cognition*,

435–64. For a classic historical application, see Alexander L. George and Juliette L. George, *Woodrow Wilson and Colonel House* (New York: Day, 1956). Motivational factors may also influence whether we attribute the actions of others to situational or dispositional factors. We are far more likely to interpret undesirable actions by people we dislike as reflecting their basic dispositions, and to interpret undesirable actions by people we like as reflecting circumstantial pressures or constraints. D. T. Regan, E. Straus, and R. Fazio, "Liking and the Attributional Process," *Journal of Experimental Social Psychology* 10 (1974): 385–97.

46. Irving L. Janis and Leon Mann, *Decision Making: A Psychological Analysis of Conflict, Choice, and Commitment* (New York: Free Press, 1977); Irving L. Janis, *Groupthink: Psychological Studies of Policy Decisions and Fiascoes* (New York: Houghton Mifflin, 1982); Irving L. Janis, *Crucial Decisions: Leadership in Policymaking and Crisis Management* (New York: Free Press, 1989).

47. Mary Maxwell, *Morality among Nations: An Evolutionary View* (Albany: State University of New York Press, 1990).

48. See, for example, Robert Folger, ed., *The Sense of Injustice: Social Psychological Perspectives* (New York: Plenum, 1984); Jerald Greenberg and Ronald L. Cohen, eds., *Equity and Justice in Social Behavior* (New York: Academic Press, 1982); Martin L. Hoffman, "Affect, Cognition, and Motivation," in Sorrentino and Higgins, *Handbook of Motivation and Cognition,* 254–80; Martin L. Hoffman, "Empathy and Justice Motivation," *Motivation and Emotion* 14, no. 2 (June 1990): 151–72; Daniel Kahneman, Jack L. Knetsch, and Richard H. Thaler, "Fairness and the Assumptions of Economics," *Journal of Business* 59, no. 4 (October 1986): S285–S300; Melvin J. Lerner and Sally C. Lerner, eds., *The Justice Motive in Social Behavior: Adapting to Times of Scarcity and Change* (New York: Plenum, 1981); Laurence Thomas, *Living Morally: A Psychology of Moral Character* (Philadelphia: Temple University Press, 1989).

49. For further discussion, see Welch, *Justice and the Genesis of War,* 18–32.

50. The most comprehensive treatment thus far is Neta C. Crawford, "The Passion of World Politics: Propositions on Emotion and Emotional Relationships," *International Security* 24, no. 4 (Spring 2000): 116–56.

51. Interviews; see also Alberto A. De Vita, *Malvinas 82: Como y Por Que* (Buenos Aires: Instituto de Publicaciones Navales, 1994).

52. Immanuel Geiss, ed., *July 1914: The Outbreak of the First World War: Selected Documents* (New York: Scribner's, 1967), 293–95.

53. Freedman and Gamba-Stonehouse, *Signals of War,* 154.

54. See p. 200, above. See also Richard E. Neustadt and Ernest R. May, *Thinking in Time: The Uses of History for Decision-Makers* (New York: Free Press, 1986); and Yuen Foong Khong, *Analogies at War: Korea, Munich, Dien Bien Phu, and the Vietnam Decisions of 1965* (Princeton, N.J.: Princeton University Press, 1992).

55. There is some indication that the junta's estimate that the international community would take no action in response to an occupation was strongly influenced by the precedent of the Indian takeover of the Portuguese colony of Goa. Freedman and Gamba-Stonehouse, *Signals of War,* 78. Indeed, a 1960s contingency plan for a military occupation of the islands, which Anaya helped to prepare, was poignantly called "Plan Goa." Hastings and Jenkins, *The Battle for the Falklands,* 31. See also Arthur G. Rubinoff, *India's Use of Force in Goa* (Bombay: Popular Prakashan, 1971).

56. There is some indication that Galtieri permitted gender stereotypes to influence his estimate of Thatcher's resolve. Haig recalls Galtieri insisting that "[t]hat woman wouldn't dare" fight to recover the islands. Haig, *Caveat*, 280.

57. I elaborate on these points in David A. Welch, "Remember the Falklands? Missed Lessons of a Misunderstood War," *International Journal* 52, no. 3 (Summer 1997): 483–507.

58. It is worth noting that even British leaders were uncertain of their capacity to retake the islands by force of arms. Although the British task force held significant advantages over the Argentine fleet in surface ships and submarines and could therefore expect to control the seas, it was outnumbered in high-performance aircraft by a ratio of more than four to one and could not be assured of maintaining air superiority. Of particular concern was the fact that the British depended so heavily on a single ship, the light aircraft carrier HMS *Invincible*. During the conflict, according to Anaya, an Argentine submarine managed to get *Invincible* in its sights, but its torpedoes misfired. This prompted Anaya to quip, "God must be English" (interview, August 29, 1995).

The British force that defeated the Argentines on land was actually outnumbered by more than two to one. Military planners generally assume as a rule of thumb that a successful offensive requires an *advantage* of three to one. For the British and Argentine orders of battle, see Martin Middlebrook, *Operation Corporate: The Falklands War* (London: Viking, 1985), 395–409.

59. See generally James G. Blight and David A. Welch, *On the Brink: Americans and Soviets Reexamine the Cuban Missile Crisis,* 2d ed. (New York: Noonday, 1990); James G. Blight, Bruce J. Allyn, and David A. Welch, *Cuba on the Brink: Castro, the Missile Crisis, and the Soviet Collapse,* 2nd ed., rev. and enl. (Lanham, Md.: Rowman & Littlefield, 2002); James G. Blight, *The Shattered Crystal Ball: Fear and Learning in the Cuban Missile Crisis* (Savage, Md.: Rowman & Littlefield, 1990); James G. Blight and Peter Kornbluh, eds., *Politics of Illusion: The Bay of Pigs Invasion Reexamined* (Boulder, Colo.: Rienner, 1997); Trumbull Higgins, *The Perfect Failure: Kennedy, Eisenhower and the CIA at the Bay of Pigs* (New York: Norton, 1987); Peter Wyden, *Bay of Pigs: The Untold Story* (New York: Simon & Schuster, 1979).

Part IV

IMPROVING THE QUALITY OF JUDGMENT IN FOREIGN POLICY DECISION MAKING

· 8 ·

Policy Planning

Oxymoron or Sine Qua Non for U.S. Foreign Policy?

Bruce W. Jentleson and Andrew Bennett

$\mathscr{T}$he dilemma of policy planning is that it is inherently one of the most difficult tasks in the making of U.S. foreign policy, yet in the absence of planning, conflicting domestic and international pressures tend to push U.S. foreign policy toward drift and incoherence. Some view the very conception of foreign policy planning as an oxymoron, so replete with internal contradictions that it simply cannot be achieved. Not only are international affairs even more uncertain and complex than domestic affairs, but as a former diplomat put it, "looking to the future does not come naturally to government officials."[1] Nor is the record of the State Department Policy Planning Staff (S/P) particularly encouraging. The most oft-cited example of S/P success was in the early cold war "golden age" with George F. Kennan as the first director under Secretary of State George C. Marshall, though Kennan himself had a more mixed view of his own efforts. The record since then is not as bleak as often portrayed, but as Robert Rothstein identified over twenty-five years ago, the dominant pattern has continued to be that "planning, prediction and a concern for the significance of long-range developments were honored rhetorically and ignored in practice."[2] The policy planning record is not much better within the Defense Department, at the National Security Council, or with respect to efforts at interagency coordination of policy planning.

Having served as policy planners, we are well aware of the challenges of effective foreign policy planning.[3] But the importance of planning at this time of global transition demands that its difficulties be addressed. Policy planners cannot serve U.S. interests well if they settle for achieving daily influence as just another operational player rather than aspiring to the unique role that Marshall and Kennan originally intended. To underestimate the problems inherent in achieving more effective planning would be unrealistic. But it is also unrealistic to underestimate the need for effective policy planning and the consequences of not achieving it, especially today. At a time in which the United States enjoys unprecedented relative power and must exercise that power amid rapid global economic, technical, and social change, foreign policy planning truly is a sine qua non for an effective U.S. foreign policy.

In making our critique and offering our proposals for change, we go beyond the usual argument that mostly stresses the importance of good relations between the secretary of state and the S/P director. This is necessary but not sufficient, as the problem is complex and more multifaceted. It is more complex in involving other relationships (e.g., between S/P and the regional and functional bureaus), other dynamics (e.g., domestic politics), and other dimensions (e.g., cognitive aspects). It is more multifaceted in going beyond the State Department and also involving policy planning in the Defense Department as well as posing key challenges at the interagency level.

We make our case in four steps. The first section of the chapter draws on cognitive and organizational theories of decision making to examine the potential role of planning in improving foreign policy judgment. The second section looks at policymakers' views on, and practice of, policy planning at the State Department (State), Defense Department (DOD) and National Security Council (NSC). The third section identifies the three major tensions and barriers inherent to foreign policy planning—operational/planning "role schizophrenia," bureaucratic barriers, and political constraints—and uses this framework to further analyze the historical record. The final section recommends reforms for improving foreign policy planning that include reinvigorating S/P within State, institutionalizing planning in the Office of the Secretary of Defense, establishing an interagency planning process under a new deputy national security adviser for strategic planning, and strengthening ties among policy planners, the policy research community, and the foreign policy staffs of U.S. allies.

POLICY PLANNING AND FOREIGN POLICY JUDGMENT

Exercising judgment under uncertainty is the essence of foreign policy decision making. The role of policy planning, ideally, is to improve foreign policy judgment by reducing the recurrent organizational and individual biases in pattern recognition, diagnosis, forecasting, and policy choice that cloud foreign policy judgments. On the organizational side, Alexander George has identified several frequent shortcomings in foreign policy decision making, including hasty arrival at a superficial consensus, consideration of too narrow a range of options, absence of an advocate for some options that are realistic or even necessary but costly, premature compromise on policy agreements at too low a level in the bureaucracy, and a narrow or even singular channel of information and advice.[4] Policy planning organizations can forestall many of these potential pitfalls by providing an independent source of advice, a quality check on the ideas advanced by operational bureaus, an occasional devil's advocate for unpopular options, and a channel for raising opposing views from outside government and dissenting views within it. In general, by diversifying the advice available to policymakers and looking beyond the short term, planning organizations can redress the well-known tendencies of large bureaucracies toward parochialism, limited time horizons, and "least common denominator" compromises that seek to prevent any "sins of commission" but result thereby in many "sins of omission" and a lack of initiative or originality.

The future is inherently unpredictable and uncertain, even more so in foreign policy than in domestic politics, and policy planners are no more capable than anyone else of making point predictions about the future. What they can do is attempt to institute more systematic processes for thinking about the future, processes such as contingency planning and scenario construction that force to the surface the key assumptions implicit in current policies.[5] The planning process can also push operational bureaus and decision makers to identify what future events might serve as benchmarks for determining whether a policy is succeeding or failing, whether one scenario is coming to fruition rather than another, and when key assumptions are being proven wrong and a reevaluation of the policy is needed. In the history of U.S. foreign policy, and even that of the great powers more generally, there are few examples of pure strategic surprise: there is almost always some information in the bureaucracy, and one or more individuals, warning that a dramatic change in the status quo is possible. The difficulty is that of making sure that warnings get a fair hearing and that low-cost preventive actions are identified so that analysts are not dismissed for the inevitable "false positives" that accompany the forecasting of low-probability but high-consequence events.

But policy planners do not and should not spend all or even most of their time on constructing scenarios and contingency plans and engaging in early warning. If planners are aware of the most common cognitive biases and have a wide knowledge of history (or better yet, historians) to draw upon, they can forestall cognitive biases and help individuals think more deeply about the past as well as the future in coming to grips with the uncertainties of the present. Four biases, in particular, have been identified in a wide variety of experimental and real-world settings, and they require vigilance: overconfidence bias in predicting future events; "loss aversion" bias, in which decision makers take much greater risks to prevent perceived losses than to achieve perceived gains (also known as prospect theory); attribution bias in attributing the behavior of others to dispositional traits and attributing one's own behavior to situational context; and biases in the (mis)use of historical analogies, including the biases of "representativeness" (judging events in relation to a seemingly "representative" mental schema or archetype) and "availability" (giving greater weight to information that is recent, firsthand, and visually and emotionally evocative).[6] Policy planners are not unique in their ability to redress cognitive biases, but what gives them greater potential to do so is that they may be freed from the pressing daily demands faced by both operational bureaus and top policymakers. Planners can scrutinize the justifications given for policies and try to identify which of these policies are particularly driven by cognitive biases as well as organizational pathologies, and they can focus their efforts on challenging the assumptions underlying these policies.

Policy planners can also contribute to better judgment by making relevant theories useful and accessible to policy makers. In recounting interviews with policy professionals for his *Bridging the Gap* book, Alexander George observed that "the eyes of practitioners glaze over at the first mention of the word 'theory' in conversations."[7] The very word evoked a sense of limited utility if not irrelevance. But it was the word and its connotations, not the notion of conceptual or generalizing thinking, which was the main problem. When he substituted the term *generic knowledge*, George found his interviewees much more receptive.

> This always met with nods of approval and understanding! I wondered why and finally decided that the explanation was a simple one. Policy-makers know that certain types of problems occur repeatedly in the conduct of foreign policy—for example, deterrence or coercive diplomacy or crisis management. These are "generic problems" with which they are familiar. To speak to policy-makers of the need to develop "generic knowledge" about each of these problems makes perfect sense to them.[8]

Whatever the term, what is needed for effective policy planning is not "Grand Strategy" or "General Theory," iron-clad laws or grandiose dictums, but midrange, well-specified conditional generalizations. By *well specified* we mean that these are more than just "maybe" statements, that the key factors that affect whether the generalization holds and the causal pattern by which they interact are identified. This kind of formulation may not tell us with certainty whether a particular foreign policy strategy is going to succeed. But it can tell us which factors and what conditions are most conducive to policy success.

Take, for example, ethnic conflict. One of the central arguments advanced in this literature is for "purposive" over "primordialist" theories of the sources of ethnic conflict.[9] The primordialist view holds post–Cold War ethnic conflicts to be primarily manifestations of fixed, inherited, deeply antagonistic historical identities. The purposive view acknowledges the deep-seated nature of intergroup animosities and unfinished agendas, but it takes a much less deterministic view of how, when, and whether these identity-rooted tensions become deadly conflicts, in which the calculations made by parties to the conflict of the purposes to be served by going violent is the dominant dynamic. In this view, civil conflicts are as much the result of political competition for power and legitimacy within groups as between them, and these conflicts arise also out of "ethnic security dilemmas," in which the optimal rational strategy for individual leaders and group members (which is to define themselves by ethnicity and take up arms to defend themselves) leads to undesirable outcomes (ethnic radicalization, arms races, and conflict escalation) when all groups practice these strategies. The policy implications of these contrasting diagnoses are profoundly different: resignation, on the one hand, and preventive diplomacy, on the other. Also with regard to later-stage conflict resolution strategies, whether one is inclined toward power sharing or partition is shaped in significant part by the underlying theory to which one subscribes.[10]

Numerous other questions being posed in today's world also require their own comparable conceptual framing and deepening. For example:

- What is the optimal balance of engagement/cooperation and containment/deterrence in relations with other major powers?
- How can force and diplomacy be used most effectively?
- When and how does economic liberalization lead to or facilitate political liberalization?
- What are the requisites for building strong and effective international and regional economic and security institutions, especially in Asia, Africa, and the Middle East, where international relations are not as institutionalized as in Europe and the Western Hemisphere?
- How can growth, equity, and sustainable development be managed cooperatively among countries at very different stages of economic development?
- Beyond rhetorical invocations, what are the requisites for conflict prevention strategies?

While phrased here generically, a name (Kosovo, China, United Nations, etc.) could be attached to each of these. But not only one name, as the issues posed are broad and ongoing and have been raised and/or will be raised recurrently. Moreover, even with regard to a particular case, policy benefits from a broad framing of the issues and from informing the particular strategy being set with more in-depth analysis. Yet this happens all too infrequently. For example, the Kosovo strategy was based on the belief that a few days of bombing would be sufficient to wring major political-diplomatic concessions from Serbian President Slobodan Milosevic. This conclusion, however, apparently was reached without much effort to inform the deliberations with broader thinking about force and statecraft and coercive diplomacy. This is where policy planning can play a key role. Yet the actual historical practice of policy planning has fallen short of the ideal, and to improve policy planning it is necessary to understand why this is so.

AMERICAN FOREIGN POLICY PLANNING IN PRACTICE

Marshall, Kennan, and the Original Model

George Kennan recounts that Secretary of State George Marshall gave him succinct advice in appointing him the first director of the newly established State Department Policy Planning Staff: "Avoid trivia."[11] This was April 1947, and Marshall had a keen sense of the need for broad strategic thinking in times of global transition and the lack of any entity within the existing State Department that could fulfill this need.

Accordingly, the new Policy Planning Staff was to have two principal functions. One, as recounted by then–Undersecretary of State Dean Acheson, was "to look ahead, not into the distant future, but beyond the vision of the operating officers caught in the smoke and crises of current battle; far enough ahead to see the emerging form of things to come and outline what should be done to meet or anticipate them"—that is, to plan.[12] The other was to be a new and key source of in-house self-assessment against conventional wisdom and policy inertia, to "constantly reappraise what was being done. General Marshall was acutely aware that policies acquired their own momentum and went on after the reasons that inspired them had ceased."[13] These overarching functions are reflected in the departmental order delineating five principal sets of responsibilities for the new office:

1. Formulate and develop long-term policies.
2. Anticipate potential threats and challenges.
3. Conduct studies on broad political-military issues.
4. Assess current policy and make advisory recommendations as to its adequacy.
5. Coordinate planning within State.[14]

S/P was intended to focus on a medium- to longer-term time frame, which operationally has translated into a window of about six to eighteen months out, often less. It is difficult to find examples of governmental policy planning, either foreign or domestic, that is longer-term than eighteen months.[15] The key point is the distinction from the short term, the immediate, the reactive, the ad hoc. By this very definition S/P's task was a very difficult analytic undertaking. In any policy context this means grappling with the inherent problems of uncertainty and complexity. "Planning," as Yaacov Vertz-berger argues more generally, "is supposed to anticipate risks and provide for their management in the least costly and most effective manner."[16] In addition, the international policy environment, with its Hobbesian anarchic nature and large number of autonomous actors, is more uncertain and complex than the domestic one. Nevertheless, as Monteagle Stearns writes, despite government officials' reluctance to look to the future, "the reason why it is better to plan policies than improvise them is that improvised policies are more likely to be influenced by events than to influence them. The very act of planning a policy requires consideration of the external resistance it will encounter, the resources that will be needed to implement it, and the ways in which it can be adapted to unforeseen circumstances."[17]

Policy planning needs to have a conceptual dimension. We mean this in two main respects.[18] One is diagnostic, to help policymakers assess the nature of the problems they face, the trends they are observing, the incipient warning signs they may be sensing. Often the problem is less a dearth than a glut of information, and the need is to discern patterns, establish salience, and trace causal connections. It is one thing, for example, to come up with an exhaustive list of many factors and conditions that are associated with the causes of war. It is quite another to hone in on key factors that are sufficiently broad to provide a sound analytic basis for policy planning but sufficiently finite to be manipulated and influenced by policy instruments.

The other aspect is prescriptive, in the sense of what Alexander George calls "the conceptualization of strategies." Such analysis, while abstract rather than directly operational, "identifies the critical variables of a strategy and the general logic associated with [its] successful use."[19] The value often is in providing the framework for putting a particular situation and strategy in the type of broader context that facilitates the design and implementation of effective policy strategies. President Dwight Eisenhower distinguished between policy plans, which could never adequately foresee all possible contingencies, and strategic thinking, which is useful even if specific plans must be adapted. "The plans are nothing," he frequently noted, "but the planning is everything."[20]

Planning can also help with drawing and using historical lessons and analogies. Failures to learn from history, the learning of the wrong lessons from history, and the overlearning of historical lessons and misapplication of them to inappropriate contexts are all inimical to effective policymaking. Policy planners, if they are sensitive to the well-documented cognitive biases that are frequently evident in policymakers' use and misuse of historical lessons, can contribute to more effective decision making by clarifying how current problems are similar to and different from the historical analogues policymakers invoke.[21] One cognitive bias is what Philip Tetlock calls "belief system defenses," which allow actors to conclude "I was almost right" more readily than "I was wrong" and which lead these actors to reject new data and bend historical lessons accordingly.[22]

Yet while operating within its more extended time frame and having a conceptual dimension, policy planning must be sufficiently connected to the current policy agenda or to the anticipated emergence of major issues so as to have "policy tangibility." In this regard, to draw an analogy with the private sector, policy planning is akin to the strategic planning divisions of major corporations. At a Microsoft or a Ford or a Siemens, it is neither the next quarterly returns nor the ten- to twenty-year long-term scenarios that define the portfolio of the vice president for strategic planning and his or her staff. The former is the domain of the sales and the other corporate divisions with more immediate performance criteria; the latter is left to the think tanks and futurists. It is the medium-term time frame that corporate strategic planners work on, that which bears on and is affected by present performance but also that can be at least partly anticipated and shaped by current actions. Even though the greater uncertainty of international politics makes foreign policy strategic planning more difficult than corporate planning, this does not make it impossible.

The last point in the Marshall–Kennan original concept was the coordinating role S/P was to play. Indeed, Kennan has recounted that S/P's key role in the Marshall Plan was less that of hatching ideas strictly on its own than that of bringing together "the knowledge and views of all these people [State Dept. bureau officials], to cull out of them a workable recommendation for the principles on which our approach to this problem might be based and for the procedure that might best be followed."[23] S/P could take advantage of its "unaffiliated" status to bring together various bureaus and experts in an integrated process more dynamic and less bogged down in interbureau rivalries than standard departmental operating procedures.

S/P after Kennan

Kennan stepped down as S/P director in 1949, and he did so with a deep sense of resignation, writing in his diary that his staff had "simply been a failure, like all previous attempts to bring order and foresight into the designing of foreign policy by special institutional arrangement within the department."[24] Paul Nitze was Kennan's successor and in this position played a lead role in the development of NSC-68. In many respects, this was the quintessential policy planning document. It embodied a broad forward-looking strategy, defining American foreign policy quite comprehensively and well into the future, even proposing to circumscribe domestic policy to the needs of foreign policy to a greater extent than any time in U.S. history outside of war. Together with the advent of the Korean War, NSC-68 contributed to a nearly fourfold increase in the U.S. defense budget from 1950 to 1953.

After Nitze's term as head of S/P in 1953, his successors up through the late 1960s (Robert Bowie, Gerard Smith, George McGhee, Walt Rostow, Henry Owen, and William Cargo) had a more difficult time making their mark on history. Subsequently, the Vietnam War and the changes in U.S. society in the 1970s made it more difficult to achieve a consensus on U.S. foreign policies, but they also loosened the intellectual and political constraints on these policies. It was in this context that Secretary of State Henry Kissinger and his S/P director Winston Lord could build on the opening of relations with China as both a broad paradigmatic redefinition of U.S. foreign policy and a concrete policy achievement. Lord had the added advantage of serving a secretary of state who dominated the policy process, although he had to contend with the resentments Kissinger's imperious style created among career diplomats.

The Carter administration further modified the framework of U.S. foreign policy, emphasizing new conceptions of American power and purpose based on human rights and, at least initially, moving away from anticommunism as the sole defining attribute of U.S. policy. In his term as policy planning director in the Carter administration, Anthony Lake sought to make long-term analytical considerations relevant to current operations by looking for "policy hooks" in ongoing policy deliberations that related to or expressed longer-term themes.[25] However, setbacks such as the fall of the shah of Iran and the Soviet military intervention in Afghanistan put pressure on S/P to become more involved in crisis management and daily operations.[26]

During the Reagan administration (S/P had four directors during Reagan's two terms: Paul Wolfowitz, Stephen Bosworth, Peter Rodman, and Richard Solomon), Secretary of State George Shultz attempted to give policy planning more long-range focus, much like a corporate planning group, while removing it from daily operations. Some analysts later argued that S/P's distance from operations made it less effective in this period.[27] Others, though, including many of those involved, see this approach as fitting well with both Secretary Shultz's management style and the nature of the Reagan foreign policy as focused nearly exclusively on the bipolar geopolitical competition with the Soviet Union.

The momentous international events during the first Bush administration led to an extraordinary period of policy planning. Views differ, but most analysts give the Bush team significant credit for managing the fall of the Soviet Union and the dissolution of the Warsaw Pact in a manner that was sensitive to both the historic and operational dimensions of these developments. The State Department under Secretary James Baker played a lead role in this, and Policy Planning under Dennis Ross was central to that role. Even so, the Bush administration was not immune to criticism that its policies amounted to tactical mastery but strategic drift, particularly in failing to define what U.S. policies were to embody the frequently invoked "new world order."[28]

In the Clinton administration, Samuel Lewis became the first S/P director under Secretary of State Warren Christopher. Lewis resigned within a year, however, in large part because of the relative disinterest in policy planning on the part of Secretary Christopher. This also in part reflected President Bill Clinton's general deemphasis on foreign policy, despite the demands of the times. James Steinberg, who succeeded Lewis at S/P, took on a highly influential role, albeit more in a counselor-like individual capacity that did not signal a major role for S/P as a whole. In 1997 after Madeleine Albright was named secretary of state and Steinberg became deputy national security adviser, Gregory Craig became S/P director. His background was much more political than typical for an S/P director; indeed, the following year he shifted over to the White House as a chief counsel defending President Clinton against impeachment in the Monica Lewinsky scandal. He was succeeded by Morton Halperin, whose strong academic and policy credentials were more typical of previous directors of S/P. While providing a longer-term perspective to ongoing policy discussions, Halperin was limited by coming into the position late in the second term of an incumbent administration.

Policy Planning at DOD

Defense Department efforts at policy planning have their own varied history. Contingency planning for military operations and planning for force structure has been carried out consistently and in great detail among the individual services, the Joint Chiefs of Staff, and the regional commands, with oversight by the Office of the Secretary of Defense. Policy planning on the political side of political-military affairs, such as that on alliance relations, burden sharing, and the political strategies accompanying the use of force, has been less consistent. When it has been carried out at DOD, it has usually been within the auspices of the Office of International Security Affairs (ISA), although even here the policy planning function has been periodically abolished and resurrected.

The post of assistant secretary of defense for ISA (ASD–ISA) was created in 1953 to coordinate DOD's role in foreign policy issues. This office played a limited role in the Eisenhower administration because of the president's own military expertise and the prominence of the State Department. ISA became a leading policy planning office in the Kennedy and Johnson administrations, however, with the appointment of Paul Nitze as ASD–ISA, the relative decline of State's role and that of S/P within it, and the growing U.S. involvement in the Vietnam War.[29] Nitze developed a close working relationship with Secretary of Defense Robert McNamara, whose assertive policy advocacy magnified ISA's influence. In the Johnson administration under John McNaughton and Paul Warnke, ISA became a strong advocate for arms control and voiced increasing skepticism of the U.S. effort in the Vietnam War. Its staff members in this period included such prominent foreign and defense policy experts as Daniel Ellsberg, Leslie Gelb, Morton Halperin, Townsend Hoopes, Winston Lord, and Richard Ullman, two of whom, as already noted, later became directors of S/P at the State Department.[30]

The role of ISA diminished in the Nixon administration due to the centralization of foreign policy under Kissinger in the White House and the appointment at ISA of Warren Nutter, a hard-liner who was out of touch with the emerging policies of détente with the Soviet Union and rapprochement with China. In the Carter administration, Secretary of Defense Harold Brown reduced the role of ISA by interposing a new undersecretary for policy between the secretary of defense and the ASD–ISA. With the partial exception of arms control policy, ISA was less influential in policy planning in this period than the corresponding staffs at the State Department and NSC. In late 1979, Undersecretary for Policy Robert Komer transferred ISA's policy planning staff to a deputy undersecretary for policy planning. The Reagan administration further subdivided ISA by creating an assistant secretary for international security policy, which subsumed the parts of ISA that dealt with the Soviet Union and arms control. In the Bush administration, Undersecretary of Defense for Policy Paul Wolfowitz drew on his experience as State S/P director to reestablish a formal policy planning unit under his principal deputy undersecretary, Zalmay Khalilzad, who built up a staff of twenty-two professionals. This staff often engaged in "Team B" exercises to challenge existing policies, which had significant analytic value but also created tensions with the regional and functional offices.

Through a series of reorganizations in the Clinton administration, this office came under a deputy for policy planning, Clark Murdock, who reported directly to Undersecretary Walter Slocombe. This office was slated to develop broad defense policy themes, provide analysis of possible contingencies in "front-burner" issues, and analyze the issues that might otherwise fall between organizational cracks. In practice the office spent much time on legislative and budgetary affairs, worked with the Joint Staff on the implications of the "Revolution in Military Affairs" brought about by new information technologies, and wrote long-range analyses of U.S. regional policies, peacekeeping, and the use of force. The vestiges of the Team B functions of this office, however, brought it into conflict with DOD's regional and functional offices, and it was disbanded. The policy planning function then moved in 1994–95 to a "Plans and Analysis Group" created by ASD-ISA Joseph S. Nye Jr., a noted Harvard professor who came to ISA after heading the National Intelligence Council, and led by Kurt Campbell, another Harvard scholar who had experience in the NSC and the Treasury Department. This staff coordinated a series of unclassified reports on U.S. regional security strategies; organized meetings with the Central Intelligence Agency's (CIA's) warning unit; summarized key debates in the open literature on defense policy; wrote speeches; and worked with ISA's regional offices to bring a long-term perspective to U.S. relations with Japan, NATO, and Latin America and U.S. policies in Bosnia. The staff was largely cobbled together from short-term appointments and detailees, however, and it dissolved when Nye returned to Harvard and ISA encountered staff reductions.

Policy Planning at NSC

At the NSC, there has been no single continuous policy planning office. At different times, one or a few individuals have been designated as planners, although these officials have often focused more on political communications and speechwriting than on classic policy planning or on efforts to oversee planning on an interagency basis. Even more so than at State, the extent and nature of policy planning have been determined largely by the intellectual orientation of the NSC adviser and his relations with the president and with other players in the policy process. NSC adviser Henry Kissinger operated very much from a strategic worldview, albeit one that was individualistic rather than institutionalized. Zbigniew Brzezinski initiated in the Carter administration the process of writing Presidential Review Memoranda, which provided a means for thoroughly reviewing current policies and revising them with a sharper focus on long-term strategic objectives. Brent Scowcroft had a less formal designation of policy planning in the Bush administration, generally seeking to develop this element closely connected to the operational aspects. Early on in the first Clinton administration, Anthony Lake came closer than his counterparts at S/P to providing a policy framework—"engagement [of current and former communist states such as Russia and China] and enlargement [of the community of democracies]"—but both the first- and second-term Clinton NSC staffs emphasized the public and political articulation of policies as much as the strategic planning of policies and the building of a bureaucratic consensus behind them.

DILEMMAS OF FOREIGN POLICY PLANNING

The preceding analysis demonstrates that past problems and frustrations have not been for a lack of trying. Nor has there been a shortage of capable and accomplished individuals serving as S/P directors and in comparable positions at DOD. To underestimate the problems inherent to achieving more effective policy planning would be unrealistic, but it would be equally unrealistic to forego planning at a time of rapid global change and given both the threats and opportunities the United States faces. For planning to be successful, it must address three fundamental dilemmas that are evident in the history sketched earlier: the tension between operational and planning roles, bureaucratic barriers to planning, and political constraints on planning.

Planning/Operational Role Schizophrenia

A first tension has been between *planning and operational roles*. The strategic analysis that Policy Planning is to provide requires sufficient distancing from the day-to-day operational aspects of policy so as to have the time and perspective necessary for this kind of analysis. On the other hand, unless there is at least some direct bearing on the operational aspects of policy, S/P runs the risk of limited relevance. As Acheson put it, "Distraction lurks on two sides; on one, to be lured into operations, on the other, into encyclopedism, into the amassing of analyses of the problems of every area and country with the various contingencies that might arise and the courses of action that might be taken to meet them."[31] Robert Bowie, Policy Planning director in the Eisenhower administration and under Secretary of State John Foster Dulles, acknowledged that Policy Planning "will have no special contribution to make if it becomes immersed in current activities," but also stressed that "if insights and thinking on long-term factors are to be effective, they must be brought to bear on such decisions as they are made."[32] Stephen Bosworth, Reagan/Shultz Policy Planning director, makes the same point but with emphases reversed, that Policy Planning "should not become yet one more aspirant for operational control over policy implementation, vying with the bureaus, neither should it become simply a long-range planning unit, producing intellectually interesting but basically irrelevant studies."[33]

In this respect, the problem as faced by Policy Planning is a particular case of the fundamental organizational dilemma that, as James March and Herbert Simon put it, "daily routine drives out planning."[34] This is especially true when organizational (and personal) prestige and power are in significant part a function of perceptions as a "player," a measure that inherently inclines much more to the operational and immediate than the analytic and longer term. Lincoln Bloomfield's analysis leans strongly in this direction:

> To be in the know, planners have to remain close to operations . . . the end result has been that many a planner has volunteered (or has been drafted) to help with current crises and to perform operational tasks. . . . The Planning Staff often as not has tended to become a high-grade pool of spare hands, available to take on some chores on current policies which the operating bureaus are too busy to handle. With this drastically amended definition of the planning function, most planners can point to substantial accomplishments in the form of policy innovations and solutions.[35]

Rothstein objects strongly to this tilt to the operational, however, and he is critical of measures of effectiveness based on perceptions of influence that are not differentially weighted by function. He notes that "influence on immediate issues as a criterion for effectiveness is hardly an unusual standard in Washington," adding that

> it is questionable, however, whether it is sufficient for a planning staff. . . . If he [the Secretary of State] thinks about his planners according to what they can contribute to immediate issues, and they in turn conceive their role in the same fashion, the result may be an influential planning staff. But the paradox is that the planning staff buys influence at the cost of relinquishing the other roles it can play.[36]

Robert Bowie, Eisenhower's S/P head, put the point vividly: "without a longer-range vision, the foreign policy bureaucracy is like a terrier, following whatever shows up."[37]

One area in which planners can contribute is the international political dimension of contingency planning. The DOD already undertakes extraordinarily detailed planning for a wide range of military contingencies, but contingency planning on the political dimensions of international crises is far less developed. In the Gulf War, for example, the U.S. military took a detailed contingency plan, Operations Plan 1003, which was originally designed for a possible Soviet invasion of Iran, and adapted it to the Iraqi invasion of Kuwait, using it to perform the complex logistical feat of deploying hundreds of thousands of U.S. troops and their equipment from all over the world. At the same time the political contingency planning for conflicts in the Gulf was so weak that U.S. leaders had to engage in an ad hoc though ultimately successful set of "tin cup" trips to round up international contributions to help finance the deployment.[38]

The balance between medium- to long-term planning and short-term policies has been a very difficult one to strike. The Kennan Policy Planning Staff is everyone's main example, albeit one more difficult to replicate than often acknowledged. Kennan's S/P operated at an extraordinary time when both the intellectual blueprint for a new era needed to be set and the main operational policies needed to be developed. There are some analogies here to the present period of momentous change, as we discuss later, but historical transition periods by their very nature are exceptional, with the previous period marked by a singular long-term threat and the present distinguished by various low-level threats and many new opportunities for the United States to use its unprecedented power to shape lasting international institutions. Other factors, such as the strong relationship between Marshall and Kennan, have broader applicability, as we elaborate below.

More often than not, though, S/P directors and their staffs have been tempted into tasks that give them influence but also distract them from their core functions and create friction with other bureaus. These include the tasks of routinely clearing memos by other bureaus, sitting in judgment on these bureaus' budgets, carrying out operational assignments, and working on relations with Congress. Planners can succeed at these tasks and thereby exercise great influence, but only with the strong support of the principal policymakers and only at the cost of a possible backlash from other bureaus should the principal policymakers waver in their support or leave office.

S/P also often has become the lead agency in speechwriting. While this provides influence over policy, planners face a management choice here that is familiar to many business managers: either they can try to enforce quality control by examining the "product" (speeches) at the end of the production line, or they can put more effort into managing the production process and ensuring quality at key intervening steps along the way. The optimal balance here is to ensure S/P involvement in the substantive components as an integral part of the drafting process. It also helps if speeches have the context of Presidential Review Memoranda (PRMs) and Presidential Decision Directives (PDDs) to draw on. S/P should limit any other speechwriting roles to the few major policy speeches.

Bureaucratic Barriers

A second set of problems that have received less attention from scholars involves the bureaucratic barriers to effective policy planning. For analytic purposes, we emphasize five such bureaucratic problems.

One is the crucial importance of a close relationship between the secretary of state and the Policy Planning director (and analogously between policy planners at NSC and DOD and their respective principals). This is the one factor that arguably is an absolutely necessary condition for effective policy planning. "The single principle on which all planners agree," Rothstein writes, is that success for Policy Planning depends on "the willingness of the Secretary to listen to it, to consult it and to protect it from enemies." This is the key reason he cites for the ineffectiveness of Policy Planning in the Kennedy and Johnson administrations:

> Dean Rusk, either because of his low regard for the staff or because of traditional views about how the Department should function, turned only to his geographical and functional bureaus for policy advice. Concerning advice on urgent issues, he did not see what the planners could do that the bureaus themselves could not do equally well.[39]

Some secretaries of state thus have had a stronger understanding of the value of strategic analysis than others. Another aspect is more one of personal rapport; this was a big part of the Kennan–Acheson problem just as it had been part of the Kennan–Marshall success. It also was key to the success of Lord–Kissinger, Lake–Vance, and Ross–Baker. The same pattern holds for DOD, with Nitze–McNamara and Campbell–Nye–Perry among the main positive examples.

A second aspect is the in-box organizational culture that, while far from unique to the State Department, is quite pronounced therein. The daily routine consists of reading cable traffic, daily intelligence reports, news clips, and occasionally more in-depth internal or open source reports and studies. Operational personnel also face many long meetings and demands for memos by COB (close of business), which require much back-and-forth within a bureau's own hierarchy even before running around to attain clearances from other bureaus. This daily routine makes anything other than cleaning out the in-box difficult. While the fundamental purpose of planning is to help manage the number and severity of problems that make their way to the in-box, the tendency is to worry about doing better with tomorrow's in-box only after today's is cleared out, which of course rarely happens.

A third part of the bureaucratic problem involves the structure of bureaucratic incentives and disincentives. Here again, influence is more obvious and measurable in operational involvements than analytic work. It thus is quite rational for career-minded personnel to opt for the operational over the analytic. In addition, to the extent that planning involves trying to alert policymakers to potential problems or crises, it can carry one of two disincentives: either the planner is viewed as the "bearer of bad news," or he or she will been seen as having "cried wolf" if the dangers they warn of fail to materialize. While loyalty often would be best served in the highest policy circles by constructive dissent, all too often dissent gets equated with disloyalty—it doesn't necessarily matter that bad news is being borne to avert its getting worse. This was one of the reasons why, for example, efforts to institutionalize a Team B/devil's advocate function for DOD-ISA did not work, creating a great deal of organizational friction. Similarly, part of the "cry wolf" dilemma is that since we cannot always know when deterrence or prevention will succeed, only in some cases are there rewards for having forewarned.

This leads into a fourth point, which is more generally the problem of intradepartmental relations with the line bureaus. Lucian Pugliaresi and Diane Berliner make the point that "as in most large institutions, the cooperation of the line bureaus is essential, not only because they can be formidable adversaries, but because their cooperation is critical in achieving successful implementation of policy proposals."[40] A cyclical pattern has emerged whereby at times S/P's clearance has been required for memos from other bureaus to go forward to the secretary of state, as was the case during the terms of S/P directors Lord and Lake, while at other times S/P memos have had to be cleared by other bureaus; in still other periods, S/P and other bureaus have had independent channels to the top. Individual secretaries of state will obviously have their own styles of processing information, and any of these clearance processes is viable if accompanied by an appropriate management structure.

Regardless of the managerial structure, it is a savvy bureaucratic strategy to raise and develop ideas in a manner that allows operating bureaus to take them on as their own and share credit and work together. This can help convince top leaders to make the initial investments of political or other resources that are often necessary to achieve long-term future gains. Conversely, without the operational offices' support, planners will have less leverage in the delicate task of talking principals out of failing policies to which these principals have been committed. Poor relations with other bureaus can also lead to a backlash against policy planning organizations once the principal policymakers leave office. The "revenge of the bureaus" was another factor in Kennan's demise at S/P—Kennan resigned when Acheson insisted that S/P memos had to be cleared through the undersecretary's staff and hence through the bureaus. If Kennan had developed better working relations with the regional and functional bureaus, his effectiveness would have been less dependent on his personal ties to Marshall. Similarly, friction with operational bureaus contributed to the periodic downsizing of the role of policy planning at DOD.

A fifth bureaucratic issue is the need for an interagency coordinating process. Acheson recounts how State played this role quite effectively for NSC-68, working collegially with DOD and running the process in a manner that allowed for input yet avoided getting bogged down.[41] State was able to do this because it was in many respects at its high-point in influence over U.S. foreign policy. Thereafter it underwent a long-term institutional decline relative to the rising influence of the NSC, which could respond more nimbly than State to the political and policy needs of presidents in a period of increasingly instantaneous global communications. State also lost power relative to DOD, which had a large and growing budget and corresponding influence in the Congress. This has created competing centers of influence over policy planning and increased coordination problems.

Political Constraints

A third set of challenges arises from the fact that policy planners must be cognizant of domestic political constraints but must not allow these constraints to overly circumscribe their policy advice. Policy planners have greater flexibility in times of growing defense and foreign policy budgets and in periods when the public is in an internationalist mood. Planners also have more political and intellectual leeway after dramatic foreign policy successes bolster the political support of the incumbent administration (as in the Bush administration immediately after the Gulf War), after dramatic failures discredit a previous administration or an outdated policy framework (as in Kissinger's policy shifts after Vietnam), or after dramatic international events and opportunities demonstrate the need for a new policy (as with the end of the cold war).

Policy planners must be aware of broad domestic trends as well as more specific political constraints evident in congressional and public opinion. It is crucial, for example, to be aware of the electoral cycle to establish a foreign policy framework early in an administration when there is more of a window of opportunity for doing so. At the same time, planners must guard against the danger of allowing their policy advice to be distorted by the lens of domestic politics. To again quote Kennan:

> In the days of my directorship at the State Department's Policy Planning Staff, I was sometimes urged to take into account, in our recommendations to the Secretary of State, the domestic political aspects of the recommendation in question. "Should you not warn the Secretary," it would be asked of me, "of the domestic-political problems this recommendation presents, and make sugges-

tions as to how they should be met?" I resisted firmly all such pressures. Our duty, I insisted, was to tell the president and the secretary what, in our view, was in the national interest. It was their duty, if they accepted the force of our recommendations, to see how far these could be reconciled with domestic political realities. This is a duty that they were far better fitted to perform than were we. And if we did not give them, as a starter, a view of the national interest in its pure form, as we saw it, no one else would.[42]

On the other hand, to ignore domestic politics is in its own way to be unrealistic. The State Department in general has long been handicapped by limited political acumen. This colors if not discredits certain kinds of input. It also weakens that input. Despite the old adage, politics rarely has stopped at the water's edge. The cold war "golden age" was more the historical exception than rule, and some accounts exaggerate the bipartisanship of this era. Foreign policy dissensus and politicization did not just start with Vietnam, and it is likely to be with us for the foreseeable future.[43] The challenge thus is to be able to take domestic politics into account sufficiently to enhance the likelihood of policies being implemented as they were originally conceptualized.

STRENGTHENING POLICY PLANNING

Our analysis leads to seven recommendations to strengthen the contributions policy planners can make to good foreign policy judgment.

Give Enhanced Importance for S/P within State

This emphasis needs to come from the top, from the secretary of state, and not just as rhetoric but through demonstrations that the secretary of state sees the value of strategic analysis and policy development and that S/P will play the lead role in this. The analogy made earlier to corporate strategic planning provides a working template, with the S/P director akin to the VP for strategic planning and his or her staff to that corporate division, and with the scope and essence of planning being to connect current issues and opportunities for action to positioning for the medium term and as possible for the longer term.

This in turn means that the secretary of state needs to be someone who conveys a sense of strategy, who is able to provide a sense of framing to U.S. foreign policy, a conceptualization of the dynamics of the era in which we live and of the U.S. national interests that is broad and encompassing yet that is articulated in a politically effective manner. This is key both internally and externally. Kennan was convinced that "no one can regiment this institution [the State Department] in the field of ideas except the Secretary . . . the only way things will work is if a Secretary of State will thresh out a basic theoretical background of his policy and then really set up some sort of educational unit through whose efforts this system can be patiently and persistently pounded into the heads of the entire apparatus, high and low."[44] The tone reflects Kennan's frustration and bitterness, and the proposal goes a bit far, but the main point about policy leadership still pertains. And while the public is not the "prehistoric monster with a body as long as this room and a brain the size of a pin," as Kennan so indelicately characterized it in one of his other books (indeed, precisely because there is a rationality and prudence to public opinion on foreign policy despite low levels of information and attention), broad frameworks and "macropolicy" leadership are crucial to building and sustaining the political support needed for an effective foreign policy.[45]

There thus is a symbiosis here between the need of a secretary of state to provide macropolicy leadership and S/P as a vital asset in doing this, and the need of S/P for a secretary of state who values policy planning if it is to be effective. A close relationship between the secretary and the S/P director, while not a sufficient condition for effectiveness, is a necessary one. While this part of the conventional wisdom is correct, too little emphasis is given to the rest of the staff. This is key to the S/P director being influential as S/P director rather than in a quasi-counselor role. Future S/P directors should strive to meet Kennan's characterization of his staff: "intellectually hard-headed people . . . sufficiently stout in argument to put me personally over the bumps, to drive whole series of clichés and oversimplifications out of my head, to spare me no complications, and to force me into an intellectual agony more intensive than anything I had ever previously experienced."[46] The S/P staff should blend insiders and outsiders, career professionals as well as scholars with strong policy interests and nongovernmental organization (NGO) professionals. It also should be multidisciplinary and covering the range of major specializations (regional, functional) while also including generalists.

One of the ways to set the tone and establish precedent right away is for S/P to be charged at the beginning of a new administration with principal responsibility within State for its input into the PRM-PDD process. This process should be carried out with full input from the bureaus, but with S/P mandated by the secretary to coordinate. In this way departmental expertise can be tapped and a message of inclusiveness sent through the department, indicating that the secretary intends to use the building while also maintaining the degree of central control needed. Thereafter, S/P can play an ongoing role of organizing periodic reviews to reassess and as necessary adjust thinking. This also should include the self-assessment function stressed in the original Marshall–Kennan concept. At times this may take a structured Team B approach; more often it should be a guiding mind-set, an analytic perspective brought to bear so as to activate the feedback loops always included in organizational diagrams but too rarely actually used.

Ensure That S/P Only Selectively Take on Operational Roles

Policy planners are a natural point of contact for the CIA's early warning unit, and they can fruitfully schedule meetings with this unit, usually including the operational offices working on the countries and issues involved in the potential crisis under consideration. They can play a crucial role in closing what Alexander George and Jane Holl call the "warning–response gap," the pattern in which the problem is less the availability of early warning from intelligence sources than its effective analysis and use.[47] The "cry wolf" danger is here, as crises are usually by nature low-probability events with high consequences. It is also difficult to demonstrate the value of crises that are successfully prevented, since it is never certain whether they were indeed prevented or were never fated to happen in any event. It is thus important to make clear that the purpose of early warning is to take low-cost steps and make contingency plans for unlikely but potentially catastrophic events, not just to cause a further flurry of warnings that the event is actually likely.[48]

In addition, policy planning organizations should participate in crisis management, but in the role most suited to their particular expertise. This is to ensure that actions taken and precedents set in crises have a sufficiently long-term view. Policy planners can carry out other limited operational assignments as needed in crises, while leaving the overall management of crises to the principals and their deputies, as is the usual practice. Two noncrisis operational functions that planners can usefully carry out are coordinating the long-term schedules of principals, ensuring that they are consistent with one another and with major predictable events in the Congress and abroad, and working with intelligence and research units to help set priorities for national intelligence estimates and for research contracts with consulting firms outside of government.

Institutionalize Policy Planning in DOD under the Undersecretary of Defense for Policy

DOD needs greater coordination on planning among the Office of the Secretary of Defense (OSD), the armed services and Joint Chiefs of Staff, and the regional and functional commanders in chief (CINCs). The Joint Chiefs and CINCs generally already have well-established planning processes, but policy planning needs a permanent institutional home in OSD as well. This function might best be placed under the undersecretary of defense for policy (USDP) and headed by the deputy secretary for policy. This office could engage in contingency planning, as USDP currently has the authority to do, at least to the extent of ensuring that the implicit political assumptions in the U.S. military's contingency plans are realistic. The military services rightly guard the operational details of their contingency plans very closely, but it should be possible to assess the political assumptions of these plans without having to broadly distribute their operational details. Stronger contingency plans on joint political goals and burden sharing can contribute to deterrence: if a potential aggressor knows that the United States and its allies have already agreed on their general goals and division of labor even before an aggressive act is undertaken, the potential aggressor has less hope of being able to divide the opposition and will be less likely to act in the first place.

Institutionalize Interagency Policy Planning under a New Deputy National Security Adviser for Strategic Planning

There are two reasons why this action is needed. One is the need for more interconnection if not integration of policy planning at State, DOD, and elsewhere in the foreign policy–national security bureaucracy. This in no way precludes or supersedes department and agency-based planning. There are many issues on which State, DOD, Treasury and others always will need to run their own policy planning, which, even when not totally self-contained, is more intra- than interagency. The innovation is in increasing and making less ad hoc an interagency planning process. One of the keys to NSC-68, as noted earlier, was how closely State and DOD planners worked together. Since so few issues today neatly segregate into diplomacy/defense/international economy, there is even greater need for structuring and regularizing interagency policy planning. Periodic interagency meetings of planners could identify the priority topics for policy reviews, share the most useful relevant articles from the open and classified literature, and coordinate the long-range schedules of their agencies.

The other key point here is the necessity of a defined and regularized link to the White House, both for helping manage the interagency process and for connecting directly to the heart of foreign policy decision making. Here, too, the argument is based in part on past experience; for example, an Interagency Planning Group set up during the Kennedy administration did not work out in large part because it lacked the White House–NSC linkage as proposed here.[49] As with all of foreign policy, little of a nonroutine nature happens without the NSC helping make it happen. Yet the NSC's increased influence has not been accompanied by any consistent role in coordinating policy planning. The very creation of the position of deputy national security adviser for strategic planning, as a second NSC deputy slot along with the existing one, would make a statement about the priority to be given to planning by a new administration. The position also would allow for close coordination with the existing deputy national security adviser, who typically chairs the Deputies Committees for high-priority immediate issues, and for interlinkage at this level as well. To be effective, though, it is crucial here as well that this be fundamentally a policy and not a political-communications position.

Conduct Better and More Regularized Outreach to the Policy Research Community

Another important task that is well suited to policy planners is that of reaching out to policy experts outside the government, including former officials, academics, and business leaders, to solicit their policy ideas and have them meet with working-level operators as well as top officials. This approach requires overcoming partisan biases and resistance to ideas "not invented here," but it can also offer a means of reviewing policies without always putting policy planners themselves in the position of being devil's advocates. Outreach efforts can serve as a two-way street as well, making outside experts more aware of the constraints that weigh against their favored policy.

Semiofficial think tanks such as the United States Institute of Peace (USIP) and the National Defense University's Institute for National Security Studies (INSS) can play useful roles in this process. Even if S/P and other governmental policy planning units really are doing planning and not just operations, they rarely have the time, perspective, or capacity to do the kind of research and analysis that research institutions can. The semiofficial status of USIP and INSS makes for a degree of collegiality and trust that can help overcome inhibitions to go outside the immediate office. On the other hand, this same status means that they may not provide the range of perspectives that unaffiliated think tanks and university scholars and research institutions can. Outreach, therefore, needs also to go in this direction.

While we all are familiar with the obstacles and the mutual stereotypes, there are benefits on both sides from the university-based academic community playing more of a policy role. Both sides will need to work at building these relationships.

Coordinate Policy Planning with Allies and Other Major Countries

U.S. policy planning organizations meet intermittently with their foreign counterparts to facilitate joint and coordinated planning, but this practice also needs to become more systematic and regularized. In particular, planning ahead for joint actions and burden sharing in foreseeable military or peacekeeping contingencies can help deter adversaries and prevent misunderstandings with allies. While the United States will continue to be the world's leading economic and military power for many years to come, the conversion of that power to influence over allies and other countries is proving to be one of the major challenges of the post–cold war era. Mechanisms for policy planning coordination can help this dynamic on an ongoing basis to the extent that they build relationships, provide forums for exchanges of views on broad strategic matters, and in other ways establish better consultations as a matter of course and not just in crisis modes.

The difference that joint planning can make is evident in the evolution of U.S.-Japanese security relations since the end of the cold war. In the Gulf War this cooperation was largely ad hoc due to the lack of advanced planning or burden-sharing agreements. The United States was ultimately successful in gaining a large Japanese contribution to the Desert Storm coalition, but the hurried nature of this effort resulted in political friction and misunderstandings. For example, the two sides failed to clarify whether the Japanese contribution was to be denominated in yen or dollars, which led to a dispute over a $700 million difference when exchange rates changed. Similarly, when the North Korean nuclear weapons crisis reached a peak in 1994, the United States found itself in the awkward position of lacking sufficient Japanese commitment to provide assistance in the event of a conflict in Korea. Since then, the United States and Japan have worked together with greater foresight, further clarifying Japanese commitments in the event of various contingencies in the Asia–Pacific region. More such advance planning could help the United States and other major allies and friends better coordinate actions in economic, environmental, and humanitarian contingencies as well.

Speak Policy to Politics

To ignore politics is to court irrelevance, or worse. Indeed, one of the continuing stereotypes is that "foreign policy types" lack any real political sense—and wonkish analysts and planners often are seen as the most glaring examples. To the extent that such characterizations continue to pervade, policy planners will continue to be handicapped in the influence they can have.

But policy planners should use their political acumen to speak policy to politics. Knowing what the political considerations are can help with knowing how to present policy arguments and analyses in ways that address these concerns in defense of the policy considerations. The policy aspects need to be gotten right and then the politics worked through, rather than starting with too narrowly drawn constraints on policy options as imposed by politics. Political constraints should not be so readily equated with fixed parameters; they should be pushed and probed for their malleability as policy goals and objectives warrant. S/P, the NSC deputy for policy planning, and others in the policy planning loop need to play key roles in this manner as well.

CONCLUSION

It may well be that "incrementalism," as Rothstein put it, "is an adequate approach to policymaking . . . in periods of great stability." But it is precisely when there is more uncertainty and instability that this take-them-as-they-come approach "leads to drift and inertia, and its reluctance to contemplate the long run ensures that problems will be dealt with only when they become crises."[50]

Ours are times of historic transition, in which we not only lack clear answers but are still figuring out what the key questions are. This is not to fall into the oversimplification of searching for a singular formulation or master paradigm into which all international dynamics fit and from which all or even most major policy strategies deductively follow. That was not true of the cold war and containment, rosy nostalgia and historical revisionism notwithstanding. And the very term *post–Cold War world* indicates that we know what this era is not, more than what it is. Still, there surely is a need for less ad hoc-ism, less reactiveness and *sui generis* case-by-case careening that too often lacks a framework, context, or strategy. If policy planners are more sensitive to the obstacles to success and take appropriate procedural and substantive steps to address them, they may for the first time in fifty years rise to the high standards for strategic judgment set by Marshall and Kennan.

NOTES

1. Monteagle Sterns, *Talking to Strangers: Improving American Diplomacy at Home and Abroad* (Princeton, N.J.: Princeton University Press, 1996), 153.

2. Robert L. Rothstein, *Planning, Prediction and Policy-Making in Foreign Affairs* (Boston: Little, Brown, 1972), 55.

3. Jentleson served on the State Department Policy Planning Staff in 1993–94 as special assistant to the director. Bennett served as a member of the Plans and Analysis Group under Assistant Secretary of Defense for International Security Affairs Joseph S. Nye Jr. in 1994–95.

4. Alexander L. George, *Presidential Decisionmaking in Foreign Policy: The Effective Use of Information and Advice* (Boulder, Colo.: Westview, 1980), 23–24.

5. One widely accepted approach to scenario construction involves seven steps:

identify driving forces, specify predetermined elements, identify critical uncertainties, develop scenarios with clear "plot lines," extract early indicators for each scenario, consider the implications of each scenario, and develop "wild cards" that are not integral to major possibilities but could change the situation dramatically if they were to happen.

Steven Weber, "Prediction and the Middle East Peace Process," *Security Studies* 6, no. 4 (Summer 1997): 172. Weber's account draws upon Peter Schwartz, *The Art of the Long View* (New York: Doubleday, 1991). See also a follow-up article to Weber's piece, Janice Gross Stein et al., "Five Scenarios of the Israeli-Palestinian Relationship in 2002: Works in Progress," *Security Studies* 7, no. 4 (Summer 1998): 195–208.

6. On overconfidence, see Lyle Brenner et al., "Overconfidence in Probability and Frequency Judgments: A Critical Examination," and Dale Griffin and Carol Varey, "Towards a Consensus on Overconfidence," in *Organizational Behavior and Human Decision Processes* 65, no. 3 (March 1996): 212–19 and 227–31, respectively. For a more skeptical view on the prevalence of overconfidence, see Robyn Dawes and Matthew Mulford, "The False Consensus Effect and Overconfidence: Flaws in Judgment or Flaws in How We Study Judgment," in the same issue, 201–11. On loss aversion and prospect theory, see Daniel Kahneman and Amos Tversky, "Prospect Theory: An Analysis of Decision Under Risk," *Econometrica* 47 (1979): 263–91, and Jack Levy, "Prospect Theory and International Relations: Theoretical Applications and Analytical Problems," *Political Psychology* 13, no. 2 (June 1992): 283–307. For an overview of the literature on attribution bias, representativeness bias, and availability bias, see Andrew Bennett, *Condemned to Repetition? The Rise, Fall, and Reprise of Soviet-Russian Military Interventionism 1973–1996* (Cambridge, Mass.: MIT Press, 1999), 89–92.

7. Alexander George, *Bridging the Gap: Theory and Practice in Foreign Policy* (Washington, D.C.: U.S. Institute of Peace, 1993), xviii.

8. Alexander George, Ohio University lecture, October 19, 1994.

9. See, for example, Bruce W. Jentleson, ed., *Opportunities Missed, Opportunities Seized: Preventive Diplomacy in the Post–Cold War World* (Lanham, Md.: Rowman & Littlefield, 1999); David A. Lake and Donald Rothchild, eds., *The International Spread of Ethnic Conflict: Fear, Diffusion and Escalation* (Princeton, N.J.: Princeton University Press, 1998).

10. See Tim Sisk, *Power Sharing and International Mediation in Ethnic Conflicts* (Washington, D.C.: USIP Press, 1996); Barry Posen, "The Security Dilemma and Ethnic Conflict," in *Ethnic Conflict and International Security,* ed. Michael Brown (Princeton, N.J.: Princeton University Press, 1993), 103–24; Chaim Kaufmann, "Possible and Impossible Solutions to Ethnic Civil Wars," *International Security* 20, no. 4 (Spring 1996): 136–75; and Radha Kumar, "The Troubled History of Partition," *Foreign Affairs* 76, no. 1 (January/February 1997): 22–34.

11. George F. Kennan, *Memoirs, 1925–1950* (Boston: Little, Brown, 1967), 326.

12. Dean Acheson, *Present at the Creation: My Years in the State Department* (New York: Norton, 1969), 214.

13. Acheson, *Present at the Creation,* 214.

14. Kennan, *Memoirs,* 327.

15. The outyear projections in federal budget planning give the appearance of long-term planning, but they actually tend to be little more than conjectures and political numbers. So, too, with the quadrennial defense review, the outyears of which bear little resem-

blance in budget figures and often in strategy to what the numbers and plans become once they are "in years." As another example, the Environmental Protection Agency (EPA) has a large planning office, but much of its focus is operational.

16. Yaacov Y. I. Vertzberger, *Risk Taking and Decision Making: Foreign Military Intervention Decisions* (Stanford, Calif.: Stanford University Press, 1998), 49.

17. Stearns, *Talking to Strangers*, 153.

18. This point draws on Bruce W. Jentleson, "In Pursuit of Praxis: Applying International Relations Theory to Foreign Policy Making," in *Being Useful: Policy Relevance and International Relations Theory,* ed. Miroslav Nincic and Joseph Lepgold (Ann Arbor: University of Michigan Press, 1999).

19. George, *Bridging the Gap*, 117–18.

20. Robert Bowie and Richard Immerman, *Waging Peace: How Eisenhower Shaped an Enduring Cold War Strategy* (New York: Oxford University Press, 1998), vii.

21. Richard Neustadt and Ernest May, *Thinking in Time: The Uses of History for Decision-Makers* (New York: Free Press, 1986), 232–46. On the (mis)use of historical analogies, see also Yuen Foong Khong, *Analogies at War: Korea, Munich, Dien Bien Phu, and the Vietnam Decisions of 1965* (Princeton, N.J.: Princeton University Press, 1992).

22. Philip E. Tetlock, "Close-Call Counterfactuals and Belief-System Defenses: I Was Not Almost Wrong but I Was Almost Right," *Journal of Personality and Social Psychology* 75, no. 3 (1998): 639–52; and Tetlock, "Theory-Driven Reasoning about Plausible Pasts and Probable Futures in World Politics: Are We Prisoners of Our Preconceptions?" *American Journal of Political Science* 43, no. 2 (April 1999): 335–66.

23. Kennan, *Memoirs*, 343.

24. Kennan, *Memoirs*, 467.

25. Anthony Lake interview with Bennett, Spring 1998.

26. Lincoln Bloomfield, "Planning Foreign Policy: Can It Be Done?" *Political Science Quarterly* 93, no. 3 (Fall 1978): 375.

27. Lucian Pugliaresi and Diane T. Berliner, "Policy Analysis at the Department of State: The Policy Planning Staff," *Journal of Policy Analysis and Management* 8, no. 3 (1989): 390–91.

28. See Terry Diebel, "Bush's Foreign Policy: Mastery and Inaction," *Foreign Policy* 84 (Fall 1991); and Thomas Omestead, "Why Bush Lost," *Foreign Policy* 89 (Winter 1992–93): 70–81.

29. Geoffrey Piller, "DOD's Office of International Security Affairs: The Brief Ascendancy of an Advisory System," *Political Science Quarterly* 98, no. 1 (Spring 1983): 62–65.

30. Piller, "DOD's Office of International Security Affairs," 68–70.

31. Acheson, *Present at the Creation,* 214.

32. Cited in Rothstein, *Planning, Prediction and Policy-Making,* 62, fn. 71.

33. Cited in Pugliaresi and Berliner, "Policy Analysis at State," 381.

34. Cited in Rothstein, *Planning, Prediction and Policy-Making,* 84.

35. Bloomfield, "Planning Foreign Policy," 376–77.

36. Rothstein, *Planning, Prediction and Policy-Making,* 61.

37. Robert Bowie, videotaped statement at a State Department conference marking the fiftieth anniversary of policy planning, U.S. Department of State, 1997.

38. Andrew Bennett, Joseph Lepgold, and Danny Unger, eds., *Friends in Need: Burden Sharing in the Gulf War* (New York: St. Martin's, 1997).

39. Rothstein, *Planning, Prediction and Policy-Making*, 60–61.

40. Pugliaresi and Berliner, "Policy Analysis at State," 380.

41. Acheson, *Present at the Creation*, 373–74.

42. George F. Kennan, *Around the Cragged Hill: A Personal and Political Philosophy* (New York: Norton, 1993), 190.

43. For further discussion of the "water's edge myths," see Bruce W. Jentleson, *American Foreign Policy: The Dynamics of Choice in the 21st Century* (New York: Norton, 2000), chaps. 2 and 6.

44. Kennan, *Memoirs*, 467 (citing his diary).

45. Kennan, *American Diplomacy, 1900–1950* (New York: New American Library, 1951), 59. For the alternative view of the more reasoning public, see Benjamin I. Page and Robert L. Shapiro, "Foreign Policy and the Rational Public," *Journal of Conflict Resolution* 32 (1988): 211–47; Bruce W. Jentleson, "The Pretty Prudent Public: Post Post-Vietnam Opinion on the Use of Military Force," *International Studies Quarterly* 36 (March 1992): 49–74; Bruce W. Jentleson and Rebecca L. Britton, "Still Pretty Prudent: Post–Cold War American Public Opinion on the Use of Military Force," *Journal of Conflict Resolution* 42 (August 1998): 395–417.

46. Kennan, *Memoirs*, 328.

47. Alexander L. George and Jane E. Holl, *The Warning-Response Problem and Missed Opportunities in Preventive Diplomacy* (Washington, D.C.: Carnegie Commission for Preventing Deadly Conflict, 1997).

48. This was done to some extent under Joesph Nye at DOD ISA, in part facilitated by Nye's having just come from heading the National Intelligence Council and being attuned to both the value of the intelligence community's work and the need for more effective policy linkages.

49. Pugliaresi and Berliner, "Policy Analysis at State," 386.

50. Rothstein, *Planning, Prediction and Policy-Making*, 25.

· 9 ·

Why Foreign Policy (When It Comes to Judgment, at Least) Is Not Pornography

Richard N. Haass

*W*as President Bill Clinton right to convene the Camp David summit and seek to bring about a comprehensive peace between Israel and the Palestinians? Is the United States right to go ahead with missile defense and move beyond the Anti–Ballistic Missile Treaty? What approach should be taken vis-à-vis Saddam Hussein? What arms ought to be provided to Taiwan? How should the United States go about contending with the combined threat posed to Colombia's stability by drugs and violence? What policy should the United States adopt to deal with global climate change?

There are no obvious or easy answers to these foreign policy questions. All, however, confront the current administration and Congress, and all require the exercise of good judgment. Yet exercising good judgment in the foreign policy realm turns out to be as difficult as it is important. It can be argued that this is as true for public policy of any sort, but foreign policy is inherently more difficult. There is often a lack of accurate information about the thinking of critical actors. This can be the result of a range of factors, including intended secrecy, deception, language, ignorance, bias, and cultural barriers. Understanding the calculations of a Saddam Hussein or a Kim Jong-Il is far from easy; appreciating how strongly mainland Chinese feel about Taiwan, or empathizing with the intensity of an Indian or a Pakistani toward Kashmir, can be impossible for an outsider.

Exercising good judgment in the realm of foreign policy is difficult for another reason, one that has nothing to do with the "foreignness" of what is at hand. For the most part, the major foreign policy questions of this or any other period—What can we expect some other government to do? What constitute America's vital national interests? What policy instruments should be used in what ways to defend and promote them?—do not lend themselves to the sort of quantitative methodologies that are useful in tackling decisions in

247

budget-driven realms. Systems analysis can be useful in deciding whether to procure one of two weapon systems, but it has little to offer when it comes to influencing whether and how to use any such capability. More generally, the number and range of factors that normally need to be considered in any exercise of foreign policy–related judgment overwhelm the capacity of systems analytical techniques; what is more, the unavoidable subjectivity and impossibility of assigning precise weights or values to relevant factors also tend to undermine the utility of formal models and equations.

HARD TO KNOW IT EVEN WHEN YOU SEE IT

So how does one identify good judgment in foreign policy? The most likely approach would be one that equated good judgment with successful outcomes—that is, those outcomes that met their stated objective at or below expected costs. This approach turns out to be less straightforward than many might assume. Success is inherently subjective. Both NATO enlargement and the U.S. Senate's defeat of the Comprehensive Test Ban Treaty (CTBT) in October 1999 constituted successes for proponents of these outcomes, but whether either represented a case of good judgment is less clear-cut. In the case of NATO enlargement, success was incontrovertible in the sense that NATO expanded from sixteen to nineteen members. But while advocates would maintain that this success reflected good judgment—it helped anchor three newly democratic countries to the West and constituted a hedge against political uncertainty in Russia—enlargement also may have diluted alliance cohesion, posed problems for the security of those countries not admitted, and contributed to the rise of more nationalist and anti-Western political forces in Russia. How these effects are weighed and over what time period would clearly affect assessments of the quality of the judgment involved.[1]

The defeat of the Comprehensive Test Ban Treaty by the Senate also highlights the difficulty in judging success because of what may be called direct and indirect considerations. For example, even someone who harbored doubts about the desirability of the CTBT—whether because of a desire to maintain an option to test nuclear warheads in order to ensure stockpile reliability and facilitate development of new warhead designs or because of concerns over the ability to verify any accord with complete confidence—might still view the Senate's rejection of the treaty as an exercise in poor judgment because of the impact of the vote on U.S. efforts to stem the spread of nuclear weapons or on how the United States would likely be perceived in the world. By this calculation, the possible benefits of rejection in the narrow could be more than offset by the broader costs to American foreign policy.

In yet another example, what one observer might judge to be a successful outcome in the 1990–91 Persian Gulf War—the liberation of Kuwait and the weakening of Iraq's military at little human or financial cost to the United States—might be judged less generously by someone who equated success with the ouster of Saddam Hussein and the installation of an enduring democratic government in Iraq. Or take the subsequent example of Haiti. It is possible to describe the 1994 U.S. intervention as a success at first, in that it helped to stabilize a country that faced a humanitarian catastrophe and threatened its neighbors with a mass exodus of people. But the same intervention looks less successful with the passage of time as it remains an open question whether Haiti can avoid sliding back into endemic poverty and political violence.

There is also an element of tautology in equating good judgment and successful outcomes. Ambitious policies are less likely to result in successes (much less complete successes) than policies defined by modest objectives. Yet to aim low when much is attainable would hardly constitute a case of good judgment if it meant that an opportunity to achieve something substantial was squandered. By this reckoning, the four days of punitive attacks launched in December 1998 against Iraq by the United States were a case of bad judgment that succeeded only in the most limited (and essentially meaningless) sense of meting out a dose of pain. Far better would have been the more demanding approach of attacking Iraq's armed forces in an open-ended fashion, be it to coerce Iraqi compliance with United Nations resolutions calling for inspection of suspected weapons of mass destruction, to stimulate a coup led by disgruntled elements of the armed forces, or both.

It turns out that the criterion of success is not enough; indeed, it can even be misleading if it is equated with good judgment. For example, a policy might turn out well despite poor judgment. Luck may have a role. Or the other side may have exercised even worse judgment. Kosovo is relevant in this regard. American and NATO officials badly misjudged how Serbia would react to the threat of force or to its introduction. Rather than back down once NATO initiated a limited series of cruise missile and bombing raids, Slobodan Milosevic ordered an intensification of the campaign against ethnic Albanians, and, in the process, created as many as one million refugees and internally displaced persons and killed some ten thousand innocent men, women, and children. After more than ten weeks, however, Milosevic capitulated, accepting NATO's demands that he cease all actions against the Kosovars, withdraw all military and paramilitary forces from the province, and accept a NATO-dominated international peacekeeping presence. The people of Kosovo were allowed to return and establish a largely autonomous society nominally under Serbian sovereignty.

NATO's ability to achieve its stated goals may for some qualify as a success. But the campaign hardly qualifies as an example of good judgment. The war was costly in both humanitarian and economic terms. It was also costly diplomatically: U.S. relations with both China and Russia were set back, in the process adversely affecting interests with greater intrinsic importance. It is also not obvious that the war was necessary: the scale of the humanitarian problem prior to NATO's bombing was relatively modest, and better diplomacy might have averted the need to use force.[2]

A second problem with equating judgment and outcomes stems from the opposite of the first: a policy initiative that appeared to end in failure. A case in point here would be U.S. policy toward Iraq in the two-year period beginning with the end of the Iran–Iraq war in mid-1988 and ending with Saddam Hussein's invasion of Kuwait in August 1990. Clearly, the attempt by the Reagan and Bush administrations to engage Saddam Hussein to encourage more moderate and constructive Iraqi behavior at home and abroad failed dismally.

Less clear is whether this policy failure constituted a case of bad judgment. The United States and Iraq cooperated in a limited fashion during the course of Iraq's war with Iran. Saddam Hussein had shown some signs of accommodation, including forcing the notorious terrorist Abu Nidal to leave Iraq. And it was not apparent that a more confrontational policy could be implemented, as the strongest advocates of trying to work with Saddam—Iraq's Arab neighbors and the principal European countries—were the very states whose cooperation would be required if a confrontational policy involving political and economic sanctions (not to mention military force) were to have any chance of succeeding.[3]

A more plausible critique of the policy is that it was implemented poorly. The problem was not so much the initial judgment to try a policy of constructive engagement—again, it can be argued it appeared better and certainly no worse than the alternatives—but rather how it was carried out. The lack of specificity as to what was expected of Iraq and what Iraq could expect in turn was an error. In addition, once the evidence began to mount that the policy was not working, it is not clear that the Bush administration reacted as sharply as it might have. Thus, the verdict is not so much one of bad policy (and bad initial judgment) as it is one of sub-optimal policymaking, reflecting less than optimal judgment along the way. The lesson is clear: the exercise of good judgment is not an event or one time act so much as an ongoing process.

A third problem with equating success and good judgment stems from a lack of transparency. Even in retrospect it can be hard to discern why something turned out the way it did and to what extent policy initiatives were responsible. Here again Kosovo is applicable. Just why Milosevic capitulated remains unclear. It is unlikely that the bombing was responsible, given postconflict reports that indicate how little was actually destroyed. It could have been Russian diplomacy, reports NATO was finally preparing a ground option, or some combination of these factors. We simply don't know.

The end of the cold war is another example in which hindsight is less than 20:20. To what extent was victory in the cold war the result of prolonged good judgment by the West? Or to what extent was it inevitable, the consequence of intrinsic flaws (prolonged bad judgment) in the Soviet system? Similarly, to what extent was the final chapter in the cold war—German unification within NATO and the peaceful demise of the USSR—the result of the good judgment of President George H. W. Bush and those around him? Or should this outcome be attributed more to poor judgment of Mikhail Gorbachev (who clearly lost control of the processes he stimulated), good fortune, or both? Did U.S. interest in funding a strategic defense system help push the Soviets over the top as some have alleged? Did the war in Afghanistan sap the strength of the Soviet system and the confidence of the Red Army? Or were these factors at most marginal in their impact? Answering these questions and determining the relative weighting in accounting for what transpired would obviously require nothing less than a massive history; what is relevant for our purposes, however, is simply the difficulty in discerning good judgment even with the benefit of the passage of time.[4]

Time introduces an additional complication. One need not go as far as Zhou En-lai (who, when asked for his views of the French Revolution, reportedly answered that it was too soon to tell) to agree with the point that some policies need years or even decades to bear fruit. This consideration helps explain the disagreement as to whether the policy of embargoing Fidel Castro's Cuba is the best policy; advocates would say yes, only that it needs more time, while critics would argue the opposite, saying enough time has passed and that the policy is not working as intended. Time can also work the other way, as what initially appeared as a success may begin to lose luster, especially if unintended consequences come to pass. Some would thus argue the "success" of supporting the Afghan resistance against the Soviets looks less complete given the subsequent rise of a Taliban-dominated Afghanistan. Again, good judgment can be difficult to certify.

MAKING IT BETTER

None of the prior discussion is meant as an argument for giving up on the grounds that defining good judgment is too hard. Policymakers must act and in so doing exercise judgment. For obvious reasons, it is better that such judgment be sound than not.

But what is good judgment? Good judgment can be defined as the ability to assess a situation accurately and, where applicable, prescribe a course of feasible policy that does the most to advance recognized interests and bring about desirable outcomes at the lowest possible direct and indirect costs.

Good judgment begins with a careful reading or assessment of the situation at hand: the intrinsic as well as indirect or associated stakes along with the likely behavior of critical actors given their known aims, capacities and constraints. Good judgment continues with a basic calculation of the likely costs and benefits of a particular course of action. Costs include but should not be limited to the financial. They are both direct and indirect, and they affect both the sending side and others, including but not limited to the intended target. Costs can encompass human life, the time and political capital of policy-makers, and the full range of interests associated with foreign policy.

A second calculation involves weighing this set of likely costs and benefits against those that would be likely to result from a range of alternative policies. For example, the exercise of good judgment requires that one compare the likely consequences of employing military force in a certain mode against using other potential types of military intervention—and then again vis-à-vis other forms of intervention, including sanctions, incentives, and various forms of diplomacy.

In this second set of calculations, it is essential that one of the alternatives be that of doing nothing (or doing nothing different than what exists or is already in train). Here the decision not to intervene in Rwanda as order disintegrated in early 1994 is a case in point. Any cost savings (soldiers and financial) derived from turning away from this humanitarian nightmare must be viewed against the horror of what transpired and the possibility that a low-cost intervention could have saved hundreds of thousands of lives.[5]

In all of these assessments, the analysis must be rigorous if it is to contribute to the quality of the judgment. As Richard Neustadt and Ernest May have written, this involves discriminating carefully between what is known and what is believed.[6] Second, the prospects of certain developments materializing need to be considered. In addition, analysis can benefit from introducing what Neustadt and May term "Alexander's question": What would need to happen to justify revising one's bottom-line judgment? Such a question can help highlight the most critical factors shaping an analysis. Last, the time horizon chosen must be meaningful and provide a fair test of what was sought.

Another perspective to bring into the decision process that could improve the quality of the judgment is that of history. Here, again, the work of Neustadt and May is useful. What is most relevant for our purposes is the need for a careful assessment of both the likenesses and differences with any historical analogies. Clearly, the two Harvard professors are as worried about the misuse of history as they are interested in encouraging its use, and for good reason. Not every compromise is another Munich; not every struggle in some far-off country risks becoming another Vietnam.

History played an influential part in controversial decisions in the 1990–91 Gulf War. In part, the decision not to march on Baghdad reflected a view that the United States had erred significantly in expanding its war aims nearly forty years before when it moved north of the thirty-eighth parallel in Korea. That decision cost the United States dearly as it led to Chinese intervention and a costly stalemate on the ground. During the Gulf War, it was argued that expanding war aims would undermine domestic and international support for the effort and embroil the United States in a costly and prolonged occupation of Iraq from which it could not easily extricate itself. Although the two situations were very different—the danger in 1991 was not external intervention by a neighboring power—there were still lessons worth bearing in mind. Above all, policymakers (including this one) were cognizant of the danger of allowing war aims to expand amidst the flush of victory.

As a rule, any change in aims should be the result of analysis no less rigorous than the analysis that accompanied the original decision to act. The failure of the Clinton administration to adhere to this rule led to tragedy in Somalia, when a limited humanitarian intervention evolved into peacemaking. Actually, it was poor judgment twice over: first, by allowing the mission to become something neither warranted by the scope of interests or necessitated by the situation on the ground and, second, by the decision not to provide the additional troops and equipment the more ambitious mission required. This line of thinking is not limited to when events are going well; indeed, the same logic would argue for not reducing strategic aims amid tactical setbacks. In this regard, the behavior of Franklin Roosevelt and Winston Churchill during World War II would seem to qualify as good judgment.

Making use of general propositions can also help improve the quality of judgment. General propositions are more concrete than theories or hypotheses, and they can be expressed as either findings or recommendations. They are often generated by the sort of research more common to think tanks and public policy schools than universities, and when adopted widely they can become part of the conventional wisdom.

One area in which general propositions exist is negotiation and conflict resolution. A common question is whether the United States should undertake an effort to settle a given dispute and, if so, with what approach. Such a decision is important, as any initiative will require time and other resources. Failure could make a bad situation worse. Or it could mean squandering an opportunity to achieve real progress—an opportunity that might not come around again.

Analysis of conflicts suggests that considerations of "ripeness"—one example of a general proposition—can aid judgment. A number of elements are central to the concept: the willingness and ability of the local parties to enter into meaningful negotiations; the existence of the outlines of compromise; the acceptability of a process.[7] Where all these factors are present, as was arguably the case in Northern Ireland in the mid-1990s, it makes sense (as the Clinton administration chose) to forge ahead; where not, diplomats are well advised to lower their ambitions, emphasize policies that can engender ripeness where it is missing, or both. Such considerations led the Bush administration to undertake relatively ambitious, face-to-face peace talks involving Israel and its Arab neighbors at Madrid in the aftermath of the 1990–91 Gulf War—and to promote far more modest arrangements involving Israelis and Palestinians during the earlier 1989–90 period.

Obviously, determinations of ripeness are in and of themselves an exercise of judgment. Each component requires separate assessment. There is no available formula or equation, but only the careful marshaling of evidence about, for example, the ability or willingness of a given leader to persuade or force his government and society to support or otherwise accept an agreement. Here there is no substitute for accurate, specific, and up-to-date knowledge of the political system and political leadership in question. Still, some degree of judgment is unavoidable given gaps in what it is possible to know and the need to weigh various considerations. At the end of the day, though, no analyst can predict with certainty what will happen. A case in point is the difficulty even the most experienced observers had in the spring of 2000 in understanding the readiness and ability of Syrian President Hafez al-Assad to enter into a peace treaty with Israel. The best the analyst can do in such circumstances is provide probabilities and identify the principal knowns, unknowns, and factors likely to prove critical. In the end, the exercise of judgment falls within the bounds of social science, with the emphasis more on "social" than "science."

Other foreign policy tools—including military force, sanctions, and incentives—also lend themselves to general propositions that can improve the quality of judgment regarding whether and how to use them.[8] Military interventions are perhaps the most closely examined sort. A review of recent interventions suggests that air power should not be asked to do too much, decisiveness is preferable to gradualism, exit dates (as opposed to strategies) should be avoided, and affecting the internal politics of a society (be it to promote integration or assist one or another faction) can be a difficult and costly job and far more demanding than promoting separation or simply providing humanitarian help without choosing sides. Keeping these and other demonstrated guidelines or patterns in mind can only help.

Serious study of economic carrots and sticks likewise suggests a set of basic guidelines. Sanctions are not appropriate for achieving ambitious goals, especially when time is short. Such knowledge might have been useful in persuading those who believed that sanctions alone would prompt Saddam Hussein to withdraw voluntarily from Kuwait. Other cases strongly argue against the use of sanctions when there is little international support. This point should caution against U.S. reliance on unilateral sanctions as a tool to be used to influence the behavior of many of the so-called rogue states. In the case of incentives, past experience highlights the importance of negotiating detailed road maps that indicate just what is expected of the target state and what it in return can expect as a reward for improved behavior—and as a penalty for continued undesirable behavior. This is akin to what the United States did in negotiating the "Agreed Framework" with North Korea in 1994, in the process resolving (at least for a time) the threat to stability posed by the North Korean nuclear weapons program. European countries appear to have departed from both dimensions of this guidance in their so-called critical dialogue with Iran, as did the United States in its approach to Iraq in the late 1980s. The fact that poor judgment led to policies that accomplished little thus comes as no surprise.

The exercise of judgment demands careful attention to specific context. What held true in the past may no longer apply. For example, axioms about the use of force might prove less valuable if relevant technologies change in important ways; not surprisingly, the greater accuracy and lethality of conventional weapons launched from great distances have stimulated questioning of existing concepts and the promulgation of new ones as regards air power. Similarly, it is possible that the demise of the cold war and the emergence of a world characterized by globalization may have consequences for policy conclusions (say, for the utility of unilateral sanctions) drawn from a quite different geopolitical setting. As a rule, it makes sense to subject propositions to extra scrutiny (but not necessarily reject them) amidst such contextual changes.

GROUP GROPES

Good judgment can also be promoted by institutional and procedural arrangements as well as by intellectual discipline. Competition is one such arrangement. It is important that judgment on critical subjects (or the application of general propositions) not be limited to one individual or group. Multiple tasking of standing bodies makes sense, particularly when the stakes are large. The quality of intelligence benefits from separate analysis conducted by the State Department's Bureau of Intelligence and Research, the Defense Intelligence Agency, various components of the Central Intelligence Agency, and the

National Intelligence Council. Standing oversight bodies, such as the President's Foreign Intelligence Advisory Board, can provide useful perspective. In special cases, ad hoc "red teams" composed of knowledgeable outsiders can be created to provide alternative viewpoints and intellectual competition. Institutionalizing a dissent channel (as is done in the Department of State) also provides a mechanism for individuals to get their assessments and recommendations known by superiors when their immediate superior—for example, the ambassador—disagrees and blocks their communication with those back at headquarters.

Consistent with the notion of competitive analysis is a form of decision making that is similarly competitive. The classic approach is an inclusive process of multiple advocacy in which all agencies with a stake in a decision get a chance to influence the policymaking process. The State Department often assigns the same issue to a geographic bureau and to one or more functional bureaus, such as those with an emphasis on policy planning or political-military affairs. The national security process (using the National Security Council and its adviser as its hub) is an even stronger example. To be sure, this method of decision making is time-consuming and leak-prone, and it requires those at the center to foster true intellectual exchange and ensure due process. The advantage of such an approach is that it subjects proposals to criticism, thereby increasing the chances that good judgment materializes. Such institutionalized competition is preferable to systems that concentrate authority in one locale or that are so disorganized that systematic give and take among appropriate agencies never takes place. The system must also be exercised regularly and not simply when the policy is first decided on; indeed, all major policies should be reviewed at regular intervals to ensure that no inadvertent drift has occurred (as was the case with Somalia policy in 1993), that the context has not changed in significant ways, and that the chosen approach still makes sense on the merits and compared with the alternatives.

POTTER'S PROBLEM

It is tempting to simply borrow from Justice Potter Stewart's assessment of pornography and accept that while good judgment in the realm of foreign policy might be hard to define, we will know it when we see it. Alas, this turns out not to be true. Good judgment is a complex, frustrating phenomenon, especially when it comes to foreign policy. It is easily confused with success. It is elusive. It cannot be produced on demand no matter how rigorous or careful the analysis or how disciplined and competitive the decision making. Nor does urgency or the presence of high stakes make good judgment any easier to manufacture. And it is inevitably and unavoidably in the eyes of the beholder.

Still, it is essential that we strive to bring about good judgment. The good news is that the quality of judgment can be improved. This may not be necessary for those few people who possess true genius. But it is relevant for the rest of us—and available to us, so long as we make certain calculations, use history, apply general propositions, and participate in competitive analysis or decision making. Even all this may not make for good judgment, but it should make for better judgment.

NOTES

1. For the best discussion of the thinking and politics behind this decision, see James M. Goldgeier, *Not Whether But When: The U.S. Decision to Enlarge NATO* (Washington, D.C.: Brookings Institution, 1999).

2. For a somewhat more generous judgment, see Ivo Daalder and Michael O'Hanlon, *Winning Ugly: NATO's War to Save Kosovo* (Washington, D.C.: Brookings Institution, 2000).

3. See the chapter by Kenneth Juster in *Honey and Vinegar: Incentives, Sanctions and Foreign Policy,* ed. Richard N. Haass and Meghan O'Sullivan (Washington, D.C.: Brookings Institution, 2000). Also see Alexander L. George, *Bridging the Gap: Theory and Practice in Foreign Policy* (Washington, D.C.: U.S. Institute of Peace, 1993).

4. See, among others, Martin Walker, *The Cold War: A History* (London: Holt, 1995); John Lewis Gaddis, *We Now Know: Rethinking Cold War History* (New York: Oxford University Press 1997); Michael R. Beschloss and Strobe Talbott, *At the Highest Levels: The Inside Story of the End of the Cold War* (Boston: Little, Brown, 1993); and Jay Winik, *On the Brink: The Dramatic, Behind-the-Scenes Saga of the Reagan Era and the Men and Women Who Won the Cold War* (New York: Simon & Schuster, 1996).

5. See, for example, *Report of the Independent Inquiry into the Actions of the United Nations during the 1994 Genocide in Rwanda.* This report was published on December 15, 1999, and can be found at www.un.org/News/ossg/rwanda_report.htm.

6. Richard E. Neustadt and Ernest R. May, *Thinking In Time: The Uses of History for Decision-Makers* (New York: Free Press, 1986).

7. See Richard N. Haass, *Conflicts Unending: The United States and Regional Disputes* (New Haven, Conn.: Yale University Press, 1990).

8. I have tried to do this in a number of books. One, on incentives, is cited in n. 3; a second, on negotiation and ripeness, in n. 7. Two other books that I authored and edited, respectively, and that attempt to provide general guidelines meant to improve the exercise of judgment in the realm of foreign policy are *Intervention: The Use of American Military Force in the Post–Cold War World,* rev. ed. (Washington, D.C.: Brookings Institution, 1999), and *Economic Sanctions and American Diplomacy* (New York: Council on Foreign Relations, 1998).

· *10* ·

Analysis and Judgment in Policymaking

Alexander L. George

This chapter addresses the relationship between analysis and judgment in high-level decision making. My interest in this question developed during the course of research on problems of foreign policymaking over a period of many years. The observations presented may well apply to other issue areas as well, but no effort is made here to examine how the relationship of analysis to judgment operates in other policy areas.

Many scholars have attempted to develop better policy-relevant knowledge of foreign policy problems that must be dealt with by decision makers. I have joined in this effort, but I couple it with a sober view of the extent to which even high-quality scholarly studies and analysis can be expected to assure high-quality foreign policy. One must not underestimate the extent to which important policies are shaped by factors other than scholarly knowledge and objective analysis. Various political considerations and psychological factors often constrain the impact that objective analysis can have on the decisions of top-level policymakers. At the very least, however, the availability of solid knowledge and objective policy analysis can reduce the detrimental impact such factors might have on decisions. I reject, as do many others, the pessimistic conclusion that policy-relevant knowledge and good policy analysis make little difference in improving the quality of many decisions.

Some students of policymaking would argue that the sole or dominant criterion of good policy should be its *analytic rationality*—that is, identifying options likely to achieve policy objectives at acceptable levels of cost and risk. Such a view, however, reflects an overintellectualized view of foreign policy. For in designing and choosing courses of action, policymakers must be concerned not solely with meeting the ideal of analytical rationality but also with several other desiderata that will be addressed here. To highlight the necessarily broader view and more complex concerns and interests that policymakers must take into account, I have coined the term *political rationality*, which is juxtaposed to *analytic rationality*. What kind of impact can scholarly knowledge be expected to have on political decision making? My answer to this question is that often it can be expected to make only a limited but still quite essential contribution. Why is this so? Scholarly knowledge can be only an input to, not a substitute for, competent, well-informed policy analysis of a specific problem conducted within the government. Policy analysts within and around the government have the difficult task of adapting available knowledge to the particular case on hand that top-level policymakers must address and decide.

Similarly, general knowledge of generic policymaking problems is not a substitute for, but only an aid to, the choice of policy by high-level decision makers. Incidentally, much the same can be said regarding the impact of the more specialized analyses produced by competent, objective policy analysts within the government. Thus, whereas scholars and policy analysts must preoccupy themselves with the task of identifying high-quality options that meet the criterion of analytical rationality, high-level decision makers must exercise broader judgments that take account of a variety of additional considerations.

What these additional considerations are will be addressed when we turn to a discussion of what is meant by the "judgment" of policymakers. In the early days of the RAND Corporation, Charles Hitch, who organized the Economics Division there, made an observation about the role of analysis in policymaking that has intrigued me ever since. Hitch was one of the founders of modern systems analysis. However, he emphasized that the results of even the best systems analysis should be regarded as an aid to the preparation of policy decisions, not as a substitute for the "judgment" of the policymaker. Deeply convinced that scholarly analysis can make important, often indispensable contributions to policymaking, I have tried ever since to understand what is meant by "judgment" in this context.

Psychologists have written a great deal about judgment and how it can be influenced and distorted by cognitive dynamics. I am conversant also with the literature on the impact that small-group dynamics and organizational bureaucratic behavior can have on the quality of decisions. I need not attempt to summarize or comment on these important literatures except to say that I have not found in them a complete or satisfactory answer to the question of what constitutes the "judgment" of policymakers.

The first task is to conceptualize and disaggregate "judgment" in ways that will facilitate development and assessment of the role(s) it plays in decision making. I have found it necessary to replace the global notion of "judgment" with seven different types of judgment, one or more of which decision makers exercise in choosing policies. I will list and briefly discuss these types of judgment and then provide a detailed discussion of the first one. In addressing each type of judgment, we should at least begin to address the difficult task of considering how analysis can be helpful in disciplining that type of judgment.

TYPES OF JUDGMENT IN POLICYMAKING

Trade-Off Judgments among Analytical Quality of an Option, the Need to Obtain Support, and Use of Time and Political Resources

In fact, three related trade-offs are at issue here. The first is the trade-off between seeking to maximize the analytical quality of the policy to be chosen (i.e., which option is most likely to achieve given policy objectives at acceptable levels of cost and risk) and needing to obtain sufficient support for the policy option that is finally chosen. Another familiar, often difficult trade-off problem arises from having to decide how much time and policymaking resources to allocate to the effort to identify the best possible option. A third trade-off problem arises from having to decide how much political capital, influence resources, and time to expend in an effort to increase the level of support for the option to be chosen.

Judgments of Political Side Effects and Opportunity Costs

Still another type of trade-off dilemma must be recognized. The criterion of analytical rationality is applied most comfortably by the policymaker when the problem in question is "bounded"—that is, when it is insulated from other policy issues that are already on the agenda or may soon emerge. But many policy issues are embedded in broader political and policy contexts. When this is so, policymakers find it necessary to consider what effect their choice on a particular policy issue will have on their overall political standing and on other parts of their overall policy program. In choosing what to do in situations of this kind, policymakers are guided not exclusively or even primarily by the dictates of analytical rationality but may be heavily influenced by their judgment of the political side effects and opportunity costs of their choices. Of course, this is not to say that a policy choice that is "best" when judged by criterion of analytical rationality always conflicts with the decision maker's political interests—indeed, it may enhance them—or that the analytically best policy choice on a particular issue will necessarily entail significant opportunity costs, but simply to recognize that such trade-off dilemmas often do arise.

Judgments of Utility and Acceptable Risk

Policy analysts provide policymakers with relevant information for attempting to calculate the utility of different options. This task is often severely complicated by the inherent uncertainties regarding so many of the factors on which decisions and choices must be based. Although policy analysts attempt to identify relevant uncertainties and possible costs and risks, policymakers often perceive other possible costs and risks and other benefits that analysts have not considered. In the final analysis, it is the policymakers who must judge what costs and risks they are willing to accept in return for payoffs to which they attach particular value. Similarly, it is the policymakers who have to decide whether to choose an option that offers the possibility of a bigger payoff but is more risky or an option that offers less of a payoff but is less risky.

Judgment about Short-term and Long-term Payoffs

Many policy problems pose a possible trade-off between short-term and long-term payoffs. The conventional wisdom is that policymakers generally act to avoid short-term losses or to make short-term gains in preference to pursuing strategies for avoiding long-term setbacks or for long-range gains. Judgments of this kind are easier to make when policymakers are more certain of obtaining the short-term payoff than the long-term one. After all, the more distant future is laden with greater uncertainties than the near term. Moreover, the short-term payoffs—either gains or avoided losses—tend to be more highly valued by most political leaders. On the other hand, there may be instances when the policymaker will forgo short-term gains or accept short-term losses if they are deemed to be modest and when long-term prospects seem to be substantial. In sum, not all trade-offs between short-term and long-term payoffs are easily resolved, and in such situations the policymaker is faced with a greater challenge for exercising judgment.

Satisfice or Optimize

Policymakers are often faced with the need to decide whether to settle for a limited payoff in a particular situation (i.e., to "satisfice") or to strive for a substantially greater one (i.e., to optimize). The literature on complex organizations emphasizes that they are generally programmed for satisficing. Political leaders, however, are able to display more variation in making such choices, and this is another type of judgment they are sometimes called on to make.

It would be useful to study the roles general knowledge and policy analysis play, or could play, in policymakers' judgment whether to satisfice or to optimize.

Dealing with Value Complexity[1]

Many problems policymakers have to address are laden with competing values and interests. (These include, of course, not only the national interests of the country, insofar as they can be assessed, but also the personal and political stakes of the leader.) Standard models of rational policymaking cannot be easily employed in such instances insofar as the multiple values embedded in the policy problem cannot be reduced to a single utility function that can then be used as a criterion for choosing among options.

In such cases, policymakers must exercise several kinds of judgment to deal with the value complexity. Can a policy option be invented that may at least partially satisfy each of the competing values and interests? When such political creativity is not possible or is not forthcoming, policymakers have to judge value priorities. Which values and interests engaged by the policy problem are more important? What criterion of importance should be employed? If not all the values and interests embedded in the problem can be satisfied by the policy option that is selected, can additional policy measures be identified and put into effect later to offer some degree of satisfaction for these other values and interests?

Once again, one asks how general knowledge of international affairs and policy analysis can help policymakers deal with difficult issues raised by value complexity?

When to Decide

Finally, policymakers are often called on to decide *when* a decision should be made. Policymakers may or may not delay making decisions to give analysts more time to come up with better policy or to muster more support for their policy choice. But here we want to call attention to the fact that other considerations may influence policymakers' sense of the timing of a decision. The urgency of the problem itself, or domestic or international constraints or both, may influence the policymakers' judgment about when to decide on a policy, quite independently of the quality of analysis available.

TRADE-OFFS AMONG ANALYTICAL QUALITY, SUPPORT, AND USE OF TIME AND POLITICAL RESOURCES IN DECISION MAKING

Academic specialists can easily fall into the error of thinking about the quality of policy decisions in too narrow a framework. Decision makers have to deal with the tension that often exists between policy quality and the need to choose one that commands enough support. Very often a measure of quality has to be sacrificed in favor of a decision that will get the kind of political support within and outside the administration that is necessary if the policy is to have a chance of being sustained.

Another trade-off in political policymaking is the one between the quality of the decision and the policymaker's sensible use of time and of analytical and political resources. A policymaker who spends a tremendous amount of time trying to arrive at a policy decision of superior quality may incur considerable costs; time is not free. Moreover, if policymakers tie up all the analytical resources at their disposal to achieve a higher-quality decision, the analysis of other policy issues may be neglected or short-changed. (This trade-off is said to have been a problem with Henry Kissinger's style when he dominated foreign policymaking in the Nixon administration.) Policymakers also face the practical question of deciding how much of the political capital and influence resources at their disposal they should expend to gain support for a higher-quality decision. They may decide to adopt a lesser policy option for which potential support is more easily gained.

These three closely related trade-off judgments are depicted in figure 10.1. Dealing with them requires policymakers to exercise ad hoc judgments, since well-defined rules for doing so are lacking. When such dilemmas arise, how, if at all, can policy-relevant theories and generic knowledge about the type of foreign policy issue in question assist in exercising judgment? This question is all the more difficult to answer because theory and generic knowledge are most directly relevant in the search for policy options of high analytical quality. This is also the focus and objective of prescriptive models of "rational" policymaking, which pay little, if any, attention to the trade-off dilemmas identified here. In fact, I know of no theory or model of decision making that tells policymakers how best to manage trade-offs among quality, consensus, and management of time and policymaking resources. What is needed and lacking is what may be called a broader theory of *effective* decision making that would subsume in some way models of analytically rational decision making.

Nonetheless, several ideas can be put forward regarding the relevance of theory and general knowledge for dealing with some trade-off problems. Knowledge can be developed about strategies such as deterrence, coercive diplomacy, and crisis management; for example, distinctions can be made between strong and weak variants of these strategies, and between conditions that favor success and conditions that are likely to hamper success. Knowledge of this kind should be helpful in deciding whether a trade-off of policy quality for enhanced support would be acceptable or whether it would jeopardize the success of the weaker variant of the strategy chosen in order to gain additional support. Of course, the need for support may sometimes push the policymaker in the other direction—toward adopting a stronger variant of a strategy when a milder one would be more appropriate.

There is another way theory and general knowledge can contribute to a

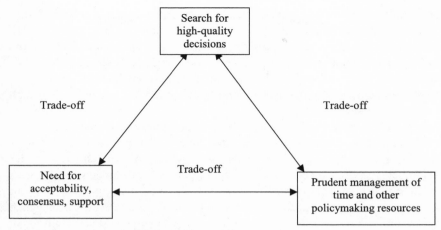

Figure 10.1 Trade-off Dilemmas in Policymaking

Source: Adapted from A. L. George, *Presidential Decisionmaking in Foreign Policy: The Effective Use of Information and Advice* (Boulder, Colo.: Westview, 1980), 2.

better understanding of the costs and risks of trade-offs between quality and consensus. As is well known, bargaining often takes place among advocates of different policy options, and at times the dynamics of bargaining weaken the role of objective analysis during the course of a search for an option that different members of the policymaking group can agree on. However, good analysis of a policy problem can equip policymakers to anticipate what kinds and degrees of effectiveness a high-quality option is likely to lose if trade-offs are made during the bargaining in order to gain broader support. In this view, *analysis is not a substitute for bargaining but serves to inform and discipline the bargaining process* in a way that helps prevent ending up with a badly compromised policy that is likely to prove ineffectual.

Perhaps this brief discussion of basic trade-off judgments policymakers often (though not always) must make suffices to provide a richer framework, albeit a more complicated one, for considering the extent to which general knowledge of foreign policy problems and policy analysis within government can contribute to the decisions of policymakers. Quite obviously, scholarly knowledge and policy analysis can contribute more to some of the judgments policymakers make than to others. Certainly, some types of judgments—particularly when strong values are at stake—are relatively insensitive to available knowledge. In other words, there can be no assurance that even a well-developed knowledge base and competent policy analysis will have impact when policymakers are impelled to make judgments in reaction to other considerations. Whereas scholars and policy analysts can and should concern themselves with identifying a high-quality policy option, top policymakers have to deal with the difficult trade-off between doing what they can to enhance the quality of a policy and obtaining sufficient consensus and support for the policy option they eventually choose. Also, top policymakers have to decide how much time and how much of the limited pool of resources to allocate to each of these efforts.

In other words, a distinction can be made between *effective* and *rational* decision making. Decision making is effective when the policymaker deals reasonably well with trade-offs between quality, support, and time and other resources. Rational decision making, on the other hand, reflects the scholar's and the policy analyst's effort to come up with a high-quality policy without reference to these trade-offs or to various political considerations with which the policymaker must deal. Although scholars have provided a number of models of rational decision making, I know of no theory of "effective" decision making that seeks to improve the ad hoc judgments top policymakers often feel obliged to make.

This remains an important problem that requires additional research and reflection. A few suggestions are offered here to stimulate efforts to link analysis more closely to judgments that decision makers are compelled to make.

SUGGESTIONS FOR ADDITIONAL RESEARCH AND REFLECTION

Cognitive psychologists have produced an impressive body of experimental research on various attribution errors and biases, but they do not seem to have given much attention to the types of judgmental problems discussed here. It surely will not tax their ingenuity and research methods to devise useful studies of this kind. Several suggestions are offered here as possibly useful starting points. First, as noted at the outset of the chapter, it will probably be necessary to disaggregate the global concept of "judgment" and develop a typology of different kinds of judgment that often enter into high-level decision making.

Second, it will be necessary to treat the level of support thought to be necessary or desirable by a policymaker as a *variable*, one that will be sensitive to the *type of policy* being addressed and to the situational context. For example, in making decisions in diplomatic crises that carry large risks, policymakers may feel it necessary to give greater weight to choosing a high-quality option rather than one of lower quality that will gain more support. For other types of policy problems, the trade-off may be weighted in favor of gaining more solid support. Moreover, the concept of "support" in a democracy such as ours itself needs to be disaggregated: *Whose* support is particularly needed by a president for different types of policies in different situations? Also, the *amount* of support judged to be necessary or at least desirable can vary for different policies and in different situations. Not to be overlooked is that in some foreign policy situations, presidents can muster more support *after* they act decisively—that is, the well-known "rally-around-the-flag" phenomenon. On the other hand, they must also be sensitive to the possibility that initial support may decline over a period of time if the policy chosen runs into difficulties and mounting costs.

A third factor that future research on questions of judgment may want to take into account is personality variables that probably affect how different individuals diagnose and deal with trade-off problems.

Experimental-type research on these questions can probably be usefully abetted by interviews with executives who have accumulated a great deal of experience in exercising various types of judgment. Do such persons operate with implicit or explicit criteria, rules of thumb, maxims, guidelines in making different types of judgment? Do they believe that they learn better judgment primarily through personal experience or also from the experience of others? Notwithstanding the limitations of self-reports in research of this kind, interviews of executives (and participant-observers of executive decision making) may yield useful hypotheses for additional examination.

One possible research design: Request executives to identify (1) an instance of what he or she considers to have been an example of his or her exercise of good judgment and (2) another example of what he or she considers to have been bad judgment. The interviewer might probe to have the executive describe his or her understanding of the trade-off faced, what it consisted of, how the trade-off was analyzed and evaluated with the benefit of what kind of information and advice, and why he or she dealt with it in the way described.

I will turn now to the question of how one might introduce the judgmental aspect of decision making into education curricula. One possibility: Public policy schools and business schools might generate case studies which report how experienced executives have tried to deal with different types of judgmental problems by making use of available policy analysis or working in the absence of such analytical studies. Such case studies might be drawn from research based on interviews with executives to which reference has already been made.

The objective of having students read and discuss these case studies would be to sensitize them to the complexity and different types of judgment executives are called upon to make and, whenever possible, call attention to the role that analytical studies of the problem played or might have played. A related question: What kinds of factual information would have been relevant and of some use?

Another pedagogical technique would make use of well-designed simulations. A variety of decisional problems that pose trade-off dilemmas could be developed. Students would be asked questions about each case designed to bring out their understanding of the nature of the trade-off dilemma, their identification of different ways in which it might be dealt with, their judgment as to how best to deal with it, and why. After each student completed the exercise, classroom discussion would follow, and an effort might be made to reach some consensus as to these questions or at least to identify the major preferred solutions. At the end of a series of such exercises, students would be asked to address the question whether guidelines for assisting judgment can be formulated and how they might be used. As a follow-up, experienced executives might be asked to evaluate the students' guidelines and, perhaps, some of the judgments expressed in the simulated cases.

NOTES

This chapter draws from previously published materials in *Bridging the Gap: Theory and Practice in Foreign Policy* (Washington, D.C.: U.S. Institute of Peace, 1993), 19–29; and "Analysis and Judgment in Policymaking," chap. 23 in *Education in a Research University*, ed. Kenneth J. Arrow et al. (Stanford, Calif.: Stanford University Press, 1996). The author expresses appreciation to the Carnegie Corporation of New York for research funds and to Kenneth Arrow, Philip Zelikow, and Deborah Welch Larson for helpful comments. In a personal communication, Herman Leonard, academic dean for teaching programs at the Kennedy School of Government, Harvard University, provided information on how the relationship between analysis and judgment is conceptualized and taught at the Kennedy School (Herman Leonard, letter to author, August 10, 1994). Paul Brest, dean of the law school, Stanford University, provided material from a seminar he teaches that touches on problems of judgment.

1. For a more detailed discussion, see A. L. George, *Presidential Decisionmaking in Foreign Policy: The Effective Use of Information and Advice* (Boulder, Colo.: Westview, 1980), introduction and chap. 2, which discusses various ways in which decision makers cope with uncertainty by adopting either psychological coping devices or analytical methods for reducing the stress created by the need to make important decisions in the face of the limits on cognitive rationality and the presence of value complexity.

Part V

REFLECTIONS ON GOOD JUDGMENT IN A DANGEROUS WORLD

· 11 ·

The World According to George W. Bush

Good Judgment or Cowboy Politics?

Stanley A. Renshon

$\mathcal{O}$n September 11, 2001, Islamic fundamentalist terrorists hijacked four planes. They flew two of them into the World Trade Center towers in New York City, causing their total destruction and resulting in just under three thousand deaths. A third plane crashed into and destroyed a section of the Pentagon with additional loss of life. And a last plane never reached its intended target because of the heroic actions of several of its passengers, who gave their lives in an attempt to prevent a fourth suicide plane crash.

Americans were traumatized. And the Bush presidency was transformed. What had been a presidency struggling to implement its agenda in the face of a divided public and contentious Congress was now a wartime presidency.[1]

It was immediately clear to observers from across the political spectrum that this was a defining moment for both Bush and his presidency (Beschloss 2001; Seib 2001; Editorial 2001b; Broder 2001a; Fineman 2001), and for Americans. The crucial issue, given the questions that had been raised about Bush's readiness for the presidency was quite simple and profound: Would he measure up?

Generally, the answer appears to be yes. He held public meetings before a stunned nation and effectively capitalized on the "rally effect" to mobilize Congress for a true bipartisan effort around the issues of American domestic and international security. After a difficult beginning, many (but not all), observers praised Bush for his forceful, steady response. Apple (2001) wrote that the Bush presidency seemed to gain legitimacy. From a solid, steady but hardly robust public approval level in the low to middle fifties, President Bush surged to unprecedented heights of public approval—at least for the short term. Whether, and for what reasons, he might be able to maintain a strong level of public support through difficult times is a critical question for his presidency and for the public's relationship to it.

President Bush said that his administration was now wholly refocused on the worldwide fight against terrorism. He himself was said to be transformed (Sanger and Bumiller 2001; Sanger and Van Natta 2001). He has used protean language casting this struggle as a "war," a "crusade," and a stark confrontation between "good and evil." Elsewhere (Renshon 1996; also see chapter 2), I have a drawn a distinction between those judgments that initially place a problem in a fitting category and those that follow. Those are *framing judgments*, and their central import lies in the understandings they reflect and the implications of these understandings for the actions that a leader takes because of them. Clearly, if there were ever a framing judgment of immense importance to the country, this occasion would qualify as one. A major question, of course, is whether Bush's framing decision is a good judgment.

The reports that the Bush presidency has been transformed seem accurate. Bush has said so, his advisers have said so, and even his critics have said so. The work of almost all the White House aides has been reoriented away from the president's previous agenda toward responding to the terrorist attack (Milbank 2001). These include a range of domestic and foreign policy initiatives including, but not limited to, mobilizing internationally and domestically to eradicate terrorist organizations and sponsors, implementing various antiterrorism legal and economic initiatives, and rebuilding the sense of domestic confidence and security that was damaged by the attack and reorienting major institutions like the FBI and INS. For a man who had often been portrayed before 9/11 as working at his job on a relaxed schedule, Bush has been very busy indeed.

It is a separate question as to whether Bush himself has been transformed, and if so in what way. Bush's judgment to wage war against terrorism may be the most important judgment of his presidency, but it is by no means the only one that he has made in foreign policy since assuming the presidency. In this chapter, I explore the question of whether Bush's judgment about going to war with terrorists is consistent with the pattern of foreign policy judgments that brought him much criticism before the terrorist attack or not. I want to argue that it is and that, to borrow Kurt Lewin's memorable phrase, "the same heat which melts the butter, fries the egg."

BEFORE SEPTEMBER 11, 2001

George W. Bush began his administration as a very controversial president, and in spite of the high approval ratings as a result of his response to the terrorist attack, he may well be so again. He was elected president but lost the popular vote by a margin of half a million votes (Associated Press 2000). He gained office by the smallest number of electoral votes in modern history—271, just one more than needed. And he gained the votes that provided his winning margin by the controversial split (5 to 4) decision of the United States Supreme Court. Accusations that Bush was not a legitimate president continued to be heard in some quarters well after he had taken his oath of office. Recounts showing that Bush would have won the Florida vote by almost any conceivable scenario have not quieted his most vocal critics. They see the fact that many intended to vote for Al Gore, but failed to do so correctly, as still undermining Bush's "moral" claim to the White House (e.g., Chait 2001; Dionne 2001).

If these circumstances didn't create enough controversy, Bush has appeared unbowed by his narrow victory margin. He began his administration with a number of far-reaching initiatives whose scope and nature are more consistent with a robust numerical mandate than with the razor-thin margin by which he gained office.

During the campaign, Bush's critics (Rich 2001; Ivins and Dubose 2000) questioned his "readiness to serve." In the area of foreign policy particularly, he was criticized as inexperienced (as most governors are), ill informed, and not an enthusiastic reader of policy papers or books. On the other hand, a number of commentators noted with approval his vice presidential selection of an experienced and "steady" hand in Dick Cheney, and they generally gave Bush high marks for selecting an experienced and intelligent foreign policy team.

Yet this selection in turn led to other criticisms. Given that Bush was known as a leader who delegated, the selection of such a senior, experienced staff meant, it was said, that Bush would be a president who passively presided over his administration. Even after his election, Bush was often presented as a man who is not interested in or in charge of his own administration's policies.

Consider, for example, the generally high marks given to Bush for his administration's handling of the U.S. surveillance plane's forced landing in China after a Chinese pilot damaged the plane in an accident resulting from his flying too close. Some not quite able to give the president credit attributed the good result to his advisers. Democratic vice presidential candidate Joseph Lieberman intimated to the *Boston Globe* that Bush was not really in charge, which in turn led to the following exchange on *Meet the Press* (2001):

> **Tim Russert:** During the whole situation with our airmen on the ground, it was concluded you told the *Boston Globe* that you really didn't know if Bush made the decisions regarding China. What did you mean by that?
> **Lieberman:** Well, they asked me how he was handling it, and as I recall the conversation, I said, you know, "We'll see what the result" [*sic*]. And, look, the result was good. But it did appear that at different times that others in the administration were playing a more active role.

Even some who might be considered sympathetic to President Bush commented on what they saw as a foreign policy lapse, one caused by the president's lack of knowledge and a result of his inexperience. When Bush (quoted in Editorial 2001c) stated rather directly that if China attacked Taiwan, "the U.S. would do whatever it took to help Taiwan defend itself," the comment caused widespread concern. Some were critical because they feared it might upset China. Others were concerned that the president seemed to be abandoning the ambiguity that had been a cornerstone of U.S. policy regarding this question.

Winston Lord (quoted in Babington and Milbank 2001), ambassador to China during the Reagan administration, came to the president's defense but in a somewhat double-edged way: "It's pretty clear to me that this was inadvertent. The language on Taiwan is very arcane, very nuanced, and people are apt to make mistakes with it. It seems to me, if this was going to be purposeful, it would be done in a different way, such as in a speech." The article added, "The dust-up appeared likely to rekindle questions over whether the former Texas governor has command of the intricate, sensitive international issues that confront presidents."

In other words, Lord, while coming to Bush's defense (or at least one assumes that is what he was doing), did so in a way that again raised the issue of the president's inexperience and perhaps as well with his ability to handle "nuance." Bush's direct response may well have been a by-product of inexperience in the "arcane, but very nuanced" language that has traditionally been used. Yet, it may also, perhaps even primarily, have been a reflection of Bush's preference for straightforward language to reflect what for him is a very clear view: This president will not allow the Chinese to militarily invade and take over an ally of the United States.

One can legitimately debate that policy statement. Perhaps it might be argued that Taiwan is not a key interest of the United States. On the other hand, letting an ally with whom the United States has had a long history of commitments be brought under Chinese control by military force would carry its own grave regional and international consequences. The blunt directness of the statement may have well upset the Chinese. However, it might also have made China more wary of forcing a military solution to the issue of Taiwan.

THE NEW DUAL PRESIDENCY

Some years ago, Aaron Wildavsky (1966; Shull 1991) wrote of "The Two Presidencies," one domestic, the other focused on foreign affairs. He argued that presidents were always more constrained in the former than the latter and would thus be tempted to turn toward foreign policy for accomplishments that were more difficult to achieve domestic domestically. Wildavsky's basic point about the frustrations of domestic policy were surely correct. However, it doesn't follow that all presidents would be tempted to "go foreign" in response or that even if they were they could do so in a relatively frustration free way.[2]

Not all presidents have the interest or skill to turn toward foreign policy, even if they are less constrained there. Among recent American presidents, Bill Clinton clearly had much more of an interest in domestic politics, even after 1994 when he had to face a Republican Congress for the remainder of his presidency. Moreover, the public's expectations for domestic attention provide an additional source of constraint even when foreign affairs may prove tempting for a president so inclined and frustrated at home. As George H. W. Bush learned, 91 percent approval ratings for enormously successful foreign policy leadership are no guarantee of reelection if the public feels that your success abroad has been at the expense of caring about problems at home. Almost eerily, his son George W. Bush faces the same circumstances with a public that strongly backs his war against terrorism but expects progress on domestic concerns as well.

Foreign policy, of course, has its own, sometimes lethal constraints. The president may have more latitude acting internationally, but in some areas, noticeably the application of military power, he operates under no less substantial restraints. Haiti, Somalia, the Gulf War, Bosnia, and Panama all involved presidential prerogatives. Yet, as these cases show, less domestic constraint does not automatically translate into clearly satisfactory successes. Indeed, *victory* itself has become an ambiguous term. The president may be able to act with less restraint in foreign affairs, but there is no immunity for unsuccessful decisions and the judgments that led to them.

This point raises the last and perhaps the strongest objection to the applicability to Wildavsky's theory to President Bush's circumstances. Whereas the American public may have given presidents latitude in foreign policy in the past, that view was based in part on a consensus that no longer exists. The presidencies of Truman, Eisenhower, and Kennedy and the first part of the Johnson administration were all predicated on the bipartisan assumptions of a bipolar cold war. The period anchored by the Vietnam War and the fall of the Soviet Union shattered that consensus.

Public expectations changed as a result. During the cold war, the public—at first reluctantly, but ultimately solidly—came to understand and support the necessity of giving the president leeway in that fight. The successful end of the cold war, however, provided a legitimate reason for Americans to do what they have always historically preferred—turn inward toward domestic issues.

By the time of the Gulf War in 1991, George H. W. Bush could not count on either an elite-bipartisan foreign consensus or much leeway from the public. He got more support from the United Nations for undoing the invasion of Kuwait than he got from Congress. After a spectacular victory with very few American causalities, Bush could not even gain a second term, because he had failed in people's minds to address sufficiently their concerns about the domestic economy.

In truth, Wildavksy's theory was overstated, not only because the historical circumstances surrounding presidential policy leadership have changed but also because his theory was anchored in the "many hats" view of presidential leadership. That basic epistemological perspective viewed the president as wearing many hats and studied each one—separately. There were studies of the president as commander in chief, as head of his party, as domestic policy-maker, and so on. Wildavsky's theory of the two presidencies fit this view well.

That view was essentially supplanted by Neustadt's (1990) classic book on presidential power. After it, no longer did scholars look across the room, see what hat the president was wearing, and analyze him accordingly. Rather, they stood behind him. From that perspective, it was clear that the presidency, no matter which role the president was playing, was occupied by one person.

This makes sense from a psychological perspective. Presidents may well have role-related considerations that change their perspective, frame their understandings, modify their calculations, and thus result in different political and policy choices. Yet it would very odd indeed if the president were to become a different person—with different ambitions, convictions and underlying ways of approaching his responsibilities—each time he addressed one of his many, and interrelated, tasks.

I want here to readapt Wildavsky's two-presidency thesis, but not in a way he had envisioned. Rather than picturing a domestic or foreign policy presidency brought about by differences in constitutional and political constraints, I want to argue that the two spheres are ever more distinguished by the requirements for successful leadership in both arenas. Foreign policy leadership in a world in which there is no consensual agreement that can operate to frame specific issues requires of the president decisiveness, clearly articulated purpose, and determination. Domestic political leadership, especially in a divided society such as the United States, must emphasize consultation, compromise, and common purpose.

The new *dual presidency* is a function not so much of constitutional mandates but of leadership psychology. It is not so much a matter of spheres of presidential activity as it is of a president's stylistic flexibility. And it is not so much a consequence of constraint as it is the public psychology that follows from public expectations. It remains for the president, who is, after all, one person—psychologically—with his singular set of ambitions, skills, ideals, and ways of carrying through relationships with all those in his personal and political world, to bridge that divide. Nowhere is this bifurcation of leadership responsibilities more clearly evident than in the presidency of George W. Bush.[3]

Bush gained office in large part because he presented himself as a person who could bring people together and bring "a new tone to Washington." He was, and presented himself as, a *reflective* leader, not a *heroic* one. He would bring people together around common ground, not a political master plan. The paradox of the Bush presidency is that he is called upon by circumstances to provide *heroic* leadership—principled, strong, and purposeful. Yet, domestically given the sharp partisanship that still permeates Washington even during a war, he is being called upon by the public, and loudly by his opposition, to develop and reflect common ground. These *are* Bush's two presidencies, and his ability to engage both of these somewhat disparate demands successfully will shape his political and historical fate.

GEORGE W. BUSH—TRANSFORMED?

The answer to the question of whether the Bush presidency has been transformed as a result of 9/11 is clear: It has. The question of whether Bush himself has been transformed is more complex. Certainly, a president's response to dramatic and extremely critical events gives us a measure of the man and his leadership. It is also true that presidential responses to even momentous events must begin with the basic building blocks and raw materials of a president's psychology, character and leadership skills.

Karl Rove, Bush's senior adviser, was asked about this:

Thomas Mann: Karl, to the outside world, it looks as if there have been two George W. Bush presidencies already, the pre–September 11 and the post–September 11. Is that simply a caricature of what we see?

Rove: Well, I'm not certain it is that much different. . . . I for one don't buy this theory that September 11th somehow changed George W. Bush. . . . But really since September 11th, I think what America has seen—and great events do not transform presidents. They bring out who they are. . . . So my view is that all this about he's changed and he's transformed, no, he's who he is, required to do more in a great crisis, so you don't manufacture these things. You don't create them. They're either there or they're not. The moment calls them out or the moment doesn't. The moment requires something of you, and you're either able to do or you aren't. (American Enterprise Institute 2001, 3)

Rove is on solid ground in one respect, but not on others. It is obviously very hard for a president or any person to change his basic psychology in response to a singular event, one that took place within the space of a few minutes. In that respect Rove is right. Bush was not a transformed person after that second plane hit the World Trade Center, but I would argue that he was a different one.

Before 9/11, Bush had many domestic policy ambitions, and several major foreign ones. After 9/11, all those competing priorities were reframed through a policy lens of singular focus: ridding the world, but more specifically the United States, of the scourge of terrorism internationally and domestically. Wildavsky's two presidencies had for Bush become one.

Before 9/11, Bush's irreverent, sometimes impish humor was frequently on display. After 9/11, it receded to the periphery replaced by a deadly serious-ness of purpose. Berke (2001; see also VanderHei 2001) reports that while Bush

> still cannot resist a joke or two (even ribald ones), dozens of friends and advisers
> who have spent time with Mr. Bush said in interviews that since Sept. 11 he has
> conducted himself far more seriously than he had before. Friends say that while
> Mr. Bush usually appears outwardly upbeat and is trying to convey a sense of
> normalcy the terrorist attacks have weighed on the fifty-five-year-old president
> far more than the lowest moments of the grueling presidential campaign.

Questions had arisen regarding Bush's level of, and even capacity for, *gravitas*—that sense of presence, standing, and authority so necessary to leaders wishing to command attention and stimulate compliance. In the hours follow-ing 9/11, a number of commentators, many critics, saw Bush as barely filling his role. Fineman (2001) wrote in *Newsweek*:

> Bush has yet to find a note of eloquence in his own voice. He is, in fact, distrust-
> ful of it, and went for Texas plain talk, rhetoric as flat as the prairie and as blunt
> as a Clint Eastwood soliloquy . . . he did not look larger than life at his Oval
> Office desk, or even particularly comfortable there.

Howard Rosenberg, a reporter for the *Los Angeles Times,* called Bush stiff and boyish, writing (quoted in Harper 2001) that "Bush has lacked size in front of the camera when he should have been commanding and filling the screen with a formidable presence; even his body language is troubling." Al Hunt (2001a), writing in the *Wall Street Journal,* said that George W. Bush's first address to Congress was "perfectly fine," but "he doesn't fill a room or a chamber." A *Newsweek* editorial noted that other leaders such as Mayor Rudi Giuliani of New York had more presidential presence.

A short time later, Bush appeared before a national audience in a prime-time live news conference. In an editorial (2001d) entitled "Mr. Bush's New Gravitas," the *New York Times* said:

> [T]he George W. Bush who addressed the nation at a prime-time news confer-
> ence yesterday appeared to be a different man from the one who was just barely
> elected president last year, or even the man who led the country a month ago.
> He seemed more confident, determined, and sure of his purpose and was in full
> command of the complex array of political and military challenges that he faces
> in the wake of the terrible terrorist attacks of Sept. 11. It was for the most part
> a reassuring performance that gave comfort to an uneasy nation. . . . He's better
> at it than he and his aides think.

Bush had found his voice as he moved from struggling to enact his political vision in a divided contentious society to a leader pursuing the larger purpose of a national mission.

In short, Bush did not become a new man after 9/11, but he certainly
became a different one. It is not possible here to explore fully the ways in
which Bush's psychology was affected by the events by 9/11. Nonetheless,
with no claim to comprehensiveness or exclusivity, it is possible to begin developing a framework for such an analysis—especially as it relates to the foreign
policy dimension of his presidency. I briefly examine those elements of interior
psychology and leadership skills that seem at this point most relevant to understanding Bush's approach to foreign policy decision making and leadership.

THE THREE PRISMS OF PRESIDENT BUSH'S FOREIGN POLICY DECISION MAKING

To the student of political psychology, a president's articulated policies, however controversial or traditional, must be reflected in and gauged against his
actual behavior. This task actually involves comparing what a president says
with what he actually does. We do so not because we expect that he will be a
slave to stated policy regardless of circumstances, but rather to gauge, over time
and circumstance, whether he acts in ways that are consistent with the views
and principles he has espoused. Strongly articulated principles of foreign policy
engagement, like their domestic counterparts, raise the issue of whether the
president is not only able to have convictions, but also to have the courage of
them.

Patriotism

Bush appears to be a real, traditional patriot. He is unabashedly proud of the
United States, clearly feels that its virtues easily outweigh its failures, respects

its traditions and institutions, and takes seriously and personally his oath to protect and preserve. Bush is not the only president to have many of these feelings, but it is rare to have a president display them so openly and often. Bush's campaign theme stressing the need to bring honor back to the White House obviously had a strategic dimension. It underscored his difference from Clinton. Yet it was very much more than just that and to miss that fact would be to miss something very important about Bush and his presidency.

Bush's love for this country is palpable, and, as with some other of his emotions, he wears it on his sleeve. Before 9/11, you could read through transcripts of his talks and interviews and repeatedly come upon his expression of how proud he was to serve the country and represent it. It was "a huge honor to represent America overseas" (Bush 2001e, 947). Or, "It's a honor to represent our nation in foreign capitals and be with foreign leaders" (Bush 2001d, 1046). One could cite many, many more such sentiments. The point here is that while many presidents might have felt it, Bush says it—often. If the same words, spoken repeatedly in different circumstances, are any indication, he truly believes it.

Given the depth of these feelings and the large role they play in shaping Bush's approach to the presidency, the terrorist attack of 9/11 could not have failed to cause him great personal anguish. But it also had the effect of providing strong emotional fuel to an already high level of resolve, framed by an intense focus on bringing those responsible, and their allies, to justice. After 9/11, Bush said that the war on terrorism was *the* focus of his presidency. These were not just the words of a leader whose country had been attacked. They were the words of a man, also president, forced to experience the vicious, unprovoked, and successful assault of a venerated object of his affections.

I think Bush's deep patriotism specifically expressed as love of country is one explanation for both his measurable rise in gravitas and his sense of mission. Gravitas reflects seriousness of purpose and a corresponding commitment that must be taken seriously by others. Bush is by nature a man with a sense of humor, but there is nothing humorous about these circumstances. The stakes could not be higher, and he recognized them for what they are: matters of life and death for this country.

American National Interest

America's interest is the primary prism through which Bush filters foreign policy debates. Yes, it is true that national interest is not always clear. It is also certainly true that one person's view of national interest is another's grave policy mistake. It is also true that "national interest" is complex, and that there are debates about what, exactly, that means in specific circumstances.[4] Yet, on a number of issues, Bush—and his advisers—have very strong views on what these interests are.

Among the many such views that Bush articulated during his campaign were the following:

1. The military was below adequate capability and needed to be strengthened.
2. The military was ill focused and ill configured, too oriented toward past conflicts and not sufficiently oriented to future ones.
3. There was too much emphasis on multilateral commitments, which, as a result, thinned out America's resources and ability to deal with problems of primary national interest.
4. Western values of economic and personal freedom are the foundation of our strength domestically—but also abroad—and trade, democracy, and free market systems are the best vehicles with which to address issues of poverty and economic development.
5. The United States has too many nuclear weapons and can therefore take steps, unilaterally, if necessary, to reduce them.
6. There is too much reliance on treaties that limit the compliant and not the cheaters.
7. In some ways because of the end of the cold war, the world is still a very dangerous place—full of unstable, violent regimes, some of which would like to humble if not destroy us.
8. As a result of issue 7, the United States had to take immediate steps to protect itself with steps ranging from creating an antiballistic missile (ABM) defense system to reviewing American defense postures and developing oil resources to decrease dependency.

Many, if not all of these views, were fiercely debated before the terrorist attack of September 11 and will most likely be debated again. However, it cannot be said that they are vague. Indeed, several points (2, 3, 7, and 8) were, in view of 9/11, prescient. Certainly, they are a clear statement of the administration's view of its definitions of national interest in these times and circumstances.

These strong views of national interest have fueled many of the policy debates and criticisms that have surrounded the Bush presidency. An ABM system? It's needed and the sooner we begin to work on it, the safer America will become. The ABM treaty? It's antiquated, a relic, and a leftover from a time with different circumstances. Global warming and the Kyoto Treaty? It isn't possible to support a treaty that will impose huge costs on the American economy—and by extension on those domestically and internationally who depend on its robustness. Nor can a serious treaty to reduce global warming ignore developing countries such as China and India.[5]

An Independent-minded Internationalist

Bush's decision to turn his back on what he and, it should be remembered, the Senate saw as a fatally flawed climate treaty was one of several such instances. His decision not to send a high-level U.S. delegation to the United Nations–sponsored World Conference against Racism, Xenophobia, and Related Prejudice was another (Perlez 2001). And there were the ABM treaty from which Bush subsequently formally withdrew, the decision to reject a Draft Enforcement Plan for 1972 Ban on Biological Weapons (Associated Press 2001c), a decision not to submit an international convention establishing a permanent international tribunal to the U.S. Senate for ratification (Alvarez 2001), the decision to continue the ban on U.S. participation in the Nuclear Test Ban Treaty that the Senate had refused to ratify in 2000 (Editorial 2001e), and his public reluctance to commit U.S. military forces to police duties. All of these decisions have been viewed and criticized by many as a by-product of Bush's unilateral style—hence the term "cowboy politics."

Discussions of Bush's "unilateral style" were temporarily suspended after the attack of September 11. Former critics hailed the president's willingness and ability to develop a broad-based coalition to fight terrorists. Bush, it was said, had learned that he could not act independently and that he had recognized out of America's hour of necessity that he needed allies.

Well, yes and no. In an interview with the *Washington Post* ("Interview" 2001, italics mine),[6] Secretary of Defense Donald Rumsfeld had this to say about the administration's strategy of working with allies:

> **Q:** I'd like to turn now if we could to some questions about your stewardship of the war. The first is this long-winded question here about turning points in the war. . . .
>
> **Rumsfeld:** First would be the September 11th attack. . . . *Another key turning point was the decision that we would not have a single coalition but rather we would use floating coalitions or multiple coalitions* and recognize that because this would be long, because it would be difficult, and because different countries have different circumstances, different perspectives and different problems, that we needed their help on a basis that they were comfortable giving it to us and we should not, ought not, and do not expect everyone to do everything. And that's fine. So if someone wants to help in this way but not that, that's fair enough. The critical element of that is that that way the mission determines the coalition. The opposite of that would be if the coalition determined the mission. Once you allow the coalition to determine the mission, whatever you do gets

watered down and inhibited so narrowly that you can't really accomplish, you run the risk of not being able to accomplish those things that you really must accomplish. That was an important decision it seems to me. October 7th really, simply happened to be the day that the bombing started.

Two different, sometimes confounded, strands of criticism are implicit in the view of Bush as a "unilateralist" (Lewis 2001). The first is that Bush goes his own way regardless of what allies suggest. The implication here is that his critics' policy suggestions are superior to his. The accuracy of these criticisms turns on the relative weight of advantages and disadvantages viewed from the perspective of the different national interests involved. Criticism of the fact that Bush followed his own assessment is not in itself evidence of the superiority of either his or his critics' positions.

It is true that Bush and his administration have come to a number of decisions that run counter to widely prevailing views. This has led to the second strand of the unilateralist criticism, which is that Bush is wrong to reject others' advice because they are allies and presumably would be upset in not having their views acted upon. Implicit in this criticism is the view that others' views of what you should do take precedence over your own assessments if they differ, or that you ought to defer in such cases out of a sense of collegiality. The latter psychology is the basis of the well-known syndrome of groupthink or concurrence seeking, which is almost universally viewed as the basis for fundamentally flawed decision making (George 1980, 22, 93–94; Janis 1972; T' Hart 1990).

International collegiality, or the lack thereof, is not synonymous with good judgment. It *may* reflect good judgment to go along with a high-quality decision that others see that way as well. It may well reflect very poor judgment to go along with a decision about which you have substantial reasonable doubts.

Moreover, the unilateralist label that has been applied to Bush does not fully or fairly describe the range of his international relations. Bush has been a very strong supporter of international trade. Trade by its nature requires collective action, and the rules that govern require widespread agreements and working partnerships. In addition, well before 9/11, he reached out in partnership to countries such as Mexico that have had an ambivalent relationship with the United States and India, with which the United States has had a cool relationship.

Bush is also a man who has placed tremendous stock in his relationships with a number of foreign leaders. He has genuinely embraced Mexico's Vicente Fox as a friend and policy partner. Earlier on, he embraced Russia's President Vladimir Putin as someone with whom he could deal—and he was right. His relationship with British Prime Minister Tony Blair is extremely close.

If Bush is a unilateralist, he is a very unusual one. His very notable tendency to reach out to varied leaders for policy and political partnerships on foreign policy issues of mutual concern is certainly inconsistent with that view. So is the same pattern that has been noticeable in Bush's relationships in Congress, where he has forged a number of diverse and different bipartisanship partnerships to address particular policy issues (e.g., tax reform, education).

There are two aspects to Bush's approach to his responsibilities as commander in chief that are critical to understanding President Bush, one growing out of how he frames them, and the other a complementary dimension rooted in his psychology. The first is anchored in his belief that America's national interest should be the first and primary, though not necessarily the only, prism through which issues should be considered. That view is clearly reflected in the president's decisions noted earlier regarding various treaties. It is also clearly and strongly reflected in Rumsfeld's remarks about the administration's approach to its allies in the war against terrorism.

The second, more deeply embedded psychological anchor is Bush's approach to relationships. I have suggested elsewhere (Renshon 1996) that a president's or any person's ways of dealing with the myriad relationships they have reflect something very basic and very important about their psychologies. The psychoanalyst Karen Horney had long ago noted that people could move toward, away, or against others, but they can also stand apart from others.

Bush is clearly a man who moves toward others. Yet, he is not a man who needs to be liked and thus tied to others' approval. He can stand to be apart from others. When he said, "I'm a loving guy, and I'm also someone, however, who's got a job to do, and I intend to do it" (Bush 2001b, 1308), he captured both elements of his interpersonal psychology quite well.

BUSH'S CHARACTER PSYCHOLOGY

There is also another reason for the student of political psychology to look to a president's behavior: to gain insight into the psychology behind his principles and their enactment. A president's worldview may provide a road map for his policy views and ambitions, but his psychology[7] is the vehicle of their realization. I don't mean that accomplishing his goals can be reduced to his psychology. I do mean that that a president's psychology—the level and nature of his ambitions, the strength of his ideals, his ability and desire to make real connections with others, and the skills (cognitive, characterological, and social) that he brings to his tasks—are critical elements for his leadership. And leadership is the personal and political vehicle for carrying through the president's judgment. What, then, can we say of Bush's psychology and its relationship to his judgment? Let us start with elements of his psychology.

Ambition

Bush is a man with more policy than personal ambition. His somewhat meandering early efforts to find his footing, emotionally and occupationally, are fairly well known and, more important, generally accurate. He was an adequate but not outstanding student at a series of excellent schools (Andover, Yale, Harvard). He was a fun-loving, hardworking, but not particularly successful businessman in a field (wildcat oil exploration) that took persistence, money, and luck to succeed. Bush had the first trait, gained access to the second in part through family associations, but never did have too much of the third. He also, by his own admission, had a drinking problem, which is generally the sign of someone who would prefer not to be in constant touch with their feelings or circumstances.

Bush, as is well known, quit drinking by stopping, period. His religious mentor Billy Graham played an important role, but that point is of less interest in this context than how Bush stopped—abruptly, totally, and without backtracking. It reflects a capacity for determination and disciplined follow-through.

It was widely said that Bush was a leader who liked to focus on articulating a few policies, pursuing them relentlessly (Seib 2002). As evidence, proponents of this view pointed to Bush's campaign for governor that featured four prominent themes: education, tort reform, strong crime control, and welfare reform (Minutaglio 2000, 277–79; Mitchell 2000, 304–5). And it is true that in his first campaign for, and in his first term as governor, he did pursue these topics vigorously.

Yet, his behavior on reaching the presidency was quite different. A superficial look might indicate that Bush was going to repeat his governor's strategy in the White House. However, as governor, he had a legislature that met every other year, and the Texas governorship is a "weak" one—with few muscular executive powers. For these reasons, Bush's time as governor proved a misleading basis of generalization.

He announced on September 1, 2001, that his four priorities for the fall were "the economy; education; opportunity, including his 'faith-based' legislation; and security, including defense, Medicare and Social Security." Ari Fleischer, Bush's spokesman, promised that the president "is going to focus like a laser" on his four categories (quoted in Harris and Balz 2001).

Yet, in reality this list did not add up to four. Only two of these, the president's education bill and his faith-based bill, were embodied in a single bill.

The other policy initiatives could only be accomplished in several other, major bills. Bush's major tax cut, for example, was viewed as a first in a series of steps. The fourth area, security, contained a number of important programmatic initiatives, among them defense strategy and reorientation. These in turn involved a number of new programs such as a missile defense system.

Additionally, Bush wanted to undertake a revamping of Social Security and the Medicare program, two politically sensitive and difficult undertakings. Small wonder that David Broder (2001b) of the *Washington Post* asked whether Bush wasn't trying to do too much with too little (political capital). Broder noted that the president had actually added to his "to do" list a comprehensive energy plan, itself made up of a number of far-reaching and controversial parts, an HMO reform bill, and a trade bill to give the president "fast-track" authority (Cooper 2001). To this list he might have added an unexpected and controversial initiative to "regularize" the status of millions of illegal immigrants in this country (Schmitt 2001); a major plan for a "new federalism" (Allen and Balz 2001); a new initiative to provide housing for people with disabilities (Allen 2001d); a new plan to enforce and refine gun control; a "New Freedom Initiative" to help people with disabilities (Hunt 2001b); and a review of a host of regulatory rules in areas including ergonomics (Dewar and Skyrzycki 2001), medical records privacy (Pear 2001), and several in environmental enforcement, including air pollution (Painin and Mintz 2001), land usage and control (Jehl 2001), and the reforming of the Endangered Species Act (Seelye 2001).

I could add to this list, but I think the point is clear. Far from presiding over an administration of limited policy ambitions, he is a president of *robust* policy ambitions. As Balz and Neal (2000) note, "Any one of Bush's major campaign planks could keep a president occupied for most of his first year in office; Bush seems determined to try to do them all at once." Indeed, it is precisely this fact that underlies his critics' complaint that he began his presidency as if he had received a large mandate. Along with questions about Bush's legitimacy after the difficulties of the Florida vote that brought him into office, the next most frequent complaint was that he was not governing in a way that was consistent with his narrow accession to the White House. Critics expected, and some demanded, a scaled-back agenda or one that was consistent with *their* views. Bush did neither, and that decision reflected another important element of his psychology.

Relatedness

President Bush is a man who likes others and gravitates toward them. They, in turn, gravitate toward him. After watching him over time on the campaign trail, one *New York Times* reporter (Kristof 2000) wrote, "Mr. Bush is a natural politician—far more so than the vice president—with a down-home, one-of-the-guys charm that puts people at ease. He loves the crowds, relishes the limelight and invariably comes across to audiences as likable, funny, sincere and decent."

It is a trait of his that was evident at Andover Academy (Mitchell 2000, 46–72), at Yale (Minutaglio 2000, 95; Mitchell 2000, 86–113), in his position as part owner of the Texas Rangers baseball team, and, of course, in the rise of his political fortunes. He is, in the view of many political pros, a "natural" (Powell 1999) and can work a room with the best of them. Yet, while Bush likes others and is drawn to them, he is not a man who needs to be liked, at least in the ways that have been true of many presidential contenders. Let me address the need to be liked first.

Some political leaders who are drawn toward others have a need to avoid conflict and to acquiesce to others, especially those who form their political or ideological group. These are not necessarily people who believe that to get along, you must go along—although persons with this psychology can be found in high-level political positions. Individuals who are conflict-avoidant are rare in the upper levels of partisan politics. The reason is simple: Politics is, and in the United States has increasingly become, a tough, sometimes brutal contest. Candidates hide their tough characterizations of their opponents with a smile or a folksy manner. A leader who cannot bear such contests and cannot defend himself, if he chooses not to attack, will, like Bill Bradley, wind up as a historical footnote. So, people with a true need to be liked that doesn't allow them to fight it out with their opponents are more likely to become accidents of history rather than its master.

When analysts mistakenly attribute a need to be liked to one or another political leader, they are often confounding a desire for validation with one of its manifestations. Validation is the larger category that simply refers to the importance of having other people acknowledge you for the things that you yourself find important. If you value intelligence before beauty, it will not help if someone tells you that you are handsome. If, like George W. Bush, you put no store in being a serious policy scholar, criticisms that you aren't won't have quite the same impact as they would on someone who takes pride in his or her detailed policy knowledge.

So, one important thing to know about a political leader is the basis for his own self-validation. What areas, what skills, what characteristics does he think are central to *his* sense of self and political leadership? The specific elements that form the building blocks of his sense of who he is and what he isn't are crucial to understanding when, to whom, and for what a president—or any leader—looks, to others. Simply equating a president's tendency, as is the case with George W. Bush, with a liking for and tendency to get along with others with a "need to be liked" simply will not do.

Even fierce political combatants can be the captives of those with whom they depend—those who support them and those whose support they want. Unable to stand apart from them, they find it hard to disagree with their friends or alienate their hoped-for supporters. The true test of personal and political independence is not so much whether a candidate or president can attack his opponent but whether he can disappoint his friends.

Standing Apart

In looking at a president's ability to stand apart from the influences that seek to shape him, it seems useful to look at three different areas: his capacity to take positions that he thinks right regardless of the public's level of support for them—even in those cases in which he has tried to build support but has not fully succeeded; his capacity to say what he thinks and present himself as he truly is—even in front of those whose support he would like to have; and, finally, his ability to stand apart from the views and policy preferences of his political friends.

In the 2000 presidential campaign, Bush, like his opponent, had to reach out to disparate groups. He had to mobilize and consolidate his base. He had to reach out to those who were not his supporters but might be. In addition, he had to address the characterizations of his opponent.

Most candidates do these things by tailoring their appeals. They stress issues that have proven resonance with the public, their supporters, and those who support they want to get. Bush did those these things, but he did other things as well. As one reporter (Kristof 2000) said of Bush on the 2000 campaign trail:

> While Mr. Bush has tacked right and left in his campaign to outmaneuver his rivals, it is striking how little he panders to audiences. Speaking to workers who worry about imports, he warmly recounts the benefits of free trade. Addressing wealthy Republicans decked out in pearls, he speaks sympathetically about Mexican immigrants and asserts that a single mother has "the hardest job in America." Before lily-white audiences that might favor English as the nation's official language, Mr. Bush occasionally drops a phrase in Spanish. The audiences stare back in puzzled silence.

When Bush turned to conservative South Carolina for a must-win primary against John McCain:

> Mr. Bush did not abandon the oratory he was using before South Carolina, and he frequently mentioned accomplishments and ideals that were not necessarily

what conservative voters most wanted to hear. He almost never talked about the importance of improving education without noting the strides that he said Hispanic and black students in Texas had made. He answered every question he received about illegal immigration—a source of intense vexation for some South Carolinians—by reminding voters that many Mexicans streamed into the United States simply to seek a better life for their children.

Bush is clearly a man who is comfortable standing apart.[8]

PRESIDENT BUSH: JUDGMENT AND DECISION MAKING

The questions that swirled around Bush during the presidential campaign concerned his experience and capacity for making good judgments. Critics said he was not particularly knowledgeable and, worse, seemed unable or unwilling to engage issues in a substantively nuanced way. He appeared intellectually hesitant and ill at ease straying too far from the messages that shaped his campaign. This led some to conclude he couldn't.[9]

Yet, in looking at whether a president makes good judgments, it is important to first see whether he is able to, and does, place the event in a fitting category. Those are framing decisions, and they are clearly central to good judgment. What, though, leads to being able to make good framing judgements?

Clear-eyed Views

It is worth pausing to consider just what it takes for a leader to have good judgment in making framing decisions. Perhaps the most important is clear-eyed sight. The leader has to see the issue before him for what it really is, not what he wishes it to be, what he hopes it might be, or what his policy or political views might find compatible. This is no easy matter. Presidents, like other people, use the frames of understanding they have developed over time as a result of experience to see the world. Clear-eyed sight requires that these cognitive aids be put aside if they don't fit, and to be used without hesitation if they do.

The morning that the two planes struck the World Trade towers, Bush was in Sarasota, Florida, at an elementary school. Karl Rove, a senior adviser to Bush, was with him at the school and recalled those first moments after the president learned of the attack:

> I will never forget the moment—I was there in Florida. We heard the word about 8:48, 8:49, when my assistant called me on my cell phone to say a plane

has flow into the World Trade Center. When Andy Card, the president's chief of staff, went in and told the President that the second plane had flown into the World Trade Center, you know, there was a lot of fog, confusion. The President came walking into the room, took one look at the television set and said, "*We're at war.* Get me the Vice President and get me the Director of the FBI." (American Enterprise Institute 2001, emphasis mine)

The president himself recalls himself thinking, "I made up my mind at that moment that we were going to war"; "They had declared war on us, and I made up my mind at that moment that we were going to war" (quoted in Balz and Woodward 2002).

It is important to emphasize that this clear-eyed decision was made in the heat of catastrophic circumstances. The World Trade towers had been attacked and destroyed. The Pentagon had been hit. There were many unconfirmed reports of further attacks, including an attempt to target Congress and the president. In a discussion on *Meet the Press* (2002) with Dan Balz and Bob Woodward, who conducted the behind-the-scenes interviews with the president and his key advisers, this exchange took place:

> **Woodward:** What we found on September 11 after the attacks—and as you may recall, Bush was flying all over the country from one military base to the next because of the fear that he was a target—you see his visceral reaction to this, the kind of sense that, "Wait a minute. This is a massive attack, people who want to die. How do we respond to them? How do we deter them," and essentially it's, "We're going to have to destroy them."
> **Russert:** It's pretty clear thinking for the first night of a crisis, Dan Balz.
> **Balz:** It is pretty clear thinking. And Bob's right, the part of what was interesting about Bush on that first day was that, in private, *he had a very clear set of kind of instructions and reactions to people.* Sometimes in the public statements, it did not come through as clearly in those first hours, but behind the scenes, he was saying and doing things which have followed through almost on a straight line since then [emphasis is mine].

There are many things that Bush might have said. There are many feelings he no doubt had and could have expressed. Yet, his first response on seeing the attack was to frame it as an act of war and to mobilize his administration to respond accordingly. And how did he respond? Not like the petulant unilateralist who has to have it his way or not at all like the person depicted in the caricatures of Bush. Nor did he respond to the attack like the impulsive cowboy that critical punditry had led some to expect. Rather, he responded deliberately, systematically, and comprehensively.

Moreover, he did so in a time of incredible tension, danger, reports of other disastrous attacks, and real fear for the safety and viability of the top layers of the American government. As *Post* reporter Dan Balz comments:

> I think one of the things that's interesting about trying to do this series was to bring back this sense of fear that was gripping not just the country but very much people in the White House during this period. I mean, it's an extraordinary moment to try to be making serious policy when you fear you are under attack, and that was really the condition that existed not just that day, but for a number of days after that. (*Meet the Press* 2002)

Secretary of War Donald Rumsfeld provided another window into the framing decisions taken at the start of the war that also sheds light on these matters. In an interview with the *Washington Post,* he was asked about major "turning points" in the administration's early decisions. He replied:

> First would be the September 11th attack. Second would be the president's decision to engage in a war against terrorism in the broadest sense, that we would use all elements of national power, that we would bring in other countries, that it would be a long, sustained effort to deal with this problem, and that a part of it would involve the use of both overt and covert military force in Afghanistan. ("Interview" 2001)

In other words, after the attack, the most important decision that faced the president was how to respond. And, to respond, he had to place the event accurately in a category that helped him frame the answer. He framed the attack as an act of a war and responded accordingly. That framing decision and its implications are likely to reshape the international system for decades to come. They have already helped consolidate the reshuffling of certain alliances and set in motion profound changes in others.

Bush's ability to reframe conventional wisdom has been evident elsewhere as well. When, after another in a long series of terrorists bombs exploded in Israel, Bush had a blunt and very clear assessment of Palestinian leader Yasir Arafat (quoted in Sciolino 2001): "He can't close the front door of his prisons and let prisoners out the back." Furthermore, "Arafat criticized us. He urged us to put more pressure on Israel. Who is he kidding? Now is his time. The spotlight is on Arafat. Performance is the key." The clear-eyed view of issues is not something that Bush suddenly developed because of the 9/11 attacks. One can look back into Bush's career and see other elements for this capacity in nonpolitical settings.

As an owner of the Texas Rangers, Bush experienced a difficult set of circumstances as his longtime friend Fay Vincent fought for his job as commissioner of baseball. It was a fight that George Bush urged him to make but that the commissioner ultimately decided not to do. One of Bush's biographers, writing about that experience, said, "When discussing Vincent, an unhappy George W. gave this clear-eyed assessment: 'He made a lot of tough decisions and because of that he was not popular. But someone's ox is always being gored'" (Mitchell 2000, 289).

Bush's relationship with his father could not be deeper and more psychologically important to him. Bush loves and respects his father and has enormous affection for him. If there ever were a relationship in which a son's view of his father might be clouded by identification, this would be it. Yet in a wide-ranging interview with the *Washington Post* Bush was clear eyed about why his father lost the presidency:

> Bush said his convictions about the importance of asserting presidential power flow in large measure from watching his father squander the high approval ratings he earned after the allied military success in the Persian Gulf War. "It doesn't matter whether you won by one point, two points, even 10 points, it's important to move as quickly as you can in order to spend whatever capital you have as quickly as possible," he said. (Harris and Balz 2001).

Pragmatic versus Intellectual Curiosity

As noted in chapter 3, Bush has often been criticized for lacking intellectual curiosity. This characteristic, it is said, reflects a lack of motivation to know what he should, a feeling that he doesn't have to know because others who advise him will, or his being just plain intellectually incapable. In short, his critics accuse him of being derelict, lazy,[10] or stupid. Extensive inquiry into these questions suggests he isn't any of these things.

Berke (2000) examined Bush's decision-making style and among other things found the following: Bush's decision-making style (Berke 2000; see also Merida 2000 for an independent confirmation of many of these points) confirms that the president carefully selects his advisers, works with them to develop confidence in their loyalty and judgment, and then relies on them. In other words, Bush works with his advisers, pays attention to what they say, and watches how well their analyses accord with events as a situation unfolds. Asked by reporter Walter Shapiro (1999) of *USA Today* how he evaluates conflicting advice, Bush replied, "It's just a matter of judgment. It's a matter of a person in my position sorting out, amongst all the voices, who's got the best judgment, who's got the best common sense."

Berke (2000) also found from wide-ranging interviews with Bush advisers that the president prefers to speed through meetings to get to the heart of the matter. He is well known to interrupt long-winded presentations to ask what the most important point is and to ask at the end whether he has been told everything that he might need to know. His advisers say that he is also not afraid to stop and ask even basic questions if he isn't sure he understands a matter.

Balz and Neal (2000) write of Bush in the period when he was preparing himself to run for the presidency:

> At times, Bush's questions can be surprisingly elementary: Just what is the Social Security debt, who is it owed to and how does it get repaid? What would happen if the United States were attacked by chemical or biological weapons and how could we defend ourselves? Why does the United States have a military? Such questions reveal Bush's lack of familiarity with many of the issues that might confront him in the White House, and are the basis for the contention by Vice President Gore and the Democrats that he is too inexperienced to be president. Bush advisers say they show something quite different, a man confident enough to show what he doesn't know, an executive who expects his advisers to know more than he does about their areas of expertise, and a leader willing to force those around him to rethink what they know.

The questions noted here reflect diverse facts about Bush. They do show a lack of familiarity with matters that might and now do face Bush as president dealing with chemical and biological weapons. Yet, why would a governor be expected to have detailed knowledge of these national security–sensitive areas? On the other hand, no such point can be made regarding Social Security debt. These questions show a man who is unclear about some basic elements of American domestic policy and is asking for information as a means to understand an important issue. One can note that he doesn't already know, which is true. However, one can also see that Bush (like Kennedy; see chapter 2) is not afraid to ask a basic question and is interested enough to do so. "Why do we have a military?" seems like a question designed to get others to reexamine their primary assumptions. Balz and Neal (2000) found that "for every sign of impatience with windy experts or extended discussions, there is a story from aides about the session that stretched into the night at the governor's mansion with Bush deeply engaged." The latter certainly comports with Mitchell's interviews with Bush's Texas advisers who were with him when he considered running for governor. She reports, "Back in 1990, when he was considering a run for the governor, he traveled to Austin to cram on statewide issues with a bunch of policy experts." That pattern persisted and intensified when he began to prepare for his presidential campaign.

> From the time he first began working toward a run for the presidency, he maintained a regular schedule of policy meetings where he gathered disparate voices in the Republican Party to hash out issues. According to many of those who

attended, George W. took great glee in assembling the most diverse group he could find and then letting the discussion fly for several hours. *He would ask hundreds of specific questions*, demonstrating the same intense curiosity that he displayed while campaigning on the back roads of West Texas. (Mitchell 2000, 333, emphasis added)

Bush's interest in diverse views appears to have carried over to his White House and Cabinet staffing (Associated Press 2001a). However, paralleling the early initiatives in developing Bush's policy thinking, they seem to have the function of exposing him to a variety of views from which he can begin to refine his own. Furthermore, it is also likely that as this process unfolded, he was making judgments about those who were talking. Who spoke most clearly? Whose arguments made sense? Whose judgment could he count on?

The "hundreds of questions" might represent the curiosity of the novice. Or, they may possibly be motivated by a more pragmatic question: What works?

It does appear true that Bush does not have the kind of curiosity that inquires deeply into the reasons why people are as they act or why circumstances have developed as they have. He does have views of these matters. However, they are not the views of someone who has immersed himself in the debates and considered in-depth the many explanations that can account for circumstances he must address. Bush is not a theoretician, but that is not the same thing as saying he is incurious. It also does not follow that his views are wrong.

Bush Is Intensely Interested in What Works

We don't often think of curiosity as pragmatic. Criticisms of the president lament his lack of interest in the nuance and detail of public policy. It is not only that he is not interested in, say, Medicaid reimbursement rate trends in Michigan. He is also not likely to enjoy and encourage, as, say, Bill Clinton did, long and often-inconclusive policy debates.

This is a potential Achilles' heel for Bush. There is, of course, a relationship between the fact that something does work and why it does. A focus on the first to the exclusion of the latter is a danger since the "why" is always connected to policy circumstances, and if they change, so will effectiveness. A leader therefore must somewhat concerned with "why" questions.

Sometimes the why questions can be answered with a principle and the view that is its foundation. Bush's policy that America must be strong is predicated on the assumption that the international system is still, in part, a hostile environment. There are countries and groups that would like to harm or destroy us. It is not an intellectually deep analysis of why, but it has proven in the wake of 9/11 to be profoundly correct essential understanding.

Blunt Talk

Clear-eyed assessments are related to an important aspect of Bush's approach to the education functions of his presidential pulpit-blunt talk. Ordinarily, Bush is considered far from fluent, although his speeches to Congress and the United Nations after the terrorists attack were considered excellent. He is better known for creative parallelisms ("Bosnaiks" for Bosnians, "Kosovarians" for Kosovars, "Gricians" for Greeks), rhetorical paroxysms, and meandering syntax. However, his combination of plain speaking and strong views give him a true "postmodern" style: With Bush less is definitely more—sometimes a lot more, moving beyond "polite" diplomatic language.

In his speech to the United Nations, Bush (2001g, 1640) thanked all those countries that had expressed condolences but went on, "But the time for sympathy has now passed; the time for action has now arrived." Speaking at Fort Campbell, Bush said:

> America has a message for the nations of the world: If you harbor terrorists, you are a terrorist, if you train or arm a terrorist, you are a terrorist. If you feed a terrorist or fund a terrorist, you're a terrorist, and you will be held accountable by the United States and our friends. (quoted in Allen 2001a)

Or consider his words to Yasir Arafat, who had long made use of Hamas terrorist actions against Israel to further his own territorial agenda: "Chairman Arafat has said he intends to fight terror, bring those to justice who are killing—murderers—in the Middle East and now is his time to perform. The world expects Chairman Arafat to lead and so do I" (quoted in Sipress 2001).

Early on the question of time was raised with Bush:

> **Q:** What do you say to American who are worried the longer it takes to retaliate, the more chance the perpetrators have to escape and hide and just escape justice?
>
> **The president:** They will try to hide. They will try to avoid the United States, and our allies, but we are not going to let them. They run to the hills. They find holes to get in, and we will do whatever it takes to smoke them out, and get them running and we'll get them. . . .
>
> **Q:** How long—
>
> **The president:** *As long as it takes.* (Bush 2001a, 1320, emphasis added)

In that same exchange with reporters, Bush referred to the terrorists as "a group of barbarians [that] have declared war on the United States" (2001a, 1320) and elsewhere as "evil" and "evildoers" (2001c, 1324). Who, after watching and listening to Osama bin Laden boasting with self-satisfaction and pleasure[11] at the thousands he had killed, might not think those words appropriate? President Bush was adamant that bin Laden be "brought to justice." How? "Dead or alive" (Bush 2001f, 1327). Asked again about the possible contributions of the antiterrorist coalition, he replied, "Thank you for your condolences; I appreciate your flowers; now arrest somebody if they're in your country" (quoted in Allen 2001c).

Black-or-White Thinking or Essential Insight?

It seems intuitively obvious that more complex, nuanced thought is to be preferred to less complex, simple understandings. After all, is not the world a complex place? And if that is true, is being capable of, and having, complex thought not consistent with the state of the world and understanding it?

Pundits are not alone in writing as if the answer to these questions is an unequivocal yes. Theories of decision making also view the decision environment as complex and in response assign complex tasks to those who would aspire to high-quality decisions. Sometimes those theories and a set of political concerns make complexity the holy grail of good decision process.

Consider in this regard Glad's (1983) long article on Ronald Reagan's "black or white thinking." In it, she details what she sees as the dangers of such a person in office, especially the presidency. Reagan "idealizes America." He has "blotted out the darker sides of the American past and glossed over the moral failures of our allies" (44). He has "painted Russia as almost all black, their goal is world domination" (44). He "divided the world into two camps, with all morality on one side, all evil on the other, with two possible outcomes—to win or to lose" (48).[12]

In Glad's view, Reagan's psychology and cognitive functioning is the cause of the worldview she describes at length. She argues, "to avoid political, intellectual, or moral ambiguities, Reagan reigns in what he perceives and what he thinks about" (50). Moreover, Reagan "embraces simplicity." As proof, Glad writes that, "he told his Cabinet to discuss the 'right' or 'wrong' of the ideas, and ignore political considerations" (51).

Psychologically, Reagan's cognitive rigidity is a defense against emotional and behavioral paralysis (Glad 1983, 51). His worldview is based on the fear that less structure would make him weak (52). Glad examines six possible explanations for Reagan's "black or white thinking": lack of sophistication, limited information sources, a career motivated instrumentality, and three others dealing with psychologically based cognitive style. Those include ambivalence toward his father, a difficulty recognizing and expressing anger, and a tendency to stereotype.

Glad clearly favors the last explanation. However, what she never seriously examines is the possibility that Reagan's worldview of the Soviet Union is correct in fundamental and important policy-relevant ways. It is only after thirty-five pages detailing her views, as noted here, that she mentions in passing that she is not arguing that "the Russians are only benevolent in their dealings with the United States, that they are not 'enemies' in reality" (69). However, cognitive processes such as Reagan's "cloud vision, as they exaggerate the enemy's evil and power, while simultaneously inflating one's own virtue and the capacity to constrain him, if one will just be strong and stand up" (69–70).

The parallels to Ronald Reagan's views and those of George W. Bush are striking. Reagan called the Soviet Union the "Evil Empire." Bush has characterized Osama bin Laden and his followers as "evil"—repeatedly. Reagan saw the world as those who were defenders and opponents of freedom. Bush warned that nations were either "for us or against us" in the fight against terrorism. Reagan thought this country embodied the highest ideals and those who relentlessly criticized it were ill informed or willfully ignorant. Bush's patriotism expressed as his love of country is palpable in the many times he says how proud he is to represent it.

On its face, it seems quite clear that both presidents share certain convictions and understandings. It follows, therefore, that a strong case could make that President Bush, like President Reagan, shares a proclivity for so-called black-or-white thinking. I use the term *so-called*, because I want to raise the issue of whether black-or-white thinking is, in some important cases, a misnomer for a process that it very essential to good judgment. Furthermore, I want to argue that it serves important leadership functions as well.

The term *black-or-white* thinking sets up a dichotomy in which whole categories of thought are purged of nuance, ambiguity, ambivalence, doubt, and thus complexity. The implication of such a term is that the user is clearly distorting reality—clearly so, because reality is complex. As a result, such a thinker is very likely to wind up making flawed decisions and exercising poor judgment.

If a decision maker truly did operate this way, it would be cause for concern. Of course, adherents of this theory, especially as it relates to high-level decision makers such as Presidents Reagan and Bush, have the obligation of explaining how people with such rigid thinking and psychological patterns have managed to rise to the top of a system that demands extraordinary flexibility. Indeed, Farnham's study (chapter 6 in this volume) of Ronald Reagan's cold war judgments suggests he had a substantial capacity to recognize changes in the Soviet Union and build on them.

Beyond the questions of a particular leader's flexibility or lack of it, there is a larger set of issues. The questions simply put are these: How do you distinguish an essential insight that weights a particular understanding very strongly and "black-or-white" thinking? How do you distinguish between conviction and rigidity? And how do you distinguish between merited confidence in your judgments and the more defensive variety that springs from the worry that you might be wrong and therefore can't stand to be challenged?

What of nuance, complexity, and choice? Decision involves choice, and choice involves simplification. It is a rare decision that can give full, or even ample, weight to all its constituent elements. The question, therefore, is not whether a judgment simplifies but whether the judgment simplifies at the expense of understanding.

Consider the response to the 9/11 attacks. Surely, the framing of the president's response—"we're at war"—gave lesser weight to a variety of elements, many of which were brought up as criticisms by others who weighed things differently. We had no incontrovertible evidence, it was said. An attack against Afghanistan would cause Arabs to see the United States even more hostilely. Our enemies hated us for reasons that would be more appropriately addressed by trying to win them over—by revising some of our foreign policies, for example. All of these considerations and others were brought up as elements that were not fully, fairly, or appropriately considered in the president's initial framing judgment.

However, we must ask then a basic question of a judgment, especially a framing judgment. Does it capture the essential elements of the circumstances in a way that does justice to their implications? Are the nuances, complexities, and ambiguities of the circumstances that might, but ultimately do not, enter into the judgment compromise in any important ways its fundamental insight?

The answers to these questions cannot be decided on an a priori basis. But they can be answered. Consider President's Bush's first response to the 9/11 terrorist attack—"we're at war."

In that moment he reached an understanding from a catastrophic event that had obviously been well and long planned and drew several important conclusions. He understood that people who would do this were ruthless, audacious, well organized, and serious about mortally wounding this country. As a consequence, he reached an understanding that the best response to this attack was not simply an emotionally satisfying but ineffective military strike, but rather a comprehensive and long-term strategy to neutralize and remove the threat that the attack represented.

That framing decision—"we're at war"—has and will continue to have the most profound implications. Is it the only framing decision that could have been made? Obviously not. It could have been considered an attack—a terrible, devastating one—but still a limited event calling for a strong but limited response. And what would have been the implications of that framing? Certainly, military action of some form—but not necessarily the long-term commitment of vast resources to a global fight.

The basic understanding reached by the president clearly had, and will continue to have, profound policy implications for the United States and the world. Yet, the president's understanding and framing of the issues had equally profound implications on his presidency and his leadership. The 9/11 attacks were, after all, attacks on the United States—its citizens, institutions, and way of life. The public had to deal not only with the physical and geopolitical realities of that attack but with its emotional consequences. So did Bush.

Consider the president's emotional state as he received the news of the attack. There is no doubt that the president, like many Americans, was deeply affected by the attack. Very strong feelings of disbelief, pain, and anger were very likely swirling though the president's psychology, as they were for many Americans.

It seems safe to say that these were very powerful feelings, perhaps especially so for the president given his strong attachment to this country. Yet, he and the public—again, he especially—faced the question of how to respond. How he chose to do so had profound implications for him and the country, emotionally and politically.

The president's framing judgment carried with it a number of psychological consequences for both Bush and the public. As a result, they also had implications for Bush's presidential leadership and his presidency. These consequences are not presented as either justification or criticism of the quality of the framing judgment he made, but rather as simply the results of having reached an understanding that confidence in it helped to consolidate. I take up three such results under the headings of clarity, focus, and resolve.

Clarity, Focus, and Resolve

Clarity requires not only that a thing be seen for what it is but that alternative understandings present no serious categorical rivalry. As noted, this does not mean that there are no unanswered questions, no concerns about whether responses that follow from that understanding will be successful, or perhaps even a clear idea at the start of what the range of those responses is or should be. In short, clarity is not synonymous with certainty.

Judgment clarity serves psychological functions. It is one way to come to grips with strong emotional currents. Understanding doubles as explanation. And explanation helps make sense of the inexplicable or, in this case, the unbelievable, if not the incomprehensible. It also serves, in a time of national crisis and trauma such as the 9/11 attacks, as a way addressing feelings of profound shock, anxiety, and loss. Judgment clarity that fits the circumstances provides answers to the most basic questions that haunt trauma victims—what happened, why, what's going to happen. Forcefully expressed, timely, basic, but accurate understandings help moderate shock, alleviate anxiety, and comfort loss.

Judgment clarity has two other by-products that, while certainly psychological, are also firmly grounded in the world of action—focus and resolve. Focus is the linchpin of action. In a world of many possibilities and even more distractions, focus is a prerequisite for sustained action.

Focus has a sorting function as well. Having reached a conclusion about what's central, the leader has, at the same time, gone some distance toward discarding what isn't. Among the many things that *might* have engaged Bush's interest and attention, many fewer—not necessarily unworthy—will do so now. What might have been legitimate, even desirable policy aspirations must now be weighed in the calculus of larger, more central purposes. A comprehensive reform of the health care system, for instance, must now wait as domestic security concerns take precedence. Moreover, the many issues vying for attention are reframed—through the prism of the framing judgment. Energy exploration, for example, takes on a new importance in light of serious questions about foreign dependency. Immigration reform through the lens of national security concerns alters what had been primarily an economic and political debate.

Focus narrows vision, but not necessarily ambition. Ridding the world of terrorists and those who sponsor them is both highly specific and largely ambitious. Highly specific but largely ambitious undertakings are difficult, and they often take long periods of time to accomplish. The successful leader must be able to sustain both his and the public's focus and commitment.

Time is the enemy of memory. So is complexity. As time passes, the sharpness of essential understandings can fade, and ambiguity obscures essential features. We recall the importance of things but not with the same sharp clarity and focus of the ways in which the various elements of an experience combined to give us an overall impression. The power of a clear and fitting framing judgment is that it helps mobilize and retain resolve and aid remembrance.

Those calculations are different, of course, for the president and the public. The president has asked the public to return to their normal lives. And many are glad to do so. Yet he has also staked his presidency in large part on a mission that requires that people don't forget. Billions for defense at home and abroad instead of prescription drug benefits or the reform of Social Security are only politically sustainable if people remember. So Bush must search for ways to remind the public that we are at war, even as time is passing—especially should there be no further major terrorist attacks on United States soil.

The president is aware that memory fades. This is one reason the administration agreed to let NBC News spend the day with him and telecast the one-hour show during prime time. It is also the reason that the administration orchestrated worldwide ceremonies three months after 9/11 (Allen 2001e). Also, it is the reason why the president often takes the opportunity to remind the American public that the United States will be in Afghanistan and in pursuit of terrorist networks for a long time (Loeb 2001, A08).

However, the president also begins with a very different highly personal experience of 9/11—along with all those others who witnessed or were directly affected. He was, after all, a likely target, and the country he was elected to protect was deeply wounded. Added to this is his very personal and strong emotional connection to this country. These are the bases for his commitment to make the destruction of terrorism his personal mission and the mission of his presidency.

Yet, it is a not at all clear that the public's memory and commitment will have the same intensity and staying power as the president's, for several reasons. Being able to continue on with life after a traumatic event is one sign of healing. People do generally have difficulty in keeping very upsetting experiences in their minds, especially if they have not been directly and personally affected. Of course, there are motivated reasons as well, ranging from self-centeredness to the press of more immediate concerns that, over time, lessen the impact of those events.

The basic understanding that President Bush reached that day—"we're at war"—is likely to be an aid in both retaining focus and supporting resolve for the president. It seems clear that the power and usefulness of a basic, clear, and fitting framing judgment as an aid to clarity, focus, and resolve is likely to be much longer than one full of nuance, complexity, and ambiguity. Sometimes, less nuance leads to better judgments and more effective leadership.[13]

CONCLUSION

George W. Bush began his quest for the presidency to a chorus of ridicule and disbelief from his critics. They, it seemed, confused their caricatures with analysis. As a result, many Americans were surprised and unprepared for seeing the real strengths and weaknesses of a Bush presidency.

It seems fair to call the president's response to the terrorist attack masterful. As a decision maker, he has responded to the circumstances by not flinching from what he saw and acting accordingly. As a leader, he has been decisive and patient. Equally important, he has understood and responded to the public's psychology in a time of trauma and war. He has shared in (not just empathized with) and acknowledged the profound grief and loss most Americans feel. He has attempted both to buttress resolve and to provide reassurance. He has done all of this, as he must, in an ongoing way, even as he finishes one battle and prepares for the others that he has said will follow.

Moreover, the public has made it clear that they expect the president to pay attention to domestic matters, while he continues to pursue the war successfully (Deane and Milbank 2001). In a December 24, 2001, *Washington Post* poll (Deane and Milbank 2001), the domestic economy (34 percent) had overtaken concern with terrorism or the fear of war (13 percent) as major American concerns. Bush's dual task of fighting a war and addressing economic and other domestic policy concerns is complicated by his having to deal with a deeply divided partisan Congress whose opposition party is united in their determination to stymie his presidency and win back control.

These are daunting tasks for any president. However, should Bush accomplish them, it will be but a small step to the historical stature and tier of a first-ranked president.

NOTES

I'd like to thank Alexander L. George and Richard N. Haass for their helpful comments.

1. Just how much of a struggle is revealed by some analysis of presidential popularity figures by Brody (2001). Calculating popularity by examining positive/negative ratings in relation to those expressing no opinion, Brody (2001) writes that in the first seven weeks of his presidency, between 70 and 75 percent of those expressing views rated Bush positive. Yet: Over the next ten weeks, from early March to mid-May, the level of "relative approval" dropped eight-plus percentage points. The polls for the remainder of May and for the last three weeks of June showed a further five to seven point erosion in his level of relative support. President Bush finished his first five months in office 17 percentage points of relative support below where he started (25).

2. In a discussion on the Bush presidency, Senior White House Adviser Karl Rove had this to say in an exchange about the application of Wildavsky's theory to George W. Bush:

Ornstein: Aaron Wildafsky [*sic*], almost forty years ago, wrote about the two presidencies, a domestic presidency which had much more trouble, and a foreign policy presidency which had much greater success. Do you see this as an important distinction, and do you see—how do you see the interaction between a President who's had an 87 percent approval rating overall, isn't quite in the same league, although he's up high, when it comes to the economy and other domestic issues; how do you relate the two now?

Rove: But you're right, I could see—you know, this President doesn't have that feeling about—for many Presidents the allure of the foreign has overshadowed the quagmire of the domestic. You know, dealing with Congress is sometimes painful, and so being able to pick up the phone and do something internationally has drawn their attention more. This President doesn't feel that. He obviously is in the moment and required to focus on international affairs, but he remains keenly interested in the domestic agenda. It's just that it's got less of his time. (American Enterprise Institute 2001)

3. George Will (2001; see also Kahn 2001) notes another element of Bush's bifurcated leadership:

> During the current war, Americans are told that it is patriotic to crank up consumption—to go to a mall, a movie and anywhere on a plane. This is the peculiar context in which the president is attempting bifurcated leadership. He must keep the country focused on war far away and involving, so far, few Americans in combat, but the country must also regain its jaunty equilibrium, meaning its money-spending ways.

4. For an excellent discussion of the many complexities involved in the use of this term for policy analysis, see George (1980, 67, 217–37).

5. The United States also objected to giving European countries a pass by making 1990 the baseline year for calculations that allowed the European Union to claim a 4 percent reduction in carbon dioxide emissions a byproduct of the closure of obsolete coal-based industries in the British Midlands and the old East Germany following the end of the cold war. Or, consider the earlier meeting in which the advocates refused to allow the United States to include carbon dioxide–absorbing forests in calculating greenhouse emissions, which would have reduced carbon dioxide emissions overall. Since the United States is 33 percent forested, this would have served to reduce our "contribution" to the effect by a substantial amount.

6. I would like to thank Tom Ricks, the senior *Washington Post* reporter who provided this interview to me.

7. I use the term *psychology* here to encompass a person's basic character elements (Renshon 1996), elements of his or her personality that are connected to character structure, and the capacities—social, psychological, and cognitive—that a person has developed. One can think of character as a person's psychological foundation and personality elements or traits as part of the superstructure built upon it.

8. This was quite evident characteristic during the 2000 presidential campaign. One example, and there are many, is contained in an analysis of the Bush campaign entitled, "Bush Targets Core Conservatives in Untraditional Election Push" (Hardwood and Calmes 2000):

> Despite much advice to the contrary, candidate Bush has refused to shrink from his conservative positions. He's pushing a sweeping tax-cut plan, even though his congressional counterparts have retreated this year in favor of more modest cuts. He's offering a controversial proposal to partially privatize Social Security that many Republicans in Congress are afraid to address. And he's resisting popular gun-control measures, despite fierce Democratic attacks. He also brushed off GOP moderates in selecting a solidly conservative, antiabortion running mate in Dick Cheney.

9. So, for example, in 1999, Jacob Weisberg was arguing in an article entitled "Do Dim Bulbs Make Better Presidents?" that the answer was no. Clearly examining then-can-

didate George W. Bush, he said, "To be sure, intelligence of the kind that might manifest itself in high SAT scores isn't the most important quality in a chief executive. Leadership, integrity, and determination are all more critical qualities. Dumb luck helps. Dumbness doesn't."

10. Crowley (2001), a photographer and essayist, was invited to spend the day with President Bush. He writes, "It was . . . a typical day, except that Mr. Bush permitted a photographer to accompany him throughout, offering an unusual behind-the-scenes view of how he conducts business." That day began at 7:30 A.M. and ended fifteen hours later.

11. In the tape, bin Laden (2001) says (see also Editorial 2001a):

> [W]e calculated in advance the number of casualties from the enemy, who would be killed based on the position of the tower. . . . I was the most optimistic of them all. . . . I was thinking that the fire from the gas in the plane would melt the iron structure of the building and collapse the area where the plane hit and all the floors above it only. This is all that we had hoped for.

12. As proof, Glad (1983) offers the fact that Reagan said, "I think there's something phony about a peace march that usually takes place carrying the flags of the enemy instead of peace flags" or his statement that "many sincere Americans who took part in the nuclear freeze movement were being manipulated by those others who wanted to weaken America" (49).

13. Consider in that regard Leon Panetta's characterization of Bill Clinton's decision process. Clinton was certainly once of the most knowledgeable and nuanced presidents to serve in that office. Yet in an interview conducted for *Nightline* (2000), Panetta had this to say:

> [T]here often wasn't a final firm decision, and no closure. Yes. He would say, "Gosh, did I make the right decision?" and he would start to really think about it and he would ponder it because it is his nature to not to bring closure. His nature is to constantly assess and assess again, depending on who's talking to him and depending on the thoughts they presented. So he would sometimes go into a very torturous process, trying to come to closure on something. And the problem is that of you are trying to move legislation, you're trying to get something to the Hill, or if you're trying to tell a congressman or senator what has to be done, or what the administration's position is, you could be floundering for a while, trying to get a decision. So that was a problem.

REFERENCES

Allen, Mike. 2001a. "From Both Sides, Promises to Fight on; Bush Says Hardest Part Is Ahead." *Washington Post*, November 22, A1.

———. 2001b. "Guest Worker Plan to Push English." *Washington Post*, September 1, A1.

———. 2001c. "Harsh Words and Holiday Cheer Bush Vows to Find Bin Laden but Revels in 'Joyous' Season." *Washington Post*, December 22, A6.

———. 2001d. "Kennedy Joins Bush in Unveiling Aid for Disabled." *Washington Post*, February 2, A2.

———. 2001e." U.S. Urges Nations to Mark Attack Anniversary." *Washington Post*, December 7, A2.

Allen, Mike, and Dan Balz. 2001. "Bush Unveils 'New Federalism.'" *Washington Post*, February 27, A10.

Alvarez, Lizette. 2001. "Bush Faces New Dispute over Payment of U.N. Dues." *New York Times*, August 17.

American Enterprise Institute. 2001. "A Discussion with Karl Rove," December 11, 2001, www.aei.org/past_event/conf011211.htm (accessed December 15, 2001).

Apple, R. W., Jr. 2001. "Bush Presidency Seems to Gain Legitimacy." *New York Times*, September 16.

Associated Press. 2000. "Report: Gore Won Popular Vote by 539, 987." *Washington Post*, December 21, A9.

———. 2001a. "Diversity Means Many Things to Bush." *New York Times*, March 29.

———. 2001b. "U.S. Rejects Draft Enforcement Plan for 1972 Ban on Biological Weapons." *Wall Street Journal*, July 25.

Babington, Charles, and Dana Milbank. 2001. "Bush Advisers Try to Limit Damage; No Change in Policy toward Taiwan." *Washington Post*, April 27, A19.

Balz, Dan, and Terry M. Neal. 2000. "Questions, Clues and Contradiction." *Washington Post*, October 22, A1.

Balz, Dan, and Bob Woodward. 2002. "10 Days in September: Inside the War Cabinet: America's Chaotic Road to War Bush's Global Strategy Began to Take Shape in First Frantic Hours after Attack." *Washington Post*, January 27, A1.

Berke, Richard L. 2000. "Gore Dots the i's That Bush Leaves to Others." *New York Times*, June 9, A1.

———. 2001. "Jokes Remain, but Bush Shows Signs of War's Burden." *New York Times*, December 9.

Beschloss, Michael. 2001. "Bush Faces the Greatest Test." *New York Times*, September 17.

"Bin Laden Tape." 2001. *Newsweek*, December 13.

Broder, David. 2001a. "A New Reality for George W. Bush." *Washington Post*, September 13, A31.

———. 2001b. "Now Comes the Hard Part." *Washington Post*, September 2, B7.

Brody, Richard A. 2001. "Is the Honeymoon Over?" *PRG Report* 24, no. 1: 1, 23–28.

Bruni, Frank. 2000. "The Texas Governor: A Borrowed Pitch Achieves the Desired Result for Bush." *New York Times*, February 20.

Bush, George W. 2001a. "Remarks in a Meeting With the National Security Team and an Exchange with Reporters at Camp David," September 17, 2001. *Weekly Compilation of Presidential Documents* 37, no. 38 (September 24): 1319–21.

———. 2001b. "Remarks in a Telephone Conversation with New York City Mayor Rudolph Giuliani and New York Governor George Pataki and an Exchange with Reporters," September 13, 2001. *Weekly Compilation of Presidential Documents* 37, no. 37 (September 17): 1291–1317.

————. 2001c. "Remarks on Arrival at the White House and an Exchange with Reporters," September 16, 2001, *Weekly Compilation of Presidential Documents* 37, no. 38 (September 24): 1322–24.

————. 2001d. "Remarks Prior to a Meeting with Easter Seals Representatives and an
Exchange with Reporters," July 16, 2001. *Weekly Compilation of Presidential Documents*
37, no. 29 (July 23): 1045–47.

————. 2001e. "Remarks Prior to a Meeting with Easter Seals Representatives and an
Exchange with Reporters," June 20, 2001. *Weekly Compilation of Presidential Documents*
37, no. 25 (June 25): 946–50.

————. 2001f. "Remarks to Employees in the Dwight D. Eisenhower Executive Office
Building and an Exchange with Reporters," September 17, 2001, *Weekly Compilation of
Presidential Documents* 37, no. 38 (September 24): 1324–27.

————. 2001g. "Remarks to the United Nations General Assembly in New York City,"
November 10, 2001. *Weekly Compilation of Presidential Documents* 37, no. 46 (November
19): 1638–41.

Chait, Jonathan. 2001. "Count down: Why the Recount Isn't Good News for Bush." *New
Republic,* November 26, 12–13.

Cooper, Helen. 2001. "New Trade Representative Faces an Old Obstacle: Fast-Track
Fight." *Wall Street Journal,* April 6.

Crowley, Steven. 2001. "And on the 96th Day." *New York Times,* April 29.

Deane, Claudia, and Dana Milbank. 2001. "Public Backs Expanded War but Wants More
Attention at Home." *Washington Post,* December 21, A28.

Dewar, Helen, and Cindy Skyrzycki. 2001. "Workplace Health Initiative Rejected." *Washington Post,* March 7, A1.

Dionne, E. J. 2001. "Lessons of the Long Recount." *Washington Post,* November 16, A47.

Editorial. 2001a. "Boasting of Murder." *Washington Post,* December 14, A44.

————. 2001b. "Demands of Leadership." *New York Times,* September 13.

————. 2001c. "Foreign Policy Missteps." *Washington Post,* May 4, A24.

————. 2001d. "Mr. Bush's New Gravitas." *New York Times,* October 12.

————. 2001e. "Reviving the Test Ban Treaty." *New York Times,* January 9.

Fineman, Howard. 2001. "End of Innocence: Can Bush Lead America through This Nightmare?" *Newsweek,* September 11.

George, Alexander L. 1980. *Presidential Decisionmaking in Foreign Policy: The Effective Use of
Information and Advice.* Boulder, Colo.: Westview.

Glad, Betty. 1983. "Black-and-White Thinking in Ronald Reagan's Approach to Foreign
Policy." *Political Psychology* 4, no. 1: 33–76.

Hardwood, John, and Jackie Calmes. 2000. "Bush Targets Core Conservatives in Untraditional Election Push." *Wall Street Journal,* August 3.

Harper, Jennifer. 2001. "Some in Media Can't Stop Criticizing Bush." *Washington Times,*
September 15.

Harris, John F., and Dan Balz. 2001. "Conflicting Image of Bush Emerges: Bush Makes
Political Investments, but Will They Make Him?" *Washington Post,* April 29, A1.

Hunt, Albert. 2001a. "All Hat and No Cattle." *Wall Street Journal,* March 1.

————. 2001b. "An Army of Opposition to Disability Rights." *Wall Street Journal,* March
15.

"Interview with Donald Rumsfeld." *Washington Post*, December 10, 2001, www.washing tonpost.com/wpsrv/nation/specials/attacked/transcripts/rumsfeldinterview_121001. html (accessed December 20, 2001).

Ivins, Molly, and Lou Dubose. 2000. *Shrub: The Short but Happy Political Life of George W. Bush*. New York: Random House.

Janis, Irving. 1972. *Victims of Groupthink*. Boston: Houghton Mifflin.

Jehl, Douglass. 2001. "White House Considering Plan to Void Clinton Rule on Forests." *New York Times*, May 2.

Kahn, Joseph. 2001. "Trying to Fight Two Wars at Once." *New York Times*, October 7.

Kristof, Nicholas D. 2000. "Political Memo: Rival Makes Bush Better Campaigner." *New York Times*, March 3, A23.

Kurtz, Howard. 2002. "At the White House, a Day to Network." *Washington Post*, January 21, C1.

Lewis, Anthony. 2001. "The Two George W. Bushes." *New York Times*, April 14.

Loeb, Vernon. 2001. "U.S. Forces to Stay in Afghanistan for a While, Bush Says; Noting 'Dead or Alive Is Fine with Me,' President Asserts Bin Laden Isn't Escaping." *Washington Post*, December 29, A08.

Meet the Press. 2001. Transcript, NBC News, April 29.

————. 2002. Transcript, NBC News, January 27.

Merida, Kevin. 2000. "George W. Bush: Is He or Isn't He Smart Enough?" *Washington Post*, January 19, C1.

Milbank, Dana. 2001. "White House Staff Switches Gears; Response to Attacks Is Now Focus of Almost All Presidential Aides." *Washington Post*, September 17, A25.

Minutaglio, Bill. 2000. *First Son: George W. Bush and the Bush Family Dynasty*. New York: Times Books.

Mitchell, Elizabeth. 2000. *Revenge of the Bush Dynasty*. New York: Hyperion.

Nightline. 2000. "The Clinton Years: Interview with Leon Panetta." ABC.com, December 27.

Neustadt, Richard E. 1990. *Presidential Power and the Modern President: The Politics of Leadership from Roosevelt to Reagan*. New York: Free Press.

Painin, Eric, and John Mintz. 2001. "EPA Seeks to Narrow Pollution Initiative; Utilities Fight Clinton Rules on Coal-Fired Power Plants." *Washington Post*, August 8, A1.

Pear, Robert. 2001. "White House Plans to Revise New Medical Privacy Rules." *New York Times*, April 8.

Perlez, Jane. 2001. "How Powell Decided to Shun Racism Conference." *New York Times*, September 5.

Powell, Michael. 1999. "The Natural: On the Trail with Bush." *Washington Post*, November 20, C8.

Renshon, Stanley A. 1996. *The Psychological Assessment of Presidential Candidates*. New York: New York University Press.

Rich, Frank. 2001. "What Big Test?" *New York Times*, April 14.

Sanger, David E., and Elisabeth Bumiller. 2001. "The President: In One Month, a Presidency Transformed." *New York Times*, October 11.

Sanger, David E., and Don Van Natta. 2001. "Four Days That Transformed a President, a Presidency and a Nation, for All Time." *New York Times*, September 16.

Schmitt, Eric. 2001. "Bush Aides Weigh Legalizing Status of Mexicans in U.S." *New York Times*, July 15, A1.

Sciolino, Elaine. 2001. "U.S. Jewish Leaders Call President Blunt in Assailing Arafat." *New York Times*, December 14.

Seelye, Katherine Q. 2001. "A Deal Protects Species from Wrangling, for Now." *New York Times*, August 30.

Seib, Gerald F. 2001. "Has the World Really Changed? Let Us Count a Few of the Ways." *Wall Street Journal*, December 26.

Seib, Gerald F. 2002. "Don't Expect the Bush Focus to Blur Much." *Wall Street Journal*, January 23, A24.

Shapiro, Walter. 1999. "Apt Student Bush Making the Grade." *USA Today*, November 11.

Shull, Steve, ed. 1991. *The Two Presidencies*. Chicago: Nelson Hall.

Sipress, Alan. 2001. "Bush Blames Arafat for Problems in Mideast Talks." *Washington Post*, December 15, A24.

T' Hart, Paul. 1990. *Groupthink in Government*. Amsterdam: Swets & Zeitlinger.

VanderHei, Jim. 2001. "President Adapts a More Serious Tone as Response to Attacks Molds His Term." *Wall Street Journal*, September 27.

Weisberg, Jacob. 1999. "Do Dim Bulbs Make Better Presidents?" *Slate*, November 3.

Wildavsky, Aaron. 1966. "The Two Presidencies." *Trans-Action* 4: 5–15.

Will, George F. 2001. "Needed: A Confidence Infusion." *Washington Post*, November 18, B07.

· 12 ·

Politics, Uncertainty, and Values

Good Judgment in Context

Deborah Welch Larson

$\mathcal{I}$n a domain characterized by political controversy, uncertainty, and conflicting values, foreign policymakers must often rely on their own judgment. Some foreign policy decisions may have domestic political implications. The president may have to consider such factors as his ability to work with Congress, the time remaining before the next election, or the position of various lobbies or interest groups when choosing an option. He must consider not only the foreign policy but also the domestic political risks. A costly military entanglement or diplomatic fiasco may damage the president's public approval rating. Launching a controversial foreign policy initiative such as trying to mediate peace in the Middle East may cost the president crucial electoral votes, whether it succeeds or fails. Foreign policy issues can therefore affect the president's ability to achieve his domestic political goals. A president has only a limited amount of political capital, and winning congressional approval of a treaty or peacekeeping mission may require him to give up something in return on the domestic side. While he may solicit the opinions of pollsters and his domestic political advisers, only the president can establish his priorities, agenda, and the amount of political capital he is willing to use to obtain a foreign policy objective. George Kennan recalls that as head of the policy planning staff, he was often asked to discuss the domestic political implications of particular policy alternatives. He refused to do so:

> Our duty, I insisted, was to tell the president and the secretary what, in our view, was in the national interest. It was their duty, if they accepted the force of our recommendations, to see how far these could be reconciled with domestic-political realities. This was a duty that they were far better fitted to perform than were we. And if we did not give them, as a starter, a view of the national interest in its pure form, as we saw it, no one else would, and they would not be able

to judge its importance relative to the domestic-political pressures by which they were confronted.[1]

Foreign policy decisions are often made under conditions of uncertainty because the outcome depends on the actions of other states. The president may be better off making some decision even if he cannot predict the outcome. War is always characterized by uncertainty, unpredictability, contingency, friction, and chance. In that respect, the war against terrorism is no different. No one foresaw the success of U.S. Special Operations forces in Afghanistan or their allies the Northern Alliance. Whether the strategy used in Afghanistan can or should be applied elsewhere, however, depends on an assessment of the particular situation.

Uncertainty means that reasonable people may differ. When the president's advisers offer conflicting diagnoses of the interests at stake and recommendations for action, the president or another high-level policymaker may then have to use his own judgment in deciding whose advice to accept. In some instances, presidents such as Harry Truman and Ronald Reagan have gone *against* the recommendation of their advisers and staff members. And it is well that they should do so, because their experience and intuition may give them a better sense of what to do.

On questions of value, the president is the one who should decide, subject to the will of the electorate. The values at stake in foreign policy such as human rights, respect for other countries' sovereignty, and economic interests often conflict with each other. While dividing up a problem into political, economic, humanitarian, and military subcomponents makes it easier to comprehend and analyze, someone, usually the president, has to integrate various considerations into a decision. Governing effectively requires achieving a balance over time among these competing goals in different contexts. The president may have to construct the national interest in a particular situation, looking at the values from the standpoint of the nation as a whole.

Classical realists such as Kennan have long advocated greater reliance on the insight and instincts of the executive or diplomatic professional rather than rules. Kennan maintains that Americans have a propensity to rationalize specific decisions in terms of sweeping general principles that can be applied to other cases, so that decisions can be made automatically, without consideration of the merits. "Seldom does it seem to have occurred to many congressional figures that the best thing to do would be to let the President, or the Secretary of State, use his head."[2] The search for rules reflects distrust of the decision maker's judgment, his ability to discern the particulars of each case and to use his common sense in deciding on appropriate values and policies.

DEFINING GOOD POLITICAL JUDGMENT

It is easier to say what good judgment is *not* than to define what it is, especially in a usable way. Above all, we should not evaluate the quality of past judgments by their outcomes. As Haass observes in chapter 9 of this volume, the outcome of a policy may also be affected by many factors and contingencies over which the policymaker has no control. For example, a good policy may nevertheless turn out badly because lower-level officials fail to implement the policy correctly in specific instances. Haass points out as well that measuring the quality of judgment by its achievement of particular objectives gives a higher rating to policies that aim at modest goals. But we would prefer that our leaders not pass up opportunities to contribute to a solution to continuing conflicts or make progress toward more ambitious economic objectives. Assessing the quality of decisions by their consequences is also subject to hindsight (i.e., viewing the alternatives with certainty derived from knowledge of how events turned out). To improve the quality of foreign policymaking in the future, we should consider the range of possibilities and considerations as they appeared to the decision maker at the time.

Good political judgment shows concern for political feasibility and costs, not only of a particular policy but also of continued deliberation. As George discusses in chapter 10, political judgment entails making numerous trade-offs—such as balancing the need to maximize the analytical quality of a decision with obtaining adequate domestic support and making efficient use of time and political capital. It would be not only unrealistic but also unwarranted to expect a policymaker to choose the "best" policy for the United States defined solely in terms of strategic interests. In a democracy, foreign policy must have public acquiescence in order to be effective. The options that would most efficiently advance national objectives may not command enough public support to be carried out effectively or consistently. At the same time, the president should know when to put aside political interests in favor of choosing what he believes to be in the national interest. The president cannot pursue an effective, consistent course of action if he is "other directed," responding to the most recent public opinion poll.

Truman showed good political judgment in the Berlin blockade in that his decisions were sensitive to the range of flexibility permitted him by the American people, and he maintained his leeway by keeping West Berlin and the German question out of the presidential campaign. He subordinated his reelection concerns to doing what he perceived to be in the long-term best interests of the United States. In contrast to General Lucius Clay, Truman understood that sending an armed convoy to bust through the Soviet traffic barriers was not politically acceptable; the American public feared war, and the risks of military engagement with the Soviets were too great. He used the airlift to provide a cushion of time that enabled him to postpone deciding whether the United States would go to war to maintain its position in Berlin. The military chafed at Truman's refusal to specify the conditions under which the United States would fight. He did not dramatize the crisis or his role in approving the airlift to avoid provoking the Soviets or stimulating Republican opposition in Congress. He managed to keep foreign policy out of the election campaign by refraining from making public statements and by consulting with Dewey to maintain bipartisan support for the policy of staying in West Berlin. In his sense of timing, balancing of foreign policy and domestic political concerns and knowledge of what was feasible, Truman showed good political judgment.

Reagan as well followed his convictions while finding ways to minimize domestic political fallout. His political intelligence allowed him to calculate how to bring his conservative supporters with him in support of arms control and cooperation with the Soviet Union. He was confident in his communication skills and ability to persuade the public to support his policies, then to use his political popularity to pressure Congress to go along.

For Haass, good judgment requires calculating the costs and benefits of a policy compared to a full range of policy alternatives, including the option of doing nothing. Costs should not be limited to financial but also include human life, the president's time and political capital, effects on countries other than the target, and more general foreign policy interests such as reputation and credibility. Such cost assessments are inherently subjective and not quantifiable, depending on the values and judgment of the individual.

Truman, for example, believed that maintaining the U.S. presence in West Berlin without a war was worth the cost of airlifting supplies and the expenditure of aviation gasoline. Truman was willing to spend vast amounts of money, $165,000 per day for ten months and to tie up all available military transport planes to reach a negotiated settlement. Although trying to feed the population of West Berlin was economically costly, the long-term political costs to the United States of unilaterally withdrawing from West Berlin in the face of Soviet pressure might have been more severe. For the U.S. Air Force chief of staff, on the other hand, the costs of the airlift in terms of wear and tear on planes and the risks of concentrating all U.S. strategic transport capability in one location exceeded the psychological value of supporting West Berlin. In deciding to stay in West Berlin and rely on the airlift, Truman disregarded the advice of experts from the army and State Department who favored withdrawal from West Berlin because it was an exposed a salient and an indefensible outpost. The army and State Department ranked values from their narrow organizational perspectives—pushing the London program to completion for the State Department, being able to carry out the strategic war plans in the case of the Joint Chiefs of Staff and military officials in Washington. Truman had to entertain a much wider range of considerations, including long-term relations with the Soviets, the opinion of Western Europeans, domestic public opinion in the United States, and the reputation of the United States for fidelity to commitments.

REQUIREMENTS OF GOOD POLITICAL JUDGMENT

Clearly, exercising good political judgment does not require a well-structured, organized policymaking system or even good advice. Truman had a small, informal White House staff system to facilitate his preference for rapid, intuitive decision making over careful analytical staff work.[3] Reagan's National Security Council system lacked any design, and the rapid turnover in his foreign policy team—six national security advisers and two secretaries of state—did not help matters. Reagan, however, ignored warnings from his conservative advisers and showed receptivity to Mikhail Gorbachev's overtures. His summit meetings with the Soviet leader played a major role in bringing the cold war to an end by promoting greater mutual trust and encouraging Soviet concessions on arms control and human rights.

Indeed, good political judgment depends on the personal qualities, experience, and interests of leaders in particular subject areas. What stands out about Truman was his ability to make major foreign policy decisions easily and confidently; he did not waver once he had made up his mind. Secretary of State Dean Acheson recalls that "with the President a decision made was done with and he went on to another."[4] Yet, Truman did not always make good decisions. According to Acheson, Truman's "judgment developed with the exercise of it." At first Truman was inclined to be hasty, perhaps out of concern that deliberateness might be viewed as indecisiveness. "But he learned fast and soon would ask, 'How long have we got to work this out?' He would take what time was available for study and then decide."[5]

Farnham credits Reagan's beliefs, personal style, and character for enabling him to respond to indications of change in the Soviet Union (see chapter 6). These aspects of Reagan's character included his ideology, antipathy to nuclear weapons, pragmatism, self-confidence, and political skills. His ideology convinced him that the tide of history was moving away from the Soviet Union and toward democracy, making him more attentive to signs of change in the Soviet Union. Reagan's belief that nuclear weapons endangered U.S. security motivated him to negotiate with the Soviet Union. That he pursued a limited number of goals concentrated his efforts and allowed him to set priorities.

Since he responded intuitively to experience rather than making deductions from premises, Reagan was relatively open to new information. Reagan's skills at reading and empathizing with people, based on his training as an actor, served him well in sizing up Gorbachev. Reagan also had some experience in negotiating from his position as president of the Screen Actors Guild. His self-confidence and ability to make decisions enabled him to alter policy toward the Soviet Union over the opposition of hard-liners within his administration.

Still, leaders who display a capacity for exemplary political judgment may also show bad judgment on occasion. For example, some historians have criticized General Marshall for being too impatient with negotiation and deciding prematurely to give up trying to reach agreement with the Soviet Union on a unified German government.[6] Marshall was also shortsighted in opposing Truman's decision to recognize the state of Israel in May 1948. Qualities of character and beliefs that are useful in some situations may prove to be dysfunctional in others. Reagan's "intuition was so sound," according to his biographer Lou Cannon, "that he relied on it too heavily, letting it lead him down paths where intuition should not go alone."[7] Reagan lacked basic knowledge on issues such as how the federal budget worked, whether the Soviets had observed arms control treaties, basing systems for land-based multiple-warhead missiles, and so on.

As Farnham writes, the ability to exercise good judgment is context-dependent. A political leader's ability to exercise good judgment depends on the "fit" between the problem and his experience, expertise, and talents. Similarly, Welch speculates that good judgment "may be a complex function of character and ability, on the one hand, and of context and experience, on the other" (chapter 7). Renshon argues that the same character traits for which George W. Bush was earlier criticized—in particular, his preoccupation with America's interests and propensity for unilateral action—enabled him to pursue a successful strategy in the war against al Qaeda and the Taliban in Afghanistan (chapter 11). Bush's delegation of responsibility to recognized experts also served him well. Bush freely acknowledges his lack of knowledge in international affairs and has chosen an experienced foreign policy team to compensate.

Truman and Reagan's presidencies marked the beginning and the end of the cold war. Each had to make major strategic decisions in an era of transition from one international security order to another, when Soviet intentions were unclear. Events were moving rapidly in an unexpected direction. Hesitation or diffidence on Truman's part might have exacerbated Western European fears that the United States was returning to isolationism. Truman later wrote:

> All the time I was President, one event followed another with such rapidity that I was never able to afford the time for prolonged contemplation. I had to make sure of the facts. I had to consult people. But to have hesitated when it was necessary to act might well have meant disaster in many instances.[8]

Reagan likewise had to respond positively and confidently to take advantage of opportunities that arose when an exceptional reformer, Gorbachev, assumed power in the Soviet Union. Bush as well has confronted an unprecedented challenge to American interests and national security. His decisions to frame the 9/11 terrorist attack as an act of war rather than a criminal offense and to go after states supporting terrorist groups marked an abrupt break with previous U.S. policy.

AVOIDING BAD JUDGMENT

Reagan's emotional revulsion against nuclear weapons strengthened his commitment to strategic arms reduction and his receptivity to Gorbachev's arms control initiatives. In other instances, however, strong emotions have impaired the objectivity and realism of decision makers. Welch's case study of the Argentine junta's decision to challenge Britain over the Falkland Islands illustrates the risks of relying on emotion and impulse. Galtieri reacted to the acclamation of cheering Argentinean crowds by announcing that the Argentine occupation of the Falkland Islands was to be permanent rather than temporary, an action almost certain to be perceived as aggressive and provocative to the British. As a professional military officer, Galtieri, like other members of the junta, did not have any previous experience in making foreign policy decisions or governing. The junta's understanding of history was distorted by the nationalistic bias of the texts they had read in school. Misinformed by nationalistic education policies, the junta saw British assertion of self-determination for the Falkland Islanders as part of a historical pattern of foreign mistreatment and victimization of Argentina. Their nationalistic culture and beliefs caused the junta to discount Margaret Thatcher's commitment to protect the Falkland Islanders and the depth of U.S. ties to Britain.

In chapter 4, Wayne argues more generally that demonizing the enemy, whether to obtain favorable press coverage or elicit immediate public support for a policy, can backfire. In the post-Vietnam era of public skepticism and distrust of government, presidents are tempted to use rhetorical exaggeration to gain support for an activist policy. But portraying the adversary as evil constrains future policy options available to the president, whereas exercising good political judgment entails maximizing one's leeway. For example, it becomes difficult to justify negotiations that might be essential to resolving a political dispute or war. The president may be placed in a position where he has the choice of taking extreme actions to eliminate the adversary or losing credibility. Using moralistic, condemnatory rhetoric can impair the president's own judgment. Vilification evokes emotions in the speaker and audience that increase the difficulty of analyzing the situation objectively. To portray the situation in terms of "good and evil" oversimplifies complex foreign policy problems that may have structural roots and that causes leaders to overlook how their own state may have contributed to the conflict.

LESSONS FOR THE FUTURE

As will be discussed later, much needs to be done in the way of systematic research and study to develop a better understanding of the sources of good judgment. But I will advance some tentative lessons drawn from the case studies and theoretical discussions. Articulating these admittedly preliminary prescriptions will at least serve to identify some of the issues.

- Domestic politics is a legitimate influence on foreign policy. Many policies require congressional action or public support for effective implementation. Moreover, only the president can decide on his political priorities and the amount of political capital he wishes to spend. The president or another high-level decision maker can ask himself a series of questions. How much time do I want to spend on this issue compared to others? Is a decision required now? How will it affect my domestic political agenda or other important foreign policy goals? Can the public be persuaded to support the policy? Will I be able to obtain allied support? And so on.
- The president should consider the effects of foreign policy decisions on his domestic political agenda and vice versa. If at all possible, he should avoid entering into a costly or controversial foreign policy undertaking when major parts of his domestic program are pending in Congress. He should not focus on foreign policy while neglecting domestic politics, as the first President George Bush did.
- The president can reduce the risk that foreign policy issues will become politicized by avoiding personalization, for instance by allowing others such as the secretary of state or the secretary of defense to take the lead and get the credit.
- Uncertainty is often unavoidable. There may be times when the president must act without knowing how events will turn out. The president should try to get the relevant facts and recommendations of various agencies. But he should then be willing to go with his "gut instincts" even against the advice of professionals, with the knowledge that he will be held accountable.
- A full analysis of costs and benefits of a policy is often unnecessary and

may waste time and analytical resources, especially given the uncertainties and contingencies involved. Too much deliberation and discussion can lead to "analysis paralysis"—that is, inability to make a decision.

- Do not announce that a policy shift is imminent, then engage in endless debate with advisers. Reports of lengthy meetings and discussions over a period of time can convey the impression of indecisiveness.
- Staff members and bureaucratic agencies have their own concerns, perspectives, and sources of information. The president needs to consider the interests of the people of the United States as a whole. Decomposing a problem into smaller parts can facilitate analysis but also cause decision makers to lose sight of the broader issues involved.
- Emotional reactions such as anger or elation can impair the quality of judgment if acted upon impulsively.

IMPLICATIONS FOR POLICY

Most prescriptions for improving the policy process aim at making the system more systematic, thorough, and objective. Having duplicate sources of information and advice can protect the president or other high-level policymaker from being manipulated by a faction trying to promote its pet policy. Haass advocates "multiple tasking"—that is, assigning judgments on critical subjects to more than one standing body. Along these lines, Jentleson and Bennett suggest that policy planners can counteract the impact of recommendations that reflect parochial bureaucratic interests by providing an independent source of information and advice (see chapter 8). Policy planners can strengthen their arguments by drawing on specialized expertise outside the government, from academia, think tanks, and former policymakers. Haass further recommends that competition between rival sources of information and analysis be encouraged and managed through selective use of what George calls "multiple advocacy," whereby different agencies or bureaus have an opportunity to debate policy options in front of the decision maker.[9]

These prescriptions should improve the quality of information and advice offered the decision maker. At the least, debate and consideration of the issues may prevent some bad judgments by providing incentives for officials to look for evidence and arguments to support their position. When decisions turn out badly, journalists invariably investigate whether there was sufficient discussion and analysis of potential pitfalls. Having a process that systematically evaluates alternative options can protect the president from the charge that a better policymaking system would have prevented misjudgment. Sometimes presidents may go through the motions of hearing alternative points of view for purposes of post hoc justification or to test their original hunches. For example, Truman recalled that he often made instinctive "spot decisions" in emergencies or serious situations without revealing them to anyone until he had called for available facts and listened to the experts or departments of government involved. Usually, Truman said, his final decision corresponded to his original "spot decision."[10]

Analytical methods of decision making are particularly well suited for long-term problems where the variables can be quantified, such as weapons procurement, the location of military bases, trade and environmental issues, and the like. On relations with China, Russia, or North Korea, thinking through the issues in advance can help improve the quality of judgment by allowing officials to rehearse their reactions to different scenarios.

Improving the quality of analysis and information reaching the president does not, however, guarantee that he will exercise good judgment. A policy-maker's instincts and discrimination depend on the range and depth of his experience in dealing with various types of situations. An expert decision maker is similar to a master chess player, who has stored in memory a catalog of games, famous opening moves, and defenses, so that all he has to do is to look a configuration of pieces on a chessboard to see familiar patterns.[11] In chapter 1, Renshon proposes that leaders deal more effectively with issues in policy domains where they have direct experience.

If good judgment ultimately resides in the experience and intuition of the president, how can it be taught? Most presidents come to office after a career in state government or Congress, with very little direct foreign policy experience. How can this barrier be overcome?

George recommends that public policy schools and business schools write case studies of important real-world decisions that required judgment. Students could be asked to write up how they would deal with trade-offs and acute uncertainty. After class discussion, the students could be told what actually happened and could then evaluate their hypothetical decisions.

Alternatively, teachers might conduct simulations of foreign policy crises and decisions. Students would be asked to identify trade-off dilemmas and ways of handling them. Ideally, the simulations should be richly detailed with realistic information. The purpose of the exercise would be to give students a chance to make mistakes and to learn without undue fear of the consequences. The U.S. Army has a sophisticated facility for simulating combat to train future commanders at the National Training Center in Fort Irwin, California.[12]

Future policymakers should also immerse themselves in reading history—not to derive any abstract rules or lessons but simply to develop their knowledge of interesting facts and contingencies so that they can recognize patterns in contemporary events.[13] History is a source of vicarious experience. Policy-makers and journalists initially compared the events of 9/11 to the Japanese attack against Pearl Harbor. Still later, as the Bush administration prepared for war against the Taliban, they sought to avoid the perceived mistakes of the Persian Gulf War and the Soviet intervention in Afghanistan. To be most useful, the history should treat events from the viewpoint of policymakers, portraying the situation as they saw it at the time. Of course, if the history they read is full of nationalistic myths and biases, it may contribute to misjudgment.

Foreign policy judgment is a more elusive subject than organizational structure and process; it is also more fundamental. Much remains to be learned by a variety of means, including case studies, experiments, and interviews. By studying exemplary cases of good judgment and comparing them with instances of bad judgments, we may find ways to improve the overall quality of foreign policy decisions, or at least to avoid egregious misjudgments.

NOTES

1. George F. Kennan, *Around the Cragged Hill: A Personal and Political Philosophy* (New York: Norton, 1993), 190.

2. George F. Kennan, *Memoirs (1925–1950)* (Boston: Bantam Books for Little, Brown, 1967), 340.

3. Clark Clifford with Richard Holbrooke, *Counsel to the President: A Memoir* (New York: Random House, 1991), 77.

4. Dean Acheson, *Present at the Creation: My Years in the State Department* (New York: Norton, 1969), 731.

5. Acheson, *Present at the Creation*, 731.

6. Avi Shlaim, *The United States and the Berlin Blockade, 1948–1949* (Berkeley: University of California Press, 1983), 93–97; Carolyn Eisenberg, *Drawing the Line: The American Decision to Divide Germany, 1944–1949* (Cambridge: Cambridge University Press, 1996), chap. 7.

7. Lou Cannon, *President Reagan: The Role of a Lifetime* (New York: Simon & Schuster, 1991), 372.

8. Harry S. Truman, *Mr. Citizen* (New York: Bernard Geis Associates, Random House, 1953), 262.

9. Alexander L. George, "The Case for Multiple Advocacy in Making Foreign Policy," *American Political Science Review* 66 (September 1972): 751–95.

10. Truman, *Mr. Citizen*, 262.

11. A. D. deGroot, *Thought and Choice in Chess* (The Hague: Mouton, 1965).

12. Major H. Gray Otis, "Developing Military Genius," *Military Review* 69 (November 1989): 43–51.

13. Yaacov Y. I. Vertzberger, *The World in Their Minds: Information Processing, Cognition, and Perception in Foreign Policy Decisionmaking* (Stanford, Calif.: Stanford University Press, 1990), 301.

Index

321

About the Contributors

Andrew Bennett is assistant professor of government at Georgetown University. From 1994 to 1995, he was special assistant to the assistant secretary of defense for international security affairs, Joseph S. Nye Jr. In this capacity, he worked on defense policy planning. His publications include *Condemned to Repetition? The Rise, Fall, and Reprise of Soviet-Russian Military Interventionism 1973–1996* (MIT Press, 1999) and *Friends in Need: Burden-Sharing in the Gulf War* (coeditor with Joseph Lepgold and Danny Unger; author of chapter on "Sheriff of the Posse: The US Contribution in the Gulf War;" St. Martin's, 1997).

Barbara Farnham received her Ph.D. from Columbia University in 1991 and is senior associate at the Institute of War and Peace Studies and adjunct associate professor of political science there. She was a postdoctoral fellow at the John M. Olin Institute for Strategic Studies at the Center for International Affairs, Harvard University and has taught at the City University of New York and Princeton and Columbia Universities. Dr. Farnham has published numerous articles on the psychology of foreign policy decision making. Her most recent book, *Roosevelt and the Munich Crisis: A Study in Political Decision Making,* was published by Princeton University Press (1997). She is also the editor of *Avoiding Losses/Taking Risks: Prospect Theory and International Conflict* (University of Michigan Press, 1994).

Alexander L. George is Graham H. Stuart Professor of International Relations Emeritus at Stanford University and a distinguished contributor to the fields of international relations, political leadership, national security, political biography, decision making, and foreign policy analysis. He has published more than sixty articles in these areas and sixteen books. Among them: *Propaganda Analysis: A Study of Inferences Made from Nazi Propaganda in World War II; The*

Chinese Communist Army in Action; The Korean War and Its Aftermath; Woodrow Wilson and Colonel House, a Personality Study and *Presidential Personality and Performance* (with Juliette L. George); *Forceful Persuasion: Coercive Diplomacy as an Alternative to War; Towards a Soviet-American Crisis Prevention Regimes: History and Prospects; Managing U.S.-Soviet Rivalry: Problems of Crisis; U.S.-Soviet Security Cooperation; Presidential Decisionmaking in Foreign Policy: The Effective Use of Information and Advice;* (with Richard Smoke) *Deterrence in American Foreign Policy: Theory and Practice* (winner of the Bancroft Prize); (with Gordon A. Craig) *Force and Statecraft: Diplomatic Problems of Our Time; Bridging the Gap: Theory and Practice in Foreign Policy; Inadvertent War in Europe: Crisis Simulation; Avoiding War: Problems of Crisis Management;* (with William E. Simons) *The Limits of Coercive Diplomacy.*

Richard N. Haass, a former Rhodes Scholar, holds a B.A. degree from Oberlin College and both the master's and doctor of philosophy degrees from Oxford University. He is currently director of policy planning for the U.S. Department of State in the Bush administration and before that was vice president and director of foreign policy studies at the Brookings Institution. He served from 1989 to 1993 as special assistant to President George H. W. Bush and senior director for Near East and South Asian affairs on the staff of the National Security Council. In 1991, he was awarded the Presidential Citizens Medal for his contributions to the development and articulation of U.S. policy during Operations Desert Shield and Desert Storm. Previously, he served in various posts in the Departments of State (1981–85) and Defense (1979–80) and was a legislative aide in the U.S. Senate. Dr. Haass is the author or editor of nine books on American foreign policy, including *The Reluctant Sheriff: The United States after the Cold War* (Council on Foreign Relations, 1997); *Economic Sanctions and American Diplomacy* (Council on Foreign Relations, 1998); and *Intervention: The Use of American Military Force in the Post–Cold War World* (Brookings Institution, rev. ed., 1999). He is also the author of one book on management, *The Bureaucratic Entrepreneur: How to Be Effective in Any Unruly Organization* (Brookings Institution, 1999). Dr. Haass also has been director of National Security Programs and a Senior Fellow of the Council on Foreign Relations, the Sol M. Linowitz Visiting Professor of International Studies at Hamilton College, a senior associate at the Carnegie Endowment for International Peace, a lecturer in public policy at Harvard University's Kennedy School of Government, and a research associate at the International Institute for Strategic Studies.

Bruce W. Jentleson holds a Ph.D. from Cornell University and an M.A. from the London School of Economics. He is director of the Terry Sanford

Institute of Public Policy and professor of public policy and political science at Duke University. He is the author and editor of seven books, most recently *American Foreign Policy: The Dynamics of Choice in the 21st Century* (Norton, 2000), *Opportunities Missed, Opportunities Seized: Preventive Diplomacy in the Post–Cold War World* (editor, Rowman & Littlefield, 1999), and the four-volume *Encyclopedia of U.S. Foreign Relations* (co–senior editor, Oxford University Press, 1997), as well as numerous articles. In 1993–94, he served on the State Department Policy Planning Staff as special assistant to the director. He was a senior fellow at the U.S. Institute of Peace and in 1999–2000 served as a foreign policy adviser to Vice President Al Gore.

Deborah Welch Larson received her Ph.D. from Stanford and is professor of political science at the University of California, Los Angeles. Her dissertation, which won the American Political Science Association's Helen Dwight Reid Award, was published as *Origins of Containment: A Psychological Explanation* (Princeton University Press, 1985). She has published numerous articles and book chapters on psychological aspects of international relations, including foreign policy decision making, belief systems and schemas, reciprocity, trust and mistrust, and the use of archival methods. She received the Erik H. Erikson career award from the International Society of Political Psychology. Other publications concern the influence of the cold war on academia and deterrence theory. She is the author most recently of *Anatomy of Mistrust: U.S.-Soviet Relations during the Cold War* (Cornell University Press, 1997), which identifies several critical cases in which the superpowers missed opportunities to resolve some of their disputes. She is currently working on a larger study concerning the use of intuition and analysis in foreign policy judgments. With collaborator Alexei Shevchenko, she has published articles on the role played by status considerations in Russian and Soviet foreign policy.

Stanley A. Renshon is professor of political science and coordinator of the Interdisciplinary Program in the Psychology of Social and Political Behavior Department at the City University of New York Graduate Center. He is also a certified psychoanalyst. He is the author of ten books (and over sixty articles), including *Psychological Needs and Political Behavior* (Free Press, 1974), *The Handbook of Political Socialization: Theory and Research* (Free Press, 1977), *The Political Psychology of the Gulf War* (University of Pittsburgh Press, 1993), *The Clinton Presidency: Campaigning, Governing and the Psychology of Leadership* (Westview, 1995); *Political Psychology: Cultural and Cross-cultural Foundations* (Macmillan, 2000); *One America? Political Leadership, National Identity, and the Dilemmas of Diversity* (Georgetown University Press, 2001 and *America's Second Civil War: Political Leadership in a Divided Society* (Transaction, 2002). His two most recent single-authored books are a full-length study of the of the Clinton presidency entitled *High Hopes: The Clinton Presidency and the Politics of Ambition* (New York University Press, 1996; updated paperback edition, 1998 Routledge) and *The Psychological Assessment of Presidential Candidates* (New York University Press, 1996, updated paperback edition, 1998 Routledge), an examination of the issue of psychological suitability in the presidency and how to judge it. *High Hopes* won the 1997 American Political Science Association's Richard E. Neustadt Award for the best book published on the presidency. It was also the winner in 1988 of the National Association for the Advancement of Psychoanalysis' Gradiva Award for the best published work in the category of biography.

Stephen Wayne is professor of government at Georgetown University and specializes in the American presidency. He received his B.A. from the University of Rochester and his M.A. and Ph.D. from Columbia University. He has written nine books and over one hundred articles, chapters, and book reviews. His major works include *The Road to the White House,* now in its sixth, postelection edition (St. Martin's 2001); *The Legislative Presidency* (Harper & Row, 1978); *Presidential Leadership* (with George C. Edwards; Wadsworth, 2003), now in its sixth edition; a coauthored introductory text, *The Politics of American Government* (St. Martin's, 1999) now in its third edition; *Is This Any Way to Run a Democratic Election?* (Houghton Mifflin, 2003); and *The Election of the Century* (with Clyde Wilcox; Sharpe, 2002). Professor Wayne has served as president of the Presidency Research Group and the National Capital Area Political Science Association. He regularly lectures to international visitors, senior federal executives, and college students in the United States and abroad on the presidency and electoral politics.

David A. Welch received his Ph.D. from Harvard University in 1990 and is currently George Ignatieff Professor of Peace and Conflict Studies at the University of Toronto. His 1993 book, *Justice and the Genesis of War* (Cambridge University Press), was the winner of the 1994 Edgar S. Furniss Award for an Outstanding Contribution to National Security Studies. He is coauthor of *On the Brink: Americans and Soviets Reexamine the Cuban Missile Crisis* (2d ed., Noonday, 1990) and *Cuba on the Brink: Castro, The Missile Crisis, and the Soviet Collapse* (2d rev. ed., Rowman & Littlefield, 2002), and is coeditor of *Intelligence and the Cuban Missile Crisis* (Cass, 1998). His articles have appeared in *Ethics and International Affairs, Foreign Affairs, The Georgetown Journal of International Affairs, Intelligence and National Security, International Security, International Journal, International Studies Quarterly, The Journal of Conflict Resolution, The Mershon International Studies Review,* and *Security Studies.*